15/-

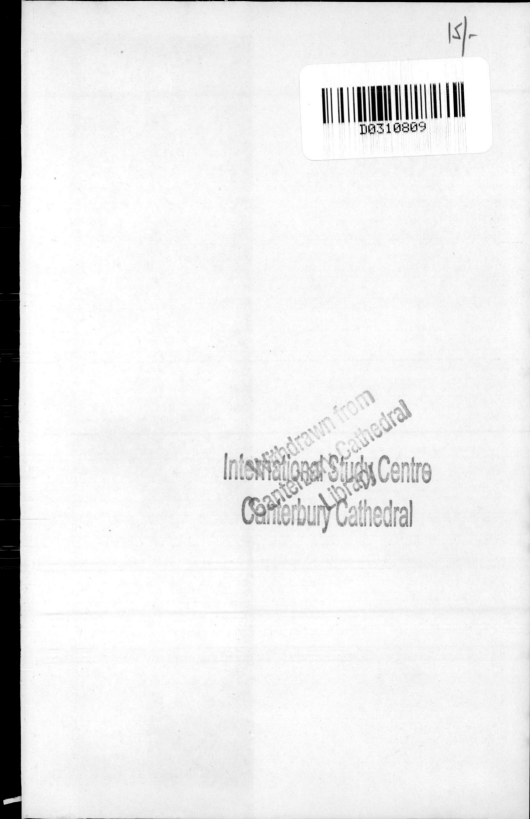

COMMUNISM
AND THE THEOLOGIANS

COMMUNISM
AND THE
THEOLOGIANS

Study of an Encounter

CHARLES C. WEST

*Assistant Director
of the Ecumenical Institute,
Chateau de Bossey,
Geneva*

SCM PRESS LTD
56 BLOOMSBURY STREET
LONDON

First published 1958

©

SCM PRESS LTD
1958

Printed in Great Britain by
W. & J. Mackay & Co Ltd Chatham

To those friends in China and in Germany
who by their life and work in the presence of Communism
have taught the author more than many books,
this volume is offered
as a small participation in their ministry.

CONTENTS

PREFACE

FROM the course of the author's many wanderings in the service of the Church, two incidents stand out which seem especially suited to form an introduction for the reader to this book.

The first was in a Chinese temple not far from a large city in the year 1949. The temple was Buddhist, but for a number of months it had been rented in part by a Christian university whose students and faculty had fled from the north as the Communists captured their city. Here, in this new environment, they had hoped to build again a community of learning and of the Spirit which would bring health to China for a few years more. It seemed indeed as if they were succeeding. Buddhist temple ceremonies and Christian life had gone on side by side in the temple throughout the winter and spring, but there was no doubt where hope and vitality lay. The microscopes of the biology department stood on the altar of the goddess of mercy, but the goddess was largely ignored. Uneducated monks chanted sutras they did not understand for pilgrims whose piety was at best nonchalant, and whose faith doubtful; while the university church in the former cowshed outside the walls met daily for prayer and preaching, and the student Christian fellowship regularly for Bible study and instruction. It was Christian students who were found in the neighbouring villages teaching the illiterate and helping with the harvest. One saw everywhere the beginnings of hope.

But at the time of which I speak all this had passed. The Communists were coming. Fear and revolt had gripped our whole community. The monks and the pilgrims had fled. A 'revolutionary committee' of the students had challenged the authority of the President, Dean and all his staff, including the missionaries. The leaders of the student Christian fellowship gathered in a deserted courtyard to share with each other their perplexity. One young woman stood out at that meeting. She poured out with tears her bitter complaint for all her Christian teachers and pastors had failed to give to prepare her for that hour. She expressed all the lostness which was in everyone's heart, leaving us with nothing but prayer to a hidden God as we parted at midday.

As we gathered again for the afternoon the girl with regained composure was studying the classical paintings on the wall of the courtyard. 'I learned to paint like that as a child,' she explained to me. 'Every stroke is a symbol, and has its place in the structure of the whole. Each style has its history and expresses the culture and tradition of our land.' Then she turned, 'But all that has no power to help us now. It has no meaning any more. It's all dead.'

The other incident took place in Berlin a few years later, at the height of the McCarthy hearings and the security fever in the United States, when East Germany for its part was facing a wave of arbitrary arrests, and expulsions from school or university on ideological grounds. A leading American newspaper arrived in Berlin with an article analysing the effect of security investigations on freedom of thought and speech in American universities. There was, said the article, a marked tendency toward conformity in themes, theses, and even in common room discussion. There was a wariness of organizations which touched on controversial questions. Students were tending to avoid commitments and opinions which might possibly, some day years hence, be held against them and cost them a job.

Some days later a group of East German students were wrestling with the problem of their Christian responsibility in the face of Communist pressure on them to conform ideologically. Should they argue and think for themselves in the required courses in Marx-Leninism? Should they write the truth and not the line required in their examinations? What attitude should they take to the 'Free German Youth' of which they were all perforce members? False steps at any of these points might lead to expulsion from the university and possibly to arrest. But the concern of the students was not to avoid these two fates, if such were the price of Christian action. It was rather that their action be a witness to the lordship

10

of Christ and thus a ministry to the Communist, not merely an act of enmity and resistance. Then one of them turned to me: 'You are a citizen of a country with long practice in freedom of thought and speech such as we have not had,' he said. 'Do you have any advice for us here?'

It is for reasons like these that the author was driven to write this book.

Communism is a changing phenomenon. The question might well be asked: is there any purpose in a study in depth, which does not pretend to be a tract for one time only, when the issues at stake may change tomorrow? As these words are written another disarmament conference has just been broken off, and the balance of military power seems to be shifting in favour of the Soviets even while there is internal evidence from the East that Communist ideology is failing more and more to hold its adherents. Yet in China the ideological front is strengthening and in Indonesia a recent election strengthened the Communist Party. By the time these words are read other events will have taken the place of these, and popular reaction will be in yet another mood.

But it is this very changing face of events which makes a long range view of the encounter with Communism so important. It is the same face which changes. Communist power may wax or wane. It may shift from the military to the diplomatic sphere and back again. But it will not disappear, nor will the non-Communist world's responsibility for containing it, negotiating with it, seeking some viable structure of order this side of total war. The question of the Christian's use of power is a long range problem. Communist ideology may change its forms, or develop its heresies. But the fact of a generation of men brought up to think in its terms will not vanish. The leadership of convinced Marxists in many countries of the world will not be abolished. Least of all will people who have lived long under Communism, even after they may have thrown it off, begin to think again like us who have never been through it. The Christian responsibility of the East German students mentioned above, to find a witness which transcends both the Communist ideology and all the ideological defences of the western world, will not cease; nor will the respon-

11

sibility of Americans, Britishers, and others who read these words, to help them at cost to our own 'security'.

Furthermore the fact of revolutionary change itself, the predicament of our Chinese girl with the cry for help it brings with it, will continue. Communism claims to organize this revolution and give it direction and meaning. But the revolution is bigger than Communism. It seethes in Russia, as it does in India and covertly as well in Britain and America. It has its post-Communist as well as its pre-Communist mood. The need for Christians who know the meaning of repentance, and who are free for endless experiments in new creation or service, will not soon be exhausted.

Theology too has changed. These pages will partly record this change, reflected in the theology of different cultures and experiences, as it meets the fact of Communism. The change could be expressed in a sentence by saying that theology has become more conscious of itself over the period of the last generation. The reader will find only brief mention of a form of Christian thinking about Communism which was highly popular twenty-five years ago: that which placed Marxism and Christianity more or less on the same level as life and death antagonists or as possible elements in a synthesis to the advantage of both. The time when both Marxism and Christianity could be considered as basically humanist philosophies at war, or in conversation about the best ideal for human society, is past. It is past because Communism has exploded in practice this false picture of what it is and intends. But it is past more surely because Christian theology has learned meanwhile that its object is not human experience, not even religious experience and practice, but God and his acts toward men. At least one of the forces which have driven it to this discovery, has been the persistent Marxist undermining of any good conscience which the Christian might have about his culture and class position, of every confidence that his doctrine is truth and not ideology, of every attempt to withdraw from submitting his faith to the test of practice in social and historical action. The greatest discovery Christians have made is their complete solidarity with a world which has lost its self-confidence in a revolutionary age, and their complete freedom to be open for what God is doing that they may

12

bear witness to it. This book is the story of this Christian discovery, in the face of the challenge of Communism, and of the ministry to the world, including the Communists, which flows from it.

The story is far from finished. Of the five major theologians with whom these pages deal, every one is still at work and may live to refute much of what is here said about him. This writer offers his apologies to each for presuming to relate their thoughts to this issue before they themselves have fully had their say. But, in my defence, the subject is too urgent to wait, and my gratitude to all of them for the guidance of their thought is too full to remain unexpressed. They have all been, personally or through their writings, my teachers.

Finally, a few words of acknowledgement are due, which may explain more than any others, the spiritual ingredients of which this book is made:

To my wife and three sons who lived with their husband and father in his often intolerable state during the months when it was being written.

To the Board of Foreign Missions of the Presbyterian Church, U.S.A., who supported the author on an extended furlough in order to give him time to complete this work, and who through the vision of their mission policies have given him many of the insights which he has incorporated here.

To Professor Roland H. Bainton of Yale Divinity School, without whose encouragement and prodding many uncertain words might never have been committed to paper, and to Dean Liston Pope, whose undeserved interest encourages the writer to publish what he has written. The substance of the book was originally presented to Yale University in partial fulfilment of the requirements for the degree of Doctor of Philosophy.

To Professor John C. Bennett of Union Seminary, whose companionship has accompanied the author at every stage of this work and before, and whose kind and careful insight into persons and social issues has corrected many misjudgements and contributed many new perspectives.

To Professor H. Richard Niebuhr, adviser in the earlier stages

13

of this volume's preparation, to whom the author owes the intangible and unlimited debt of a student to that teacher who has opened his mind to new worlds of thought, and has imparted to his spirit that desire on the one hand to love and appreciate them, and on the other hand never to rest in them, which is the mental discipline of every Christian.

To Professor Reinhold Niebuhr. The reader of the chapter of this book devoted to Niebuhr's thought will recognize in it the author's struggle with himself and his own heritage. Niebuhr's dialectical manner of finding the critical point of Christian obedience, his uncompromising solidarity with those who bear the burdens and responsibilities of our common life, and even his suspicion of theology which does not prove itself in responsible action, belong indelibly to this writer's sense of what the Christian faith is and means. Every criticism of Niebuhr's theology which this book contains, every attempt to show him as the Barthian he truly is, is an expression of undying gratitude for the spiritual impulse his teaching, his action in society, and his books have given, and is meant in loyalty to his true intention.

To Professor Karl Barth. More space has been devoted to him in this volume than to any other theologian, partly because he is less well known in the Anglo-Saxon world, but mostly because in the broad vistas of his *Dogmatics* a new perspective emerges and a new horizon becomes visible whose potentialities the Christian world is only beginning to explore. It may be beyond the capacity of any Christian to bring every thought so captive to the mind of Christ and to live so utterly from the centre of God's redemption in Him as Barth would have us do. The great theologian himself would be the first to admit the possibility of an area where he himself does not succeed, though he might not agree with this writer's contention that politics is that area! But it is Barth more than any other thinker of modern times who opens the Christian imagination to the boundless resources for practical living in the fact that his life is in the hands of a redeeming God. His theology forms a seedbed in which the Christian insights of other men can reach a fuller flower, and the Christian encounter with Communism find firmer roots in reality.

Finally, to the many friends who cannot be named here, whose lives are one continuous encounter with and ministry to the Communist world in the name of Christ. It is these men whom this study exists to serve first of all, by exploring the resources of Christendom which might help them with their task, and by making known to the rest of Christendom by what standards and in what spirit they live and work. The judgements and ideas this book contains, so far as they are my own, have been forged in constant and grateful companionship with them in their action, thought, and prayer. Where the judgements err and mislead the fault is mine. Where the ideas contribute to the knowledge and practice of others concerned with this encounter, I shall have succeeded in conveying to the reader something of the work of the Holy Spirit which I have seen and heard among these companions who carry on their ministry on behalf of us all.

CHARLES C. WEST

Bossey, 1957

15

INTRODUCTION:

COMMUNISM VERSUS THE THEOLOGIAN

THE purpose of this study is not to add another to the long list of Christian and other analyses of Communism in theory and practice. That field has often been ploughed, by every conceivable theological, philosophical, and experiential point of view. Nor does it aim to orient Communism and the Christian faith theoretically to one another. Rather it seeks to meet a more concrete need: the need of Christians who cannot escape the fact of Communism in their daily lives, and the need of other Christians who are tempted, because the Communists are so far away, to oversimplify or to forget it. In the centre of this work we seek to place no theory or analysis, but the living response of Christians to the living force of Communism in the present-day world, as it is illuminated by the theologies which have had most to do with this response. This is the meaning of the word 'encounter' in our title. In using it we have already assumed one conviction which Communism and the Christian faith hold in common: that the true, the good, and the real are to be sought in no realm of ideas, in no system of doctrine or philosophy, in no order of society or culture, but in the living relation of concrete human beings.

We must assume this common conviction. Without it whatever response to Communism Christians develop will be response to an abstraction—the reflection of our fears or the construct of our minds—rather than help for people confronted with the Communist movement itself. Communism is more than a social philosophy which can be refuted. It is more than a power movement which can be resisted, or a false religion which can be outpreached. It is a living force which combines all these factors in an organic whole which proves itself on the field of historical human action. Here it must be encountered.

But we must assume this common conviction more basically

because it is a Biblical conviction first of all. It is the Bible which first refers men to the action of God in history as the place where truth and goodness are to be learned and reality to be met. It is the Bible which first exposes the group-interested nature of our ideas, even our religious ideas and practices, and the self-justification of our justice. These insights reappeared in Marxist form in an age when the Church had blinded itself to a whole sphere of human suffering and revolutionary hope by forgetting them. For this reason of course we cannot allow the Marxists to define for us the encounter we are seeking. We must seek to understand this world, in which the Communists continue to be so powerful, in the light of God's work in it, that is, theologically, just at those points where we also recognize the validity of a Marxist challenge or insight. To acknowledge Marxist insight theologically is, in the same act, to place Marxism in the perspective which most profoundly refutes it. Yet we must distinguish this from the creation of one more 'Christian answer to Communism'. All the differences in Christendom are already reflected in the 'answers' which we have, and many of the weaknesses and unsolved problems of Christendom show up there. We need at this point rather to listen carefully to this Communist reality before us, in order to purge and refine the expression of our faith, that it may be more useful to the work of Christ who is Lord over Communists and Christians, and more helpful in their concrete encounter as God wills it to take place.

Three major kinds of questions concern us in this task:

1. We must ask of each theologian whose encounter with Communism we examine, what sort of experience gives direction to his thought. How fully does it include the many-sided reality of the Communist movement itself? What correction does it need? How deeply has the challenge of Communism and of Marxism penetrated into the centre of his thought?

2. We must ask how adequate the resources of each theology are to meet Marxism at those points where it makes its strongest challenge. Christian thought largely agrees that this challenge is religious in a double sense. On the one side prophetic elements have entered into Communism's formation and development: it speaks

to the bad conscience of the Christian. On the other side it has become itself something of a counter-faith with its own view of man and history, and its own demand for commitment to itself.

With this however little has been said. The recognition of Communism as a religious phenomenon has had a chequered history. It has been used to praise the movement, and to damn it. It has served to dispose of the serious claims of Communism and Christianity together, and to exalt a Christian culture over a Communist one. It has been cited as evidence of a deep bond between the inner meaning of Marxist socialism and Christianity, and as evidence of the unceasing and ultimate conflict between them.[1] One task before us is to penetrate this confusion; to clarify what it means for Christian theology that this other faith, so explicitly atheistic yet so analogous to Christian faith in its structure and hope has arisen, like Islam centuries ago, out of the soil of a Christian culture. This leads to three theological questions:

(a) How far does Christian thought meet the challenge of the Marxist doctrine of ideology in general and the Marxist criticism of religion in particular? In its sharpest form this doctrine forms the heart of Marx's 'scientific materialism':

'The sum of . . . production relations forms the economic structure of society, the real basis upon which a juridical and political superstructure arises, and to which definite forms of consciousness correspond. . . . It is not the consciousness of men which determines their existence, but on the contrary, it is their social existence which determines their consciousness. . . . One must always distinguish between the material transformation in the economic conditions essential to production—which can be established with the exactitude of natural science—and the juridical, political, religious, artistic, or philosophical, in short ideological forms, in which men become conscious of this conflict and fight it out.'[2]

[1]Examples of these various uses of the 'Communism is religious' theme are:
John Macmurray, *Creative Society* (London, 1935).
Fulton J. Sheen, *Communism and the Conscience of the West* (Dublin, 1948).
Charles Lowry, *Communism and Christ* (London, 1954).
Emil Fuchs, *Marxismus und Christentum* (Leipzig, 1953).
Erwin Metzke (ed.), *Marxismusstudien* (Tübingen, 1953).
[2]Marx, Introduction to *The Critique of Political Economy*. English translation quoted from Eastman, *Capital and other Writings by Karl Marx* (New York, 1938).

If this combination of misused natural science and materialist philosophy were all we had to deal with in Marx and in the Communist movement, our task would be simpler than it is. The encounter of the last thirty years has taught us that the Marxist claim to be a science of society is not one which the Christian need take seriously as such.[1]

But the Marxist doctrine of ideology is older and greater than this materialism. The heart of it, from the days of young Marx down to the poets and idealistic Komsomols of present day Russia and China, is prophetic rebellion against the bourgeois world's idealizing of itself—its deification of its own spirit, typified for Marx in Hegel—in the name of real concrete men who are being exploited and enslaved (estranged from themselves as he put it) in this world. 'I intend a ruthless criticism of everything which stands', he wrote in 1843, confronted with what he regarded as a monolithic system of bourgeois society, Prussian state, and Hegelian philosophy, the last surrounding the other two with a closed system of illusions and self-justification.

'I am not in favour of planting our dogmatic flag—on the contrary. . . . Our slogan must be: Reform of the consciousness, not through dogmas, but through analysing the mystical consciousness which is unclear about itself, whether that consciousness takes a religious or a political form. . . . It is a question of *repentance*, nothing more. In order for its sins to be forgiven, mankind needs only to recognize them for what they are.'[2]

From the perspective of the proletarian, estranged from possession of the manner and fruit of his own labour, and hence from himself,

[1] The disappearance of the whole Christian-Marxist movement in England under the leadership of John Macmurray, John Lewis, Joseph Needham and others, and the gradual movement of the Fellowship of Socialist Christians in America away from Marxist premises, are symptomatic. In the post-war period only Alexander Miller, in *The Christian Significance of Karl Marx* (London, 1946), maintains among Christian thinkers that Marxist analysis is a science of society. Miller can only do so however, by confusing prophetic understanding of nineteenth century capitalism, which Marx had and which still judges society today, with scientific analysis.

[2] *Marx-Engels Gesamtausgabe*, Erste Abteilung, Band I, Zweiter Halbband, pp. 573, 575 (Berlin, 1932). The statement is from a letter to Arnold Ruge concerning an editorial venture. Marx's italics. This and all other German quotations in this book are translated by myself, unless otherwise stated.

philosophy, religion, law, politics, and all the rest, are exposed as the consciousness of one possessing class, and the instrument of its interests. Reality comes into view as the natural relations of men in society acting, producing, and striving to overcome this self-estrangement into which they have fallen. Truth, as against the 'mystification' of the philosophers, becomes the ideology of the dispossessed class of men, stripped of all vested interest and illusion. It becomes response to the real demands of human beings thus revealed, a matter of changing the world. 'The revolutionary practice of millions of people,' wrote a modern practician of Marxism, 'is the only standard for measuring truth.'[1]

Thus Marx set out, from the abstract categories of Hegelian idealism, to find his neighbour. The fact that he did not find real human beings, but only another person-enslaving concept of man; the fact that he did not find empirical reality, but only the Hegelian system once more reflected in the so-called 'material' world, cannot obscure the searching question which his doctrine of ideology continues to put to Christians everywhere.

This challenge becomes still more specific in the Marxist criticism of religion, which, he assures us in an early work, is the beginning of all criticism, and an application of his doctrine of ideology. If God exists as creator and source of grace, then the human being becomes less important, or indeed nothing, along with nature.[2] Marx sees here an either-or, reinforced by the actual function which religion has in his mind, as the ideology of a given society. 'It is the imaginary realization of humanity, because that humanity possesses no true reality itself.'[3] It has a certain positive function in holding the vision of human reality before dehumanized man. But to turn men to the changing of their society, is to start with disillusioning them about this world to which religion gives a

[1]Mao Tse-Tung, Hsin Min Chu Chu I (New Democracy) p. 1. (Included in *Selected Works*, Vol. II, London, 1954). Cf. Marx and Engels, *Theses on Feuerbach*, in English translation of *The German Ideology*, Parts I and III (London, 1947).

[2]Marx, *Nationalökonomie und Philosophie*, edited by Erich Thier (Cologne and Berlin, 1950), pp. 197–8.

[3]*Gesamtausgabe*, Erste Abteilung, I/1, p. 607. From the *Einleitung: zur Kritik der hegelschen Rechtsphilosophie*.

kind of illusory sanctification in the very act of relating it to a vision of something higher. This is the sense in which Marx regarded it as opium for the people. Religion, he charges, is perhaps the most understandable illusion of all; but it is nevertheless still an ideology. In its very pessimism about 'this vale of tears', in its very contrast between heaven and earth, it justifies, gives an 'appearance of holiness' to this world through its theological explanations and sacramental comforts.

Thus Marx. He was the mildest, in some ways the most understanding and therefore the most searching of all Communist critics of religion. But the challenge is no less real today. Communists everywhere maintain their inner discipline and train people under their control partly by constant 'criticism and self-criticism'. The object of this is to bring about soul-searching, moral analysis and repentance for past wrongness in attitude and conduct. There is no distinction in these sessions of criticism between moral and ideological evils. In Communist doctrine they have the same root: a consciousness still determined by bourgeois or feudal society, not yet purged of selfishness and attachment to 'imperialist' social forms which separate one from true dedication to the people. Here once again the Christian is charged with the ideology of his religious belief, and the behaviour of his church. Here in dead earnest the Communist believer may struggle for the soul of a Christian, seeking to make him give up 'the burden of his superstition'.

How fares the Christian's conscience in this situation? Does his theology and witness express in truth only God's work in Christ, or does it reflect the interests of some social group, some other ideology over against the Communist one? Does his faith explain the world to him, justify it and separate him from the needs of his neighbour who is out to change it?

'All our indignant crusades' writes Helmut Gollwitzer, 'cannot get rid of the fact that those people over there have a kind of good conscience about their repudiation of religion, which is customary among those who think they are on the trail of a swindle; people who claim to have exposed a deception or, better, a self-deception.'[1]

[1]'Christentum und Marxismus', in the magazine *Unterwegs*, 1951, Heft 1, p. 8.

To take away this Communist good conscience about their ideology and their judgement on the Christian faith; to confront it with a witness which is not another system of ideas pretending to be objective truth and value while it in fact reflects and covers the interest of one social group, is the task of Christian theology here.

(b) How effectively does Christian thought meet the challenge of the Marxist doctrine of history, with its capacity to strain every nerve of society toward revolution and the classless society? Here also there is a later 'scientific' form of the Communist understanding of history which endows the developments of the class struggle with a deterministic inevitability capable of prediction; and there is an earlier form of the same doctrine wherein Marx expresses primarily his moral outrage at the way in which a system of economic exploitation deprives man of his true humanity, explains how this came about, and exposes the inevitability of its destruction. It is this prophetic Marx who concerns us, not only because he stands so close to the Christian faith in pulling the Hegelian dialectical pattern of historical conflict out of the realm of ideas into that of material reality, but also because this note of prophetic moralism sounds down through Communist history, despite their explicit denials of it, into today's world. The attraction of the Communist doctrine of history for many a Chinese was primarily its expression of his outraged sense of justice and his hope for a better life for his fellow men. The fact that Communism has expressed the power of a disinherited proletariat in its will to change society, has impressed itself also on Christian minds. So we must ask the theologians:

(i) How effectively do their doctrines of history understand the revolutionary ferment of our time, to the expression and leadership of which Marx gave his life, and the Christian's place in it? How free is the theologian's mind and life from values and social forms which reflect his own cultural background and interest, eternalized in his theology itself? How clearly can he place himself vicariously in the proletarian situation?

(ii) How effective are they in facing the problems of social and cultural construction in a chaotic and changing world? The Marxist vision of a classless society has caught the imagination and energy of millions, and even for many who have reason to fear it, it seems to represent the only hope for society.[1] How does the Christian hope engage itself with the lives of these people?

(c) The third theological question is the static relational side of the second: How effectively does Christian thought about man in society confront the promethean humanism which has marked Communism from the early Marx down to present-day Russia?[2] This humanism is to be sure both collectivist and abstract, prepared to sacrifice real human beings for the proletariat or 'the people'; prepared to make them conform to a Communist ideal of what man should be. But this does not obliterate in the least the actual attraction of Communist humanism when it reveals to masses of men a vision of what they shall become in contrast to what in non-Communist society they are. It does not dull the prophetic edge of the Marx-Feuerbach affirmation of man. Therefore we must ask: (i) How effectively do our theologians take account of the facts of economic determinism, and the material aspect of man's existence? How seriously are social institutions dealt with as instruments not only of order but also of exploitation, as embodiments of social group interest? How clearly is concrete man seen in the framework of his real, not his ideal, social bonds and relations? How far does their Christian view of freedom reckon with these bonds and relations, and with the disciplined group responsibility and action they imply? And in a Communist society on the other side, how helpful are these theologians to the Christian who must make practical decisions under Communist power?

(ii) How effectively do our theologians affirm and love all the

[1]The author is drawing here on personal experience in China with a number of intellectuals themselves western in training and orientation, lovers of democracy and freedom of the mind, who nevertheless could see no solution of China's social problem other than Communist victory. For a Christian plea along this line cf. Hromadka,'The Church of the Reformation Faces Today's Challenge', in *Theology Today* (January, 1950).

[2]Very little of this unbounded optimistic humanism, this worship of collective man, has come to us across the Iron Curtain. Some hint of it is found in John Somerville, *Soviet Philosophy* (New York, 1946). But for its full impact one would have to read the poetry and literature of the Soviet Union.

fulness of human life? How effective are they in reaching men captivated by the Communist vision of what man can be, with a Gospel of more real humanity, and a more realistic means of expressing it?

(3) With this we come to the more concrete side of this encounter: Christian action in the face of present-day Communism. We face here three basic questions:

(a) The question of the Christian's responsibility for power, both for the power in his hands or with which he is associated, and the power of Communism which it may be his duty to contain. It might be otherwise stated: what is the challenge which anti-Communism presents to Christians today? How realistically do Christians come to grips with the needs and experiences of men who have fled from Communist tyranny, who have awakened from the betrayal of their minds and spirits by Communist ideology, and who still suffer under the practice of a Communist state? How do they answer these people who are asking what the Christian may and must do to help the neighbours who have fallen under this rule and to prevent others from succumbing as well?

This is first of all a question about the Christian's realism in power conflicts. But it may also be a question about his use of powerlessness and suffering, of little bits of opportunity to serve a neighbour or bear a witness in a totalitarian situation. We must ask the relation of this, as well, to the will of God.

(b) The question of creative alternatives to Communist order in the state and to Communist community among its adherents. What relative importance have the Church and the civil community in this connexion? What safeguards can we propose that these alternatives—whether Christian community or secular democratic state—may not themselves become group-interested expressions?

(c) Finally, the question of the Christian's ministry to the Communist as a person. How can the Christian relate this ministry creatively to action toward the Communist as the representative of political and ideological power he is resisting?

Such are the questions of this study. But the sceptic might well ask how much Christian grist there is for such a mill as this. It has

25

not been Christians on the whole who have produced the most penetrating analyses of Marxism, but rather radical empiricists.[1] Even the spiritual problems of encounter with Communism, the definition of its power and appeal, and of the plight of the bourgeois world against it, have been more effectively portrayed by an Arthur Koestler than by any Christian. The dilemmas of those who are caught in the meshes of the Communist system have found no convincing answers, Christian or otherwise. And no common spirit seems to distinguish the conflicting Christian advice which non-Communist statesmen receive about relations with the Communist world.

It is rather when we look to the future that the special relevance of this study becomes clear. For as time goes on, those responses to Communism which are not based in another faith tend less and less to commend themselves to those who must deal daily with it. They contain illusory hopes and analyses which spoil quickly in the heat of real encounter. Men are looking more and more for such a faith as will sustain them in meeting the reality of Communism without illusion and without despair; such a faith as God himself offers through his victory over the world in Jesus Christ the crucified. This is why the halting response of Christians to Communism contains such a responsibility, and such a promise, that out of it may grow a life and hope adequate to the world in which Communism is rampant. Under this promise we turn to our study.

---

[1]Among the best of these are:
Mandell M. Bober, *Karl Marx's Interpretation of History*, 2nd Ed. rev. (Cambridge, Mass., 1948).
George H. Sabine, *A History of Political Theory*, 3rd Ed. (London, 1951). Chs. 33–34.
Karl Popper, *The Open Society and Its Enemies*, Vol. 2 (London, 1945).
Joseph Schumpeter, *Capitalism, Socialism and Democracy* (London, 1943).

1
COMMUNISM AS THE ENEMY

A POLEMICAL response to the challenge of Communism is in one sense the oldest and most natural reaction for the Christian world. From the time of the younger Marx, Christians have met the Marxist attack on religion by accepting the absolute conflict of system with system, by condemning Communism as atheistic in theory and immoral in practice, and by defending as one united whole their faith and their 'Christian civilization'. Were this all the substance of this point of view today we would not have to consider it here, for it is not a genuine encounter with Communism but rather a refusal to understand it, or to engage the mind and spirit with the problems it raises. This kind of anti-Communism fights a blind rearguard action against the rapidly changing realities of today. We can ignore it, for it has nothing to teach us.

The spirit of anti-Communism however, is in another sense something new in the post-war world, because it is based on a real and bitter encounter. Its representatives today are no longer only comfortable people who stand to lose their property and status, but Korean prisoners of war shouting down their Communist persuaders, East European refugees from destroyed or satellite societies, ex-Communists shaken in spirit by their break, and ordinary people behind the Iron Curtain robbed of every normal security in life, hoping for a day of liberation. It is the encounter of people like these—the encounter of conflict and rejection out of bitter experience, and the struggle to save precious things from Communist power—which is given theological form by the writers with whom this chapter is concerned.

1. PERSPECTIVE ACROSS THE BATTLE LINE
The foremost of these is Emil Brunner. Communism, for Brunner, is the most consistent and thorough example of the principle of

27

totalitarianism in all history. It outdoes even Nazism. If the totalitarian state itself is 'the omnicompetent state', 'the politicization of all of life' which 'takes upon itself to form men as it will' and 'lays claim to them body, soul and spirit',[1] Communist totalitarianism is its logical perfection:

'Control of all the means of education and control of opinion by the state; state monopoly of all the middle schools, universities, the press, books, wireless, cinema and theatre, for the purpose of creating *a new type of human being* (Brunner's italics), i.e. the "Communist" type—the person whose actions are determined solely by state orthodoxy, and who can and will no longer think except on "orthodox" lines.'[2]

Totalitarianism is therefore injustice *per se*. It 'is identical with the denial of those rights of the person *vis à vis* the state which we usually call human rights.'[3] It is fundamentally inhuman and denies human dignity. It is essentially atheistic even when it tolerates the Church and does not stress atheism in theory; because it claims the total allegiance of man which belongs to God alone, thereby setting itself in the place of God. Such a state is the Communist state. From this flow all the terrible evils, Brunner believes, of which we hear year by year: concentration camps, secret police, slave labour, the uncertainty of law and of daily life, the warping of minds, and so on.

For this reason the Church itself, he says, cannot be neutral in the struggle of 'the West' to maintain its traditions of respect for freedom, human rights, and the democratic form of the state. The conflict indeed cannot be stated in terms of 'East' and 'West':

'It is', he says, 'a question of humanity which is denied by the Communist total state. Those who take up an attitude of apparent impartiality and superiority in relation to this opposition between East and West, and suppose that they must justify it on Christian grounds, do not observe how they are committing treason against a blessing which the peoples of the West owe to the gospel of the Bible.'[4]

[1]*Justice and the Social Order* (London, 1945), p. 180.
[2]*Our Attitude as a Christian Church to Communism*, statement for an informal staff conference of the World Council of Churches (W.C.C. Study Dept., Geneva, 1950), p. 2.
[3]'An Open Letter to Karl Barth', in *Against the Stream: Shorter Post-war Writings*, by Karl Barth (London, 1954), p. 110.
[4]*Communism, Capitalism and Christianity* (London, 1949), p. 28.

But this conflict need not be described only in terms of totalitarianism. An American writer, Charles W. Lowry, starts from the principle that Communism is 'the newest of the universal salvation-religions'. He is at pains to explain Communism as springing from, parallel to, and opposed to the Christian faith, as an anti-faith. He presents a table of parallel doctrines.[1] But the implication is the same explanation of the Christian-Communist encounter as an absolute conflict of systems, as Brunner also gives:

'The tragedy of Communism, and of our tortured contemporary world, is that the denial of love as the first law of man's being has become a fixed dogma around which the most titanic and herculean efforts are being made to reintegrate the whole of human life and culture. It is this denial which is Antichrist, and which must be resisted by all possible means (save by surrender to the Enemy's own principles) and with all the energy and resolution which free men and lovers of their kind can muster.'[2]

The same point of view is more eloquently and fully presented in the widely publicized attitude of Whittaker Chambers, one of the few ex-Communists who have found their way into a non-Roman-Catholic religion. Chambers knows why Americans, especially American intellectuals of good family in the 'twenties and 'thirties, became Communists. He does not begrudge his former Communist colleagues the respect due to men of integrity and conviction. Nevertheless one receives from him, more than from many more vigorous polemicists, the impression of a great struggle between God and the devil in modern society. His diagnosis puts it thus:

.'The revolutionary heart of Communism . . . is a simple statement of Karl Marx further simplified for handy use: "philosophers have explained the world; it is necessary to change the world." Communists are bound by no secret oath. The tie that binds them across the frontiers of nations, across barriers of language and differences of class and education, in defiance of religion, morality, truth, law, is a simple conviction: it is necessary to change the world. . . . It is a simple rational faith that inspires man to live or die for it.
'It is not new. It is, in fact, man's second oldest faith. Its promise was

[1]*Communism and Christ* (London, 1954), pp. 54 f.
[2]Ibid. pp. 175 f.

29

whispered in the first days of Creation under the Tree of Knowledge of Good and Evil: "ye shall be as gods." It is the great alternative faith of mankind. . . . The Communist vision is the vision of man without God.'[1]

This faith challenges man to prove his superiority

'by using the force of his rational mind to end the bloody meaninglessness of man's history—by giving it a purpose and a plan . . . by reducing the meaningless chaos of nature, by imposing on it his rational will to order, abundance, security, and peace. It is the vision of materialism.

'Hence the Communist Party is quite justified in calling itself the most revolutionary party in history. It has posed in practical form the most revolutionary question in history: God or man? This vision *is* the Communist revolution, which, like all great revolutions, occurs in man's mind before it takes form in man's acts.'[2]

As Chambers has pictured Communism, so he pictures the Christian encounter therewith. The world is in deeper crisis than any in past history—a total crisis, religious, moral, intellectual, political, social, and economic. The issue in this crisis is:

'whether this sick society which we call Western Civilization, could, in its extremity, still cast up a man whose faith was so great that he would voluntarily abandon those things which men hold good, including life, to defend it.'[3]

The root of this faith Chambers finds in God. God is the nemesis of the Communists. When they break, they break because in spite of all their human logic and confidence, the inhumanity of their system communicates itself to their souls. His key illustration is that of a pro-Communist German diplomat who turned against Communism. 'He was immensely pro-Soviet, and then—one night in Moscow—he heard screams. That's all. Simply one night he heard screams.'[4] When the Communist hears these screams, he must stifle their implications in his soul at once or they will question his faith in Man, History, and Reason, 'the only vision that has force against the vision of Almighty Mind'. He will stand before the fact

[1]*Witness* (New York, 1951), p. 9.
[2]Ibid. p. 10.
[3]Ibid. p. 4.
[4]Ibid. p. 14. Cf. Also Koestler, *Darkness at Noon* (London, 1940), for Rubashov's recurring vision of the *Pietà* upsetting his Communist reason. But Koestler draws no such theological conclusions from it as Chambers.

of God. Therefore 'faith is the central problem of this age. The western world does not know it, but it already possesses the answer to this problem. But only provided that its faith in God and the freedom he enjoins is as great as Communism's faith in Man.'[1]

With this eloquent testimony we are already amid the implications of this experience of Communism for Christian faith and social analysis as a whole. It starts from a groundwork of total conflict. There are strong differences of emphasis among the anti-Communists of this school, but they agree in regarding Communism as a total enemy, and as *the* enemy, in struggle with which the Church is as surely locked as is western civilization as a whole. These conservatives are all distinguished by the absence of such an encounter with the insights of Marxism as we shall describe in future chapters. Their encounter with Communism is undialectical rejection. They experience not the Communist but the soul-destroying power of his ideology.

2. THEOLOGY FOR THE CONFLICT

It is not surprising therefore that this pattern of conflict is reflected in the views of truth, history, and society, which underlie the efforts of this group to explain and oppose Communism, primarily in the thought of Brunner.

Brunner, to be sure, denies that his absolute 'No' to Communism limits prophetic criticism of the West. He calls the terrible fact that part of the working class seems to prefer a totalitarian state to the lack of social justice in a liberal state, 'a judgement on the wretched moral condition' of modern capitalist society, and 'a judgement too on the Christian Church and its powerlessness to direct the moral forces of society'.[2] The 'capitalist spirit' (which Brunner opposes to the technical functioning of the capitalist system which might, in the hands of good Christians, bear another spirit) is based on the principle of profit, not livelihood, which, compounded by money and credit into the accumulation of capital, looses all restraints on

[1]Chambers, *Witness*, p. 6.
[2]*Justice and the Social Order*, p. 182. Cf. also *Christianity and Civilization*, Vol. II (London, 1949), pp. 96–97.

the acquisitive instinct. Money, the abstraction, and credit and capital, the higher abstractions, break the organic ties between a man and his property or his work, which usually limit cupidity. A class arises whose income is unearned, and other classes neither profit from their labour, nor have a propertied stake in society. The proletariat arises which is unfree because of its dependence on the labour market. The spirit of calculation, which replaces social responsibility, drives the whole process to extremes of individualism which are a cover for the disproportionate power of big business in the total life of the world. This is the tendency and temptation of an uncurbed capitalist economy. Its most disastrous consequences are moral: (a) the concentration of possession and power in the hands of a few who have not shared their gain or responsibility; (b) the growth of income without labour; (c) degradation of the worker into a factor of production rather than a responsible co-worker; (d) raising of material values of gain and security above free personal values, hence the breakdown of all community. Communism has a natural appeal to human beings so secularized and afraid as to value only security, and so cut off from meaningful responsibility and a fair share in the economy as to place the (illusory) hope of more justice above all freedom.

The hand of Marx is visible in this analysis, though Brunner takes his analysis of capitalism's ethical dynamic largely from Werner Sombart.[1] Indeed Brunner credits Marx with being a moral prophet who first invented the concept of capitalism and accurately described its evils for his day. On the other side however, Marx, in Brunner's view, was himself in the tradition of the progressivist, individualist, equalitarian rationalism whose phenomena he was opposing. Behind him lay the break of this humanism with its roots in Christian revelation, its trend through idealism with its subjectivist idea of truth, its confidence in the goodness of rational human nature, its faith in historical progress, its natural harmonies between individual and community, and its justice grounded only in human nature; and the breakdown of this idealism into naturalist positivism with its relativism about truth,

[1] *The Divine Imperative* (London, 1937), p. 665. See also *Der Kapitalismus als Problem der Kirche* (Zurich, 1947).

evolutionary theory with its a-moral overtones, and finally materialism. Marx operated, says Brunner, with a thoroughly individualistic ideal. 'Man is free only if he owes his existence to himself' (Marx). Therefore he could not accept a God on whom man is dependent. Therefore he saw man's religious dependence as a reflection of his economic dependence in the capitalist system, and man's hope in the absolute equality which would follow the abolition of exploitation and the establishment of absolute freedom. Communism was to be the means to this; Brunner holds Marx to be a progressivist trying to save the progress theory by his doctrine of inevitable revolution.

In this understanding of the world as it now is, on the other hand, Brunner sees Marx as in sharp reaction against the idealist humanism of his predecessors. His concept of man in present history is collectivist and materialist. His concept of truth is objectivist, with the material man of appetite and of the mass as object. From this combination of individualist ends and collectivist means flows inevitably the totalitarianism that Communism is today. Rationalism has left no place for revelation, and has destroyed humanism by leaving no ground for objective ethics. Individualism and equalitarian ideas of justice have destroyed all vision of plural community; of persons related to each other in different, complementary orders. Truth itself becomes instrumental by way of positivism. The extremes meet. The total state becomes the logical means toward an illusory end which is individualist humanism. In the process man is depersonalized and the human is destroyed. 'Only a Communist state can be completely totalitarian.'[1]

[1]*Christianity and Civilization*, Vol. I (London, 1948), p. 115.

We are criticizing here the general tendency of Brunner's theology rather than its details, so that a critique of his highly questionable analysis of philosophical history in the last 500 years is not in place. Lest silence be taken for agreement with his picture of Marx however, the following seem to me to be its errors:

1. There is no basis for calling Marx an individualist. Man is, for him, in ideal essence a 'Gattungswesen': a being in union with another. The socialist man of the post-revolutionary period will be a new creation, an absolute harmony of the individual and collective. Marx is more a promethean, collective humanist.

2. Marx was no equalitarian. He regarded equality as a bourgeois

What, then, is Christian responsibility in the face of this massive accumulation of the apostasy of the whole post-Reformation age behind the Communism which Brunner has described? For this we must draw on certain principles of his social ethics which bear on Christian responsibility in a world of such titanic conflict as this.

There has been a certain development in Brunner's ethical thought. In his earliest work on ethics, *The Divine Imperative*, there is a dialectical tension, if not a contradiction, between the Divine Command as the basis of ethics, and the orders of creation. The Divine Command, the will or act of God, said Brunner at that time, constitutes our knowledge of the Good. It is always specific. Christian ethics therefore is no new principle. It is decision in obedience to God. 'The Divine Command is absolutely concrete, it cannot be formulated in general terms. But since the will of God which demands obedience is the same as his will which gives, he cannot command anything but the obedient imitation of his activity as creator and redeemer.'[1]

The immediacy of the Divine Command, this openness to concrete decision in faith beyond all principles, seems to have been lost in Brunner's later thought. In *The Divine Imperative* it was balanced by the orders of creation, a concept which is the basis of Brunner's rejection of revolution, and his conservatism. God commands us to revere the form of creation in which we find ourselves, as we perceive this in the light both of Scripture and experience.

'We are to allow ourselves to be limited by this given form, and to respond to the claim which it lays upon us through the existence which it

---

moral concept. It would be more to the point to find the source of Communist totalitarianism in the fury of a utopian idealism, religious in its claims and hopes, than in the meeting of collectivism and individualism.

3. Marx never really accepted the challenge of materialism in science and empiricism in philosophy or ethics. Brunner forgets, in his generalizations about the history of philosophy, the Anglo-Saxon tradition of empiricism from David Hume, through one side of the Utilitarians, notably Mill. From this angle Marx's error is his failure to take scientific objectivity and respect for the material world, and the relativity of all our ethical standards and hopes, seriously enough. He remained a Hegelian dialectician about science and material things.

[1] *The Divine Imperative*, p. 122.

shares with us and through that in which it is distinct from us. We are to range ourselves within this order.'[1]

It is the will of God to conserve creation by his orders, and to redeem them from within. To be sure each order makes allowance for human sin. Some of them (how many is not certain) will be abolished in the last day. But until that time, as the example of Philemon in the New Testament shows, to escape from the orders is worse than to suffer under them. Brunner describes the Christian however, as a 'conservative revolutionary', because he sees the orders under the aspect of Christ's redemption and seeks always to transform them from within by his love of the neighbour. 'The Divine Love is . . . that which enters into the world by sacrifice in order to tear it out of its present accursed existence.'[2]

It is this side of his thought which Brunner has developed in later works, in which he has dealt with the Communist problem more in detail. His post-war work, *Christianity and Civilization*, adds a third to his basic principles :

'A spiritual impulse capable of relating all the other impulses in the right proportions and unifying them in such a way as to produce a truly human life. . . . An understanding of man which gives to all the elements of human life . . . their full chance, and which at the same time subdues all of them to that which guarantees true humanity.'[3]

The New Testament conception of man, in this view, is one which forms and moulds culture and civilization. There are limits to this. A civilization does not require a 'Christian' element in order to exist for it is one of the orders of God's creation. The New Testament is firstly concerned with the kingdom of God, not the formation of culture. Nevertheless there are Christian criteria for civilization, and a Christian idea of it, which is dynamic in its formation. A civilization, such as that of the West, which has been so strongly influenced by this idea can, with due caution, be called a 'Christian civilization'.

It is this last principle which seems to dominate Brunner's recent

[1]Ibid. p. 125.
[2]Ibid. p. 130.
[3]*Christianity and Civilization*, Vol. II, p. 129.

writings. From it (against the background of the orders of creation) he evolves three more specific principles for the guidance of society.

A. The principle of federalism—a pluralism of communities prior to the state. These are the positive mores-forming agencies from which come customs, contracts, ceremonies, and rights. The health of society depends on the state co-ordinating and coercing where it must, but not usurping the functions of the family, the local community, and other groups. For the modern centralistic state which unites unrelated individuals is well on the way toward totalitarianism.

B. The principle of personal freedom in community. The community of persons is Brunner's Christian antithesis to both individualism and collectivism. This means the control and limitation of those powers, economic and political, which deprive persons of their free participation in responsibility for the community. Brunner deals especially with capitalism in this connexion. He recognizes that the description of its spirit and tendency given above no longer applies, having been modified by trade unions, state regulation, and the conscience of capitalists themselves. Nevertheless he suggests three further reforms: (*a*) The capitalist's power over his property should be limited in the interest of workers and consumers; (*b*) The worker should be treated as the subject of the economy, as the responsible actor in it, and not merely as an object tossed about by the laws of capital; (*c*) Anonymous capital control should be limited in the interests of workers in the factory.

C. Justice does not imply equality, but a proper ordered functional hierarchy based on the orders of creation. All men have equal dignity before God. But a man has only such rights as come from God's grace to him in his due place in the community. So for instance different rights pertain to father, mother, and children in a family, yet these are complementary to the fulfilment of all, and recognize the personal worth of each. So also with justice in connexion with work, which is a specific personal service performed for the community. A system which destroys this meaning must be opposed.

Such in broad outlines is the Christian civilization which Brunner would oppose to the totalitarian Communism he condemns. He does not pretend that such a civilization now exists in the western world. He does claim however that ideas such as he has described have been active and more or less normative in forming the traditions of the West. He attributes the survival of healthy pluralist societies, despite the tendency of our time toward collectivism or individualism, to this Christian influence. Many a time he draws on examples from his native Switzerland to illustrate this Christian ideal. It is not surprising that his programme for Christian action in society is essentially individual and conservative:

'The primary function of the Church is not to change structures, that is, legal and organized systems, but to change the intention by the vital union of individuals and the community with the living and present Lord Jesus. Where there are people permeated with the Spirit of Christ, right relationships, laws, and arrangements always follow. This does not mean that the Church has to disinterest herself individualistically from the questions of the true order, the creation of better laws and industrial organizations. It does precisely the opposite most effectively when it equips its members in their situation within economic life . . . with that spirit which qualifies them for co-operation with and the capacity to learn from others, because it awakens in them the awareness of responsibility for a better order, and unites the different groups, workers and contractors, "capitalists" and "proletariat" in the common search for the best way.'[1]

Thus Brunner explains the theological conflict with Communism in which Christians stand, and proposes lines of action for renewal within and the battle without. Let us look at his analysis critically in the light of the challenge of Marxism described in the introductory chapter.

A. Brunner does not face the challenge of Marx's doctrine of ideology to his own thought, about the orders of creation, his ideals for the Christian community, or about totalitarianism and the course of recent history. His own answer to the question of the roots of ethical and social knowledge (given in *The Divine Imperative*) lies in his emphasis on the concrete command and gift of God's

[1]*Communism, Capitalism, and Christianity*, pp. 43–44.

grace which is beyond all principles and which reflects God's activity. In this he is one with Karl Barth. But he balances this with reverence for orders of creation which are elaborated not only by suggestive analogy to Biblical example subject to the activity of God in Christ (as with Barth), but a combination of Biblical authority and natural reason which lays him open to the charge that his own social experience and position have been formative here. This is even clearer when he begins in recent years to speak of ideals for society in Christian terms. The neatness with which he describes the Christian as a 'conservative revolutionary', the thoroughness with which he condemns the secular dynamics of recent history, and the authoritative way he feels free to expound the content of the orders of creation, all mark him as one who has not felt the impact of that fundamental doubt about human capacity to express social truth free of social interest, which a full encounter with Marx's doctrine of ideology arouses.

B. The same pattern is visible in relation to the question of history. Brunner's own doctrine of history in general emphasizes the fulfilment of history in the decision of man according to his dual relation to the Church and the world; the decision of faith in the single concrete event, Jesus Christ, who confirms history's linear character and meaning as history. He proclaims eschatology, the knowledge of redemption held in hope, against theodicy.[1] Yet in the historical analysis we have examined above, this theology of history gives way to:

(i) A picture of the historical struggle in terms almost of Manichean dualism. Brunner's emphasis on the fact that modern western civilization has heard the message of Christ, is matched by the heightened seriousness he gives to atheism. Today paganism cannot be merely a-theistic; it must be anti-Christian, 'consciously and aggressively pagan'. The paradox of his thinking is that Christ's lordship over history only heightens the crisis in history, and absolutizes the struggle between Christian and anti-Christian forces. The other possibility, developed by all the other theologians we are to consider, that modern paganism, notably Marxist atheism, may owe its historical dynamic to reaction which God permits

[1] *Man in Revolt* (Philadelphia, 1947), esp. Ch. XIX.

38

against 'western' identification of partial interests and structures with God's will, appears on the edge of Brunner's thinking, but does not become part of its structure.

(ii) Conservatism, which seeks to protect and restore the pluralist personalism that he imagines to have been active in the Christian tradition, and which in any case abjures the possibility of revolution even in the face of injustice. Brunner's attitude toward revolution parallels that of the early Barth. But Barth disclaimed social revolution as another ideology which therefore was not revolutionary enough. Brunner disclaims it because it is irreverent toward the sustaining grace of God expressed even in unjust order, and the assertion of human power from without instead of the truly 'revolutionary' influence of the Spirit from within.

(iii) Idealism which lacks clear reference to a future hope. The note of judgement is conspicuously absent when Brunner starts describing the kind of society a Christian can approve, or even the reforms necessary in modern western society. The eschatology of his theology fails to penetrate his social ethics.

c. When Brunner turns to the question of man in society he is basically concerned with the Christian conception of a civilization, its principles and criteria. But he draws these largely from his own social background. The social action to which he calls the Christian is: (i) Mild reform of the capitalist system along the lines already achieved; (ii) Return to the spiritual foundations of this civilization to prevent the acids of liberal-rational equalitarianism from furthering its decay; (iii) Vigorous defence of this civilization against the totalitarian menace of Communism.

Brunner recognizes that the first two of these may be the best means to the last. But his whole picture of ideal social conditions circumscribes human freedom by leaving out very real questions about the operation of interest and power in society. Too much is credited to the Holy Spirit immanent in the arrangements of a plural free society, and too little to the free work of that Spirit in the power sphere of his enemies. The real problems of society are always falling outside Brunner's conceptual analysis. Despite what he says about individualism, he emphasizes individual influence changing the attitudes and spirit of other individuals, as the key to

39

social change; and thereby by-passes the whole problem of power. In short we have here a typical example of conservative idealism, peculiarly open to all the Marxist charges that it fails to understand and change reality in a largely socially determined world, and helpless before the vigour of Communist power to build new societies on the strength of a future hope.

It is not surprising therefore that Brunner has little to say about the whole range of strategic problems which arise in the Christian-Communist encounter. He removes all the questions and restraints on total opposition to Communism, but he leaves open the form this opposition should take. In this situation we find two lines of strategy flowing from his theological attitude.

3. STRATEGY OF THE CONFLICT

The first of these is expounded by Mr John Foster Dulles. Mr Dulles is explicitly opposed to any crusade to eliminate Communism from the earth by violence. His aim is so to neutralize Russian power that a situation of free competition between ideologies may be set up, where the influence of example and of the spirit may be felt. He recognizes that Communism is a stimulating competition for the West, and has many social achievements to its credit.

Nevertheless Mr Dulles belongs to the company of those whose anti-Communism is a matter of absolute principle, not of practical realism, because his own faith is so closely bound up with the ideals of the American tradition. Like Brunner, against a slightly different background, he fails to perceive the relativity of these ideals. In the case of Dulles however this failure of insight is rooted in a faith which emphasizes the Law at the expense of the Gospel. His religious premises are three:

A. There is a universal moral law which has influence also upon those who deny it. Therefore there is such a thing as a world conscience.

'The need is for more effective political use of moral power. The moral law, happily, is a universal law. But Christians believe that, through Christ, the moral law has been revealed with unique clarity. The Christian churches ought, therefore, to be specially qualified to help men to form moral judgements which are discerning and to focus them at the time and place where they can be effective.'[1]

B. America has lost the faith she had in the spiritual power of her ideals and democratic experiment in the nineteenth century. Her sense of mission to the world and her moral prestige in the world has waned because she is being tempted by material prosperity. This makes her anxious, valuing security above creative effort, and invites disaster. 'As a nation, although still religious, we have lost the connexion between our religious faith and our practices. . . . We can no longer generate a spiritual power which will flow throughout the world. . . . We have no message to send to captive peoples to keep their faith and hope alive.'[2] So the great materialist power, the Soviet Union, has become the nation which seems to have a world mission.

America must recover this faith, Dulles believes, and express it in modern terms. She must 'have a faith with spiritual appeal that translates itself into practices which, in our modern complex society, get rid of the sordid, degrading conditions of life in which the spirit cannot grow.'

C. The western world needs a new faith in itself and its values, as a foundation for more adequate world organization. 'A world of free societies could be that foundation, and free society depends in turn on individuals who exemplify Christian qualities of human brotherhood, and who treat freedom not as licence but as occasion for voluntary co-operation for the common good.' Christians must produce the moral vision which will undergird peaceful change as opposed to revolutionary upheaval.

Dulles recognizes material problems which America must tackle within herself. He mentions the race problem and uncontrolled business cycles as examples. But the main enemy is the Communist system. Since it recognizes neither God nor moral law, and operates by class warfare toward world revolution, it is a self-professed enemy, which knows no limits save those of superior

[1]'Christian Responsibility in our Divided World', in *The Church and the International Disorder*, in the series *Man's Disorder and God's Design* (London, 1948), Vol. IV, p. 113.
[2]*War or Peace* (London, 1950), p. 259.

power, and recognizes any means as valid in the struggle. At the same time the 'great Russian experiment' has a spiritual attraction, fostered by clever propaganda, as great as that of the 'great American experiment' of the nineteenth century. It seems to be the great dynamic idea for today.

Strategy for dealing with this Communism is on two levels. Christians and Christian nations must beware of falling into the Soviet thesis that violent conflict is inevitable. They must not declare total war, cold or hot, on Communism. Foreign policy must aim, despite Soviet politics, at building up a world situation in which peaceful change can take place in an ordered way and in which a 'peaceful competition of ideologies' will be possible. This must be the object of the containment of Communist power, not the crushing of Communism itself.

On the second level, however, Christianity, or the rejuvenated faith of the western world, is locked in a life and death struggle with Communism. On the side of the West is the moral conscience of the world. America must make herself respectable before it. She must conduct her policies according to the Moral Law and not merely by expediency. She must strengthen institutions, such as the United Nations, in which the moral power of the world can work in the interests of peace. She must above all prove that peaceful change is possible in the framework of western international order, giving hope to the poor and weak of the world. 'We must effect peacefully those reforms which Soviet leaders claim can only be effected by violent means.'

There is a contradiction between these two levels of strategy. On the one side Dulles follows men of broader philosophy than his, such as George F. Kennan and Dean Acheson, in refusing to project the ideological conflict into American foreign policy. The faith of the Christian who realizes that the ideological conflict is not absolute in God's eyes, and the realism of the statesman who knows the horror of atomic war as well as of Communism, meet in the politics of 'containment'. On the other side however Dulles' faith, like Brunner's, is linked to an idealized civilization of the West. To be sure he, like every conservative, inserts the warning at some point that no civilization can be called Christian in the New Testament

42

sense. But he leaves no doubt of his belief that the Moral Law is expressed with a special adequacy beyond the stresses of special interest, in the foreign policy of the United States, and in the United Nations of which he was a co-architect.[1] He would find no difficulty with Dr Lowry's claim that:

'There is no question of contradiction between democracy and Christ . . . (there is) a relationship of enlarged and deepened affirmation as between the truths of the Declaration (of Independence) and the perspective of the mind of One who came as "the way, the truth, and the life".'[2]

For the other line of strategy which flows logically from Brunner's point of view—that of irreconcilable conflict whether in cold war or hot, in resistance active or passive until the day when Communist powers are overthrown—we take an illustration from the propaganda of the Free Europe Committee, which expresses the attitude of many Christians. Before the revolt of October 1956, this committee developed a highly successful system of distributing in Czechoslovakia and in Hungary a series of practical immediate demands, each representing a goal which might be, in a relative sense, achievable by pressure on the government from within the country and which would relieve the plight of the people in some concrete way without necessarily overthrowing the government.

[1] An outstanding example of foreign policy according to the Moral Law, is, in the opinion of Mr Dulles, the Peace Treaty with Japan signed in San Francisco in 1952. Here, he maintains, the principle of forgiveness overcame that of vengeance. The victor powers renounced the rights to which a retributive justice would have entitled them, and welcomed Japan once more as a partner (*The Christian Century*, 19th March, 1952). Nothing could make clearer the delusions of this kind of conservative moralism operating in the name of Christian faith. Perhaps it was God's will that the Japanese Peace Treaty be signed as it was. But the motives behind it were at least ambiguous: the fear of Russia, the desire to shift the cost of defence more on to Japanese shoulders, the hope of engaging Japanese nationalism in our cause; these mixed with the purer Christian motives Dulles described. And the results were two-sided as well: conservative big business control of the government, revival of religious nationalism, increasing censorship, and the like, as well as national independence and status. In the face of these things one might still call the treaty on the whole a good thing. But Dulles hails it as a triumph for the Moral Law through Allied politics.

[2] Lowry, *Communism and Christ*, p. 145.

43

But the Free Europe Committee is at pains to let the world know that the relief of human need is only a by-product of its real aim:

'We raise our voice at a time when the Opposition of the Hungarian people has achieved concrete results of which the whole world takes note. The Communists retreated in July 1953—but not enough. The regime can be forced into yielding (a series) of concessions; but these can be extracted from the regime only by broadening and strengthening the national opposition.

'Kossuth said of his movement, "it arose spontaneously". So also the National Opposition Movement sprang from the will of the people, to weaken the Communist system, quietly, relentlessly.'[1]

It is the spirit of these words which is basic—the spirit of implacable enmity which turns every negotiation, every act of bargaining, every assertion of truth and justice, into an act of war. For these people, largely refugees, there are no terms under which peace might be made with Communism; no basis for reconciliation, but only absolute conflict, in the service of which every temporary agreement, every immediate demand, is a tactical instrument. This is, in reverse, exactly the Communist attitude toward the non-Communist world. It is the attitude which Dulles, so far as he supports the policy of containment of his predecessors, is concerned to overcome. The Hungarian revolt of October 1956, with its costs in life, in shattered hopes, and in lost opportunities for slow progress towards a more humane society, is a tragic footnote to it. But Dulles is the prisoner of his principles, the logic of which is not really containment, but total conflict. He shares with the refugees the conviction that the struggle with Communism in the modern world is absolute, and must end in victory, or in the destruction of Christian civilization. His policy therefore is weak toward the criticism that any given common meeting ground, agreement, or deal, betrays the moral principles of the anti-Communist cause.

4. CRITIQUE

There is, of course, great difference among the men who share the general point of view we have been describing. Some are apologists

[1]The newspaper *Free Hungary* quoted in 'Operation Focus', in *News from Behind the Iron Curtain* (New York, December, 1954), Vol. 3, No. 12, p. 41.

for capitalism, others regard it as the forerunner of Communism. Some speak of the western tradition as a democratic revolution, others regard revolution as *per se* evil. But all of them agree in finding a specially intimate connexion between the will of God, the Moral Law, faith in God, or whatever their description of Christianity may be, and the spirit or institutions of western civilization. They all, in varying degrees, recognize that this civilization is threatened by loss of faith, by a rash of false faiths, and by the decay of its institutions, and that Communism is the most consistent and absolute expression of this process. All of them seek to rescue civilization by undergirding it with Christian faith once more, and to recall it to its past values and beliefs; therefore, to put Christian faith at the service and in the defence of the western way of life.

What, then, is the value of this conservative reaction to Communism, for the Christian encounter as a whole? Let us recognize clearly that it has value.

First, it has made it impossible any longer to take lightly the fundamental challenge which Communism presents to western institutions and values. We recognize in retrospect how completely such Christian leftists as John Macmurray, Harry F. Ward, Hewlett Johnson, or in Switzerland Fritz Lieb, failed to grasp the meaning of Communism when they harmonized it with Christian ethics. No one will doubt the sincerity of Macmurray's or Lieb's desire to bring about genuine encounter and mutual enrichment between Christianity and Communism. But the encounter took place in these men's minds, and the men themselves were used by popular front movements so long as Soviet authorities deemed this useful. The conservatives in this chapter have helped to show more clearly the way in which the Communist mind is warped and determined by what is in fact a new idolatry backed by power, which requires therefore an indirect approach which does not presuppose common ground. They have taught the importance of distrusting promises and appearances, and of seeking hidden connexions. They have forced the world to weigh more heavily the fact of terror and oppression, and have prevented our consciences from writing off the fate of millions of men against technical and social improvements.

45

They have reminded us of the necessity of meeting power with power against an opponent who respects nothing else.

Secondly, these conservative writers remind us of the human values in western civilization. One may differ with their attempts to give these values a more absolute status than any human creation may have before God, but anyone who has compared in experience life on both sides of the Iron Curtain learns to thank God for things which never occurred to him before in the relatively free world: for the direct contact with other people unhampered by fear of informers or police; for demonstrations in public which are free and undisciplined; for the profusion of clashing advertisements and the rank growth of competing literature in any large city; for the right to a private life and private plans, even to private prejudices and tastes. These and many others could be named without even listing the traditional principles with which we are wont to describe the virtues of our society. Helmut Gollwitzer, himself far from the conservatism we are here describing, reports his five year long imprisonment in Russia with profound Christian sensitivity, without resentment, and with due appreciation of the problems of Russian life. But the final incident, his reception in West Germany with his comrades, he describes as follows:

'Then we stood before the gates of the American demobilization camp Hof-Moschendorf. The German camp leader greeted us and gave us the first instructions: we were all to proceed to the camp office to give personal data about ourselves. The true data that is. In other words, whoever up to now had been going under a false name, now no longer needed it, "for you are now in a world in which justice and freedom rule".

'At this sentence there broke out among the hundreds of men a storm of cheers. Although this warning only applied to a few of us, it was for all of us the sign that the barbed wire was gone. The long-suppressed joy broke through; we threw ourselves into each other's arms and, for the first time, moved into a camp laughing.'[1]

Such experiences as this are the background of truth in the conservative position. John Foster Dulles is wrong when he calls America to recover a faith in its spiritual world mission comparable to that which it had in the nineteenth century; but it is because he

[1] *Unwilling Journey* (London, 1953), p. 309.

has confused faith, which can never be offered to a nation, and love. Love is not blind to the need for repentance and renewal, or the possibility of judgement. The patriots who loved Germany most truly in the last war came to hope for her defeat, for they had accepted its necessity. But love is fully appreciative of that which it loves, rejoices in it, seeks to fulfil it and affirm it as God affirms his creation. Much of the neutralism, the existentialism, and the popular nihilism in the West today is a failure of this love, disguised as that realism which claims to have given up the illusions of a false faith. It is a refusal to take the responsibility which love demands for one's neighbour, or for that collection of neighbours in their mutual relations which is a nation or a civilization. He who, in the western world, works out the implications of loving his neighbour will be tempted by Brunner's ideal of personal community as a vision for his own society. He will find new meaning in the institutions which protect and help his neighbour. He will be grateful in a new way for relative and partial justice, and for openness to repentance and change, wherever he finds it. He will find new resources in his own society and new responsibility for it in time of its danger.

Yet it is this very criterion of love which must also be the centre of our criticism of the conservative kind of opposition to Communism. For this 'No' is grounded on two crumbling cornerstones. The first is hate and bitterness; total rejection of Communists because of their Communism. The men we have been describing tend to regard Communists as creatures of their Communist ideology and Party, forgetting that they are also creatures of God whom he seeks in Christ. They tend to regard Soviet power as an indivisible system informed by the demonic power of its faith and purpose, forgetting that it is at best the resultant of the struggle of this ideology and will to power against the realities of a world God created and loves. They fail to encounter Communists as full human beings because they are determined by their opposition to Communism. To be sure all Christendom is at a loss in the problem of understanding and reaching Communists. There have only been isolated instances of success in this field so far; we dare not underestimate the power of Communism over the human spirit. But we know enough by faith and by centuries of Christian experience to seek the way not by a *witness* which declares war, but by that depth of understanding and service to the real person behind the Communist, which is the fruit of Christian love.

More seriously yet, however, this kind of absolute opposition fails to understand the life problems of the people who live under Communism, and to take what realistic steps are possible, to help them. To be sure, many of these absolutists are refugees who know the mind and attitude of the people from whom they come. Their crusading enmity toward Communism and all its works reflects the reaction of masses of people in Eastern Europe and the Soviet Union itself. As during the second world war millions of White Russians and Ukrainians welcomed the German armies as liberators, so now there are millions waiting for the American armies; millions to whom the horrors of total war weigh light in the scale against the hope of their liberation. These are often devout Christians, whose total hope is set on the day when this war will start and Russian tyranny be broken. But these reactions, hopes and hatreds, are themselves the products of confusion. They are an embarrassment to responsible western policy, not to mention the peace of the world. They are an embarrassment to the Church because the motives behind them are anything but Christian, and their hope for war as the price of liberation is an appalling choice of values. They are, finally, an embarrassment to the people who are ruled by them. Few are so masochistic as to rejoice in the sight of Soviet weakness in 1953, which expressed itself in purges and waves of arrests in Poland, Czechoslovakia, and Eastern Germany, as the Free Europe Committee does; or to welcome the famine which follows the breakdown of Communist rural economy. Another voice comes to us also from across the Iron Curtain: help us in our immediate need; understand us in our confusion, from your wider perspective; and forgive us when we give way under pressure.

It is this real need of the people behind the Iron Curtain which is aggravated by crusaders in the West. False hopes are raised, and hatreds fanned to futile self-destructive acts of rebellion. Food packages become the instrument of cold war strategy, which leads to Soviet reprisals, and brings suffering and loss to more thousands.

48

The process is the exact counterpart of the Communist strategy of increasing the tensions and conflicts of capitalist society, the misery of its workers, in order to hasten the revolution. The sufferers however, are living human beings. They are being asked to engage in a kind of total resistance, passive or active, which has no hope of being supported or protected against reprisals, by the western powers. They are being led to hope for a liberation which is not on the horizon, and to believe in a war which we in the west are trying desperately not to have to fight. In all this they are being encouraged to neglect the business of living and producing as members of a society which must exist no matter who its rulers are. The field of action for all men, including Christians, under Communist power today, lies rather in the difficult business of making out as well as possible in a total state, keeping as free as possible of its man-destroying influences, and performing as independently as possible, some service to fellow men; not, with a few exceptions, in underground resistance movements and guerilla warfare.

The second crumbling cornerstone is what German theologians have defined as *Kulturchristentum*—culture Christianity—the confusion of Christian faith and ethics with the values and traditions of western culture, and Christian action with the defence of western civilization, so that one is never quite sure which is primary. This is more than love for one's native land, community, and neighbours. It is a faith which limits love, because it cannot break through to encounter human beings who are conditioned by needs and traditions outside this western society. George F. Kennan expresses a practical statesman's objection to it thus:

'Whoever says there is a law must of course be indignant against the lawbreaker and feel himself morally superior to him. And when such indignation spills over into military contest, it knows no bounds short of the reduction of the lawbreaker to a state of complete submissiveness—namely unconditional surrender. It is a curious thing, but it is true, that the legalistic approach to world affairs, rooted as it unquestionably is in a desire to do away with war and violence, makes violence more enduring and more terrible, and more destructive to political stability than did the older motives of national interest. A war fought in the name of high moral principle finds no early end short of some form of total domination.'[1]

[1]*American Diplomacy, 1900–1950* (New York, 1953), pp. 98–99.

This shaft strikes Dulles directly. Although Kennan is an outspoken relativist in world politics, his criticism of moral absolutes reflects the Christian insight that no law, no set of principles or ideals, no concept or set of standards for culture and civilization and no dynamic principle of social relations (such as Lowry's 'Democratic Revolution') can be so purely conceived and explicated as to provide an objective standard of the Good, on the basis of which to judge between ourselves and our enemies. Every such attempt is partly the justification of the culture and social power out of which it arose. Every such Christian is tempted to explain other men in terms of principles which screen the real man from him more than they explain him. The consequence is rigidity in world politics where flexibility is of the essence, and self-righteousness which aggravates conflicts, and fails to recognize the evil consequences of necessary actions.

The same issue is at stake in the verbal duel between Barth and Brunner on the question of Barth's attitude toward Communism in post-war Hungary. Brunner claimed that the Christian must declare his absolute opposition to totalitarianism *per se*, so that what was said about Nazism applies, *mutatis mutandis*, to Communism in the present day as well. Barth however, refused to judge the historical reality, Communism in Hungary, by the principle.

'The Church must not concern itself eternally with various 'isms and systems but with historical realities as seen in the light of the Word of God and of Faith. Its obligations lie, not in the direction of any fulfilling of the law of nature, but towards its living Lord. Therefore the Church never thinks, speaks, or acts "on principle". Rather it judges spiritually and by individual cases.'[1]

Barth was certainly less right than Brunner about the nature of Communism when he wrote these words. But he was in a better position to learn, because Brunner's mind is enclosed in a system of principles, of which totalitarianism is one, whereas Barth is open to further experience of the Word of God and the concrete situation. In the next chapter we turn to those Christians to whom Barth was concerned to minister—those who have said a basic 'Yes', as Christians, to Communist dominated society.

[1]*Against the Stream*, p. 114.

2

COMMUNISM
AS JUDGEMENT AND HOPE

THE encounter with Communism which forms the antithesis of that in the preceding chapter has a long tradition in theology. Christian pro-Communists have always sought to find in Marxist doctrine and later in the practice of the Soviet Union a truth and value which can somehow be integrated with a reformed Christian faith and practice. But, as with anti-Communism, it is something new in the post-war world as well; for it represents the experience of those who have faced the determining power of Communism in their own societies, and have sought some *modus vivendi*, some way of life for the Christian conscience, acceptable both to Communist power and the Christian faith. Its chief theological spokesman, Josef Hromadka of Prague, like his antithesis Brunner, improves on the tradition he has inherited. He rejects the attempt, so popular in pre-war years, to reconcile Christian and Communist world views on the basis of a liberal theology. He does not try to harmonize Communist practice with the Christian ethic, or the classless society with the Christian hope, as do such familiar leftist clergymen as John Macmurray, Harry F. Ward, Emil Fuchs, or Hewlett Johnson.[1] Hromadka approaches Communist reality from the perspective of a theology of crisis which sharply distinguishes Christian faith, hope and obedience from such political movements and structures as may be found good in their time. His encounter is both contemporary—it has not lost its influence under the pressure of historical events as have most of the more liberal pro-Communist theologians of twenty years ago—and it is theological: consisting in an encounter between Christian revelation and the

[1]Cf. Macmurray, *Creative Society* (London, 1935).
Johnson, *The Soviet Power* (London, 1940).
Ward, *The Soviet Spirit* (New York, 1945).
Fuchs, *Marxismus und Christentum* (Leipzig, 1953).

reality of Communism, and not in an attempt to accommodate one to the other.

1. THE CRISIS OF CIVILIZATION

In his experience however, Hromadka is rather the antithesis of such a man as Whittaker Chambers than of Emil Brunner. From both men comes the conviction that the old civilization to which we belong is enveloped in a total crisis, and that Communism is this old civilization's nemesis. 'The crisis of our civilization is deep,' wrote Hromadka during the war,

'. . . deeper than many of us are prepared to admit. The civilization as it existed prior to 1914 and, in a way, until 1930, is gone. The cathedral of common norms and ideas, standards and hopes, disintegrated from within. The present world war manifests in an unparalleled way the destruction of the (certainly imperfect yet real) unity on which the community of the civilized nations had rested. . . . We are living on the ruins of the old world, both morally and politically. Unless we understand this state of affairs, we cannot help groping and stumbling at noonday as in the night. All is literally at stake. No one single norm and element of our civilization can possibly be taken for granted.'[1]

Western civilization's moral and spiritual unity, on which its political and cultural unity rested, has crumbled. It no longer recognizes a common authority in God. It no longer adheres to a common view of truth, or even of the importance of truth. The great dominating ideas of the bourgeois era which were new and dynamic a century ago—those of 'free, autonomous, self-determining humanity'—have become dead and powerless. First, the moral prestige of the West has suffered by its failure to keep the peace and to understand the aspirations of the rising masses, aroused by the Russian Revolution.

These 'might have been guided into more or less normal channels of human progress if the western nations had shown a far-sighted understanding of the downtrodden and oppressed peasants and workers of the central and southeastern areas of Europe.'[2]

[1] *Doom and Resurrection* (London, 1945), pp. 118-19.
[2] 'Christian Responsibility in our Divided World', in *The Church and International Disorder*, in the series *Man's Disorder and God's Design* (London, 1948), Vol. IV, p. 122.

Second, a fundamental doubt exists that western democracy can organize a new order on the basis of 'real social justice and equal opportunity'. There is fear that fine slogans hide material economic interests, and a retreat into oppressive reaction. Third, the spirit of western democracies seems to have become that of mere defence : negative and hostile, and hence weak and blind.

'What the peoples of Europe . . . badly need is a spiritual, intellectual, moral power to cope with their national, political, cultural issues. . . . What is it that the Western man really believes in ?'[1]

The world is in revolution. The classes which have been oppressed have become conscious and are rising up and taking over power—the proletariat and the masses. This comes as a judgement on the bourgeois world, especially in Czechoslovakia, out of whose experience Hromadka speaks.

'We set up various philosophies of history, but we did not understand real history. We greeted Fascist movements in various lands with joy. We Christians considered our national cultural life as firm and normative. But now the moment has come for us Czechs, when we have to deal with real history. History itself has attacked and overpowered us.'[2]

The Czech bourgeoisie simply collapsed. It had been undermined by its softness toward the anti-Communist crusade of Hitler. It wanted only to preserve an old form of social stratification and an old culture. It was helpless and lost before the new socialist aspirations and powers of the times.

Despite all this, however, Hromadka is not specific in his indictment. He does not analyse political strategies and power balances, cultural expressions or economic facts. His words give generalized impressions of culture and politics, in terms of the breakdown of one organizing spiritual power and the rise of another. But nowhere does he say exactly who, from a Christian as distinct from a Marxist standpoint, belongs to the 'bourgeoisie'. He does not analyse creative and destructive movements within Anglo-American or European society. This vagueness makes possible a

[1]Ibid. p. 124.
[2]'Ruf zur Glaubensentscheidung', in *Unterwegs* (Berlin), 1951, Heft 2, pp. 113–14.

Marxist interpretation of what he says, despite his theological terms of reference.

Further, Hromadka is not clear in his understanding of civilization's crisis, as to whether the bourgeois liberal world is to be condemned because it is weak, or because it is evil.

'The fear and anxiety of a Maginot-line mentality which tries to preserve old treasures and values instead of creating new ones are not strong enough to meet the challenge of the present day. They reveal a spirit of self-defence. The people who are afraid and uncertain about what they believe or what they ought to establish are under a constant temptation to yield to a political or social reaction, or to an urge to stop the morally and socially justifiable processes of history. They will yield to the peril of being destroyed by the explosive elements accumulated by blindness and weakness, instead of shaping and forming the fluid lava of the present spiritual and social life. From my own experience I know of many instances—even in my own country—where the non-Communistic groups have failed precisely because of their lack of common convictions, and of a united, morally and politically dynamic, programme; whereas the Communists know what they want, are well disciplined, and are hard-working people.'[1]

This quotation is a typical mixture of Hromadka's ideas on this subject. He demands a common spirit, faith, body of convictions and common allegiances, which will bind a culture together, give place in it for all classes, and enable it to conquer the forces of nihilism in philosophy, disorder in politics, and lack of organic fellowship in economics and culture. Because the bourgeois liberalism of 'the West' has failed to provide this kind of integrating power, it has failed in history. It is therefore to be rejected, at least in Czechoslovakia, in favour of a new power which can so integrate, even though the forms of this power may often be cruel and its ideology inadequate.

In all of this Goodness and Power are so mixed that one cannot tell which is determinative in Hromadka's mind. Has the 'bourgeois' West failed because it was ruled by unjust, exploiting groups, or because it failed to create and enforce a *kulturchristliche* unity of common aims, laws, loyalties and values through indoctrination as a base for its political and military power? Does it not

[1]'Christian Responsibility . . . ', p. 124.

54

occur to him that the kind of integrating spiritual plus political power he longs for is the most dangerous of all rivals to God the Father of Jesus Christ, and the exploiter of the needs of real human beings? Could not the weakness, the diversity, the balance of interest against interest in western society, reflect a profounder wisdom, more potentiality for the just solution of social problems, and more openness to the Word of God, than either the 'cathedral of common norms' whose crumbling he deplores, or the unity of Communism whose coming he regards as inevitable and hopeful? All these questions are overridden by the conviction that through the revolution, God has spoken:

'We cannot go back. We cannot save civilization by conservative caution or by reactionary devices. We cannot impose our abstract formulas and blueprints on the events of current history. Behind the history, the Risen Lord is doing his work.'[1]

In short, Hromadka's consciousness of the total crisis of western civilization is a highly personal response to his own experience with it, not the fruit of social analysis. In this however he represents a large group of Christians who have come to the encounter with Communism basically disillusioned with the only alternative society they know, fundamentally insecure, and without a world view which would give explanation and hope to the events of their time. The failure of liberalism in China to create forms of political order and power, and the hopelessness of the Kuomintang government over against the military, political, and spiritual power of Communism, created the same basic experience as was Hromadka's. But the most vivid parallel is the experience of certain Hungarian leaders, notably the Bishops Berecsky and Peter, whose influence, though diminished by the revolt of October 1956, in which Bishop Peter was deposed, still plays a role in the churches of that country.

Their point of view also starts with a theological interpretation of the events of recent history. The Church in Hungary deserved total judgement from God for its failure to proclaim and live the Word of God in the feudal, semi-fascist society of Hungary before

[1] *Doom and Resurrection*, p. 21.

the war, a society doomed for its oppression of the poor, the smug indifference of its middle classes, and climactically, for its willingness to join in persecuting the Jews. Berecsky recaptures for us the sense of total judgement in which he lived in those last days of Nazi domination. His experience, though personal, represents the group we are describing. The shame he felt for his nation's degradation deprived him of all human hope:

'One day I saw in front of our church a naked corpse which was flung on the pavement, and all I had to say to my family was that when our corpses will lie in that manner, there will be nothing else to say but this: "Lord God Almighty, true and righteous are thy judgments." . . . My farewell to the congregation was this word: "There shall not be left one stone upon another." '

But God chose instead to spare his Church and the Hungarian people. Berecsky realized this when the first Soviet soldiers broke in on his family. He expected to be killed outright. But instead the soldiers smiled and started to play with his grandchildren.

'In that very moment, a new reality began to dawn on me. . . . It was the kindness of these Soviet soldiers to my grandchildren which brought hope into my consciousness. Perhaps, after all this destruction, there will still be a church, a nation, a future.'

Since that time the Bishop has been 'liberated':

'I was liberated from my shame which turned into repentance. . . . There will be no future until we willingly condemn that past which was judged by God.
'I was liberated from the fear of my people's complete annihilation. I do not envy the man who has never felt this fear, for he cannot know what God's real deliverance means.
'I was liberated from fear of my church's breakdown. I knew and I know that the church has work and service in this world insofar as she is renewed in repentance and thanksgiving, and accepts from God's hand that great opportunity which he is always ready to give to a church which wants to serve and not to rule.'[1]

The keynote therefore of the Church's word in the post-war Hungarian state must be, says Berecsky, repentance for the blindness, the fruitlessness, of the Church in the old society and joyful

[1]'I Was Liberated', in *Five Years of Hungarian Protestantism* (Budapest, 1950). Reprinted in the *Hungarian Church Press*, 1st April, 1950.

gratitude that the Church may be allowed to live and serve God in the new.

2. HROMADKA'S PICTURE OF COMMUNISM

Over against this indictment of the past bourgeois society, Hromadka places his analysis of the Communist revolution in his country and the world, with its relation to the task of the Christian Church. The present revolution is, to him, unavoidable and morally justified. It is the historic mission of the Communists to be the instruments of the socialist reconstruction of society when its foundations have rotted away. Russian Communism offers the most radical plan for rebuilding Europe, corresponding, Hromadka says, to the dynamic will of the oppressed classes. These new classes do not respond to our sense of values. The liberal era is gone, with its freedom 'to believe whatever you want to'.[1] The reconstruction of today demands first of all an integrating principle, an order which incorporates the will of the masses of people for social justice and liberation.

This historical mission, Hromadka claims, determines the nature of Communism itself. Communism must be understood as an organic whole in historical movement, not merely in terms of its own, often inadequate, ideology.

'Communism is also the dynamic—so difficult to define—of contemporary history; it is that which is in the air; it is that which, humanly speaking, acts as an irresistible effort to put the disintegrated world not on the basis of personal privileges, interests, profits, and advantage, but on social equality, security, and collective co-operation of the popular multitudes.'[2]

It is therefore 'partly an heir of the age-long craving for social justice and equality, partly a child of the errors, blindness and greediness of bourgeois society'. 'Communism reflects, in a very secularized form, in spite of its materialism and dictatorship, the Christian longing for the fellowship of full and responsible love.' Its thinking is instrumental, its

[1]'The Church of the Reformation Faces Today's Challenge', in *Theology Today*, Vol. VI, No. 4 (January, 1950), pp. 457–58.

[2]*Komunismus a Krestanstvi* (Communism and Christianity) (Prague, 1946). I am indebted for this and other translations from the Czech to Miss Marianka Fousek.

'atheism is, in large measure, rather a tool and weapon of an anti-bourgeois or anti-feudal political propaganda than a distinctive faith or metaphysic'. Its driving force is 'an engrossing, fascinating idea of a society in which man will be free of all external greed, mammon, and material tyranny, and in which a fellowship of real human beings in mutual sympathy, love and goodwill would be established'. . . . 'It tends—in its philosophy—towards the total liberation of the individual man.'

To understand Communism thus as a broad social historical movement is to understand its ideology, Hromadka believes, as essentially relative to that broader movement. Marx and Lenin gave systematic form to the movement of the proletariat. They did not set up a philosophy which was absolutist or totalitarian in principle, even though the government of Russia may at the moment take this form. They did not raise any earthly reality to a metaphysical absolute. In this, so Hromadka claims, Communism differs fundamentally from Hitlerism. Marx-Leninism moves within the plane of history, not beyond it.

'The main point of Marxism is that it wants to interpret history from within history itself. . . . It does not recognize the eternal truths and norms which are above history.'[1]

So conceived, Marx-Leninism is, in Hromadka's opinion, relatively helpful in bringing out the importance of the economic factor in history. It helps Christians also to interpret the great philosophers of the past against the background of their society. Furthermore, it is right that philosophy must be placed in the service of building a better social order. The true Communist, whom Hromadka distinguishes from the adherent of the Communist Party, who is so often spoiled by opportunism, 'should be dear to us'. He needs the help and positive criticism of Christians because his rise to power as leader of thousands of workers represents effort toward progress in social life.

All this does not mean however that Hromadka harmonizes Christian theology with Communist doctrine or Christian ethics

[1] Quotations in the above two paragraphs from: 'Between Yesterday and Tomorrow', in *Christianity and Crisis*, 24th May, 1948, p. 69; 'Christian Responsibility . . .', pp. 128–9, 132; and *Komunismus a Krestanstvi*. Quotations below from the last-named source.

with Communist practice. He makes a strong point of his conviction that Communism is only a secularized reflection of some of the themes of the Christian faith.

The writings of Marx, Lenin, and the Russian Communists reflect 'the echo of the prophets and the apostles. Communism as we know it from its theory and practice, with its whole dynamic, is unthinkable in lands which have not known the Gospel of the sovereign God who descended into the dark valley of human life.'

Therefore 'human reality, both past and present, social and personal, transcends the concepts and the categories of what we call dialectical materialism. . . . Its philosophy does not suffice for the explanation and transformation of the *real* world.' Dialectical materialism is like a train which stops before it reaches the last station. It can help us on our way but it cannot help us 'to understand humanity in its depth and height, misery and nobility'. Its very greatness as a historical philosophy reminds us of that 'monstrous philosophy of history' of Hegel from which it sprang, 'without beginning or end, personality, or right and wrong'. It has no answers for the ultimate questions of life, however provisionally helpful it may be on some social issues. Therefore even the social issues cannot finally be dealt with on its basis alone.

'Human dignity, the ideal of social justice and brotherhood, cannot receive their *raison d'être*, cannot be guaranteed theoretically and morally by the mere Marxist method.'

Something else is needed. This something else can only be the living tradition of faith. The best accomplishments of Communism cannot be saved without the 'deep moral fires' and the 'devotion to trans-historical ideals' of Christianity, and without knowledge of human guilt and sin taken up in the forgiveness of God. The same faith which now sees the historical importance of Communism as an expression of the world's revolution 'is a guarantee that our history will not stop at Communism. The movement for justice and freedom will go on, measured and limited only by the Kingdom of God.'

The Christian therefore, in Hromadka's view, must guard Communism against the tendency to claim religious validity.

'If Communism becomes a religion, itself the highest norm, it will be transformed into an idolatry and tyranny, and idolatry and tyranny bear in themselves the seeds of disintegration and death.'

And the Christian must say 'No' to Communist philosophy at three basic points.

'1. State and society can claim no such loyalty, as would be unlimited. However powerful they may be, they can never be final authority or highest destiny. The eschatological witness of the Church has things to say here which stand in radical opposition to Marxist dogma.

'2. The value of man can never be anchored in man himself, nor even in the human collectivity. The Church preaches that human worth is based only in Christ.

'3. Even in a classless society the witness of Jesus Christ will remain necessary to salvation, and will continue its work there. For the root of human misery is not the class, but man himself.'[1]

But this criticism must be offered positively, in the name of what Communism essentially is with its present historical mission.

We find the same pattern in Hromadka's evaluation of Communist practice. He does not blink the fact that the Soviet regime in Russia is 'strict, and at times harsh'. But he explains this as 'a historical necessity in a country consisting of multiple ethnic, and in part culturally backward elements, and in a nation which for many reasons had not been privileged to enjoy political liberties and popular education.'[2] He invites the Christian to look not so much at this, as at the tremendous progress being made in all fields. It is the motifs and aspirations which are at work in this Communist world which make it basically a hopeful one, the beginning of a time of reconstruction. In Russia, he claims, we see a tremendous development of literacy, of culture, of knowledge in all fields, which includes the minority nations in the Soviet Union as well as Great Russia. Constructive optimism is the rule. Over-critical or pessimistic voices are frowned upon. The contribution of Christianity to the historical development of Russia is now more appreciated. Family life is cultivated and sex morality is cleaner than in

[1]Hromadka quoted in 'Erklärungen aus Genf', in *Evangelische Welt*, Jg. VII Nr. 16, 16th August, 1953, p. 472. Statement made to the World Student Christian Federation in Lund, 1952.
[2]'Christian Responsibility . . .', p. 131.

many bourgeois lands. And the Church stands—on the fringe, but it stands—bearing witness to its Lord and to the fact that even a revolutionary materialist society must have to do with the Lord of history.

By analogy with this latest phase of Communism in Russia, he finds that Czechoslovakia too is 'on the threshold of a new era.'[1] The churches are offered officially a part in the reconstruction of this new era, through the new church laws. Everything depends on an atmosphere of mutual trust and good will, of co-operation on common tasks, being built up within the framework of these laws.

Hromadka recognizes certain evils and dangers which lurk in this Communist practice. The concentration of power which we find in the hands of Soviet leaders may tempt them, despite the Communist rejection of the idea of personal dictatorship, to world domination and catastrophe. The philosophy of historical materialism, since it denies all norms beyond the process of history itself, may break down self-control and conscience, leaving the world a prey to animal passions. It is doubtful whether the revolutionary tradition and Marxist materialism can protect human freedom or appreciate human personality. The Communist methods of dealing with minorities and adversaries often disturb honest men. In such cases as these the Church must raise a prophetic voice in warning.

'The Christian faith calls out to the revolutionaries: Avoid new injustice, for the wrath of the Holy Lord will come upon you and your children if you arbitrarily and arrogantly trample upon eternally valid laws of right and mercy and truth. It reminds the victorious revolutionaries: Do not boast of your victory. Do not consider yourselves anything more than servants of men. And especially do not think that your revolution is the last stage in human history! The Lord God is Lord even over Communism, and already today is preparing new forms of social life which will grow high above even the best that Communism can offer.'[2]

[1] Cf. 'On the Threshold of a New Era', tr. from *Krestanska Revue*, October 1949, and mimeographed by the World Student Christian Federation (Geneva). The article welcomed the new church laws in Czechoslovakia which put the essential finances of the churches, including pastors' salaries, into the hands of the state, and provided for state supervision in the selection of clergy and other church matters.

[2] *Komunismus a Krestanstvi.*

However this warning again must be couched in terms which recognize the basically constructive impulse in Communism:

'Let us once more appeal to the leaders of the Soviet community and of the communistic parties to rely less on the violent methods of agitation, threat, deportation, trials and police control, and to arouse in man his noblest sentiments of sympathy for the poor, the weak, the helpless and the miserable, to awaken him to what is after all the core of socialistic humanism.'[1]

Thus Hromadka's picture of Communism. Once again it is representative, of appraisals both in Hungary and in China, although in neither country has so outspoken a critic of certain aspects of Communism arisen among the 'progressive' Christians. In China it is the devotion, discipline, and the selfless spirit of the Communists which has most impressed these Christians, and has helped to convince them that the heart of Communism is the service of the people in the hope of a strong socialist China, rather than its dictatorship, its oppression or inhumanity. In Hungary the transfer has been natural from gratitude for God's grace in not destroying the Church utterly, to gratitude for the privilege of aiding in the 'construction of the socialist society'. The following criticisms therefore, apply to a certain extent more widely than to Hromadka himself.

A. In the first place he evokes an image of the Communist movement which identifies it with a kind of ideal moral-historical force of his own definition, rather than with the reality, either of the proletarian revolution, or of the Marx-Leninist Communist Party. Had he started with the proletarian revolution, he would have had to raise the serious doubt, whether in fact the Communist Party or philosophy is any longer the expression of that revolution. As it is he takes this problematical fact for granted. Had he started with the Communist party as a reality, he could not have interpreted its movement so freely in terms of moral purposes, nor could he have called its atheism purely instrumental.

B. Hromadka is of course right that Marx and Lenin regarded theory as inseparably bound to practice, and the consciousness as a reflection of material existence. But he is wrong in assuming that

[1]'Christian Responsibility . . .', pp. 141–2.

therefore Communism differs from Nazism in not raising any earthly reality to a metaphysical absolute. Marx-Leninism is not a science designed to be helpful in explaining the economic background of social action, and in achieving a generally recognized ideal society. It is a 'science' whose object of investigation and allegiance is, not economic reality and human welfare as a whole, but the experience and success of a particular movement in politics led by the Communist Party, which is presumed *a priori* to represent the proletariat. Hromadka completely misses the heretical nature of Communism as a counter-faith, in the very act of calling it a secularized version of some Christian themes, because he does not see through the pretensions of this counter-faith to absoluteness as a science. He does not see the way in which these Christian themes still are dogmas in their secularized state. Therefore he gravely underestimates the difficulty of the Christian-Communist encounter and mutual interaction.

c. Basically, Hromadka comes out with a two-story universe in relation to Communism, which leaves ultimate truth, final goodness, and eschatological hope to Christianity, while granting to the Communist movement and ideology the right to interpret and control the immediate movements of history. Although he may not find the materialist interpretation of historical movements congenial, he nowhere offers his own interpretation of these movements such as might be compared with the Communist one. We are not shown where Marxism fails in its analysis of social reality, despite the general statement that it lacks the capacity to understand that reality in its fullness. We are left with the image of a train which is on the right track, moving with proper speed and power, but which stops before the last station. Christianity is needed, on the political level, to complete the revolution which Communism has begun.

D. It is not surprising therefore that, in his analysis of Communist practice, Hromadka is urgently concerned to find grounds for basic optimism; and that he does so by ignoring the basic problem of power in a totalitarian state. During the war he contrasted his hopes that a spiritual though socialist Russia would emerge from the war, with the possibility that she might become instead more intensely imperialistic, dominated by lust for power and dominion. But he dismissed the latter possibility with the remark that internationalism would be helped far more by faith than by 'cynical realism'.[1] This could be applied to the post-war world. The new church laws in Czechoslovakia provide that ministers are to be paid by the state, which also is to have a say in their selection. To regard this, as Hromadka does, as an opportunity for the growth of co-operation, mutual trust, and good will, is faith. To regard it as state control over the Church with the sinister implications this bears, is cynical realism. For the western nations to negotiate with Russia on the basis of the latter's proposals for German unification, would be faith. To seek such conditions for for German unification, as Russia could not violate, would be 'cynical realism'. The pattern repeats itself continually in Hromadka's thought. The question of power realities is overridden in his mind by his basic sense of the historical rightness of the Communist revolution. In this process concrete human beings and human problems fail to come into focus.

3. HROMADKA'S UNDERLYING THEOLOGY

We have already described Hromadka's encounter with Communism, despite his basic approval of it, as theological. Before turning to his strategy of Christian response to Communism therefore, let us look more closely at the theology which underlies it.

A. The concept of crisis is for Hromadka theological as well as political. His answer to the Marxist criticism of religion and doctrine of ideology is, therefore, to refer the Church to the total crisis in which it stands before God.

'What is going on at the precise point where the personal vertical challenge of the Living God cuts across the very existence of our personal life? What does it mean that God, *the God*, and not our *idea* of the Prime Cause, not our idea of the Holy, not our better self, nor the Spirit of Nature, nor the Harmonizer of the Universe, encounters us and demands a personal, inescapable life and death decision? A decision *hic et nunc*, at the present moment, a decision that cannot be shirked or delayed or postponed? These are the central questions of theology.'[2]

[1]*Christianity and Crisis*, 24th January, 1944.
[2]*Doom and Resurrection*, pp. 91–92.

In this crisis of decision neither Marx nor the Church as it has existed is justified. This is the ultimate dimension of revelation by which every human truth, not least religious truth embedded conservatively in a culture and social order, is called in question, and given new existence.

In an early work, however, Hromadka gives a special dignity to the natural knowledge of God, the reason of the Enlightenment, over against the false pretences of the 'religion' of Schleiermacher, Schelling, and Hegel with its idealism and pietism. Natural reason, he maintains, has a positive relation to God's revelation, because it gives knowledge, not of God the Creator himself, but of his works, traces and hints of his activity. It is possible because God is the Creator. It has the character of a church porch. It depends on the background of divine revelation in Christ, through whom the the Creator is known. But it reminds the believer of the works of creation.[1]

No mention is made of Marx in connexion with this essay. Very little is said, except by way of rejection, about Hegel's historical dialectic. Yet we can see here the sense in which Hromadka later can accept Marxism in place of, or in addition to Enlightenment reason, as a porch of the church which is God's revelation. We can also see why his thought was able to take in Marxism so uncritically on its own level. As with Enlightenment reason earlier, Hromadka's highly existential crisis theology accepted this relative 'science', without gaining from his theology itself the basis on which to question its credentials on the level of social and economic reality.

B. But the centre of Hromadka's theology is his doctrine of history. The historical Word of God which he is concerned to proclaim, separates him fundamentally from those liberal theologians who have sought a synthesis between Christian and Communist theory. The roots of his theology are in the heritage of the Czech reformation, and the crisis theology of Karl Barth. From the former comes his faith in the lordship of Jesus Christ over all powers on earth, and his instrumental view of the Church as servant of his lordship. Hence also 'reserve and mistrust over against the world,

[1] 'Prirozene nabozenstvi' (Natural Religion), in *Sbornik K Prvnimu Desitileti Husovy Fakulty 1919/20, 1928/29* (Prague, 1930).

combined with consciousness of the responsibility for proclaiming and asserting the royal rights of Jesus Christ.'[1] From Barth comes his sense of the total crisis in which human life stands when God speaks to man, in which he found a theological interpretation of the crisis of western civilization as seen by men like Dostoievsky and Thomas Masaryk. In this total crisis relative degrees of human goodness, relative values in social life are revealed in God's total judgement on them. But this judgement itself is only revealed in a 'yes' which God speaks to man in Christ's cross and resurrection; a 'yes' which we may take up in every human situation, serving and bearing witness to Christ in and through all the social catastrophes and new orders of history, and seing the hand of God in them.

Therefore the Church of Jesus Christ cannot

'. . . be at home under any political regime nor under any social and economic order. . . . She does not complain and she is not afraid when something unexpected takes place, when horizons are covered with clouds and the earth quakes. She marches quietly and courageously toward the heavenly Jerusalem.'[2]

But the Church, precisely because it lives in the presence of its Lord,

'. . . has a peculiar mission: to go down to the very abyss, where men commit clumsy blunders and make inescapable personal decisions. This is exactly where the prophets and apostles have sent her. The Lord of holiness, justice and mercy has descended from the heaven of heavens into the darkest valley of human corruption and sin, and has broken the bondage of guilt and death exactly where the power of godlessness and destructive evil seemed to triumph invincibly over Christ and his kingdom.'[3]

The Church, says Hromadka, must understand and stand with the oppressed masses in order to bring the Gospel to them. She must recognize and rejoice in the judgements of history, out of her sovereign freedom, and must act in the light of them. This the Church should be able to do more completely than any other community, for only the Christian believer is free enough from the

[1]*Unterwegs*, 1951, Heft 2, p. 113.
[2]*Theology Today*, January, 1950, pp. 449–50.
[3]'Christian Responsibility . . .', p. 117.

determinism of history to dare look upon the naked brutality of all its facts without losing his faith. 'The time of the Church and the time of the world are not identical, and yet they have something to do with one another. . . . The line of Jesus Christ and the line of the world cross every so often.'[1] So it is that at the moment the path of Christian decision and the path of Communist activity run parallel. Tomorrow they may part, because they are of essentially different natures. God is the Lord of history; but this fact does not excuse us from taking the power political developments of our time, its mass revolutions and social changes, seriously. It rather forces us to do so.

This is the theological background of Hromadka's reaction to the history of our times. In theory it retains a robust independence of political influence. In practice however this picture of the two lines of Church and world seems almost dualistic. Although Hromadka proclaims the Christian's urgent involvement in the world in the name of Christ, this involvement has more the flavour of subjection to an alien law and alien hopes—for the building of great societies and cultures—than the flavour of service to the Lord of history according to his will in his domain. To be servants of Christ is to be free from reliance on any earthly order; free to see reality as it is. But reality itself in history retains an independent, in this case largely Marxist, structure. Even its provisional hopes—of a classless society for example—are given their structure not by the redeeming work of Christ in human politics, free of all ideologies, but by an earthly ideology.

From here it is just one step, which Hromadka hints at but does not take, to the endowment of 'socialist reconstruction' in a Communist society, already possessed of a historical necessity of its own, with a positive relation to the Christian hope. Bishop Berecsky is less guarded. He asserts a 'positive correlation between the history of salvation and world history.' And Bishop Peter, though he guardedly praises the policies of his government only in political terms, finds them in unqualified harmony with Christ's redemption:

'All our work in the church, the presence of Jesus Christ in his Word and by the Spirit in our services, are but a foretaste of and a pointing to

[1]*Unterwegs*, loc. cit.

67

that work of world redemption which was made perfect by his sacrifice, and which he is unfolding to our eyes and fulfilling in the general history of mankind.'[1]

c. It is not surprising, against this background, that the view of man in society which Hromadka and these Hungarians share emphasizes the fullest kind of Christian involvement in the world, in the complete confidence that Christ is sovereign over it and asks of his Church a joyful affirmation of the creative possibilities inherent in the new society which the Communists are building. This is the key to their relation, both to the ecumenical movement, and to the state and society in which they live.

These church leaders have declared themselves, in word and deed, against all pressures and difficulties, to the concrete expression of their faith in one Holy Catholic Church, by active participation in the ecumenical fellowship of the World Council of Churches. The unity of the Church, explained Bishop Berecsky in 1951, is not a task to be mastered but a given reality which we must recognize in faith. This is the fundamental idea of the ecumenical movement. Intercession must never cease that this unity may be recognized, and Hungarians must never forget their responsibility for its expression:

'Our way of expressing our responsibility, arising out of our solidarity with the Church Universal, is to strive that our church may become in ever greater measure such a Church of God, which looks up to her Lord, obeys her Lord, performs her service at her appointed post in the light that she receives from the Word of God by the Holy Spirit.'[2]

Over and over again, these men commend themselves to Christians in the West in words such as these, asking believers in the wider Church to share responsibility for the Church in Hungary, in prayer, love and trust, as for a brother who seeks the way of Christian obedience under different conditions.

But this sense of solidarity and of collective personality, over against the individualism of the western bourgeois tradition, applies to both church and nation. Peoples as well as churches can

[1]'The Way of the Hungarian Reformed Church', in the *Hungarian Church Press*, 15th December, 1951.
[2]'The Church and the Churches', ibid., 1st to 15th July, 1951.

have a collective personality. Therefore a given church and a given nation can sin, repent and be forgiven as a unit. This sense of solidarity, parallel to but more complete than Hromadka's, is borne out in all of Berecsky's writings. It helps to explain the total and unanalytical nature of his reactions to political events, his total shame and despair for his people in 1944, his self-identification with the Communist social order today, and the depth of his allegiance to the ecumenical movement despite profound differences of mind and conscience with it. Yet the danger of a split with other Christians is more conceivable for him than a split with his nation. In condoning Dr T. C. Chao's resignation as a President of the World Council of Churches he wrote:

'Professor Chao is a Christian, but *he is a Chinese Christian who is living in the fellowship of his people.* (Italics his.) And once he has had to face the question whether he should stand on the side of his own people and preach the Gospel to them, or whether he should make a stand on the side of the World Council, the choice is not difficult. We must never forget that the World Council is not identical with the *Una Sancta.*'[1]

In Berecsky's mind this clash of solidarities is overcome by a wider and deeper understanding of Christ's sovereignty over the whole world. The Church is the servant of the Word, not its master. The promises of God are for the world. The Hungarian Committee which dealt with the World Council preparatory commission on international relations for the Evanston Assembly in 1954, used this theological point as the base of its criticism, rather than any 'eastern' political analysis of its own. It objected sharply to the idea that common moral codes or 'turning to God' are essential presuppositions of the 'temporal, relative, and provisional reconciliation' which is possible among nations. Christ has provided *all* the conditions for human reconciliation. God can use those who do not turn to him, by the grace of Christ. In him the reconciliation is already effected between East and West, among races and nations. Therefore we can speak with one another, lessen world tensions, and forbear one another in love. The Committee suggests that the Church Commission on International Affairs abandon the anxiety inherent in their concern about population pressures, and

[1] *Hungarian Church Press*, 1st September, 1951.

about the problems that would still remain if war and tyranny were banished from the earth. It warns against the religious pretension of using the United Nations to 'express the moral judgement of mankind'. This whole approach to world problems, in the Hungarian Committee's judgement, represents a failure to grasp that the primary power at work in the world is Christ's lordship, and not the moral efforts and concerns of men for the preservation of societies they deem to be good.

At the same time the Hungarian bishops have no doubt that the fruit of true Christian repentance means the support of the Communist kind of socialism. To seize the opportunity to serve which the socialist society offers her in its guarantee of religious liberty and countless aids to church life, the Church must truly repent, and no longer depend on the privileges of the past. It must repent by saying 'Yes' to socialist reform, in the school question for example, or the land reform, even at her own expense. The Church must take her stand within the socialist society, with all the earthly insecurities it brings, rejoicing in the grace of her Lord. Berecsky puts it thus:

'Our Church, by the judgement and grace of God, lives on that spot of the earth where, among two struggling giants, there is not the slightest doubt as to which is the sphere of power in which we live. We belong to the Hungarian Reformed Church which, in her earthly life and service, shares the destiny of the Hungarian people. Our task is to be Christ's Church in this part of the world; to stand here in that tension of prophetic service. . . . We must stay on the critical spot where the Church of the apostles and prophets discharges her double task; that is, to proclaim God's Gospel and law, and to intercede, in repentance, in the sight of our forgiving and gracious God, for our people. . . . Our Church is not between East and West; our Church is in the East. She must serve here, and she must accept from God's gracious hand all struggles, travails, positive achievements, of the great transition in which we live, as opportunities to serve.'[1]

Such is the way of repentance for the Church. The way the bishop outlines for the world is similar. The revolution is not limited to the east. Colonial peoples are rising throughout the world. The question for the ecumenical movement is whether she

[1]'On the Prophetic Service of the Church', *Hungarian Church Press*, 1st February, 1952.

70

will find true repentance in time to meet this movement creatively. Hungarian church leaders continually charge ecumenical agencies with insincere repentance; with critical statements about the West carefully qualified so that those who are at home in a system of capitalist exploitation will not be truly challenged by them. They question the support which western Christians give to the policies of their nations, and defend the Communist-sponsored programme, always by pointing to this issue. So the silence of western churches on the admission of China to the United Nations and the re-armament of Germany, and above all the Toronto statement of the World Council Central Committee supporting the United Nations' action in Korea, are traced to Christians' lack of real freedom from bourgeois domination, which can only come when they truly repent.

4. THE STRATEGY OF CHRISTIAN WITNESS

Such is the involvement of man in society from this Czech and Hungarian point of view. What then, must the Church do to bear its witness to a Communist society? It must first of all, says Hromadka, preach the Gospel in a positive way, not obscuring the ideological differences between Christianity and Communism but subjecting the Communists to a helpful critique. The leaders of the new Czechoslovak government for example are indeed devoted to a new ideology, but they are honest hardworking men who are still making their way. They are not certain that their ideology, which calls for a 'religionless' state, will prove correct. This is an area which 'they lack the culture of the heart' to understand.[1] They need constructive education as much as criticism. The Church must assist with her prayers and the activity of her members the building of a socialist society to the end that exploitation, injustice, and violence be abolished and a classless society be created. She must 'help the aspirations' of the Communists and 'purify them of human faults'.

In doing this, the Church must speak the truth as it is in Christ, and must therefore criticize, as Hromadka continually does in his

[1] Remarks by Hromadka in Minutes of the Central Committee of the World Council of Churches, Chichester, July, 1949.

71

country, the Communist ideology. But Christians must also be quick to help victims of injustice, to intercede with the government for individuals who suffer unfairly, and to exercise brotherly love toward all, be they Communists or reactionaries.

'Of course,' he writes, 'we must be objective and precise when we deal with these things, especially when we make them public. When we have seen a clear injustice happen, we have the possibility of turning to a Party member or government official. We have contact with some of them. We know in fact that we should make much more use of these possibilities than we do.'[1]

Hromadka claims that he intercedes in cases of injustice 'almost every week'.[2]

There is also a moment, in any society, when the Church must say an absolute 'No':

'. . . if someone tries to lead her away from God's authority and to subject her to a human authority. The Church accepts the social reconstruction even if many of her members look upon it with antagonism. But the Church is not mute, especially when she sees injustices done wilfully, when human dignity is maliciously trampled upon, when people seat themselves upon the throne of God (Ps. 73. 4–5). Whenever the authority of the living God and the validity of his Word are questioned, the Church, and especially the Church of the Reformation, has to speak clearly and definitely.'[3]

For this great 'No' the Church must purify her position in order that its motive be not mistaken. But her primary work is her 'Yes' to Christ who called the needy in high and low position to himself. She must not demand an irresponsible freedom which might interfere with the attempt to build a socialist society. It is her task to serve all people, to have 'honest conversation with the Gentiles', to 'be the transforming power, and keep the new socialistic and communistic order free from spiritual stagnation and impotence'.

Hromadka also includes in his writings a plea to western non-Communist society. 'Let me repeat over and over again: all

[1] *Evangelische Welt*, p. 473.
[2] From the report of a lecture in Budapest before a preparatory study conference for the Evanston Assembly of the World Council of Churches, February, 1954.
[3] *Theology Today*, 1950, p. 459.

Europeans, eastern not less than western, would be terribly impoverished, intellectually, morally, and politically, if the 'West' should break down under its own weariness, exhaustion, and lack of vision.'[1] Many of the values and achievements of the West are missing in the Communist world. But the West must search back into the dynamic of its own traditions—its great philosophers and its Christian heritage—to reform itself. Here it must find not only freedom, but social security, organic fellowship, and 'a deep faith, warm conviction, and an ardent hope', out of which will come new planning and strength to mould the future. This is, in other words, not the Christian faith, but a culture religion which Hromadka hopes we will recapture. He is not satisfied that the West has succeeded in the post-war years. The remilitarizing of (West) Germany, the failure to seat 'democratic' China in the United Nations, lack of support for the Stockholm Peace Appeal, and the Korean war, are all for him indices that the spiritual diseases of the West continue unabated. In the self-criticism of the West, even by Christians, he finds largely pious phrases which do not press to action, by which he usually means acceptance of the Communist programme and demands.[2]

5. CRITIQUE: THE PROBLEM OF COMMUNICATION

Such are the convictions of Christian pro-Communists within the ecumenical movement. One hears them with a double reaction. On the one hand they lay claim to our serious thought by the cogency of their theology, which owes its inspiration in large degree to the teacher and friend of all these men, Karl Barth. We know it to be true that the Christian must obey God and witness where he is placed, concretely, and not in terms of the principles of a bygone or far away social order. We know that repentance is the starting point for Christian prophecy. We share the conviction in the West that Christ's lordship makes men free from dependence on the security of a social system or culture—even a 'Christian' one. We agree that the judgement and grace of God are to be found in

[1]'Christian Responsibility . . .', p. 124.
[2]For a clear example of this spiritual questioning in terms of Communist politics, see *The British Weekly*, 25th January, 1951.

the events of history, not least in revolutions. We cannot but accept the right of fellow Christians to ask, as these men do, about the sincerity of our repentance, and the genuineness of our freedom in Christ from the fears, appeals, and ideologies of a bourgeois capitalist society.

Yet when we pursue the conversation to which this challenge gives rise, we quickly realize that a common theology does not by itself create communication among Christians. For Josef Hromadka and the Hungarian bishops have chosen a side, and their minds have been determined by that choice. To be sure even here, both claim to have affirmed only God's grace active in the Communist society. Not conflict and separation, but 'seeking the welfare of the city' is their theological starting point. Yet despite this claim that the choice is a relative one made in Christian freedom, each of them is involved, not only with the human situation in Communist society as God sees it, but also with the ideological movement of Communism itself. Their 'Yes' is not only to the state as God would have it be, but to the state as the Communists conceive and rule it; not only to God's purposes for the Communists, but to the Communists' purposes for themselves. Their thinking involves a kind of Platonic realism about social powers and movements, as if they were entities in themselves before God instead of the efforts of human beings. Their Christian freedom expresses itself therefore in terms of participation, suffering, and transcendence of Communist society but not in terms of the daily impact of the kingdom of God on the world in the life and work of a Christian who is a citizen of both. Communication fails with such men as these because their conception of the worldly realities with which we have to do, the forces which are moving current history, the very facts of life, seems to us distorted. Despite their theological transcendence these men continually treat the ideological concepts which the Communists have taught them—socialism, the rise of oppressed classes in Communism, the Communist Peace Movement, and the like—as God-given 'scientific' axioms.

The same applies to the Hromadka-Berecsky concept of repentance. When Hromadka attacks 'the disquieting self-assurance of . . . too many "Western" churchmen and theologians that they are free

74

of any self-imposed prejudice and that only "the other side" might be a victim of propaganda pressure, a police supervision, and a systematic indoctrination',[1] he points to a real theological failing in the West. There is too little concrete radical repentance prepared to respond to the will of God free of that kind of identification with human culture and ideals which we have described in the preceding chapter. Yet Hromadka's and the Hungarians' own repentance, for all its Biblical sound, follows too closely the requirements of adjustment to the power of Communism to be wholly convincing. It is repentance for past sins, for dependence on a dying social order with its injustices, not for present sins in a new order. As far as it goes this is valid, because one of the great spiritual temptations Christians face behind the Iron Curtain is to oppose the 'Christian' social order of the past, with its comforts and personal securities, to the atheist order of the present, instead of seeking freedom, in Christ, from both. But these pro-Communist spokesmen fail to face the problem of repentance for a much more immediate sin—that of accommodation to the demands and blandishments of a powerful new social order, with its own total claims on human allegiance. Many words are said about concrete repentance and action. Yet we have hardly a clue to the pastoral guidance these churchmen would offer the Christian who faces the indoctrination of his child in school, the collectivization of his farm, the pressure to inform on his neighbour for the police, and the hundreds of other practical dilemmas of life in a Communist state. This theology of the concrete Word of God remains curiously pious and abstract. It challenges the West with the East, but it challenges the East with nothing concrete.

This is partly due to the psychological pressure of living as a man of influence in Communist society. Judgements must be formed on the basis of propaganda alone. Each question and decision involves the ideology, which in turn involves the question how far one is loyal to the whole Communist system. Enthusiasm, confusion, misinformation, and concern for strategy in one's utterances, all may play a role in making open contact with outsiders difficult even when no informer is within earshot. The most

[1] *The British Weekly*, 25th January, 1951.

amateur social scientist could demolish Hromadka's analysis both of Communism and of western society. Certain areas of reality seem not to be present to his mind—the scope of Communist injustice, the totality of ideological pressure with its total disregard for truth, the trend and perversion of Communist power, to name only a few. But Christian friends in the West will never be quite sure—and perhaps Hromadka is not sure himself—how far he and Hungarian and Chinese leaders who speak as he does, are expressing genuine convictions, and how far they are paying the price which a Communist government demands for their participation in the ecumenical fellowship at all. Are there political facts which these men will not recognize because it would not only be unsafe, but (much more important) would interfere with their effective ministry to a nation whose knowledge of political facts is circumscribed by Communist information services on the one hand and wild rumour on the other? How far are they setting devotion to truth aside in order to use words in the service of a more urgent ministry, that of love for neighbours who can only be concretely served at the price of verbal accommodations to and deceptions of the prevailing Communist power? In short, how do these fellow Christians want to be understood and answered by their brethren in the West? These questions, to which there are no clear answers, should give us pause in judging the men behind the point of view with which this chapter deals.

Nevertheless a final theological criticism applies to the point of view itself. The theological position of Hromadka and the Hungarian church leaders is, in the tradition of the Reformation, grappling with the concrete situation of a church, once primarily feudal in structure, now plunged suddenly into a Communist society. This is its great strength and fertility, and the source of the validity of the questions it raises. Yet it must be asked how far the naïve unanalytical picture of social history which these men express, their silence in the face of flagrant violations of other men's freedom and welfare, their total lack of searching critique toward their own society, and their acquiescence in government control in the Church itself, give a false meaning to a theology which is in theory valid. Karl Barth has been the staunchest defender of both the Hungarian

76

and Czech attempt to free themselves of a bourgeois past in order to find a positive relation to Communist society.[1] But it is he who raises the question with Berecsky, whether the Hungarian churches' enthusiasm for the socialist society does not take the place for them, in practice, of the Christian hope, and whether Communist analysis and social power are not becoming for them in practice a second revelation, much as Nazi ideology was for the 'German Christians' of Hitler's time.[2] He notes an utter lack of prophetic criticism of the Communist state in the *Hungarian Church Press*. He notes silence over against obvious injustices where the Church should speak, and increasingly indiscriminate paeans of praise for the socialist society and its benefits.

In other words, behind the orthodox crisis theology of both Hromadka and the Hungarians, lurks a longing for a *kulturchristliche* unity of religion with social power, such as we have already found in the anti-Communism of Brunner, Chambers, and Dulles. It is the breakdown of this kind of social power which has turned Hromadka from the West, and from bourgeois liberalism. It is the recovery of this kind of power, even if it be united with the surge of Communism, for which he hopes, in East and West. When John Foster Dulles challenges America to recover that dream for society, that sense of her destiny as a moral leader of mankind under God in the struggle with Communism, he is speaking the same language as Hromadka, and taking up his challenge. Hromadka would least of all accept the answer which Dulles proposes. But in the last analysis both men, the extremes of Christian pro- and anti-Communism, think in terms of a faith which is less than the Christian faith, a faith in culture, society, and politics informed by a unifying religion, which will meet Communism as friend or enemy, on its own level. In both, the Christian remains bound not to Christ in the world, but to the world of Communist power and pretension, itself.

[1]Cf. *Against the Stream*, pp. 101–24, for Barth's support of the Hungarian Churches. His support of Hromadka is cited by M. Spinka, *Church in Communist Society* (Hartford, Conn., 1954), p. 34. Spinka refers to the Czech paper *Kostnicke Jiskry*, 15th April, 1948.

[2]'Letter to Berecsky', in *The Christian Century*, June, 1952.

3

RELIGIOUS SOCIALISM: PAUL TILLICH

1. THEOLOGICAL CATEGORIES

PAUL TILLICH has been, throughout his life, a theologian and philosopher first of all. But his thought and message, from the end of the First World War until his exile from Germany in 1933, were informed by a vigorous political conviction and commitment. Heir of the more naïve religious socialism of Hermann Kutter and Leonard Ragaz, he gave the German movement its philosophical foundation and its realism. Like Marx, he did not believe that theory and practice are separate:

'In the life of religion . . . theory means something other than philosophical contemplation of Being. In religious truth the stake is one's very existence and the question is to be or not to be. Religious truth is existential truth, and to that extent it cannot be separated from practice. Religious truth is acted . . .'[1]

Therefore his early philosophy, which went under the title of Religious Socialism, though highly theoretical, was yet thoroughly involved in the social and political movements of inter-war Germany.

In this, as in all his thought, Tillich had a typological, a theoretical framework for the description of historical development, which he applied to concrete events. Modern society, he believed, is characterized by the victory of the Unconditional Demand (*unbedingte Forderung*) over the power of Origin (*Ursprungsmacht*) to such an extent that society has been emptied of its inner structure, has become dynamic and unstable, seeking with endless dissatisfaction to find its own end in itself. This is the bourgeois spirit.

These terms require closer definition. The power of the Origin is like the power of nature. It is that aspect of Being which holds us

[1] *The Interpretation of History* (New York, 1936), p. 18.

in the order out of which we have arisen. It is responsible for our sense of belonging. It is, so to speak, the substance of Being which must be fulfilled and not denied:

'The Origin will not let us go. It is not something that was and no longer is, now that we have taken charge of ourselves. Rather we remain continuously in the Origin; it bears us; it allows us in every moment to grow out of itself, and therefore it holds us fast. No living being goes beyond that which is posited by birth; development is the growth and decay of that which comes out of the Origin and returns to it again.'[1]

Over against the Origin however stands the Unconditional Demand. This arises when I and Thou confront one another and I recognize that the other person has the same value (*Würde*) as I. In other words the Unconditional Demand is the Demand for justice (*Gerechtigkeit*), and 'Justice is the true power of Being'. This points back to an ambiguity in the Origin. 'The actually original is not the truly original,' Tillich distinguishes. The truly original is the fulfilled Being, that toward which the Unconditional Demand points, but which the Origin could never fulfil simply by the power of its own Being. Therefore the Demand creates a break with the Origin. It introduces freedom into human life and places the Origin under criticism in the name of its own fulfilment. An unconditional element enters into a basically conditioned circle of Being. The infinite becomes related to the finite and yet at odds with it.

All this is rather imprecise, whether in German or English. Tillich rigorously holds to discussion of concepts without referring to the people in whom they play their roles. He is trying to be at once ontological and existential. The doctrine of *Selbstentfremdung*, estrangement from oneself, due to the powers of history which are a necessary consequence of the very structure of Being itself, and which lead to eventual completion of history on a higher level, seems to underlie this conceptual structure, as it did the historical

[1]*Die Sozialistische Entscheidung* (second ed., Offenbach-am-Main, 1948), pp. 18 f. A somewhat inaccurate translation of this section of the book is found in *The Interpretation of History*, pp. 206 ff. The original book was first published in 1933 and represents the fullest flowering of Tillich's socialist thought.

thinking of Tillich's predecessors Hegel, Schelling, and Marx. This doctrine contains an echo in philosophy of the Christian doctrine of the fall of man, but it differs in that faith does not regard the fall ontologically but dramatically.[1]

However Tillich's concepts are best appreciated, and if need be criticized, when they are seen in his concrete analysis. Historically speaking he points to the Old Testament as the first expression of the Unconditional Demand breaking the power of the Origin. 'Prophecy transforms the Origin into the beginning of the historical process, Creation, which is taken as itself the symbol of an historical act.' It stands over against the tendency of the Origin under the influence of human consciousness and freedom, to become mythical, imperialistic, priestly.

Christian history however poses a different problem, because it depends on Christ as the centre of history, the *kairos* or time in which unconditioned meaning is fulfilled in history determining both beginning and end of all history. All history is divided into periods of preparation, which are characterized by demand and by expectation, and periods of fulfilment in which meaning which has appeared in the *kairos* is actualized in culture. Christ's coming is the centre and standard of this process for all history. He is the New Being, the fulfilment of the true Origin, in the light of whom all history becomes the history of salvation since his appearance. Within this history, to be sure, the struggle between the divine and the demonic continues.

'The only unconditional prospect is the promise and expectation of the supra-historical fulfilment of history, of the Kingdom of God, in which that which has not been decided within history will be decided and that which has not been fulfilled will be fulfilled.'[2]

But Tillich's distinctive contribution is the doctrine of the secondary *kairos*, and the movement of history since the coming of Christ between the poles of theonomy and autonomy. This absorbs

[1]*Die Sozialistische Entscheidung*, pp. 27, 29. See Niebuhr's criticism of Tillich on this point: *The Theology of Paul Tillich*, ed. Kegley & Bretall (New York, 1952), pp. 222 ff.

[2]'The Kingdom of God and History', in the Oxford Conference on *Church, Community and State*, Vol. V (London, 1938), p. 141.

so much of his attention that his emphasis on the final hope tends to fade into the background. It is the sense of this secondary *kairos* underlying his analysis of modern history and his call to religious socialism which gives his message its urgency in his earlier writings.

Tillich defines *kairos* in this secondary sense, by distinguishing it from other views of history. It is not the revolutionary-absolute type which denies the past and affirms the future, whether in history or beyond (as Christian sects and Communists do). It does not set up one historical reality as absolute at the expense of all others (as the Roman Catholics do). It does not establish the *kairos* as given in every moment of history, thus being indifferent to 'the special heights and depths of the historical process' (as he believes the Barthians to be). It does not relativize the historical crisis so that

'Crisis becomes restricted criticism, radical change becomes slow transformation, the ideal is projected into a remote future, the enthusiasm is replaced by the clever calculation of possibilities, the belief that the turning point has arrived is exchanged for the certainty of a continuous progress.'[1]

Over against all of these the secondary *kairos* is that moment when a crisis of history, a period of expectation informed by the prophetic demand, passing judgement on the failures of a fading structure of social existence, is met by the power of a new creation for which the time is ripe, and which, although 'conditioned, surrenders itself to become a vehicle for the unconditioned'. When this happens this new power is *en kairō*, and the period which follows is a new theonomy—a period of 'fragmentary actualization of a new principle of meaning'. Thus the interpretation of, and acting in, a *kairos* is always a venture of faith. There is no certainty connected with it. It may not be a correct interpretation, and even if the interpretation is correct the time of the *kairos* may pass without being grasped because the faith of those *en kairō* was not great enough. Furthermore a theonomous period of history brought on by the *kairos* cannot be said to be a realization of the kingdom of

[1]*The Protestant Era* (London, 1951), pp. 45 f. Subsequent quotations in this section are taken from this book, pp. 45–53, or from the article mentioned in the previous note.

God. The power of a particular, concrete demonic force may be broken but the realization of meaning remains partial. The consciousness of not being the unconditional, of standing under judgement, of living from the forgiveness of God, is essential to the very understanding of the *kairos*.

A theonomous period of history nevertheless is one conscious of the Origin and of the Unconditional Demand so that the latter fulfils the former according to the standard and measure of the New Being in Christ. It is a period in which 'the divine is not a problem but a presupposition'.

'The separation of subject and object is missing; things are considered more as powers than as things. Therefore the relation of them is not that of technical manipulation but that of immediate spiritual communion and of "magical" (in the larger sense of the word) influence. And the knowledge of things has not the purpose of analysing them in order to control them; it has the purpose of finding their inner meaning, their mystery, and their divine significance.'

Individual religion, culture and interests are in this situation impossible. The spirit of the whole carries the individual. 'Such an age, in all its forms, is directed toward the divine.'

Over against this however stands the principle of autonomy. Here an analogy to Nicholas Berdyaev is to be seen. For both men humanism is basically autonomous, and autonomy starts with the assertion of human freedom and creativity seeking to realize, to objectify, the unconditional meaning (to use Tillich's phrase) in existence. Autonomy rationalizes and analyses. It destroys magical and original ties in order to put the parts together again rationally, and to form social groupings by personal decision, even when these social groupings are religious. Autonomy is not in itself irreligious. It is obedience to the *logos* principle in the Unconditioned, and involves 'asceticism toward the *kairos*'. It is indirectly religious, through its respect for this form of justice, order, beauty, scientific method and the like. Nevertheless autonomy is basically critical, not substantial. 'Autonomy is the dynamic principle of history. Theonomy, on the other hand, is the substance and meaning of history.' Autonomy does not have creative power. At best it clears the ruins of an old theonomy away, when it has lost its inner power to hold allegiance and has become therefore heteronomous. It prepares the way of a new theonomy. 'Theonomy is the answer to the question implied in autonomy.'

Heteronomy is the truly demonic condition of society in history. Although Tillich on occasion applied the word 'demonic' to late forms of autonomous culture, he really meant the heteronomous elements present in them. Heteronomy is the conscious attempt to suppress autonomy, to limit creativity and subject human life to a law which is alien to its internal consciousness. It sets up authority which forces obedience and belief. This is the type of authority which Tillich finds in the Nazi attempt to reimpose myths of origin on the German people, but equally in the image of the Father-God in the Old Testament. In his assertion of man's freedom, even if necessary over against the Bible, and his search for the fulfilment of human life in the communion of this life in its depths with the depths of the Unconditioned, Tillich comes close to Berdyaev and both owe a great deal to Jakob Böhme. Tillich however never attains that self-confidence in freedom which enabled Berdyaev to burst the bonds of all systems. 'That all autonomous thinking is accompanied by a consciousness of guilt,' confesses Tillich, 'has been a fundamental experience of my own life.'[1] Tillich has organized this theory more tightly than has Berdyaev. He has remained within the framework of Being, although he recognizes the often tragic conflict between the depths of Being and that which exists on the surface. He lacks that historical dualism which makes Berdyaev's thought unremittingly revolutionary. There are extremes of the demonic before which Tillich's mind stops, for he can see no further into their inner spiritual workings.

Nevertheless Tillich inherits from his German Protestant background a certain realism about political (and by implication other social) power and authority which Berdyaev does not have.

The ambiguity of every social power (*Macht*) is that it rests in every case on a sub-group within the whole state, and at the same time gives the whole state its existence. 'It can be understood as the expression of the collective will of a group, or as the production of this will through the ruling group.' This power demands some

[1] *The Interpretation of History*, p. 23.

83

form of a loyal opposition—which puts it under the criticism of the Demand, and this principle must somehow be recognized in the formation of any power in the state. In other words right (*Recht*) and power depend on one another. Without a fundamental basis of consent a state organized primarily around a ruling group degenerates to mere force (*Gewalt*) and loses eventually its power to a revolutionary group with a greater power to be in itself. Nevertheless force is always a factor in the state. Force and right go together in breaking the power of resistance such as would undermine the existence of the state's power. One without the other is insufficient. At the same time this whole analysis is not as nominalistic, or as out of keeping with Tillich's other social philosophy, as it seems. For power finally exists only by the renunciation of power, that is, by the surrender of its allegiance to that which is sacred to it and which therefore has a right to determine it. It is the theonomous orientation which saves social power from being a demonic assertion of some group as an end in itself. Such a sacred allegiance sets up a demand over against the state in which the power of the state becomes aware both of its responsibility and of its brokenness.

'Here the brokenness of the situation is the expression of a structure of the state which corresponds to Protestantism. . . . The tension between democracy and the group which bears power is, when seen from this depth, the tension between criticism and realization, the tension between valid demand and the immediate power of being, the tension between the law (*Recht*) of the Ought, and the law of Being. The mere law of Being is demonic-destructive; the law of the Ought is abstract and empty.'[1]

We are now in a position to turn to Tillich's analysis of the present social situation against its historical background. He mentions two periods of theonomy which lie in the background of the modern age. The earlier one was the culture of the Middle Ages which however, turned to heteronomy in its reaction, first

[1]*Religiöse Verwirklichung* (Berlin, 1930), p. 228. In a recent work, *Love Power, and Justice* (London, 1954), Tillich goes even further in describing the ontological foundation of true power as the 'power to be', the power of self-fulfilment. His sociological existentialism gives way more and more in later works to ontological essentialism.

to the autonomous impulses in the Renaissance, second to the Reformation. The second period was the Reformation itself and its fragmentary actualization. Luther, says Tillich, was *en kairō*. He brought about a new interpretation of the centre of history. Because of him the modern age can in one sense be called the Protestant Era. One great line of historical development, giving form and meaning to this age, has been the working out of the Protestant principle in concrete structures of grace (*Gestalten der Gnade*), and the decay of empirical Protestantism into arbitrary heteronomous forms (Biblical fundamentalism, confessionalism, and, to a certain extent, 'dialectical' theology in Barth and others) or washed-out autonomy without depth (liberal theology). Nevertheless, Tillich believed, in his period of religious socialist activity, Protestantism, like socialism, is today *en kairō*. In the Protestant principle alone are the resources to understand and interpret to itself the extreme autonomous condition of the world today, and to lead it over into a new period of reception and creation.

For the Protestant principle drives man first to the boundary of his existence where every sacramental expression of religion, every philosophy and social order, is confronted with the prophetic Demand that it 'realize the true, and actualize the good' and with judgement for its failure to do so. It demands that man take the full responsibility of his freedom on himself, denying himself all the devices of escape from it. In this boundary situation, Being is called in question. Doctrines, even the most orthodox, are revealed as ideologies, as ways of salvation by intellectual work. The tragedy of nature's growth and dying, and even more the fate which overcomes all human endeavour, good or bad, drives one to despair. The very prospect of God's inescapable and all-seeing presence into the inner structure of ourselves becomes intolerable. The situation demands the break-through of a New Being which is grace and truth.

To proclaim this grace, which comes to man in the boundary situation, is the greatest task of the Protestant message.

'Protestantism must proclaim the judgement that brings assurance by depriving us of all security; the judgement that declares us whole in the disintegration and cleavage of soul and community; the judgement that affirms our having truth in the absence of truth (even of religious truth); the judgement that reveals the meaning of our life in the situation in which all the meaning of life has disappeared.'[1]

As the boundary situation, so also the Protestant message of salvation is, for Tillich, something more inclusive than the drama of the forgiveness of sins. It is first of all epistemological and ontological, an answer to doubt. For the very seriousness of one's questioning about the meaning of life is only possible by the truth in which one lives, just as sin is known in its fullness only against the love of God in Christ. God is that which cannot be finally doubted—the very power or ground of Being itself which is that by which we are enabled to doubt. The word 'Unconditional', which Tillich often prefers to 'God', carries the idea of justification in this ontological sense in it, because it refers to that 'quality which we experience in encountering reality, for instance in the unconditional character of the voice of conscience, the logical as well as the moral',[2] which is at the same time the ground and meaning of our own Being.

The message is, secondly, broadly social in a sense not limited to the visible Church. 'No realm of life can exist without relation to something unconditional, to an ultimate concern.'[3] Thus we have a 'religious situation' in all the fields of culture and society, the church included. Here we have the questions asked to which the act of God is the answer, which judges and fills with new Being. The Protestant Church is called to proclaim the act of God and promote its realization in society or culture, and only in so doing does it become the holy society over against the profane. Only by denying this difference before God is it correctly established. Society as a whole is justified by God's grace, and the Church is called to make this known.

Thirdly, the Protestant principle and message is called to proclaim the New Being of Christ, and to live out of its power alone. This, says Tillich, 'is the richness of Protestantism which is the correlate of its poverty.'

[1]*The Protestant Era*, p. 202.
[2]Ibid., p. 37.
[3]Ibid., p. xxx. See also *The Interpretation of History*, p. 219 ff.

'Protestantism neither devaluates nor idealizes culture. It tries to understand its religious substance, its spiritual foundations, its "theonomous" nature.'[1]

The form in which it does this is the structure of grace (*Gestalt der Gnade*). This structure, which is really the same thing as theonomy, is the form which faith takes when it acts to realize that unconditional reality which has grasped it. It is the finite form in which the divine, the transcendent meaning, appears. It is the object of imaginative perception and action involving a certain risk. It unites protest and form within itself, trying to be transparent for a meaning beyond itself rather than absolute in meaning itself. Thus the religious element in it must always be questioned by a secular. Tillich calls this kind of structure-creating perception and act 'belief-ful, or self-transcending realism'. It is realism in the fullest sense because it is limited by the two factors which one cannot deny—the Unconditional, and the other person.

'Neither by criticism nor in formative influence (*Gestaltung*) may the Church place itself on the same level with other spiritual and social powers. The Church is not a party, not even when it takes up the concern of a party in its prophetic criticism and makes clear its transcendent meaning; not even when it comes close to some rational structure in its imaginative suggestions about formation. When the Church becomes concrete, when it takes form, it does not unequivocally declare for one concrete form of Being. Rather, precisely there, where a concrete de-decision is called for by the Church, it means the transcendent meaning in the form of being, not the form of being itself.'[2]

This is the sense in which Tillich called Christians to religious socialism.

2. BOURGEOIS PRINCIPLE AND PROLETARIAN SITUATION

The influence of Protestantism however is only one side of the historical analysis of modern society. The other is the development of autonomous humanism to the time of its present crisis in bourgeois capitalist order. Humanism, originally, he points out, 'can be

[1] *The Protestant Era*, p. 203.
[2] *Der Protestantismus als Kritik und Gestaltung* (Darmstadt, 1929), p. 34.

understood as a defence against religious demonism, i.e. against the attempt to shatter the human essence which is Being and Freedom, for the sake of that which is "beyond Being and Freedom. . . ." Therefore non-Christian humanism is a form of Christian development: it is the specifically Christian and therefore the first complete carrying out of autonomy, of the humanistic attempt to place the human essence on its own foundation.'[1]

Thus we have, in the Enlightenment, a belief in reason, freedom and progress which is filled with religious fervour and revolutionary power. This was the age of revolutionary reason undergirded by an implicit belief in the sustaining (*tragende*) power of natural harmony. In this period the theories of *laissez-faire* economics, democratic politics, sovereign states, and congregational church polity developed.[2] This gave way to a more limited technical reason however in the nineteenth century. Reason became no longer concerned with the ends and principles of life. It was limited to the service and development of the existing order, of production and exchange. This machinery, this system produced by this reason has become for man a 'second nature' which rules him and subjects him to a kind of impersonal fate. Man has lost control over his historical existence. This is the demonry of the bourgeois period. It is driving itself to destruction by its inner laws. This is the crisis which has produced Marxist socialism. It needs to be more closely described.

Tillich describes the bourgeois principle in an early work as 'self-sufficient finitude' (*in sich ruhende Endlichkeit*), and in a later one as 'autonomous this-worldliness' (*autonome Diesseitigkeit*).[3] In either case it is the same. Its religious situation is

'. . . that endless procession of man's attempts to fulfil his meaning in that which has an end; that ever restless dynamic of existence, which stretches over all reality, in order to find in it the rest of unconditioned fulfilment. But such a rest is nowhere to be found.'[4]

[1] *Religiöse Verwirklichung*, pp. 195 f.
[2] See 'The World Situation', in *The Christian Answer*, ed. H. P. Van Dusen (New York, 1945).
[3] The former phrase is from *The Religious Situation*, translated by H. R. Niebuhr (New York, 1932), p. 71. The latter is from *Die Sozialistische Entscheidung*, p. 49.
[4] *Religiöse Verwirklichung*, p. 198.

In this activity is expressed the broken inner relation between man and his Origin, between man and things. In the pre-capitalist world these original social ties, and the property a man possessed, expressed to him a transcendent meaning. They were symbols of his participation in the world. The capitalist system and the bourgeois spirit destroy all these meanings.

'Its principle is the radical dissolution of all original bonds and forms, of all that was originally given, into elements which can be rationally controlled; and then the rational conjunction of these elements into instrumental structures for thinking and acting.'[1]

Nature and society are made into mere things (*Verdinglicht*— Tillich uses Marx's word).

'Things become wares—objects whose meaning lies in the production of profits in transactions of buying and selling, not in the enrichment of personal life. They are acquired and disposed of by their masters, not by beings who have some kind of community with them, hence there is no limit in their acquisition. Free economy tends necessarily toward infinite commercial imperialism.'[2]

This has the positive effect of exalting personality above the realm of things and denying things any holy character of their own. Yet it enslaves man to an endless 'ever-increasing, life-consuming activity in the service of unlimited wants'. The economic function dominates life, and human personality is left with only desires and no transcendently directed love.

At the same time the individual is left alone and in conflict with all others. Such is the inevitable principle of capitalism, which is seen more clearly now that the faith in natural harmony, whether idealistic (Hegel) or liberal (Smith, Mill, etc.) has broken down. The individual seeks, in his predicament, the solidarity of common interest groups. But these are temporary, and without transcendent meaning. He may seek deliberately to throw himself into the mythology of bourgeois nationalism. This has become a new demonic force in modern society. But finally this is also an illusion because it denies and curbs the meaning of human life.

[1] *Die Sozialistische Entscheidung*, p. 49.
[2] *The Religious Situation*, p. 72.

'So man swings to and fro within himself, surrounded by an endless void. Into all his struggle toward meaning penetrates an icy breath of meaninglessness which paralyses him. . . . That is the situation on the ground of Christian humanism which has lost its religious tone, and of the rule of the capitalist system.'[1]

This places us in the midst of class war and the proletarian situation, which is the point in existence (as Protestant Christian faith is the point of view), from which Tillich claims (in the days of the Weimar Republic) to be speaking. This situation is one of existence (*des Seins*). It is created in the capitalist system and is, seen from this objective angle,

'the situation of that class within the capitalist system whose members are dependent exclusively upon the "free" sale of their physical ability to work and whose social destiny is wholly dependent upon the turn of the market.'[2]

In human terms however, it is the 'place where the threat to human Being is a continuously experienced reality in the form of unavoidable social threat'. It is the uncovering of the actuality (*Wirklichkeit*) of class war which is the secret condition of all capitalist society, although the bourgeois hide this from themselves. Tillich describes it with four terms: (i) Insecurity (*Ungesichertheit*—more accurately un-securedness). No common social or economic values remain to protect the proletarian against the threat to his existence. And he is left fundamentally without means of changing his condition. (ii) Rejection (*Ausgestossenheit*—literally, the condition of being cast out). Especially in Eastern Europe, the proletarian is no longer included in the unity of society. 'The inward, natural affirmation of his place by the other levels of society is lacking.' (iii) Hopelessness (*Hoffnungslosigkeit*). He is a victim of the system's mechanism which holds him to the minimum of existence. (iv) Meaninglessness (*Sinnlosigkeit*) in which all these others are summed up.

This is the fate and reality of the proletarian. He cannot escape from it except by the way of class war. All attempts to ask him to

[1] *Religiöse Verwirklichung*, p. 199.
[2] *The Protestant Era*, p. 241.

desist from this warfare are basically heteronomous, a further threat to his existence itself.

At the same time the proletariat is an ideal type (*idealtypischer Begriff*), a fighting concept (*existentieller Kampfbegriff*). This means that it is not simply subject to empirical verification and definition. It is a concept which gives meaning to the empirical situation. It is a concept the meaning of which is only fully understood by those who identify themselves consciously with its condition.

'Therefore the proletariat is as much a creation of socialism as socialism is a creation of the proletariat. Both are posited in and with each other. Socialism is the knowledge of the proletariat about itself, and precisely as such, is its foundation as a proletariat. For the foundation of a human-social Being is always at the same time a foundation of a consciousness in which this Being fulfils itself. For human Being is conscious Being.'[1]

Tillich therefore does not share Marx's more extreme expression of materialism. But he incorporates into a coherent theory the Marx-Leninist thesis that one can choose the proletariat, although one is not driven into it by circumstances, and that such intellectual leadership as comes to the proletariat in this way, i.e. its party leadership, is the expression of its true self-consciousness.

3. MARXIST SOCIALISM

Tillich understood Karl Marx basically as a prophet standing on the spiritual foundation of a bourgeois society, and the socialism which he founded as 'prophecy on the grounds of an autonomous, self-contained world'.[2]

Therefore he does not argue with Marx as does Brunner, nor does he recoil from the 'one great lie' of Marxist atheism as does Berdyaev. Rather he interprets the whole of Marx and the spirit of socialism, in the light of the younger, pre-materialist Marx. From this perspective he discovers a 'structural analogy' between Judaeo-Christian prophetism and Marxism, especially at three points which correspond roughly to the three points of theological analysis with which this study is concerned.

[1] *Die Sozialistische Entscheidung*, p. 60.
[2] Ibid., p. 86.

A. Tillich finds a structural analogy between the Christian and Marxist ideas of truth as a unity of theory and practice. Marx's perception that truth is revealed only in the business of acting on it, and that it furthermore comes only to the group whom history has placed in an ideology-unveiling situation, Tillich believes to be a parallel of the Christian-prophetic insight that truth is response to the New Being in Christ, and is known only to the elect group and the spiritual man. All truth must be in one sense ideological. It can be known only from some 'absolute standpoint in Being'[1] and not in the abstract. It is furthermore dynamic, truth for a particular time and place, not universal law.

Christians must recognize with Marx that the proletarian situation today, the situation of a 'broken finitude, namely a finitude which is opened for the infinite by suffering, where ideology and rationalization have become impossible,'[2] is the favoured place, from which truth about present society is to be known, in the prophetic sense, which involves action in changing that society.

The same is true in a negative way, Tillich believes, of the Marxist criticism of religion and all other 'ideology'. Any system of truth which sets itself up as a closed system of doctrine and tries to make itself independent of the situation of the knower, becomes an instrument of the power of one group defending its position against another. 'Luther's warning against the self-made god means in religious parlance exactly what ideology means in philosophical language.'[3] The temptation to this creation of ideologies is nearly irresistible in the non-proletarian classes, because these classes have so much to rationalize and defend by incorporating it into an ideal system. Religion especially must recognize the degree to which it has succumbed to this temptation. Tillich understands Marxist opposition to religion as basically a class reaction to the actual alliances which the Church has made with feudal or bourgeois structures of power.

Therefore the Christian answer to the charge of ideology against

[1]'Ideologie und Utopie', a review of the book of this name by Karl Mannheim, in *Gesellschaft*, Heft 10, 1929.

[2]'Man and Society in Religious Socialism', in *Christianity and Society*, X (Autumn 1943).

[3]*The Interpretation of History*, p. 63.

all religion must rest in the realization that this tendency to ideology is 'implied in the structure of every religion which has become a social phenomenon'. It must prove itself not by the defence of its traditional rights and institutions or even of its traditional dogmas and perspectives, but by the effectiveness of its prophetic self-criticism in the light of the proletarian situation. This means not only criticism of its tendency to uphold conservative social forces. It means the examination of honest convictions to see in how far they are 'self-made' answers to psychological needs. It means on the philosophical level that:

'Christian theology must first of all *give up its alliance with idealistic metaphysics* which interpret existence as the appearance of an essence or an idea, thus idealize given reality and support an anti-revolutionary conservatism. Christian theology must, secondly, give up such conceptions of transcendence as weaken the *unconditional significance of social aid and political achievement* by stressing an other-worldly utopia and a purely individual solution. This leads on to the third and most fundamental challenge: Christian theology must show that *it does not hold to a second world* next to or beyond the world of experience, but that its contents are symbols for the transcendent meaning of the one world of experience.'[1] (Tillich's italics.)

When this has been done, to be sure, Christians can counter-attack. For Marxism must admit a more fundamental criticism than its later forms allow. It also, like every other prophetic movement, tends to become an ideological and conservative force as soon as it becomes a social institution. But in this counter-attack Christians are participating in the Marxist-socialist movement itself, and purging it from within.

B. Tillich finds a structural analogy between the prophetic Christian and the Marxist views of history. Both are truly *historical* interpretations. They understand that history has a beginning, a middle, and an end: and that it has a meaning of its own, toward which it develops and which becomes visible in its centre. Both regard the content of history as being the struggle of good and evil forces; both envisage the ultimate victory of justice, but regard the

[1]'The Attack of Dialectical Materialism', in *The Student World* (2nd Quarter 1938), pp. 117-22.

existing order as unjust, and challenge it concretely. Both believe that only catastrophic events will bring a change from the present stage in history to its fulfilment. Both believe that a certain minority group within an elect nation or class bears the destiny of all history and is the instrument of its fulfilment. Both believe, finally, not in a mechanical historical determinism, but in an expectation with which all historical happening is pregnant, of the fulfilment of history.[1]

The Marxist expectation reflects the Christian hope, in not being merely an abstract demand placed upon the social situation—the demand of an ideal which has no relation to the movement of historical forces, such as the utopians have always made and never fulfilled—but a promise inherent in the movement of Being in history itself. 'In it also Being must be moving toward what is demanded, so that the demand may not remain abstract and powerless. . . . Out of the analysis of Being itself arises socialism as promise for man.'[2] This is the sense, Tillich believes, in which Marx's economic analysis must be understood. It is not an attempt to elaborate an independent economic science, but to express in economic terms the tendencies in the human historical situation which are working to remove the self-estrangement of the proletariat, and create a new humanism, or a fulfilled existence of man. The prophetic humanism of the early Marx remains the 'hidden presupposition' of all his later politics and economics.

The Marxist view of history therefore, says Tillich, has that combination of demand and promise which has always characterized historical prophecy. It has taken the Hegelian system with its intimate connexion between historical analysis and moral demand,

[1]This summary is taken from *The Protestant Era*, p. 278. Tillich maintains (*Die Sozialistische Entscheidung*, p. 100) with considerable emphasis that Marx did not regard his own interpretation of history as an infallible science; that he reckoned more than once with the possibility that a return to barbarism rather than socialism could be the end of the capitalist development. He gives no references in Marx however, for this statement, and he is the only student of Marx in this writer's knowledge who has made this point. Is he perhaps overstressing a few passages out of Marx's earliest thought to fit his 'religious' interpretation of him?

[2]This and the two following quotations are from *Die Sozialistische Entscheidung*, pp. 91, 92, 93.

but in which 'the Ought is engulfed by Being', and has placed it under the demand of justice, showing how Being is not fulfilled but still awaits fulfilment. 'He gave to Expectation (*Erwartung*) again the right it had in prophecy and faith in Providence, and even in the beginnings of the Hegelian dialectic.' It is to be sure a prophetic movement within the framework of autonomous rationality. Therefore 'the prophetic substance is expressed rationally' in this-wordly (*diesseitig*) pictures of a better world which is continuous with this one. But this is a valid protest, typical of all prophetic movements, against a false concept of the other world (*Jenseits*) which separates it from effectively acting on this world. The socialist hope of a classless society, Tillich declares, is symbolic and eschatological as well as this-worldy. In Marxism the *Diesseitig* and the *Jenseitig* remain in creative tension and this reflects the character of all human hope. 'Human expectation is always at once this-worldly and other-worldly; more exactly: the antithesis does not exist for expectation.'

Therefore, Tillich believes, Marxism has a value for the Christian understanding of current history, which outlives the accuracy of Marx's original predictions. These have indeed been shown to be erroneous, although he was a good analyst of nineteenth century capitalism. But Marxism continues to have power because he saw history 'in a way which makes even his erroneous prophecies significant,'[1] namely as a movement in which the proletariat is a group called to the achievement of justice through revolution toward the fulfilment of human life.

c. There is thirdly, according to Tillich, a structural analogy between Christian prophetism and Marxism in their doctrine of man. Both believe that man is not what he ought to be. 'His true being and his real existence contradict each other. Man is fallen. . . . He is estranged from himself and his true humanity, he has been dehumanized, he has become an object, a means of profit, a quantity of working power.'[2] Both agree that man's historical existence, and not some other, is decisive for the doctrine of man. And both agree

[1]'How much Truth is there in Karl Marx?' in *The Christian Century*, 8th September, 1948.
[2]*The Protestant Era*, p. 279.

that man is not definable as an individual, but only also in terms of his social existence. Tillich maintains vigorously that Marx's historical materialism, in contrast to that of many later Marxists, was not an assertion of the primacy of movements of material and of the purely reflective character of human consciousness.

'Man, the man who produces in society, is the material of all history. But just this man, and not some weird combination of animal and spiritual nature, which shows human lineaments neither on the one nor on the other.'[1]

Here again Tillich interprets the whole of Marx in the light of the younger Marx. There is no division of 'spirit' or 'idea' from 'matter' or 'economy', just as there is no division of Being (*Sein*) from Consciousness (*Bewusstsein*). Tillich claims that Marx's whole point was to stress this intimate together-ness of both, so that a spirit or mind could not be something by itself but only the spirit or mind of some Being.

In these three points Tillich regards Marxism as basically a prophecy which has become the valid expression of the proletarian movement. Because of them he calls Christians to participation in the Marxist-socialist movement, to basic common action and conversation with Marxists. This does not mean that he is unaware of the hardening of Marxist dogma which began in Marx's time and has continued since, or of the points at which both Marxist socialism and Communism have come to take basic issue with his prophetic-religious interpretation of the basic impulse behind their movements. But Tillich differs from Berdyaev, with whom he otherwise shares so much, in believing, at least until the end of the nineteen-thirties, that the basic historical impulse in Marxist socialism is not the demonic one represented by Soviet Communism, but the *kairos* in which the proletariat stands, on the verge of a new theonomy, as understood by religious socialism. All Tillich's criticism and all his interpretations of Marxist shortcomings, therefore, presuppose this spiritual solidarity with socialism as an historical movement, and with the basic insights and vision of Karl Marx. 'Nobody can understand the character of the present world

[1] *Die Sozialistische Entscheidung*, p. 96.

revolution who has not been prepared for it by the Marxian analysis of bourgeois society, its contradictions and its decisive trends.'[1] There is no religious position beyond the class war.

'It is the task of religious socialism to carry through a radical criticism of socialism, but on the ground of socialism itself. Its criticism may not weaken the passion of the proletarian struggle. Rather it must strengthen this passion in that it deepens it; in that it holds up to socialism what the true meaning of its movement is, and makes this meaning the critical standard of the actual facts.'[2]

The criticism starts with recognizing an inner conflict within the principle and movement of socialism itself. This conflict (*Widerstreit*) is not, Tillich emphasizes, contradiction (*Widerspruch*). It is the tension of historical existence which nevertheless must be brought to consciousness and resolved. The basis of this inner conflict is that socialism is fundamentally religious, according to the definition of religious which Tillich regards as the only admissible one: 'living from the roots of human Being', from the power of the Origin, and hence having an unconditional concern. But socialism cannot admit this religious character; it can form no alliances with the pre-bourgeois traditions and forms because all of these have been dissolved into bourgeois class instruments, and the proletariat has been disinherited. The proletarian situation is the radicalization of the bourgeois principle.

'The proletariat must deny the very reality by whose strength it fights the Bourgeois Principle, the Origin; and it must affirm the reality it wants to shatter, the Bourgeois Principle. This is the inner conflict of its situation.'[3]

This conflict shows itself all along the line of socialist theory and practice.

A. It shows itself in the place of science in socialist thinking. The Marxist socialist not only employs science as a method. He *believes* in science—his own Marxist science. This is the bourgeois

[1]*The Protestant Era*, p. 284.
[2]*Religiöse Verwirklichung*, p. 208.
[3]The following points and quotations are drawn from *Die Sozialistische Entscheidung*, pp. 63, 81, 103; and *Religiöse Verwirklichung*, p. 206 ff.

principle carried to its extreme. The bourgeois was a devotee of natural science but was prepared to refrain from being too 'scientific' about the social and spiritual realms. The Marxist finds in Marx's consistent application of scientific methods to the analysis of society not only illumination, but the exposing of a false bourgeois ideology by the means of science itself. He believes therefore that he has found the finally valid science, the science which is a symbol and dogma of the fulfilment of his Being. But there is a conflict in this, a faith in the miracle of a *Sprung* from a purely scientific relative insight, to an absolutely religious one.

B. It shows itself in the unsettled attitude of socialism toward traditional forms of community and toward the Party. It must carry through the bourgeois principle of the atomization of life, to reveal the class-interested character of every traditional social form —family, estate (*Stand*), village, *Volk*, and nation. Yet it endows its own Party, nominally only an instrument of class war, with the characteristics of a religious community in which the meaning of existence is found; or else it supports national or other groups in spite of itself.

c. It shows itself in the socialist hope for a coming world harmony, which 'reckons with a *Sprung* which cannot in any sense be made understandable from the given present reality.' Socialism today takes the bourgeois principle to its extreme by expressing its hope exclusively in terms of a classless society which will be a this-worldly rational social order; where power will be no longer a problem and the state will be purely functional until it withers away; and where absolute economic reason will guide its planners. Yet it attempts therewith to express an eschatological, an other-worldly (*jenseitig*) hope. The consequence is continual oscillation between the poles of premature satisfaction with relative goals— the 'petit-bourgeois character' of much social democracy, in which 'relative successes obtain unconditional meaning'—and the 'metaphysical disappointment' which may come from the failure of an idolized historical reality.

In this Tillich sees German Social Democracy as the type of socialism. The Communist Party however, in his opinion, during the Weimar Republic

'. . . escapes this conflict no more than does socialism. . . . Socialism stays closer to the liberal democratic foundation which the bourgeoisie and the socialists have in common. Communism is more ready to renounce it for the present, because it has a stronger faith in the miracle which will restore it in the future. . . . But the opposition is not absolute. Social Democracy too is ready, under certain circumstances, to give up its liberal element completely; and Communism can never give an unbroken approval to the restoration of powers of origin.'

Tillich recognizes at this time a kind of dogmatic Marxism which refuses every intellectual discussion as superfluous ideologizing in favour of revolutionary strategy. But, he says, 'The history of the German Communist Party shows that, in Germany at least, this will not work. The dogmatic foundation is too weak to carry a successful practice.'

D. It shows itself in the *Sprung* involved in the socialist understanding of man. The empirical side of the bourgeois principle is taken to its extremes to break the bourgeois confidence in human reason, and to show man as a creature primarily determined by his drives for economic satisfaction. Since being in this sense determines consciousness, human reason cannot be the source of harmony and reasonable order. Yet the socialist view of man involves a miraculous *Sprung* into rationality, whereby precisely this liberal bourgeois man shall be constituted. Socialism in fact depends heavily on a liberal psychology and on education, without relation to the deeper aspects of human personality.

4. THE *KAIROS* OF RELIGIOUS SOCIALISM

Where this inner conflict of socialism shows itself, religious socialism, in Tillich's view, receives its task and opportunity. At all these points the proletarian world is revealed in a boundary situation, an historical crisis in which everything depends on whether it will break through to a theonomous awareness of its own unconditioned ground in Being; its religious roots. Only so can socialism escape its 'philistine this-worldliness', its imprisonment in the bourgeois way of thinking, against which its whole being is a rebellion, to discover the true depths of its creative *kairos*. Only through such a socialism, whose expectation becomes

99

the vehicle by which the Unconditioned invades the world at this point in history, is there hope for the reconstruction of society. Socialism is *en kairō* because the power of Being expressed in the proletarian situation is expressed in it. If socialism grasps the depths of this Being and realizes it in society, a new theonomy may break on the world. If not, the world may turn to a new barbarism. The task of religious socialism is to bring this awareness and this direction to socialism as a whole.

This means, first of all, a theological critique of Marxism, in the interest of bringing out the unconditional concern, the religious depth of Marx himself: 'to take Marxism out of the narrow dogmatism into which it has fallen among the followers, and place it in the breadth which it had in the young Marx.'[1] This means accepting Marx's demand for unity of theory and practice, or 'existential thinking', but rejecting the distortion of this into a 'sceptical relativism according to which all thinking is only the expression of a special kind of being'. It means that Marx is right in emphasizing the basic importance of material production, but that 'the distortion of this insight into a mechanistic economics or into a metaphysical materialism must be rejected'. It means that the dialectical method is also helpful in describing the tensions and movements of history, the way in which any given structure drives beyond itself. But the erection of dialectic into a calculable mechanism of change must be resisted. It means finally recognizing the value of Marx's method of economic analysis, without worshipping the results of his analysis in detail.[2]

It means further taking Marxism beyond itself, for not even Marx recognized the prophetic depths of his own insight. Marxism was suspicious of transcendence and knew nothing of eternity breaking into time, shaking and transforming time and society. Its criticism of religion therefore was of a distorted, narrow religion, and its own hope was distorted in a number of ways by being forced into a purely this-worldly pattern. Religious socialism must maintain over against Marxism that 'history is fulfilled from beyond

[1] *Die Sozialistische Entscheidung*, p. 103.
[2] The points in the preceding and following paragraph are drawn from *The Protestant Era*, pp. 280–3.

history, not within history'. It must point out that 'the turning point of history is not the rise of the proletariat but the appearance of a new meaning and power of life in the divine self-manifestation'. It must point out the relative and time-limited nature even of the socialist *kairos*. Special forms of injustice and evil power may be overcome and a new principle of meaning may be realized in it, but injustice and the will to power themselves continue. The socialist principle must also be subjected to rigorous examination for its ideological elements. It must look forward to a fulfilment beyond every concretion of its principle if it is to be true to its own expectation.

'Socialism is not the end for socialism. . . . Especially here religious socialism has laboured to permeate and purge the socialist faith. It has tried to make clear the limits, but also the right and the meaning of socialism's concrete expectation, through the idea of the *Kairos*. . . . The expectation is always at the same time bound to a concrete situation, and reaches out beyond every concretion.'[1]

Beyond this critique however, Tillich outlines a social and intellectual strategy for religious socialists and implicitly for the socialist movement as a whole, which gives some indication of the form of the new theonomy toward which he looked.

A. Socialism must not depend on the absolute proletarianization of all other classes. It must make alliances with those social groups (Tillich mentions for example small farmers) which carry within them still a pre-bourgeois connexion with the power of social Origin, and tend to express it in some form of political romanticism. These groups will give structure to the classless society, to be sure, and militate against the equalitarian ideal. But labour itself is developing a kind of social structure, and it is right and creative that these pre-bourgeois functional and natural groups form a tension with the proletariat in a socialist society.

[1]The following points and preceding quotation are drawn from *Die Sozialistische Entscheidung*, pp. 104–30. Eduard Heimann refers to two writings of Tillich—'Principles of Religious Socialism'—which would give his picture of socialist society in much richer detail, but which unfortunately have been lost. See Heimann, 'Tillich's Doctrine of Religious Socialism', in *The Theology of Paul Tillich*, Ch. 14.

B. Socialism must free itself from a concept of man which regards him as a sociological thing, or an attitude which refuses to think about a doctrine of man at all until after the revolution. The element of prophetic expectation which Marx preserved, Tillich believes, by speaking of the real needs of man and regarding him as an indissoluble unity of Being and Consciousness, must be rescued from the psychological determinism into which much later Marxism has fallen. Man must be understood as 'finite freedom'[1] subject to structural but not mechanical necessities in history. The importance of personal life must be recognized for society and social change. Man's needs (*Bedürfnisse*) must be seen whole, in the light of his loyalties and his values, as well as his pleasures and his basic living requirements. The complex interaction of spiritual and material needs must be understood from the standpoint of a doctrine of man which is more adequate than the bourgeois economic one which socialism has borrowed.

C. Socialism must understand power as 'the realized social unity'. It depends on a basic group which is its carrier, which is able to take the leadership and establish order in society. But it is vital for the revolutionary power of socialism to be the bearer of a general justice for the society it will bring into being. This justice however must be specific and concrete, for this age and this society, not some abstract ideal. The bearers of power in this socialist state must also be subject to the democratic corrective, exercised not as a constitutive but only as a corrective principle, which protects the demand for universal justice.

D. Socialism must go into the churches both to spread the socialist idea with its prophetic power there, and to seek in the churches the religious depths of its own principle. Out of this will come new symbols around which culture and education can form a 'harmony (*Zusammenklang*) of religious and profane symbolism'. In an early writing Tillich also called, in reverse, for Christians to seek new forms of church community which would be free of the bourgeois ideology and culture which pervades existing congregations. It would then be up to the broader *Volkskirche* to carry the tension

[1]'Man and Society in Religious Socialism', in *Christianity and Society*, Autumn 1943.

between these two forms of Christian community in itself.[1] He claims not to be advocating here, however, a new type of socialist *Kulturchristentum* (although Karl Barth accuses him of this). 'The symbol,' he emphasizes, 'creates no heteronomy.' Every symbol stands under the corrective of autonomous reason, which, although it cannot constitute culture, 'is the judge of every foundation and of every construction.' Only such symbols as are genuinely Protestant, reflecting without claiming to be the Unconditional, can survive this criticism, and mediate cultural fulfilment to all humanity.

E. Socialism must learn how to fulfil all of the *Ursprungskräfte*—family, and *Volk* community especially—which have been turned into bulwarks of the bourgeois way of life. Socialism must be carried through in the nation. 'Socialism must affirm *das Volk* more deeply than nationalism can.' This affirmation is a part of prophecy, for prophecy is always spoken to a nation even when it is spoken in judgement. So also in the family it is not enough for socialism simply to carry the bourgeois principle of individual equality of the sexes to extremes without considering a new ethic of the family itself as a group.

F. Socialism must turn from the essentially bourgeois search for a 'pure economic reason' as centre for a planned society, to consideration of the concrete Being of the form of production with which it has to deal in a given society, and the forces which control production with their interests. 'Only a concrete justice (*Recht*) and a concrete economic structure can be actualized, in which the leading forces of production find expression.' Tillich gives four examples of what this may mean: (i) Needs will be more standardized in a socialist society because of greater equality of income and priority, given by central decision, to more basic needs. The constant creation of new demand to stimulate new production will tend to diminish. (ii) Technical development will depend less on the pressure of competition, and more on the interaction of a tradition of human demand established through the market, and the decision of responsible authorities. It may be that this will cut down somewhat the rate of technical progress, but it will eliminate its arbitrary wastefulness and its disregard of human labour. (iii)

[1] *Der Sozialismus als Kirchenfrage* (Berlin, 1919).

103

The motives of labour will be shifted from threat and insecurity, to an understanding of the production process of which the labourer is a part, and his stake in it. (iv) Primacy would still be given to the economic needs of the nation or social unit in which the socialist society was responsible. But its aims would be more truly in the direction of a world economy than the bourgeois individualism which it has superseded. Here also a creative tension would prevail.

5. CRITIQUE

This, in essence, is Tillich's religious socialist encounter with Marxist socialism, at the height of his political activity in the nineteen-thirties. From it two lines move forward in time toward the present day encounter with Communism to which this study is devoted, one which remains a lasting contribution to this encounter, and another which has proved itself inadequate to the realities of history and has lost itself in history's fortunes.

The first of these is Tillich's exposition of the prophetic-religious character of the early Marx, and his conviction that with Marxism defined essentially in these prophetic terms, Christian faith belongs in a relationship of fruitful give-and-take. Since the end of the Second World War a number of writers have followed Tillich's lead, returning to the early Marx in search of the key to the spiritual continuity and power of Communism today, as well as of the points where Christians might make contact with it.[1] All of them share the conviction with Tillich that the whole Christian-Marxist encounter of today can be illuminated from this point.

---

[1] The first of these was Fritz Lieb, *Russland unterwegs* (Basel, 1945). Lieb's intention was to show that a new humanism was developing in Russia which, with reference to the younger Marx, would make post-war spiritual co-operation possible. More realistic was Walter Dirks, 'Marxismus in christlicher Sicht', in *Die Frankfurter Hefte*, February, 1947. The following quotations in this section are taken from this article. See also Erich Thier's new edition of Karl Marx, *Nationalökonomie und Philosophie* (Berlin and Cologne, 1950); introduction by Erich Thier covering Marx's early development to the time when he wrote this book. See also *Marxismusstudien*, ed. Erwin Metzke (Tübingen, 1954), especially Friedrich Delekat—'Vom Wesen des Geldes, eine theologische Marxanalyse'. In England the same subject has been opened up by Alasdair MacIntyre, *Marxism: an Interpretation* (London, 1953).

Most of them however, are no longer captivated by Tillich's assumption of a continuity of Being which creates a common participation in the same reality. One illustration will show the difference.

A decisive essay for the whole post-war German Christian thinking on this subject has been that of Walter Dirks, the Roman Catholic editor of *Die Frankfurter Hefte*: 'Marxismus in christlicher Sicht'. Dirks shares with Tillich the point of view that the proletarian standpoint in our day is especially qualified to be that of Christian understanding and social reconstruction. It corresponds most closely to both the positive and negative picture of human nature and the Christian view of existence as we see it in the Bible. The bourgeois is the rich man who has secured his life through his effort and his property.

'The bourgeois world has spoken its heathen "Yes" to the world,— and has isolated the Christian "No" in religious orders, or dehumanized it in alms and charity offerings. The bourgeois cultural accomplishments, admirable as they are, cannot hide the fact that his own law of life was indeed well suited to dissolve the medieval world in the ferment of freedom and at the same time develop itself widely and deeply; but that it is ill suited to become a positive law of order in the whole of society.'

The Christian is therefore called to see the world from the standpoint of a Christian and a proletarian at once, and to contribute to the reconstruction of society according to this point of view. Dirks also agrees with Tillich that the Church has failed in its task at just this point, and must learn from the early, prophetic Marx. For Karl Marx was the first who, after having experienced the ripe fullness of bourgeois thinking in Hegelian idealism, deliberately identified himself in thought with the proletarian existence: 'radical thinking out of the existence of the helpless and exploited ... which undermines the bourgeois social world.' This, says Dirks, was an act of love, 'an act which is profoundly related to an essentially Christian act: an act of solidarity with the other, with the neighbour, a sacrifice.' No Christian thinker in the nineteenth century set Marx an example in this way toward his neighbour. Only now, much later, Christians are beginning to free their existence as Christians from dependence on bourgeois idealism and security.

Only now, under Marx's challenge, they are beginning to set concrete man in the centre of their thought, not some social or religious idea. Only now they are beginning to see that the true image of man is 'man in his greatest need in the lostness and dishonour of the proletariat', not 'the normal, socially adjusted and secure man'. Only now they are beginning to recognize that their religious idealism was an ideology. All of these things are negative similarities, where Christian faith draws close to the early Marx.

Dirks also follows Tillich in recognizing positive similarities between Christian and Marxist insight, at two points. First, the younger Marx led the way for Christian thinking in opposing his type of materialist view of history to Hegel's idealism. This early Marx did not regard human nature as a pure case of materialist determinism. His 'material' was human relations in production, which in fact are more spiritual than material, even though the spirit which governs them be 'the Prince of this world'. Marx described the real world of power conflicts and selfish drives, without idealizing it.

Secondly the younger Marx calls the Christian to sober obedient realism about his responsibility in this world of power conflicts and economic forces, for the whole life of man in body and spirit. Not just any social ideal, but the strategic next step in the light of the forces at work in society, lays its moral claim on the Christian.

The central point of Dirks' criticism of Marx is his continuation of Hegelian pantheism, in spite of his efforts to break through to concrete reality. Because Marx lacked a real faith in salvation, because God was not a reality for him, he was reduced to believing in an immanent goodness to be developed in the classless society. Because Christ as the truth was a deception to him, he sought certainty by equating scientific accuracy with historical necessity— a synthesis which no later Marxist has been able to hold together, for history does not develop according to absolute pantheistic categories. Because Marx confused spirit with ideology, he forgot about a whole dimension of human nature, that of freedom, sin, salvation, and life in God's grace.

All these points Tillich also made. But Dirks' thought represents the break with Tillich's religious socialism which

106

characterizes most post-war thinking on this question. For Dirks understands Karl Marx, not as the prophet of a socialist movement whose inner conflicts are to be resolved by deepening its own religious perspectives, but as the apostle of another faith which confronts the Christian faith at once with humbling examples of love and devotion, and with distorting and limiting perspectives and actions. Dirks does not posit a common ground in undifferentiated Being for Marxist and religious socialism, reference to which makes them, despite themselves, participants in a common movement. He does not theorize about a socialist movement of history in both being and consciousness, which leads Tillich to define Marxism as *the* necessary expression of the proletarian consciousness.

Consequently the problem of the Christian-Marxist confrontation takes another form for Dirks. He recognizes, as Tillich did not, that direct encounter of minds is not possible at first. The Christian must rather start to live his faith, as honestly as the Communist, from the proletarian situation, until he can solve problems better and think better than the Communist does, in the midst of a revolution in which all men become poor and insecure. 'Only in social behaviour in the midstream of this development shall we become credible over against Marxism.' This implies no counter-theory of 'religious socialism' or any other principle, but an open and flexible approach to social reality with only the Word of God as guide. Only so will the Christian eventually pierce the armour of the Marxist's total claim on truth and social power, and bring about an honest and fruitful discussion. This encounter will then not presuppose the world-view of Marxism or any other, but will be one in which faith will recognize faith, and test it against reality.

This is the fruitful Christian understanding of the prophetic elements in Marxism, seen from the perspective of the younger Marx, of which Tillich was the pioneer. By contrast, the religious socialist movement which Tillich founded, and the religious socialist theme in Tillich's own later thought, have proved less influential and relevant to Christian decision in the face of Communist reality. This is evident first of all in Tillich's own social thought in

107

the face of Nazism, the Second World War, the challenge of Communism, and finally the post-war tension between Russia and the U.S.A. *Die Sozialistische Entscheidung*, his most political work, was written in 1932 and published as Hitler was already beginning to make most of the hopes he expressed for Germany vain. Tillich's coming to America further upset the clear socialist challenge which he had formulated in Germany, because the American class structure differs so from the German, and the lines of connexion between social existence and social theory are so much harder to determine. By 1943 he was evolving, still in the name of religious socialism, a far more generalized picture of human freedom and the content of social change, one less linked to an historical analysis of the powers at work in history bearing fruit in a *kairos*, and more in line with American 'pragmatic' thought about social problems. At the same time his concept of the proletarian situation underwent a significant change.

'Religious socialism also asks the question of the favoured place or of the liberated finitude without being able to identify it with a special sociological group. Religious socialism is inclined to believe that the broken people in all groups are the favoured place in our present historical situation.'[1]

This was symptomatic. Tillich's confrontation with Communism in its Soviet form proved equally unrealistic. Learning from Berdyaev,[2] he interpreted its rise in Russia as a special situation, as

'. . . the form in which the principle of rationality succeeds for the first time on the grounds of a social situation determined by myths of origin, and takes over itself the unbroken powers of origin.'[3]

This alliance of Communist rationalism with *Ursprungs*-mythical forces produces a healthy tension between the planners and the peasants. But its attempt to sanctify the state in its atheism by forced education expressed the tendency of every totalitarian system to become a state religion.

[1]'Man and Society in Religious Socialism.'
[2]Berdyaev contributed an essay on 'Die russische religiöse Idee' to the collection of religious socialist essays which Tillich inspired and edited under the title, *Kairos: zur Geisteslage und Geisteswendung* (Darmstadt, 1926).
[3]*Die Sozialistische Entscheidung*, p. 65.

Tillich understands Communism also therefore as a religious movement standing, with all its dangers, in the socialist *kairos*. Christians must combat its aberrations—the raising of earthly leaders to saviours, Marxist doctrines to creeds, and the Party or state to absolute authority. They must challenge activities based on lies and tyranny. But they must do so without giving preference to the anti-revolutionary system of power. Church authorities, he wrote in 1936, must 'publicly join and transform the Communistic criticism of the present social demonries, and the religious heresies linked to them', and at the same time 'publicly challenge Communism for its own demonic and heretical elements';[1] Christian laymen 'may become Communists and try to unite the Christian principles with the principles of Communism', even if the Communists reject them and their success is small, for the sake of the apologetic effect this will have on the masses alienated from Christianity. The Church should support this attempt with sympathy, even though she cannot take it as a task for her whole self.

The unrealism of this kind of advice has been shown by history. Tillich never quite came spiritually to grips with the kind of revolution which Communism is. His categories did not provide for it. After the war he hoped for a new conversation between Russia and the West, each learning creatively from the other; and a new opportunity for socialism, deepened into religious socialism, to grasp the *kairos* of our time.[2] But he was not too optimistic and his hopes were dashed by the overriding importance of the American-Russian conflict. In 1948 he confessed that there was no possibility of a religious socialist spirit penetrating East and West with a new outlook. The hope of the *kairos* had been shattered for the second time.[3] Still, he maintained, religious socialist principles are the only ones on which Europe's social and economic life can be

[1]'The Churches and Communism', in *Religion in Life*, Summer 1937, pp. 347–57.
[2]See 'The Christian Churches and the Emerging Social Order in Europe', in *Religion in Life*, Summer 1945.
[3]'Beyond Religious Socialism', in *The Christian Century*, 15th June, 1949. Tillich protested against this title. 'If the prophetic message is true, there is nothing "beyond religious socialism".' *The Theology of Paul Tillich*, p. 13.

successfully built up. Therefore the Christian must wait and not act. The *kairos* has been replaced by a 'sacred void'.

This concept of the 'sacred void' however, throws doubt on Tillich's whole religious socialist interpretation of present history, above all on his doctrine of the secondary *kairos*. What evidence is there finally, apart from Tillich's own word, that there ever was a *kairos* in which socialism stood? As we have seen from Dirks, full justice can be done to the prophetic qualities in Marx and his movement, without assuming that Marx was the appointed bearer of an historical promise which would be decisive for the growth of a new theonomous culture. Tillich's obvious reply, that the present age has missed the *kairos*, and has opened the way to a new barbarism—not least the barbarism represented in the Soviet Communist hardening of a socialist dogma—is rather an escape from the problem than an answer to it. For Tillich earlier gave us to understand that the powers of Being itself, reflecting the power of the New Being in Christ who was the primary historical *kairos*, were moving in socialism toward fulfilment, so that religious socialism corresponded to the very dynamic of history itself. On the contrary it has shown itself to correspond far more closely to the very kind of utopianism which Tillich most roundly condemned— that which represents a demand of an ideal nature, unrelated to the actual forces which are moving history and therefore unable to guide them. Tillich's attempt to combine theological understanding with a philosophy of the trends of present history, has led him to impose on recent history an ideal pattern which, far from being fruitful for Christian encounter with Marxism, has led to discouragement and withdrawal in the face of it.

The deepest root of Tillich's failure to come to grips with Communism as a reality, however, lies in his ontology itself, which is a combination of Christian faith in the dynamics of God's act in and through Being, with generalized philosophical categories of Being itself. The Being which Tillich posited, as underlying both Marxism and religious socialism, and as realizing itself in the proletarian situation toward a new theonomy, was an illusion, and not real existence. It was an *a priori* of Tillich's mind, which made him incapable of understanding the real issues which Marxism raises for the Christian encounter as another faith, and another organizing centre in society. In the long run Tillich remains enclosed in his own ontological system, and the encounter which he has with such a movement outside this system as Marxism, is encounter with a Marxism which has been 'religiously' re-explained so that it is no longer truly itself. Tillich's contribution, therefore, to our understanding of the religious qualities and roots of Marxism is great. But his faith that the world is basically a system of Being in motion corresponding to his philosophical understanding, closes his mind to the human realities of Communism when they fall outside this system.

APPENDIX: NICHOLAS BERDYAEV

A few words must be said, before we leave the contribution of the continental religious socialists, about another thinker loosely associated with their way of thinking, though from a different background—Nicholas Berdyaev. Berdyaev, though neither a theologian in the strict sense, nor a thinker representative of anyone but himself, was the pioneer who blazed several theological trails in the encounter with Communism, which have since been followed by others. At the same time his philosophy, growing out of the Orthodox tradition conditioned by the nineteenth century radicalism he himself describes so brilliantly,[1] remains a challenge and a goad, at several important points.

In the first place, Berdyaev was the first Christian thinker to take with full seriousness the revolutionary aspect of the Marxist challenge, both in its attack on religious ideologies and its working view of history. Berdyaev is fundamentally revolutionary, more deeply so than Marx, whose impulse in this direction he catches up and develops. For him all historical concretions and achievements violate the transcendent communion of personal subjects in the Spirit, while at the same time it is through earthly history that celestial history—the fulfilment of life of persons in community in

[1]See especially *The Russian Idea* (London, 1948). His earlier work, *The Origin of Russian Communism* (London, 1937), tells the same story in shorter form. For an account of Berdyaev's own personal development and intellectual Odyssey see his autobiography *Dream and Reality* (London, 1951). This book is a key to all his thought.

communion with God—reveals itself and gives to each moment of time its essential meaning.[1] On the one hand Berdyaev was fundamentally in revolt. He revolted against history, but also against objective social structures, which seemed to him to violate the meaning of personal community, against external authority in religion, in fact against the very image of a Father God whose judgements condemn and who demands obedience. He revolted against the doctrine of Providence, in fact against Being itself, so far as this is conceived rationalistically and objectively, and against the processes of nature which presented an objective fetter on the personal spirit. But he made this revolt in the name of freedom for the human personality, and in longing for a transfiguration of this world by the fire of human creativity. It is this which makes his revolt revolutionary toward the world, and eschatological in its historical expression rather than escapist mysticism. He proclaims the value of the free creative life of concrete human beings above all the philosophies, movements, and powers of history, and judges the latter by the former. In this he expresses a Christian concern in a way which raises a question to every theological attempt to set up or justify a system which fetters this freedom, or sanctifies any historical order. He does so, to be sure, with reference to heretical doctrines. His concept of meonic freedom as the chaotic non-being which forms the background and antithesis of God's creation[2] has a Platonic flavour. His subjective union of God with man in 'theandric' personality above and apart from objective creation[3]

[1]Berdyaev's first essay on the question of history, *The Meaning of History* (London, 1936), written in the early revolutionary period before 1920, speaks much more positively about the relation between celestial and earthly history than later works, such as, for example *The Fate of Man in the Modern World* (London, 1935).

[2]The most systematic presentation of Berdyaev's basic position with regard to being, creation and freedom is found in *The Destiny of Man* (London, 1937).

[3]The most radical statement of this theme is in his earliest book, the last to be translated into English, *The Meaning of the Creative Act* (London, 1955). 'Man is not a fragment of the universe, but a complete small universe.' See also *Solitude and Society* (London, 1934), and 'Das Problem des Menschen' in *Kirche, Staat und Mensch: Russisch-Orthodoxe Studien* (Geneva, 1937). 'Man is a Microcosmos and a Microtheos. God is the Macroanthropos' (p. 181).

avoids the question of sin and forgiveness, with all the problems in practice which attend it, of the proper use of power and the place of objective authority. Tillich himself points out that (*a*) Berdyaev underestimates the break between divine consciousness and human consciousness, and produces a kind of idealistic epistemology; (*b*) he neglects the creative character of natural and empirical forms in favour of their symbolic transcendence. There is some question whether Berdyaev really loved the concrete human being as much as he loved the transcendent image of divine personality. Yet when all this is said, Berdyaev's philosophy poses to all Christians still the question implicit in the fact that God revealed himself through a cross. We have seen already two opposing cases—that of Brunner and that of Hromadka—in which the theology of the Reformation has led great theologians to subject themselves to the powers of this world at the cost of true sensitivity to the concrete condition of their fellow men. Can a less heretical theology than Berdyaev's do justice to that basic revolt against every violation of man by other men, which springs from God's purposes for men themselves?

In the second place, it was Berdyaev who first understood and expounded Marxism and Communism as a religious movement, with all that this implies. This, in his view, explains both its strength and its demonry. 'In Communism,' he begins one of his books, 'there is a whole series of truths, and only one single lie. Yet this lie is so tremendous that it outweighs all these truths and spoils them.'[1] The truth, like the lie, is in the realm of morals and spirit. Marxism was right and prophetic in attacking the *Verdinglichung* of capitalist society and pointing out how it dehumanized man.[2] Its exposition of class ideology was inspired. Its criticism of religion, Berdyaev was the first Christian writer to acknowledge, contains a judgement of God on churches which have not sought to transform human social life, and have excused themselves theologically for their neglect. Communism is right in its unity of theory and practice furthermore toward a radical transformation of

[1] *Die Wahrheit und Lüge des Kommunismus* (Darmstadt and Geneva, 1953), p. 9. The essay was written before 1932.

[2] 'Human Personality and Marxism' in *Communism and the Christians* (Westminster, Maryland. 1949. Translated from the French of thirteen years previously).

this world. 'The whole world is burning, thirsting for transformation, seeking a new and better life. The strength of Communism lies in its having a complete design for reconstructing the world's life, in which theory and practice, thought and will, are one.'[1]

But the lie of Communism, in Berdyaev's view, is its denial of both God and man (Feuerbach had at least still affirmed the latter) in the name of an inhuman collectivity which is its God. 'Marxism gave economics a metaphysical and even religious colouring. The messianic hope is bound up with them. The Five Year Plan, whose prosaic object is to industrialize Russia and which, objectively, is not socialism at all, but state capitalism, is experienced as a religious emotion.'[2] Marxist dogma hypostatizes certain concepts which lose more and more of their correspondence with the real world as they become more and more the rigid tools of propaganda and standards of belief. Marx was right in declaring the dependence of consciousness on Being. But his assumption that Being was material only has led his followers into a kind of sectarian idolatrous religion which has its own Scriptures, catechism, Messiah, and inverted theocracy, its own inquisition and eschatology. This picks up traditional Russian messianism and gives it a collectivist instead of communal, an imperialist instead of redemptive power.

The relation of this technological idolatry to Christianity is twofold, Berdyaev believes. On the one hand it is drawn into inevitable conflict with Christian faith, precisely because it is another religion. 'It is the very religious character of Communism which makes it anti-religious and anti-Christian. A Communist society and state professes to be totalitarian. But only the kingdom of God can be totalitarian.'[3] Communists may disguise their persecution of the Church with political reasons, but fundamentally it springs from their need to maintain their orthodoxy against 'heretical' belief. On the other hand, however, Communism as a religion is curiously dependent on the religious energies of the people. It attempts to enlist them in the service of an idol but it cannot produce them. An

[1] *The Russian Revolution* (Essays in Order, London, 1931), p. 79.
[2] Ibid. p. 86. See also *The Realm of Spirit and the Realm of Caesar* (London, 1952), pp. 126 ff., and *Christianity and Class War* (London, 1933), *passim*.
[3] *The Origin of Russian Communism*, pp. 185 f.

idol has no grace, no spiritual food to give. 'That is the fatal side of the worship of false gods. Religious psychology remains, only religious ontology is lacking.'[1] As Russia succeeds in turning its society into a vast machine and man into a rational economic robot, creativity and revolution come to an end. The human problems of man are left unsolved and the dehumanizing tendencies of bourgeois capitalism are intensified and clothed with an incongruous messianic radiance.

Thus Berdyaev's picture of what the religious character of Russian Communism means. His third great contribution is his realism about Christian encounter with it. On the one side his analysis of Communist revolution contained a realism which not even Brunner or Whittaker Chambers could excel. Here is no illusion that Communism can be understood piecemeal or co-operated with in a limited way. Berdyaev does not share Tillich's concept of an underlying union in the *kairos* between this Communism and other socialism. On the other side however it was a basic tenet of his view of history that the Russian revolution must be accepted as the judgement of God, as an internal apocalypse in history, which was inevitable even though not 'good' or creative in itself. It was the fate of Russia to become Bolshevist, prepared by the moral condition of the Russians themselves. 'God, if I may dare say so, transferred authority to the Bolshevists for the punishment of the people. This is why their power possesses a mysterious strength which the Bolshevists themselves cannot understand.'[2] Christians therefore, said Berdyaev already in 1923, cannot wish to go back before the revolution, to things which are judged and dead. They must meet the revolution from a post-revolutionary standpoint, having shared its suffering from within, having repented and having found the new life which transcends the hatred, vengeance and blood of revolution itself. 'A counter-revolution must not be a contrary revolution, but the contrary of a revolution.'

This does not mean accommodation to Communism. It may

[1] *The Russian Revolution*, p. 47.
[2] *The End of Our Time*, lectures given in Berlin directly after Berdyaev's expulsion from the Soviet Union, to other emigré Russians (London, 1933), p. 138.

mean resistance and martyrdom when truly sacred things are challenged. But it does mean seizing the creative opportunity given to Christians by the fact that Communism cannot carry through the spiritual promise of its own faith, and that Bolshevists more and more fail to bring forth creative power. 'Groups of believers are the web on which the new material of society will be woven; they will hold the social threads together when the old states finally collapse.' It means seeking out creative forces among those who have been through the revolution and have been chastened by it, and working with them in hope. Berdyaev's radical personalist philosophy, his revolt in the name of freedom against all objective authority combined with his complete involvement in history toward its transfiguration, saved him from both the Brunner and the Hromadka antithesis toward Communist revolution, and made him the first to express the insights which inform the most effective Christian witness behind the Iron Curtain today.

4

AN AMERICAN ENCOUNTER:
REINHOLD NIEBUHR

REINHOLD NIEBUHR differs from all the other theologians in this
study in taking as his primary datum neither a theological conviction
about grace, as does Karl Barth, nor a vision of what society might be,
but the social relations in which he stands. This is his starting point,
and this is his final test of the relevance both of Marxist insight and
of theology. He has resisted every movement and philosophy, Christian or Communist, which would over-simplify or escape from the
practical problems of the Ford workers in Detroit in the 'twenties,
the urban proletariat in the 'thirties, or a nation caught in the
dilemmas and responsibilities of great power in the post-war years.

Niebuhr has therefore always had a practical measuring rod
against which to place Marxism. He does not find in it, as does
Brunner, the incarnation of an evil principle. He does not absorb it,
like Hromadka, as part of his own historical fate; nor does he
combine these two approaches, as does Berdyaev. He does not
wrestle with Marxism's appeal as a total philosophy of life, as does
Tillich. He decries Barth's attempt to place a new theological
reality over against the world, which changes the whole picture of
conflict and human responsibility. But in the same way, Niebuhr
has resisted from the beginning the temptation of Communism as
a philosophy of life, or as an historical power with a mystic force of
its own. Primary reality lies for him not with the power of social
movements toward revolution, nor with the present victory of a
risen Christ, but with the immediate struggles of men in their sin
with the social powers and responsibilities before them.

1. SOME BASIC PRINCIPLES OF NIEBUHR'S EARLY
SOCIAL ANALYSIS

This does not mean that Niebuhr operates without principles of
understanding in the social situation. These principles derive,

however, neither from the structure of Marxist philosophy, nor from the revealed Word of God, but rather from the wellsprings of American social gospel liberalism deepened by an intense Christian consciousness of human sin. As such his encounter with Communism is a profoundly American one, representative and exemplary of the best American experience in its strengths and weaknesses. Its earliest principles bear examination in more detail.

A. Niebuhr owes least to Marxism in the basic ethical standard he has brought to all his thought from his background in the Social Gospel: the absolute moral imperative of love in human relations and the compulsion to act toward its realization. In strong contrast with Tillich and Berdyaev, who wrestled in their own souls with Marxist ideals, he seems never to have been tempted to express the demands of Christian love in Marxist terms. There is not the slightest suggestion in any of his works that he was captivated by the ideal of a classless society, the liberation of self-estranged man, or the subjugation of nature through science to the boundless development of man.

In fact the law of love is for Niebuhr an intrinsically dynamic, eternally challenging standard which cannot be captured in any ideal structure. He nowhere describes the outline, even of a tolerable reflection of the kingdom of God, such as we find in Brunner's person-in-community, in Berdyaev's personalist socialism, or in Tillich's theonomous culture. His earliest work symbolizes it rather as that form of social imagination which sees all human beings as personalities to be revered and thus 'qualifies the individual's will to power so that his life can be integrated with other lives with a minimum of conflict'. It breeds a 'spirit of humility which regards every moral achievement as but a vantage point from which new ventures of faith and life are to be initiated'.[1] But his classic formulation is that of the 'impossible possibility' of the Christian life in *An Interpretation of Christian Ethics*. Here the law of love is neither (as with Brunner) the benevolent conservatism of an 'order of creation', nor (as with Barth) the sustaining grace of a forgiving God, but the ethic of Jesus in the Sermon on the Mount. Love means imaginative insight into the true life of others to the point

[1] *Does Civilization Need Religion?* (London, 1928), p. 55.

118

where one affirms the life of others equally with, or at sacrifice to one's own. It is a command which contradicts our basic will to survival and self-assertion, and equally our partial and particular loyalties. The way of the Sermon on the Mount is not a way to success in this world or in any extension of its society. Nor may it be an escape into a more satisfactory 'other world'. It is the ultimate ideal of this world which inspires, judges, and transforms every achievement of relative justice. Humanity therefore faces a double task:

'The one is to reduce the anarchy of the world to some kind of immediately sufferable order and unity; and the other is to set these tentative and insecure unities and achievements under the criticism of the ultimate ideal. With Augustine we must realize that the peace of the world is gained by strife. That does not justify us either in rejecting such a tentative peace or in accepting it as final. The peace of the city of God can use and transmute the lesser and insecure peace of the city of the world; but that can be done only if the peace of the world is not confused with the peace of God.'[1]

So Niebuhr cannot start his social analysis, as does Barth, by considering the relation of the Church to the world, any more than he could presuppose a Marxist proletariat. For him neither Church nor proletariat is such a community as to escape the tensions of this world in the power of a new reality. His whole theology itself arose in the search for answers to the social-ethical problem raised by the gap between the world of sinful power conflicts and God's law of love. This is why he has resisted from the beginning, and continues to resist, every attempt to soften this tension or escape from it, whether the attempt be liberal theories of natural harmony, Marxist dreams of the classless society, or Barthian affirmations of *sola gratia*. It is this dynamic impossible possibility of the law of love which makes Niebuhr the consistent exposer of all social irresponsibility or love of security, even when it clothes itself as piety; and a leader in Christian decision and action, despite the realism and relativity of his theology.

B. Niebuhr's analysis of society in terms of the conflict and balance of powers is also fundamentally non-Marxist, although he

[1] *An Interpretation of Christian Ethics* (London, 1936), p. 71.

119

gave it a Marxist application to the economic struggle in the 'thirties. Every society, in his early view, depends on some form of coercion because the will to power is basic in human society. At the same time coercive power is dangerous, because every group which wields it uses it unjustly for its own interests at the expense of others. 'Any kind of significant social power (for example military, economic or priestly) develops social inequality.' This power may appear to have the consent of the ruled as long as it maintains stability and as long as the rulers mix in one community with the ruled, protecting them from outside danger. But it destroys its *raison d'etre*, for it feeds on itself until

'. . . it destroys the social peace of the state by the animosities which its exactions arouse, and it enervates the sentiment of patriotism by robbing the common man of the basic privileges which might bind him to his nation.'[1]

Society, therefore, 'is in a perpetual state of war'.

'Lacking moral and rational resources to organize its life without resort to coercion except in the most immediate and intimate social groups, men remain the victims of the individuals, classes, and nations by whose force a momentary coerced unity is achieved, and further conflicts are as certainly created.'[2]

This posed for the early Niebuhr the ethical problem in society: to achieve such a balance of power in society as will contribute to a relative justice, and lend the support of society's coercive forces to those standards of reason and morality which would be ineffective if no such social interest were behind them. It is the problem of creating enough justice and peace to save society from the opposing disasters of despotism and anarchy. It involves accurate insight into the tendencies and dangers of the powers at work in society, both those working for change and those working to conserve, and political action at that point where a relatively greater justice may be achieved or where catastrophe may be averted by timely action in the interests of the underdog. But this is a perpetual problem of Christian action, not one tied to Marxist analysis of present society. It is neither optimism nor pessimism about this

[1]*Moral Man and Immoral Society* (London, 1933), p. 11.
[2]Ibid. pp. 19–20.

world. It points beyond itself to the hope of the kingdom of God at the end of and fulfilling history.

c. So it is also with reason and conscience. Niebuhr rebelled against the liberal tradition which puts all its confidence in these forces, but he never fell into that complete relativism which led Marx to economic determinism and moral instrumentalism, and Barth to a totally theological orientation of all thought and morals. On the one hand Niebuhr saw reason, making man aware of the needs and demands of other life, and conscience affirming a duty toward this life. Together reason and conscience regulate, extend human impulses and approve those most universal. They strengthen the resisters against unjust power. But on the other hand they can do these things with only relative efficiency. 'There is no miracle by which men can achieve a rationality high enough to give them as vivid an understanding of general interests as of their own.'[1] The very faculty which makes it possible for man to understand the interests and claims of other men over against his own, leads him to fear these others as threats to himself, and to universalize his form of life by subjugating theirs. Reason, even moral reason, can operate as an ideology, justifying one group's interest and will to power, when opposing reason is not backed also by power. Christian action therefore, in Niebuhr's early view, must neither reject the guidance of reason nor trust it overmuch, but seek that power balance in which it and conscience can provide a maximum of society's cohesive power, and educate both with the imaginative insight of Christian love.

d. The above points have all described the dialectical tension which, in Niebuhr's mind, determines the Christian's responsibility in all human societies in all times. To them Niebuhr added a fourth: radical analysis of present day ideologies and powers which place society in historical crisis and threaten it with revolutionary change. Here most clearly he placed himself in the dynamics of this change, but once again, neither basically in Marxist nor in theological terms. In *Moral Man and Immoral Society* he ranged through history and over the globe collecting examples of the hypocritical morals of nations and privileged classes, but the hand

[1]Ibid. p. 45.

121

of Marx is less evident in his choices than his own genius for spiritual insight on the basis of his liberal heritage. He recognized in Russia a privileged class arising whose power is not first of all economic. He rejected dialectical materialism as a 'science' and refused to understand social existence exclusively as a function of the relations of production. Yet it was his immediate experience in Detroit of the nineteen-twenties that economic privilege was a primary force in creating vested interest and ideology. In seeking explanation of and guidance in the crisis of that society, Niebuhr was led to Marxist analysis and strategy, just as pondering its deeper implications, he was led to elaborate his theology of historical judgement and grace.

2. CHANGING APPROACH TO MARXISM

Chronologically, Niebuhr's encounter with revolutionary Marxism has been through three stages. The first was his pre-Marxist period of religious liberalism and struggle as a young pastor with the problems of a labourers' parish. Here is where the problem of social justice and of American capitalism first presented itself to him. His first effort to meet it shows some awareness of Marxism but depends basically on a deepened liberal faith, a chastened moral sincerity, and a new religious asceticism which will 'produce spiritualized technicians who will continue to conquer and exploit nature in the interest of human welfare, but who will scorn to take a larger share of the returns of industry than is justified by reasonable and carefully scrutinized needs.'[1]

In his second stage of political realism and deepening Biblical faith, Niebuhr found in revolutionary Marxism a guide to political and economic reality in capitalist society and a religious utopianism whose dangers became increasingly apparent to him as his experience with it broadened. However his picture of this revolutionary Marxism was not that of the closed system of power and ideology centred in Soviet Russia which today goes by the name of Communism. His encounter was rather with the ideology of a social class whose insights expressed, he believed, a valid judgement on present society, whose power was basic to social change,

[1]*Does Civilization Need Religion?* p. 229.

whose cause is more nearly moral than that of any other class or movement, and whose utopian illusions and pride are subject to the dangers and corrections which apply to those of any other class. In so understanding Marxism Niebuhr always distinguished himself from 'the Christian Left' in Great Britain and from such men as Harry F. Ward in the United States. He refused to identify the coming of socialism by revolution with the more metaphysical claims which Marx makes for it, or the socialism of Soviet Russia with a secularized expression of the Kingdom of God.[1] He was concerned with the whole social problem, including other classes than the proletariat, even in his most Marxist period, and he dealt with it in the light of his basic principles which use, but are not captivated by, Marxist analysis.

Despite their close companionship, Niebuhr differs here from Paul Tillich. He has always lacked Tillich's profound understanding of the detail of Marxist philosophy because he has not allowed Marxism to define for him the proletarian situation, as Tillich has done. Niebuhr could never designate socialism as *en kairō*. Tillich's encounter, as we have seen, was that of an inner affinity with Marx's doctrine of self-estrangement against the background of his own struggle with the problem of autonomy and heteronomy. Tillich saw the social-ethical problem of the working man through philosophical Marxism. Niebuhr saw it directly in experience and found Marxism helpful in its analysis. Tillich shared with Marx a view of the determining importance of ideas in action, which is common to German idealism, but which is not convincing to the more directly moral and empirical American background out of which Niebuhr comes. We find Niebuhr using Marxism therefore without being shaken by its total question to his existence or its total claim on his consciousness.

The third stage of Niebuhr's encounter with revolutionary Marxism has seen him re-orient his social-ethical analysis from a radical base, in the explication of which Marxist theory played a strong role, to a pragmatic base whose effect is often conservative. The object of his social-ethical concern has changed from the

[1]'Socialist Decision and the Christian Conscience', in *Radical Religion*, III (Spring 1938), pp. 1–2.

problems of working men seeking social change, to the preservation of the genius of a democratic tradition in a mixed economy, and its inner improvement. Socialism therefore becomes just another ideological illusion which interferes with this pragmatic task. Marxism becomes misleading analysis, and Communism a religious utopian threat with which no real encounter is possible, although Niebuhr still recognizes that Communism has the characteristics of a Christian heresy and is fed by the self-righteousness of Christians.[1]

In travelling this path, Niebuhr is the leader and representative of a large group of Christians on the left in both Britain and America, who have taken revolutionary Marxism seriously without becoming its fellow-travellers in the past thirty years. Their environment differs from that of the European continent or of Russia in being filled with more or less practical socialist and semi-socialist liberalism of non-Marxist origin, some of it Christian in inspiration. Ideologies have not dominated political movements and social democracy has shown far more strength than in Europe. The revolutionary pressure of the depression which led many to co-operate with Communism gradually dissipated in the New Deal reforms. The social conflict lost its acuteness and the acute Marxist consciousness of the way in which vested interests rationalize their power faded as well. At the same time Communism showed itself more and more clearly to be an ideological and political totalitarianism. Its party members proved untrustworthy in common causes and uninterested in the common welfare. In this field of experience the Christian encounter with revolutionary Marxism, never as intimate as that of the German religious socialists or that of Berdyaev in Russia, has become more and more external and unfriendly. Communism has shown itself on the one hand irrelevant to the problems of society in their variety and relative technical nature, and on the other hand threatening to both justice and freedom in its total claims. It has been accepted as an enemy, not as a challenge.

This is an American encounter with Communism. The question may well be asked, as it is indeed asked by Christians from other

[1]'The Relevance of Reformation Doctrine', in *The Heritage of the Reformation*, ed. F. J. E. Arndt (St. Louis, Missouri, 1950), pp. 254–5, 262.

lands, is it a *Christian* encounter? Is it a true encounter with Marxist insight and Communist reality? When pragmatism combines with theology to drive socialism from its place of judgement over society's *status quo*, the result is a typically American approach to knowledge and social action. It pretends to be free of all presuppositions except real social situations. But does it in fact depend on unexamined values and structures organic to American traditions which are themselves hiding special interests? Does Niebuhr, in abandoning socialism, fall back on these, and lose thereby his stature as a prophet? Is the theologically grounded pragmatism of his social ethics free enough from the world to understand the revolutionary crisis in which the world stands today, as well as he understood the American crisis of the nineteen-thirties, and to speak wise prophecy to it? When these questions are formulated, any American Christian left of centre can recognize them as questions and challenges also to himself. This chapter must attempt some answer to them.

3. NIEBUHR'S MARXIST ANALYSIS OF SOCIETY

No clear line can be drawn between the Marxist and non-Marxist elements in Niebuhr's thinking of the nineteen-thirties about society. Even when he accepted the proletariat as the basic group in society working to redress the inequality of power and so toward justice, and when he accepted socialism as the proletariat's justified goal, he was echoing the conviction of Walter Rauschenbusch.[1] But at this point Niebuhr moved from the realm of theory to that of social action by aligning himself with the Socialist Party and the Labour Movement, not because, according to the liberal pattern, it was composed of men of good will with a common aim, but because it was 'the only potentially powerful organized group whose enlightened self-interest coincides roughly with the best interests of the majority of men.'[2] Here the categories of the 'Social Gospel' no longer proved adequate for his guidance. He accepted a Marxist

[1]Walter Rauschenbusch, *Christianity and the Social Crisis* (New York, 1907), pp. 401 ff.
[2]'Statement of Principles of the Fellowship of Socialist Christians', in *Christianity and Society*, XI (Winter 1945–6), pp. 33–37.

picture of social conflict and change, precisely because it expressed most truly, for him, God's historical judgement.

A. This was expressed first in Niebuhr's conviction that capitalism was through as a tolerable social system. 'We are living in a period in which the anarchies of capitalism have reached an insufferable proportion,' he wrote in 1936.[1] 'We cannot go on with the present social organization.' 'Fear of disaster' he continued later, 'ought to drive us toward socialist decision even more than the hope of justice. Capitalism is incompatible with the necessities of a technical civilization.' With its creed of bourgeois individualism it has, to be sure, not always been self-destructive. It was bourgeois individualism which discovered the value of the individual over against his previous limitation to a status and function in society. It fathered humanitarianism, which condemns the brutalities of collective life and appeals to reason and sympathy to mitigate them. The political power of the bourgeoisie, derived from its economic base, was accepted because of the 'plausibility of its claim to government and the willingness of society to accept that claim'.[2] But the dynamics of power have done their work on capitalism. Its struggle for profits has collectivized and mechanized society beyond the power of private initiative to control the resulting overproduction, unemployment crises, and the breakdown in the system of distribution. Although capitalism did not create imperialism, the capitalist form of modern imperialism, whereby backward nations are first exploited as markets, then develop as competitors whose competition can only be hindered by lending them money to buy our goods, is ridiculous and self-destructive.

B. Nevertheless the exposure of the self-destructive nature of capitalism does not guarantee that it will be eliminated without violence. On the contrary the capitalist's fear of growing opposition to his injustice and anarchy produces in him a more frantic will to power. He may appeal to the wise rationalist for advice in his problems, but he cannot follow this advice when it leads him to surrender any of the power of his position, nor can he any longer

[1]'The Idea of Progress and Socialism', in *Radical Religion*, I (Spring 1936), pp. 28–29.
[2]*Reflections on the End of an Era* (London, 1934), p. 151.

tolerate a prophet whose criticism is implemented by the power to realize it. Therefore the liberal planners of remedies for capitalist society (John Maynard Keynes, the Roosevelt New Dealers *et al.*) will have little success short of becoming revolutionaries. The essential requirement for any effective action on the social problem is a transfer of economic power from capitalist hands to other classes, which means a change in the ownership of that productive property which is the source of this power.

For the same reason Niebuhr was sceptical at this period of democracy's ability to stand the strain of the coming power conflict. Political power is commanded in any society by that group which commands the most significant non-political power, he believed. Democracy may indeed register other classes' lack of confidence in the ruling bourgeoisie. But it cannot sustain a social revolution because all the power of the prevailing economic order will be brought to bear to prevent this revolution, violating democracy if necessary. This was Niebuhr's Marxist explanation of Fascism at this time. Furthermore the constitution of a capitalist democracy itself excludes a vote which would destroy the social system:

'Every constitution is no more than the rational and legal codification of a given equilibrium of social power. A completely new equilibrium cannot therefore be established within terms of a rational justification of the old one.'[1]

With this Marxist picture of revolutionary necessity Niebuhr the socialist scorned the New Deal as a confused attempt to apply palliatives to a sick society, without changing any of the real structure of power.

c. The problem of revolutionary violence concerned Niebuhr deeply however. The proletarian, in Niebuhr's view, is created by the pressures of capitalist industrialism which destroy the organic relations of medieval times. He sees his hope entirely in terms of a struggle for power, not in an appeal to human morality. He expects a violent revolution and tends to regard as traitors those who accept moderate reforms from capitalist regimes. His loyalty to his class and its struggle is based on hope for a transvaluation of its disinherited

[1] *Reflections on the End of an Era*, p. 55.

127

existence, a glorification of its propertylessness by the possession of all things, in the classless society. This struggle is bitter and admits no qualification, because it is inspired by the religion of Communism. 'The executors of judgement in history are always driven by both hunger and dreams, by both the passions of warfare and the hope for a city of God.'[1]

Niebuhr regarded this proletarian state of mind and politics as both tragic and helpful. Its combination of moral cynicism with apocalyptic idealism is tragic. But its realism is helpful in forcing on softer minds the brutal conflicts of power as basic to history. The Marxist proletarian

'. . . is right not only in the projection of his social goal (of justice through revolution) but in his insistence on the urgency of its attainment. Comfortable classes may continue to dream of an automatic progress in society. They do not suffer enough from social injustice to recognize its peril to the life of society. . . . Thus it is the proletarian who predicts disaster for modern society (and may actually become the instrument of catastrophe), who is potentially the strongest force of redemption in society.'[2]

In all these points—in his analysis of the dynamics of capitalist society under historical judgement, in his belief that the primary task was to change the base of economic power in society, probably by revolutionary means, and in his acceptance of the socialist proletariat within which to work—Niebuhr was Marxist during the depression years in his working analysis of and strategy for society. The Fellowship of Socialist Christians, he wrote,

'. . . are socialists because they believe that it is the duty of a Christian to affirm the highest possible justice in every society; and they regard socialism, that is, the social ownership of the means of production, as a minimal requirement of social health in a technical age.'[3]

[1]*Reflections on the End of an Era*, p. 140.
[2]*Moral Man and Immoral Society*, p. 166.
[3]'The Creed of Modern Christian Socialists', in *Radical Religion*, III (Spring 1938), pp. 13–18. In *Reflections on the end of an Era*, Niebuhr puts it even more sharply: 'The political task of dealing with the roots of social injustice must precede the moral task of building imaginative justice upon the foundations of the rough justice of politics' (pp. 234–5).

This is not in the spirit of Marxism. But it is Christian prophetic action operating on the basis of a Marxist analysis. Niebuhr realized that this socialist commitment was relative and might be wrong. But he regarded any failure to go this way as more of a temptation:

'Those of us who seek justice in the name of the love commandment must inevitably view our task as an effort to realize the prophetic principle in Christianity against the constant tendency of the Church to identify the *status quo* with the Kingdom of God. Our moral decisions are therefore efforts to realize our Christian imperatives. They must be made even if subsequent history will prove them to be more relative than they now seem.'[1]

4. SOCIALIST CHRISTIAN ACTION IN THE NINETEEN-THIRTIES

Nevertheless, to decide for socialism as a Christian was to seek to guide, moderate, and redeem the socialist movement from within, to save from its vengeance what is valuable in the old society and to mitigate the harshness of the new. This Niebuhr and his colleagues sought to do in four political ways and one religious one.

A. They sought to rally all the forces of religion, morality, reason, and social tradition within the non-proletarian classes, to acquiesce in the necessary shift of economic power, so that as little violence as possible might be necessary to achieve this change. Czardom breeds Communism. Therefore

'It must always be the purpose of those who try, in a measure, to guide the course of history, to check the desperate brutalities of a dying civilization in order that the new which emerges may not be too completely corrupted and blinded by the spirit of vengeance.'[2]

It is not normal for the ethical imagination even of the most sensitive bourgeois to go beyond personal sympathy to the roots of social inequality. He must be forced to do so by the dual shock of revolutionary power and moral command.

B. They sought to educate the proletariat as well, and especially

[1]'Socialist Decision and the Christian Conscience', in *Radical Religion*, III, pp. 1–2.
[2]*Reflections on the End of an Era*, pp. 140–1.

to wean it from Russian Communism's fanatic erection of the principle of proletarian existence—collective propertylessness—into a universal principle. The Communist undermines the revolution itself by rejecting the ideals and principles of all other dispossessed classes—the farmer's love for his soil, the devotion of the believer, the natural patriotism of the citizen, the ties of the family. He forgets 'the egoistic elements in his spirit of justice, the very elements which change justice into vindictiveness'.[1] This uncritical class egoism can be morally comfortable exterminating its enemies, collectivizing farmers 'for their own good' against their will, and in forcing its materialist determinism on all; but it antagonizes other classes whose interests are naturally common with the proletariat and turns them toward Fascism.

Therefore Niebuhr was sceptical, even at the height of the popular front period, of co-operation with the Communist Party. A front for specific purposes uniting responsible socialist and Communist leaders might be advisable. But Communists are unreliable allies, because their 'dogmatisms and oversimplifications are so false to the political realities of western society, that their political emphasis, for all its vitality, may help to create Fascism'.[2]

c. The socialist Christians sought to develop all the possibilities society offers for peaceful change through all the reforms they could contrive, so that the final revolutionary transfer of power might involve as little violence as possible.

'No community can live in a permanent state of civil war which would result from a revolutionary socialism unable to press through to its goal. If violence can be justified at all, its terror must have the tempo of a surgeon's skill and healing must follow quickly upon its wounds.'[3]

D. Socialist Christians sought to bring about such a socialist society as would avoid the obvious danger which comes with the centralization of economic power.

'With the elimination of that specific cause of anarchy (capitalism), mankind will advance to a new level of maturity; but not to a new level of

[1] *Reflections on the End of an Era*, p. 168.
[2] 'The Question of the United Front', in *Radical Religion*, I (Winter 1935–6), p. 2.
[3] *Moral Man and Immoral Society*, p. 220.

frictionless unity and tensionless innocency. In some respects a socialist society with its higher cohesiveness will be more perilous than a capitalist society; just as a capitalist society contains greater perils than a feudal society. . . . Slighter dislocation can produce more harmful effects.'[1]

From here, Niebuhr and the Fellowship of Socialist Christians moved to conditions on the kind of a revolution they were prepared to support. The F.S.C. Statement of Principles early in 1938 declared itself for 'a co-operative society along socialist lines',[2] and differed from 'doctrinaire collectivist philosophies' in seeing the 'danger of unnecessarily mutilating organic forms of life by coercing them into mechanical moulds'. It questioned the advisability of collectivizing agriculture or retail trade. And finally Niebuhr expressed the Fellowship's concern for the control of power in a socialist society. 'They want to equalize economic power but not at the price of creating political tyranny in a socialist society. They do not trust any irresponsible power in the long run, whether it is wielded by priests, monks, capitalists, or commissars.'[3]

In short, these socialist Christians in the middle 'thirties were attempting, after the prophetic dynamite of Niebuhr's political books had cleared the ground, to express an independent Christian interpretation of the social revolution which they regarded Marx to have illuminated and the proletariat to be bearing, and to put forth a genuinely Christian policy for it. Here we see at its best the way in which the two political consequences which Niebuhr drew from his basic sense of tension between the law of love and the necessity of relative decision, interact. Niebuhr remained a realist about human nature. He allowed himself no illusions about the continuing problems of justice in a socialist society or the difficulties of power control after the revolution. But his realism about power, and his politics for its control, were driven by a sense of crisis, of the dynamic movement of God's judgement in history which found its form in the socialist decision.

It is therefore the socialist Niebuhr of the 'thirties who can speak

[1]'The Idea of Progress and Socialism', in *Radical Religion*, I (Spring 1936), pp. 28–29.
[2]'Statement of Principles of the Fellowship of Socialist Christians', in *Radical Religion*, III (Winter 1937–8).
[3]'The Creed of Modern Christian Socialists.'

effectively with Josef Hromadka. The two men share the same theological rejection of Communism. Yet they involved themselves in the revolutionary struggle with basically the same response to the demand of an historical crisis before God, for a social decision in terms of the powers which hold the future. Niebuhr, however, retained throughout his capacity for critical analysis on the basis of his realism about all power and its pretensions. Where Hromadka lyricized about the proletarian movement, Niebuhr spoke of mitigating the vindictiveness of the victims of injustice. Where Hromadka saw Soviet Russia bathed in the morning sunlight of a great new hope, despite its cruelties, Niebuhr saw it thwarting the revolution with its dogmatic utopianism. Where Hromadka lived for a great new hope for the total cultural development of mankind, Niebuhr rejoiced rather in the relativities of politics where in daily life God's grace covers man's sin, and held his hope strictly eschatological.

5. CHRISTIAN RELIGION AND COMMUNIST RELIGION

The religious task which the socialist Christians of the nineteen-thirties set themselves was to combat the utopian illusions of of Communism about the perfection of a socialist society with the greater realism of Christian insight; in other words to oppose Marxism's false religion with Christian truth.

Niebuhr has regarded Communism as a religion at least since the beginning of his career as a teacher. Central to its faith is the eschatological vision of a classless society combined with a realistic pessimism about the present. This makes Communism more than a sterile determinism, more than a 'science'. 'A world view which is at the same time pessimistic and optimistic is alone pregnant with moral incentive.' The link between this pessimism of the present and optimism of the future is a metaphysical faith in the dialectical process. This is, to be sure, secured, as in so many religions, by a concrete authority which is the source of interpretation and action, and which tends more and more to absolutize its own decisions and position—the Communist Party. But this Party's faith and discipline qualifies the will-to-live and turns it to social ends while at the same time asserting this will and absolutizing it in social terms.

'Unlike modern liberal rationalism, its interpretation of life and history is dogmatic rather than scientific. Like all vital religion it engages the entire human psyche and offers its interpretation of life and the world in order that it may challenge to action in conformity with its "truth".'[1]

Nevertheless Communism, in Niebuhr's view, is not a 'high' religion, because it is not 'dualistic'. It does not, in the first place, give any place to the transcendent freedom and destiny of the individual. It does not consider the whole problem of time and eternity. It is a religion of groups. It universalizes the struggle of a proletarian class, and eventually sanctifies a party and a state. In the second place Communism is a faith limited to history and this world. It shares with many other expressions of religion, including corrupt forms of 'high' religion, the tendency to identify some relative and partial historical and earthly good with the absolutely good and true. Like all naturalism it seeks to derive this good from the self-explaining process of the great unconscious world of nature, and to explain human nature and destiny in these terms. Despite its provisional realism about class conflict its hope deserves the title 'utopian', because it is a dream of perfect harmony and progress in society, of innocence in human nature after the elimination of property, which on the one hand obscures the facts of human sin and power conflicts, and on the other hand absolutizes a particular power and group interest. In recent years Niebuhr has tended to describe Communism primarily in these terms:

'We do not understand Communism if we fail to realize that it is a variant of the same utopianism with which the whole liberal world is infected. Communist tyranny, in other words, grows out of habits of thought which rendered our generation incapable of anticipating or understanding Nazi tyranny. Communism turns the soft utopianism of modern culture into a hard and truculent utopianism.'[2]

These have remained the more or less constant factors which have defined Communism's religious character for Niebuhr. It is

[1]'Christian Politics and Communist Religion', in *Christianity and the Social Revolution*, ed. John Lewis (London, 1936), pp. 461 ff.
[2]'Two Forms of Tyranny', in *Christianity and Crisis*, 2nd February, 1948, pp. 3–4.

his attitude toward religion which has changed and with it his judgement on this religious character. In the 'thirties he balanced the resources of Communist religion against those of 'high' religion for social living and reached well nigh an impasse. For high religion has many resources which society may not lose. They are, first, the resources of transcendence: the knowledge that the Absolute is personal will, that life for the spirit is not to be fulfilled within the bounds of nature and history. They are, secondly, the resources of love which stimulate our imagination and sensitize our moral judgements toward higher possibilities in the affirmation of human personality in lives other than our own, and fuller community with them. Niebuhr links this love with individualism because conscience sharpened by religious insight condemns the brutalities of collective life against the human spirit. They are, thirdly, the resources of repentance and grace: the knowledge that all our achievements are distortions of love, that sin distorts all human effort, that no person or group is good enough not to stand under the judgement expressed by effective correcting power in the hands of those who suffer from him; and the knowledge of God's forgiveness which makes the tension of this everlasting moral struggle tolerable.

'Perhaps the most sublime insight of the Jewish prophets and the Christian gospel is the knowledge that, since perfection is love, the apprehension of perfection is at once the means of seeing one's own imperfection, and the consoling assurance of grace which makes this realization bearable.'[1]

On the other hand high religion can be a social liability. The basic problem of religion in our society, Niebuhr maintained in his earliest work, significantly entitled *Does Civilization Need Religion?* is not the scientific attack on it, but the fact that Christianity has become morally irrelevant, especially to the proletariat, in a world where moral problems are complex and relative. Throughout this period Niebuhr seems haunted by the fear that this may be so. On the one hand its transcendence makes relative judgements of good and evil questionable, and its command of love rules out the effective use of power against power toward relative justice. On the

[1] *Reflections on the End of an Era*, p. 285.

other hand it easily becomes a cover for the power interests of ruling groups. 'No sound principle of political change emerges anywhere in Christian thought,' he concluded, after a survey of Christian political attitudes through the centuries.[1] Reverence for authority easily becomes reverence for a particular authority now in power. 'The fact of the sinfulness of the world was used as an excuse for the complacent acceptance of whatever imperfect justice a given social order had established.'[2]

Against these weaknesses Niebuhr saw the religion of Communism arising at first as a violent but necessary correction, both of the conservatism and the bourgeois moralism with which so much Christianity, liberal and orthodox, is infected. 'The conflict between Communism and the Christian world,' he wrote in 1931, 'is one between brutality and hypocrisy. The Christian world is less brutal than the Communist world, but it is more brutal than it is willing to admit.'[3] The same could be said for Communist and liberal-Christian illusions. For a brief time Niebuhr even went so far as to assert that a certain degree of illusion, like a certain degree of brutality, is necessary to produce the social power necessary for change. 'Nothing is ever as true as it must seem to be to compel action,' he said bluntly in an early article. The fact that this illusion is always dangerous, that it stands under the judgement of the insights of 'high' religions whose lack of social realism and dynamic its own revolutionary power judges in turn, expresses society's religious dilemma.

Niebuhr's concern for effective social change, in other words, was so basic to his thought and action, that for a while religion itself was regarded as instrumental to this end. In this he both adopted and adapted a piece of Marxism. His description of Marxism as a religion was itself non-Marxist to be sure, not only because Marxism considers itself a science, but because Niebuhr placed himself outside the Marxist utopian ideology and judged it as an instrument among others. Even when he treated this utopia as a necessary illusion, the illusion was for him an instrument, replac-

[1] *Reflections on the End of an Era*, p. 221.
[2] *An Interpretation of Christian Ethics*, pp. 151 f.
[3] *Atlantic Monthly*, April, 1931.

ing the illusion of eternal progress in the bourgeois world, and not an object of belief. Nevertheless Niebuhr used Marxist tools of analysis in describing the way in which conventional Christian orthodoxy and liberalism become the ideological fronts of conservative powers. He wove the Marxist picture of the relation between religion and social interest so into his point of view that he was faced with a real problem of relativism in his own faith, the more so because he could not accept the Marxist hope as a solution.

What then is the true religion which leads beyond this dilemma? What truth gives adequate expression at once to the drive of the Marxist proletariat toward shifts in power, to the realistic pessimism of this proletariat about the morality, reason, and religious hypocrisy of privileged classes, and to the transcendent character of a God who is love, judging all sinful human efforts to embody the ideal in a system, enforcing humility and contrition, stimulating the imagination beyond all achievement, and raising the individual above all social bonds? To this question Niebuhr developed two kinds of answer: one dominated by his concern for a truly radical politics, expressed primarily in the pages of the journal *Radical Religion;* the other a quest for a theology adequate to undergird the Christian in all the tensions of his social responsibility.

The first of these represents the highest fruits of Niebuhr's encounter as a Christian with the fullness of revolutionary Marxist faith and criticism in the 'thirties. The name he gave to it was prophetic, or radical, religion. It encounters Communism in four ways.

A. It recognizes, in the first place, the validity of much of the Marxist criticism of religion. It claims in fact to know these things by virtue of its Biblical insight even more acutely than do the Marxists. It recognizes that every church has a sociological basis which tempts it to sanctify particular interests. It 'does not imagine that a religious institution which is completely enmeshed in a civilization is able to present such a civilization with an effective challenge.'[1] It recognizes that Christian pessimism about human nature, although honest and true, has been used to soften the demands of the law of love to such an extent that often 'justice

[1] 'Is Religion Counter-Revolutionary?' in *Radical Religion*, I (Autumn 1935), pp. 14–20.

meant merely that social relations should be ordered and decent within terms of the presuppositions of this society.'[1] It knows how this removal of the *status quo* from moral criticism 'both because it was hopeless and because it was God-given' becomes a mockery when it is used to sanction a bourgeois capitalist order which in itself is chaotic and self-destructive, giving those it oppresses no stability even in their oppression.

In all this criticism of religion, however, prophetic insight goes further than Marxist criticism, in Niebuhr's opinion. Christians, he wrote, 'accept the Marxian theory of the ideological character of all moral idealism as roughly similar to the Christian idea of the sinfulness of man'.[2] But they carry the criticism further. Moral idealism is not only, or even mainly, a fruit of Christianity. It flows rather from the rationalist culture of our time, and has infected liberal Christianity from there. It is furthermore not only a disease of idealists as opposed to materialists or naturalists. 'In the modern day the physical and economic basis of all culture is more frequently obscured by empiricists than by old-fashioned philosophical idealists.'[3] The illusion of a pure moral reason must be exposed wherever it arises. It is furthermore the ideology not only of economic interests but of all interests.

B. In the second place however, prophetic religion recognizes the permanent validity of some religious insights regardless of the fact that they may be a danger to radical politics. These are, especially, a genuine pessimism about the possibility of any perfect society on earth, an other-worldliness which sees how the perfection of the kingdom of God and the horizon of his grace transcend every historical achievement, and an individualism which recognizes that the human spirit under God cannot be fulfilled within the bounds even of the finest social harmony. Niebuhr recognizes in the late 'thirties that all those Christian emphases qualify the Christian's loyalty to any political movement—in itself a change from his position in *Reflections on the End of an Era*.

From this, Niebuhr reached a position which recognized the

[1]'Christian Politics and Communist Religion', op. cit. p. 447.
[2]'The Creed of Modern Christian Socialists', *Radical Religion*, III.
[3]'Is Religion Counter-Revolutionary?'

value of a vocational ascetic witness, much like his recognition of vocational pacifism during the Second World War; provided this witness was realistic in cutting social ties and recognizing the sin of irresponsibility which it incurred in so doing. Such an ascetic witness is necessary over against a revolutionary movement.

'No community of the ideal can ever be fully conscious of the ease with which natural and inevitable human loyalties are transmuted into sinful and socially dangerous forms of imperialism, if a portion of the community does not, by the ardour of its discipline, reveal the subtle peril and the stubborn inertia of egoism in even the most natural and praiseworthy collective enterprises.'[1]

Furthermore, Christian pessimism about perfection in society expresses itself validly in helping man to live a human life in spite of injustice.

'Once it is recognized that the socialist society which we intend to build will not be a perfect society, and that it will not be able to save individuals from many frustrations, unfulfilled hopes and unrealized dreams, it must also be conceded that individuals are bound to express themselves not only by setting goals for a better society, but by finding ways of bearing the injustices and frustrations of the moment in terms of a faith which sees life in its essential rather than in its existential reality.'[2]

c. In the third place, prophetic religion turns its instruments of criticism, sharpened and partly formed by Marx himself, on Marxist Communism as a religion. Socialist Christians 'think it slightly pathetic that Marxists who pretend to defy "bourgeois ideology" on every front, should have such a touching confidence in bourgeois rationalism and naturalism as a philosophy of life.'[3] From this comes its romanticism about human nature and its own ideological taint. 'The same natural relativists who are afraid of every transcendent reference, end by dreaming of an unconditioned social order in which perfect justice and perfect peace will be achieved. The Marxians significantly speak of a dialectical process which ends with the revolution.'[4] 'After the revolution the Marxist becomes half Catholic, half liberal.' His institutions are the Kingdom

[1]'Christian Politics and Communist Religion', op. cit. p. 456.
[2]'Is Religion Counter-Revolutionary?'
[3]'The Creed of Modern Christian Socialists.'
[4]Ibid.

of God for him. He hopes for continued natural progress in the socialist society. The result is a sanctified state ruled by priest-kings with a holy power more complete than any genuine religious authority ever was, because there is no transcendent object of worship beyond the state itself. All of this the socialist Christian must resist in the name of the revolution itself.

D. In the fourth place, the socialist Christian finds in his prophetic religion the resources not only of criticism and transcendence but of revolutionary action as well. Its heart, in the spirit of the Hebrew prophets, is in the dynamic relation between God's love and justice and man who is called in question along with his whole society. Man experiences the forgiveness and grace of God not as a possession or datum, but as a rescue from despair, and as strength to go on living in this tension.

'In that capacity for judging all relative and partial values and in the humility which does not claim to reach an absolutely pure judgement itself even while it sees what is partial and incomplete in every culture; in these lie the genius of prophetic religion. In them lie also the guarantee of perpetual revolution, protest, rebellion, and criticism in human affairs.'[1]

Radical, prophetic religion therefore, as Niebuhr expressed it in his more political writing of this period, is a religion of humble self-criticism, but nevertheless of fundamental criticism and revolt, because the Christian knows himself involved in the action of God's judgement and cannot be an observer. He suspects himself of ideological distortion even in the expression of his faith, and knows that he must prove himself to the secular radical by effective and radical social action. Yet he knows that the realism of Christian insight is necessary to purify radicalism itself, which in this case takes a Marxist form; and he struggles so to express this insight in thought and action that it will be proved, by secular acceptance and by its fruits, to be a genuinely unideological force for justice and truth.

6. IDEOLOGY AND CHRISTIAN TRUTH

Such was Niebuhr's response to the challenge of the Marxist doctrine of ideology, based primarily on his sense of the present

[1] 'Is Religion Counter-Revolutionary?'

judgement of God in history. He paid it the high compliment of not trying to refute it with another doctrine alone, but with more effective and realistic radical practice. But Niebuhr's theological answer to the problem of ideology is differently motivated from the beginning. No longer does he operate under that sense of crisis which calls even his own beliefs and thought processes in question in the interests of social change. Rather he seeks a dialectically balanced formulation of truth which shall be beyond the criticism that it is ideological because it expresses in itself the proper tensions between reason and revelation, law of love and relative decision, judgement and grace as these are found in every historical situation. Search for the standard by which to judge revolutionaries, conservatives, and liberal reformers alike, gradually replaces radical politics as his primary concern.

In this search Niebuhr does not abandon the base-line of his thinking: human experience in society, as a reality independent of all preconceptions of its meaning, and incapable of being reduced to any system of rational coherence. In this he differs from Barth for whom revelation is a first datum of human experience itself. Reason, in his developed view, is involved in a continual dialectical struggle with ideology. On the one hand, enlarged to true wisdom, by its capacity for self-transcendence, it points beyond itself toward a fulfilment of life's meaning to be revealed and known by faith. On the other hand, having recognized this need for a saviour, it is constantly tempted to find this power in some rationally comprehensible principle of meaning and ethical system which obviates the need for living by faith. So the perspective of a group is again universalized and becomes an ideology imposed on the world.

'It is this capacity of self-transcendence which gives rise both to the yearning after God and to the idolatrous worship of false gods. It leads both to the expectation of Christ and to the expectation of the false Christ who will vindicate us but not our neighbour.'[1]

Modern scientific liberalism and Marxism both appear to Niebuhr in this context as attempts to impose a premature coherence

[1]*The Nature and Destiny of Man*, Vol. II. *Human Destiny* (London, 1943), p. 65.

on life at the expense of empirical facts in their variety and unique-
ness, which means therefore also, at the expense of human freedom.
For liberalism in all its forms this coherence is embodied in the
processes of nature and history, themselves redemptive through
the march of progress. Truth which fulfils life is found by rational
men using the scientific method. Marxism has the advantage over
this of being 'a purer derivative of the prophetic movement', and
showing a certain provisional realism about evil in society. But its
way of knowing truth and meaning is after all of the same stripe.
It is a prime example of a system in which a messiah is expected
because the brokenness of human knowledge and goodness is recognized, yet where his coming is blocked by resolving this expectation into a rational principle which expresses the interests of a
single social group. Marx's insight into the relation of reason to
social interest is prophetic, but Communist messianism hardens
and makes absolute the illusions of the bourgeois world view.
Natural harmony of social forces becomes dialectical movement
toward this harmony by way of total conflict. The goodness of all
men becomes the goodness of the proletariat. 'The Marxist spon-
sorship of the theory of ideology was unfortunate, for Marxism
discredited itself so quickly by becoming the prisoner of its own
ideological presuppositions.'[1] Marxists tried to escape from the
problem of ideology too easily by positing a material reality in
dialectical movement knowable 'scientifically', and explaining
ideological taint in purely economic or class terms.

There is, in fact, Niebuhr believes, no science of society; no
objective point from which to see the truth about policies and judge
among values, free of all ideological taint. Judgements in this field
are all value judgements given by participants. The conflict of
values between individual initiative and social security which
divides every society, for instance, cannot be resolved by any
appeal to social science. The reason of both sides is ideological.
Reason can only exercise a relative empirical function in the midst
of conflicts of interest, to mitigate them in the name of a more
objective and inclusive truth. And it can do this best when it refuses
to force the world into premature patterns of coherence, maintains

[1]*Christian Realism and Political Problems* (London, 1954), pp. 76 f.

141

a healthy scepticism about the moral pretensions of every social ideal, and remains open to new realities which reflect the action of human freedom, prepared to mediate morally between the conflicting human values they express.

Unideological truth therefore is the truth of revelation; not rational propositions, but events in the drama of God's encounter with man, whose meaning man can never fully grasp or exhaust. There is no way of comprehending human freedom, or human evil. There is no way of proving that human history or human life is meaningful or good by reason alone. Revelation shows the ideological character of all such attempts. Its first word is spoken against the structures of reason and society which man has set up, though man's reason may understand that such a word must be spoken. God is revealed as a Lord whose power is revealed in suffering, not as a Messiah who fulfils the desires of those who expected him. He shows himself to be the redeemer who does not help the righteous to victory, but forgives the contrite and gives promise of the day when 'the evil in every good and the unrighteousness of the righteous is to be overcome'. As God who suffers he reveals the seriousness with which God takes human freedom and autonomy, yet the operation of his redeeming love upon them. In all this the radical character of human repentance is emphasized again and again. There is no apprehension of the truths of revelation, no appropriation of God's mercy and grace, no new wisdom, so long as man's self-esteem, security, and systems of meaning in life, have not been brought to despair.

Furthermore the new truth we then find in Christ is also subject to the dialectic of sinful distortion, judgement and forgiveness. There is no refuge from ideology in a system of thought and action based on propositions of revealed truth, for though we are given this truth we do not possess it. We 'hold the truth in unrighteousness' even as believers.

'The truth, as it is contained in Christian revelation, includes and recognizes that it is neither possible for man to know the truth fully, nor to avoid the error of pretending that he does.'[1]

[1] *Human Destiny*, p. 225.

We are called as Christians to embody our faith in thoughts and actions which make use of reason to work out faith's implications. Yet faith tells us that in doing this we are corrupting truth again with our interests. Prayer and consecrated thought help to make us aware of these corruptions, but only if humility and contrition operate alongside of faith's conviction, so that we forgive and learn from those who hold what we believe to be untrue convictions. This is the perpetual dialectic of Christian knowledge.

The same is true of grace, in Niebuhr's view. It is the power of God in us, yet it is known only in the faith which contritely recognizes man's tendency even to misuse this gift and which therefore seeks ever again forgiveness for this misuse. Here also it is the unbelievers and moral sceptics through whom God reminds Christians of the way they turn even the central truths of faith into ideologies. So for example the profound moral scepticism of Marxism is the judgement which the sentimental morality of liberal Christianity and the conservative piety of Christian orthodoxy have brought upon themselves.

This dialectic is Niebuhr's answer to the problem of ideology. The prophetic sense of God's historical judgement and grace in an historical situation has been generalized into a method: empirical reason encountering revelation, both deepened by dialectical tension, to express that truth which is beyond ideology. Out of this comes a perpetual correction of false allegiances, radical or conservative. It is not surprising therefore that Niebuhr defends the relative value of natural empirical reason as staunchly against what he regards as irrational absolutes in theology, as he attacks any simple continuity between rational systems and revealed truth. A truly empirical method, in his view, can be faith's handmaiden—a reflection of that residue of *justitia originalis* still present in man—because on the one hand it never ceases to seek such rational coherences as are present in human life and history, and on the other hand it posits no total system of truth. It seeks constantly correction for the inevitable distortions of perspective, the 'ideological' elements which creep into its understanding. It supports in social ethics an open society in which power is balanced against power, and no one concept of social truth or welfare dominates the state. It recognizes the necessity of encounter between person and person, idea and idea, and the relativity of all man-made systems. The mystery of God's revelation in Christ, therefore, imposes no irrational dogma on this empiricist. It places his thought rather in the framework of his whole existence so that relativism becomes faith in God's free act, and tolerance becomes contrition wrought by God's mercy in Christ.

'There is no possibility of fully validating the truth in the foolishness of the Gospel if every cultural discipline is not taken seriously up to the point where it becomes conscious of its own limits and the point where the insights of various disciplines stand in contradiction to each other, signifying that the total of reality is more complex than any scheme of rational meaning which may be invented to comprehend it.'[1]

The truth of the Christian Gospel must be related meaningfully to the reason of the whole secular world. It must be validated in responsible decision in all parts of society. Only so is it saved from becoming just another cover for the interests of some men against others.

Is this an adequate answer to the challenge of the Marxist doctrine of ideology? The answer has two sides. On the one side, no other theologian in this study makes the way of love revealed in Christ on one side, and the problems of responsible social action in the world on the other side, so completely the starting point of all his thought, as does Niebuhr. In his thought are exposed more mercilessly than anywhere else the devices which even Christians use to justify their own social power or privilege and deny their responsibility for their neighbours. Nothing arouses Niebuhr's opposition more quickly than the attempt, which all the other five men in this study make in one way or another, to escape from the burdens, tensions, anxieties and relative decisions of this world in some theological or churchly way, leaving less pious people to bear them. 'Freedom over law', he writes impatiently to Karl Barth,

'. . . cannot mean emancipation from the tortuous and difficult task of achieving a tolerable justice. It is certainly not right for Christians to leave it to the "pagans" of our day to walk the tightrope of our age which

[1]*Christian Realism and Political Problems*, p. 184.

144

is strung over the abyss of war and tyranny, seeking by patience and courage to prevent war on the one hand and the spread of tyranny on the other, while Christians rejoice in a "revolutionary hope" in which all these anxieties of human existence . . . are overcome proleptically.'[1]

In all his works Niebuhr declares his solidarity with the 'pagans' of this world wherever they are honestly engaged in dealing with the problems of our time—with responsible statesmen, reforming politicians, farmers, businessmen, soldiers, and human beings in all the dilemmas and tensions of life. His finest ethics are found where he analyses the particular problems of these people, bringing the insights of the Bible to bear on discerning the forces at work, the dimensions and limits of possible action, and the false ideals or principles which becloud the issue. His finest theology is in those sermons where he reaches up on behalf of this 'pagan' world to lay hold on the promise of God:

'The weakness of Christ is not merely the weakness which God's revelation in history makes necessary. It is in part the weakness of God as he is in his nature. It is the weakness of his forgiving love. . . . The mystery lies in the fact that this mercy is partly the fulfilment and partly the contradiction of the justice which punishes. . . . The words of derision, "He saved others, himself he cannot save," give us a clue to the innermost character of a man in history who perished upon the cross. They also give us a clue to the mystery of the very character of God.'[2]

In all this Niebuhr fulfils the first and basic requirement of an effective Christian encounter with Communism, and answer to its doctrine of ideology. If empirical reasoning, the Cross as the final meaning and fulfilment of history, and democracy as a social system, emerge as carriers of all Niebuhr's thought, this is precisely because each of them is conceived, not as a human system,

[1]'We are Men and not God', in *The Christian Century*, 27th October, 1948, p. 1139.

[2]*Discerning the Signs of the Times* (London, 1946), pp. 126–31. Cf. also p. 21: 'Religion as such is no cure for human pride and pretension. It is the final battleground between pride and humility. There is no form of the Christian faith, no matter how profound its insights about the finiteness and sinfulness of man and the majesty of God, which can prevent some devotees of that faith from using it to claim God too simply as the ally of this or that partial human judgement.'

but as a guide for responsible action in the endless complexities of human society. Because his faith shares every burden of this world, even the burden of its uncertainty, its realism about the world must be the starting point for any effective Christian action.

But, on the other side, Niebuhr's deficiencies are the reverse side of his contributions. There is missing, complains Karl Barth, a third dimension, beyond the dialectical balance between creation and corruption, sin and grace:

'The Word of God, the Holy Spirit, God's free choice, God's grace and judgment, the Creation, the Reconciliation, the Kingdom, the Sanctification, the Congregation; and all these not as principles to be interpreted in the same sense as the first two dimensions, but as indications of *events*, of concrete, once-for-all, unique divine *actions*, of the majestic mysteries of God that cannot be resolved into any pragmatism.'[1]

These events are of course present for Niebuhr. He is as concerned as Barth to present truth as God's act, as historical dramatic event, and the Christian response as repentance and new life out of encounter with this God. Both men are in the full sense theologians of revelation. But Niebuhr, the Christian-in-the-world, does not allow himself the joyful abandon of Barth, the preacher-in-the-church. Suffering love on the Cross can be shown as relevant to the decisions of life, and meaningful in the promise it contains. But in Barth's emphasis on the datum of the Resurrection victory, he senses a certain irresponsible lightness toward real human beings and their problems.

This is the point where Niebuhr fails to draw on the full resources of the Christian faith in meeting the Marxist challenge. He long ago repudiated the idea that belief in an illusion, such as the Marxist utopia, might be necessary to motivate needed radical social change. Yet there was an insight in this point which he has failed to transmute into his theology, just in so far as 'illusion' can be understood as a transcendent given, which requires a response of faith prior to all experience. For we find Niebuhr in uneasy alliances with illusions of this sort right down to the present day. To be sure, despite his fierce defence of *justitia originalis*, no system

[1] Karl Barth, 'Continental versus Anglo-Saxon Theology', in *The Christian Century*, 16th February, 1949, p. 203.

of natural law survives in his tension between Christ's law of love and the relativity in sin of social action in the world. But ever again we see Niebuhr implicitly taking his commandments from somewhere in history itself rather than from Christ's relation to the redeemed man. At first Marxism provided for him a clear analysis and point of contact for the Christian ethic. Now that Marxism has been discredited we find him more and more seeking the concrete will of God, despite all his dialectic, in the organic development of a pragmatic democratic tradition. One of America's leading New Deal liberals expresses his profound gratitude to Niebuhr at just this point in the following words:

'Niebuhr showed that the refutation by history of democratic illusions need not turn into a refutation of democracy; that the appalled realization that man was not wholly good and reasonable need not turn into a repudiation of man as wholly evil and impotent; that men and women could act more effectively for decency and justice under the banner of a genuine humility than they had under the banner of an illusory perfectibility. His penetrating reconstruction of the democratic faith—in the context of Roosevelt's brilliant invocation of democratic resources against the perils of depression and war—absorbed and mastered the forces of disillusion and preserved the nerve of action. With his aid that faith emerged from two anguished decades far better armed than before against future ordeal and challenge.'[1]

This is, to be sure, the story of what Niebuhr did for a New Dealer's faith, and not of Niebuhr's faith. Niebuhr is too profound a Christian analyst to share this new liberal religion his theology has helped to found. The concept of irony which he applies to the liberal, responsible America in which he most believes,[2] is full of foreboding that our civilization may fall, despite its moral superiority, to a demonic foe, because it trusts in its own virtue overmuch. But his anxiety before the judgement of God on those who erect a relatively greater good into an ultimate good, does not liberate Niebuhr from bondage to this relative good. The 'necessary illusion', though tempered with anxiety, remains until revelation is

[1]Arthur Schlesinger, 'Reinhold Niebuhr's Role in American Political Thought and Life', in *Reinhold Niebuhr, His Religious, Social and Political Thought*, ed. Kegley & Bretall (New York, 1956), p. 150.
[2]Cf. *The Irony of American History* (London, 1952), *passim*.

allowed to bring its own testimony to a new reality, a truth on the plane where these illusions have tried to operate, which gives human experience a new meaning, free of dependence on overt or covert ideologies. Only Redemption is truly radical.

7. MARXIST AND CHRISTIAN VIEWS OF HISTORY

The same pattern which we have just described, is that of Niebuhr's relation to the Marxist view of history. He was spurred to reflection on history by the demands of concrete prophecy. In his earlier years he was confronted with a society which he believed to be under the inevitable and just judgement of God. Its disintegration was a datum of his social experience. Its moral necessity and justness was a datum of his conscience. He confronted on the one side a complacent or unrealistic liberal moralism, within the Church and without, which failed to see this crisis; and on the other side an individualistic orthodoxy which separated the world of the spirit from the world of politics and history. In this situation he felt the power of what he then called the Marxist 'mythology'[1] in the Communist movement, as a secularized version of the Christian hope. Here, where Christians had abandoned them, Biblical insights into the meaning of history were being secularly reaffirmed. Divine Providence becomes the self-contradictions of capitalism leading to revolution. The promise to the meek and suffering becomes the hope for the proletariat. Confidence in God's act alone becomes economic determinism. The fulfilment of history becomes the promise of the classless society. Niebuhr was not enamoured of this power. He saw the danger in its self-righteous illusion. He described the rise of the Marxist proletariat by analogy with the barbarian invasions of Rome. But the urgency of this historical crisis was central to his thinking. He called Christians to understand the historical forces playing around them, to take their part in softening the fall of one social order and its replacement by

[1] *Reflections on the End of an Era*, p. 122. The term 'mythology' was a misnomer. Niebuhr was referring not to Grecian symbols of the forces eternally playing on human life, but to the adequate expression of the prophetic Hebrew-Christian sense of the movement of history toward a goal through judgement and redemption, which sense is not bound to a literal interpretation of the Biblical account.

another, and to inform the society to come with that depth of Christian insight into its true purpose and meaning which would save it also from destruction. Under this pressure his theology of history developed.

When we turn to this theology, however, we find, as with the question of truth and ideology, another motive also at work. His search turns from seeking a response to historical realities adequate to the revolutionary situation of which Marxism is the most potent expression, toward seeking a view of history which, by understanding it whole, will provide a sound basis for responsible living in any age, and will refute both Marxism and liberalism. This search is indeed dominated by the desire to do justice to the dialectical encounter between Providence and human freedom, meaning and mystery, God's purpose and human purposes, which makes history what it is. Niebuhr finds the problem of history posed by the ceaseless search of modern man for a formula whereby history, as revealed to us by our Hebrew-Christian background, can be rendered totally intelligible and meaningful by some principle within itself. So it is with the liberal doctrine of progress, with philosophies of emergent evolution, with the rational union of Being with Becoming in Hegel, and so it is also with Marx's dialectical materialism, despite its note of provisional judgement. All of them 'exalt time into the position of God by making it the clue to existence'.[1] Against them all Niebuhr proclaims in the name of moral realism and responsibility the 'irrational' sovereignty of a God who in the cross of Jesus Christ 'embodies the perplexity of history into the solution',[2] by giving history the meaning and fulfilment from beyond itself which it cannot have within itself. History needs a saviour, for every attempt to make moral sense of events, or to set up a working justice, must reckon with the morally irrelevant fact of power, and the rebellion of men against the laws of their own existence.

Christ therefore, gives to the continuing time scale a new, a theological, significance. In him God puts a final end to historical messianisms by revealing human history on all levels of its achieve-

[1] *Faith and History* (London, 1949), p. 48.
[2] Ibid. p. 161.

ment to be in contradiction to God, needing repentance. In him also God reveals a new reality—suffering love, *agape*—as the norm and source of the new life which is the fulfilment of history. Thus the Christian is able to grasp by faith the hope of the resurrection without denying the sinful and contingent character of historical existence.

'He is persuaded that a divine power and love have been disclosed in Christ which will complete what man cannot complete; and which will overcome the evil introduced into human life and history by man's abortive effort to complete his life by his own wisdom and power.'[1]

On the other hand, however, this event changes the relation between man and God in history less, in Niebuhr's view, than one might suppose. For the drama of Christ's life, death, and resurrection is for him symbolic as well as historical. It shows the way God suffers under the rebellion of men, and yet the sovereignty of the sufferer over history. The kingdom of God is a symbol of the supra-historical character of God's will which yet enters history and works in the consciences of men. Its conquest is always an immediate possibility:

'Civilizations and cultures in their larger historical development are never destroyed by external enemies without having first destroyed themselves. The force of their destruction is . . . the loss of their moral authority under the challenge of those who speak against their power in the name of the Kingdom of God.'[2]

But it is never a success story. History will only be fulfilled as it is judged at its end, expressed in the symbols of Christian eschatology which neither separate eternity from time and devalue history, nor justify unambiguously any achievement in history. But eschatology must, above all, be understood symbolically. Faith in the coming again of Christ is

'. . . an expression of faith in the sufficiency of God's sovereignty over the world and history, and in the final supremacy of love over all forms of self-love which defy, for the moment, the inclusive harmony of all things under the will of God.'[3]

[1] *Faith and History*, p. 170.
[2] *Beyond Tragedy* (London, 1938), p. 285.
[3] *Human Destiny*, p. 300.

The last judgement 'affirms that the ultimate mercy does not efface distinctions between good and evil'.[1] And the resurrection of the body symbolizes that all nature, purged of its tendency to make itself the centre of existence, is taken up into the fulfilled meaning of history.

In all this, Niebuhr's pattern of history is one of continuous dialectic between the absolute standard of God's *agape* and the ambiguous pattern of man's search for self-fulfilment. History develops ever greater human capacities for creative accomplishment, and equally great corruptions of these capacities. The pattern does not reorganize itself when God's act in Christ enters it. Christ rather illuminates it in all its ambiguity, like a divine searchlight. The cross stands, in Niebuhr's phrase, 'on the edge of history', showing its true meaning, establishing a new hope by faith, and setting up a new tension between imaginative love and the world. It shows the judgement over all history to be one of grace. But the cross leaves man where he was before in the complex of historical forces. It lifts no burden from him. It clarifies, but does not essentially change his responsible action toward the powers of this world.

In short, Niebuhr's picture of history places us perpetually in the twilight position of standing under the Cross, looking forward toward the Resurrection. The decisive event, without which our faith is vain, hangs over the historical process in tension with every part of it, offering a symbolic promise to the whole. The Cross, and the Man on it, remind the reader more strongly of an ideal state of human relations—that of selfless love poured out for others—than of the full person of the Son of God. There are passages where God seems to be interpreted in terms of the Kingdom of God the trans-historical realm of true justice and mutuality by whose standards earthly powers are judged and inspired—rather than the other way around. One can understand Niebuhr's concern in all of this, lest too unguarded an affirmation of Christ's victory in the Resurrection play into the hands of some human interest which is less than God's, and excuse Christians from wrestling with the duties and conflicts of this sinful world as responsible neighbours. Yet, paradoxically, in this very concern, Niebuhr has generalized

[1]*Human Destiny*, p. 303.

151

the sense of historical crisis which drove him to seek a theology of history, into a symbolic explanation of the perpetual forces at work in history which leaves the question of concrete action open.

This did not make Niebuhr immediately a conservative, however. In his greatest theological work—*The Nature and Destiny of Man*—and the books which followed it, we find a careful balance between support for organic tradition and revolutionary change. On the one hand the way in which 'history had to stumble by tortuous processes upon the proper techniques for avoiding both anarchy and tyranny'[1] deserves respect. On the other hand these very processes have included and sometimes justify revolution.

'Such rules of justice as we have known in history have been arrived at by a social process in which various partial perspectives have been synthesized into a more inclusive one. But even the inclusive perspective is contingent to time and place. The Marxist cynicism in regard to the pretended moral purity of all laws and rules of justice is justified.'[2]

At this point Niebuhr absorbs Toynbee's view of a historical pattern in which civilizations rise, break down, and eventually disintegrate due to forces of the spirit within the range of their moral responsibility. But, in criticism of Toynbee, he grants even the creative period of a civilization no moral authority of its own:

'Ruling oligarchies within a national community and hegemonic nations within an imperial community are never purely creative even in their heyday, except "by grace". The grace which makes them creative is the historic coincidence between their will to power and the requirement for wider unity within a nation or community of nations which that will to power serves.'[3]

Ruling classes and nations have their time, by grace, of fulfilment. But they continue in history only by 'dying to self' in response to the challenge of new, previously subject, groups with new demands for justice.

'Marxist collectivism was, on the whole, a healthy and inevitable revolt against bourgeois individualism. The new class of industrial workers . . .

[1]*Human Destiny*, p. 278.
[2]Ibid. p. 262.
[3]*Faith and History*, p. 252.

knew themselves to be members of one another. They also sensed their true relation to the vast forces of historical destiny, which human decisions may deflect and affect, but not negate.'[1]

On the other hand new social forces, instruments of divine judgement though they are, 'are always involved in the same idolatries as the forces against which they contend'.[2] Utopia, Niebuhr cites Mannheim, is the ideology of the dispossessed. The illusory self-righteous hope of absolute justice and harmony accompanies every revolutionary movement, Communist or not, just as the self-righteous pretension to be just and harmonious accompanies the defence of the *status quo*. The Christian must act as a dialectical balancer of the forces of order and of freedom against their tendencies to turn respectively into tyranny and anarchy, putting himself now on the side of organic tradition, now on that of revolutionary change. In this work he may hope that the forces of tradition may so repent and accept the new power and its interests into their structure that they may be 'reformed rather than destroyed by the bludgeonings of history',[3] or that the powers of revolution may turn from dogmas about a new social order to more concrete and humbler goals.

8. MAN IN SOCIETY

What, then, is the substance of human freedom and responsibility in society? Here Niebuhr extends the perpetual tension of God's relation to man and man's relation to his fellow man into social analysis. As the word of revelation spoken against man's reason leads to the correctness of empirical thinking as a method, so the word of God's judgement against human systems of social order validates democracy as a method and calls men to work always for a balance of powers. This does not mean that Niebuhr calls men back from pursuing false gospels (revolutionary or conservative) to the law. His ethics are not without vision; no law could adequately express the subtlety of his insight into the moral

[1] *The Children of Light and the Children of Darkness* (London, 1945), p. 44.
[2] *Faith and History*, p. 258.
[3] Ibid. p. 261.

issues at stake in society. Yet something of the burden of the law remains in the way the law of love, which in New Testament revelation stretches the imagination and upsets earthly justice, interacts with the power facts of society.

It interacts first as standard and obligation, the source of that disinterested concern for others which approves what contributes to their fulfilment. Justice is first of all the elaboration of love into custom and law for a whole community.

'Community is an individual as well as social necessity; for the individual can realize himself only in intimate and organic relation with his fellow men. Love is therefore the primary law of his nature; and brotherhood the fundamental requirement of his existence.'[1]

Here is the suggestion of an absolute natural law.

This absolute however stands in tension with the competing vitalities of people and groups in society. Every actual achievement of relatively just order has been the result of the interaction between the moral sense of competing groups and the balance of their wills to power. Furthermore every statement of the absolute is partial and interested. Therefore every statement of principles of justice relative to a given social order must recognize the right of other groups to criticize and to organize power against it, to redress its moral pretensions and its actual injustices. Structures of freedom which provide for effective change in the balance of power belong to any system of social justice.

In the relativities of political justice, however, equality—of rights, of status, and of power—remains for Niebuhr a guiding principle. This is less than love: 'the fence and the boundary line are symbols of the spirit of justice.' It is furthermore an unattainable balance, became firstly inequalities of ability and function exist and tend toward other inequalities; secondly every power balance is dynamic—a potential conflict. Formulated as an absolute it becomes the ideology of a revolutionary group (as in the Communist image of the classless society); just as any natural law which justifies functional inequalities—Niebuhr mentions Brunner in this regard—becomes the ideology of dominant groups. Never-

[1] *Human Destiny*, p. 253.

theless equality is at work in the social conscience of men and participates in the formation of social order.

Government is involved in the same dialectic as other social forces. It has on the one hand a divine authority as an organizer of order and justice among competing vitalities; as the enforcer of society's traditional wisdom, the fruit of adjusted past conflicts; and as the centre through which society can shift disproportions of power in order to preserve its own health and safety. Yet it contains on the other hand the most dangerous possibilities of injustice when it makes order—a relative good—into an absolute tyrannical power coercing society. Political power must always therefore be guarded against too close alliance with one power group or another in society, if Marxist cynicism about the state is not to be justified. And furthermore the majesty of government, like the authority of natural law and the validity of reason, only reigns if it has built-in provisions for correcting its own abuses; constitutional checks on the power of the governors.

Democracy therefore, as the political method and framework for the endless experiments which are necessary to achieve a just balance among the changing power groups and vital interests of society, is for Niebuhr the Good in politics.

'It is the highest achievement of democratic societies that they embody the principle of resistance to government within the principle of government itself. The citizen is thus armed with the "constitutional" power to resist the unjust exactions of government . . . (for) government has been so conceived that criticism of the ruler becomes an instrument of better government and not a threat to government itself.'[1]

This does not mean democracy as a panacea or an ideal state placed over against the Communist ideal. In contrast with Karl Barth, who otherwise shares his view about democracy, Niebuhr will not even accept the reality of man redeemed in Christ as a starting point of political thinking. The fanaticism or the irresponsibility of all idealists imperils democracy and can be broken only by knowing the judgement of God over the best of human societies and our inevitable involvement in them. But for those who know these things, 'the real point of contact between democracy and

[1]*Human Destiny*, p. 278.

155

profound religion is in the spirit of humility which democracy requires and which must be one of the fruits of religion.'[1]

9. CHRISTIAN REALISM IN POWER POLITICS

Is this theological perspective as a whole an adequate response to the challenge of Communist revolutionary doctrine and power? Does it speak to the needs of men confronted with this challenge in the work of society? Let us look at this question from three points of view, that of realism in the face of Communist and non-Communist power; that of creative alternatives to the Communist programme and hope; and that of ministry to the Communist as a person.

It is to the first of these that Niebuhr has made his greatest contribution. The whole force of his profound involvement, dictated by his theological perspective, in the problems of achieving relative justice in the American society in which he stood, and in the world as a responsible American, led him gradually to reject Marxism as a tool of social analysis, and the Marxist statement of the historical crisis in which society stands. The Second World War confronted him with an historical crisis which was inexplicable in Marxist terms and which raised a host of questions about the continuing vitality of a free economy. By 1944 he was analysing property in terms of a balance between socialist concentration under public control, and liberal distribution to a large number of small private owners, though he still affirmed Marx's description of property as social power tending toward injustice.[2] In 1948 he reaffirmed his socialism, but in terms which moved a long way toward redefining it:

'We continue to be socialists, in the sense that we believe that the capitalist order of society stands under divine judgement and that there is no justice in technical society without a completely pragmatic attitude toward the institution of property. It must be socialized wherever it is of such a character that it makes for injustice through inordinate centralization.'[3]

[1]*The Children of Light*, p. 104.
[2]Ibid. Ch. 3.
[3]'Frontier Fellowship', in *Christianity and Society*, XIII (Autumn 1948).

But these were transitional thoughts. In 1949 Niebuhr threw over even this pragmatic socialism as a programme and even this highly Christianized Marxist sense of judgement on American capitalism in favour of a purer pragmatism such as he found embodied in the New Deal's experimentation with mixed economy, averting a crisis in capitalism.

'The issue in America', he wrote, 'is the right and duty of democratic society to achieve economic justice under the conditions of a technical society. The task cannot be performed if the conscience of the nation is confused by either of the contrasting dogmas (capitalism and socialism) which have brought civil war into western civilization.'[1]

There are two sides to this pragmatism. One is its dependence in Niebuhr's mind on the genius of a democratic society for developing organic institutions capable of furthering a wise balance of power with power in defiance of all theories and dogmas. This is the questionable dogma underlying it, as we shall point out below. The other side is its analysis and action in social reality today. Here, it seems to this writer, the instinct which led Niebuhr to break with the Marxist categories of his youth in order better to understand the problem of planning in society, is clearly valid. Niebuhr follows his theology of the state even in this pragmatism He does not reject the basic responsibility of government for the economic order. He reinterprets this responsibility to take account of two facts: (1) the importance of a certain free play for motives of profit, because 'the self-interest of men . . . is too variable and unpredictable to be simply controlled'; and (2) the incapability of any one planning centre to balance all interests fairly against one another, to know the whole good for the economy or to avoid the temptations of power.[2] Therefore planning for society must not always mean socialization or control. It may mean permissive legislation for the organization of special interest groups such as labour. It may mean regulation of private business in its own interest. It may mean intervention in the price or production system at specific points on behalf of the general welfare. Only experience

[1]Editorial in *C. and S.*, XVI (Winter 1950–1), p. 4.
[2]'The Christian Faith and the Economic Life of Liberal Society', in *Goals of Economic Life*, ed. Dudley Ward (London, 1953), pp. 446–8.

with concrete social forces can determine under different conditions what combination of freedom and planning works best.

Niebuhr's pragmatism is valid as well, in contrast to Brunner who shares many of the same social insights, in its refusal to set up even the principles of a mixed economy as ideal principles, and above all its sharp break with the moralistic illusions of a 'Christian politics'. All generalized programmes, even those of a Fellowship of Socialist Christians,[1] which claim moral sanctity, become ideologies. They clothe some partial interest and become its tool. The Christian will therefore be impelled by love to ask the right questions of the secular world, to analyse it more accurately, and to set up norms of justice in the light of God's grace toward man in concrete situations. But

'. . . the whole capital of religious sanctity must not be invested in these norms. For these systems and structures of justice are not eternal norms to which life must perennially conform, but *ad hoc* efforts to strike a balance between the final moral possibilities of life and the immediate and given realities.'[2]

Thus much for Christian action within a nation in the face of Marxist socialism as an alternative. But Niebuhr's pragmatic realism has contributed more to the Christian encounter with Communism in recent years, in the international scene, at three major points.

First, Niebuhr is of all the six theologians with whom we have to do, the sharpest analyst of world Communist power and of Christian responsibility in the face of it. He does not change his analysis of Communism in the post-war period, but he gives it a new urgency and direction—toward explaining why this utopian dogma has replaced Nazism as the greatest single threat to world peace and order.

This threat comes partly because a utopian ideology removes all the controls of conscience on the ruling group through its inade-

[1] 'A certain taint of this moral ideology is evident in the earlier pronouncements of our Fellowship (of Socialist Christians) and indeed in all pronouncements of the Christian left.' *Christian Faith and Social Action*, ed. J. A. Hutchinson (London, 1953), pp. 231–2.
[2] *Goals of Economic Life*, p. 451.

quate doctrine of man. Because Marxism believes all power to be economic or a reflection of it, and the root of all evil to lie in private property, therefore it imagines that the post-revolutionary society is one with no problem of power and only a residual problem of human evil. Because the Communists, following Marx, believe that a single proletarian class is the sinless carrier of the revolution which will establish the structure of the ideal society, therefore they see no need to balance its power against that of other groups in society. Because the monopoly by this class of power and righteousness becomes the monopoly of the party, and then of the ruling oligarchy in the party, or a single tyrant, there develops a more absolute division between the powerful and the powerless, a more absolute use of some men for the interest of others than ever before. Because the world is divided into absolutely good and absolutely evil camps in conflict, every kind of inhumanity, hypocrisy, hatred and oppression is justified if it serves the ends of this conflict. Because absolute power is linked to an absolute system of 'science', Communism has no resources for self-reformation and inner change. Because the realities of society are bound to frustrate and defy this idolatrous 'science', the power of the Communist oligarchs becomes all the more dangerous and unpredictable when they are faced with this frustration. All of this adds up to a system which is worse than simply unjust. It has the dangerous dynamic of a fierce self-righteous power convinced of its mission to mould the world according to its pattern, convinced that its devotees have taken 'the leap from the realm of necessity to the realm of freedom'. This is why there can be no mutual confidence in relations between Russians and the West, and negotiations only on the basis of positions of strength.

But Communism is more dangerous than Nazism, Niebuhr believes, secondly, because its utopianism has a seductive appeal to the liberal and the idealistic mind. Marxism is a kind of religious apocalypse, he says,

'But it is a very modern kind of religious apocalypse; for it contains the dearest hope of all typical moderns, Marxist or non-Marxist. That hope is that man may be delivered from his ambiguous position of being both creature and creator of the historical process and become unequivocally the master of his own destiny. The liberal culture has been informed by similar hopes since the eighteenth century.'[1]

Hard utopianism has a fascination for the soft utopians. They are constantly tempted to excuse its brutalities in the name of its ideals and goals. The fifth column for the Communists is made up of misguided idealists, not of cynics and opportunists. But it also appeals to nations where social chaos reigns and other channels for the resentments of the oppressed are blocked. It appeals to poor agricultural nations in their relations with rich ones, though its analysis is less true there than in an industrial society. It offers unity amid confusion, and a channel of historical action linked with a total 'science' which seems to emancipate the world at once from old religious and social fatalism. In short Communism tends to draw all the frustrated humanistic hopes, and all revolutionary resentments in East and West, to its combination of utopia, power and ideology. For this reason the international power struggle cannot be carried on by physical strength alone. The basic economic and moral health of non-Communist nations, above all their provisions for effective protest and change in the light of their own weaknesses, are as important as military balance.

In this situation Niebuhr has consistently supported the policy of containment toward Russia over against suggestions of preventive war, or of compromise. He belongs himself to that group of men who once supported Yalta, who ended the war with modest hopes that Communist dictatorship would be easier to get along with than were the Nazis because of its disciplined ideology, and its need of peace for internal reconstruction; and who has been disappointed in these hopes.[2] More than any other theologian he has 'walked the tightrope of our age which is strung over the abyss of war and tyranny' with the most sober and humble of western statesmen, supporting their creative efforts (Truman doctrine, defence of Berlin, Marshall plan *et al.*), defending them against dogmatic criticism from right or left, reminding them, in scores of concrete

[1]*The Irony of American History*, p. 57.
[2]'The Russian Enigma' in *Christianity and Society*, XI (Winter 1945–6).

analyses, of the perils of claiming too much sanctity for their programmes, and of the variety of problems yet before them. 'The
kind of patience required for living in an insecure world,' he wrote
in relation to the question of preventive war, 'and for meeting
truculent adversaries with forbearance as well as firmness, is a
religious rather than moral achievement. It accepts the moral
ambiguities of our situation as our fate and does not try to achieve
goodness, either by fighting Russia in the name of justice or capitu-
lating to Russia in the name of peace.'[1] In all this thinking about
Communism Niebuhr has remained within the framework of power
politics. But his writing has served to remind Christians everywhere who have any sort of political power or responsibility, both
of the central importance of maintaining a power balance over
against world Communism, and of the peril of claiming too much
sanctity for our cause.

Niebuhr's second contribution is his criticism of the moral pretensions of Western policy, and of moral principles in general as
direct guides to foreign policy. No American reader of *The Irony of
American History* can doubt that Niebuhr's pragmatism reveals the
instability of social traditions as effectively as his earlier Marxism.
In it he attacks, to be sure, most of the usual criticisms, Marxist or
otherwise, of the impact of American society on the world.
American achievements in the pragmatic approach to problems of
justice, says Niebuhr, belie both our consistent bourgeois ideology
and foreign criticism of us as the centre of capitalist injustice.
American foreign policy is more informed by irresponsibility toward power than by lust for it. American technical development
and high standard of living over against poor Asian countries, is
not related to exploitation of them. In fact imperialism economically speaking is not the unmixed evil which Marxism paints. Her
highly technical civilization is not simply another form of de-
humanization, comparable to the Russian one. In all this Niebuhr's
pragmatism works to exalt America's practice, where it has not
been spoiled by America's theory, and to break down most of the
usual categories of moral judgement on American society. This is a
questionable business, and gives a certain questionable background

[1]Editorial in *C. and S.*, XIII (Spring 1948).

to the concept of irony which he then substitutes. Yet this concept of irony remains a devastating critique of the moral pretensions of a relative social and political virtue.

The heart of it is that America stands in danger today, not because of her failures but because of 'achievements in which she takes an inordinate pride'; not because of evils comparable to those of a Communist system, but because of illusions of a perfect innocence and virtue which cannot deal with the ambiguities of power politics, and the give and take of international life. She faces world Communism with a 'soft' version of the same illusions which inform its aggressive mission, for Communism is the absolutized version of the liberal view of life. This illusion of innocence and virtue in her creed is less evil than Communism because it is less consistent, but it equips her neither to deal with the terrible reality of Communist power, nor to live creatively with non-Communist neighbours. The American attitude toward the power in her hands is schizophrenic: sometimes imagining that a purely rational harmony of interests or world organization will solve all problems, sometimes bordering on the Communist combination of cynicism and idealism, whereby any means are justified to achieve her righteous ends.[1] She imagines that the relative social peace which stems from an expanding economy and the careful balance of interest against interest, is the result of her doctrines of free enterprise and opportunity. Americans tend to equate economic prosperity and security with moral goodness and to regard themselves as 'tutors of mankind in its pilgrimage to perfection'. Therefore the continuing frustration of international tension and distrust baffles them, as it baffles the Soviets. They are tempted, as are their opponents, to attribute it to the machinations of a selfish and malignant power, and to project on to this power the anxieties which beset them because they are in history where absolute meaning, happiness, and peace are bound to evade all men.

'We can understand the neat logic of either economic reciprocity or the show of pure power. But we are mystified by the endless complexities of human motives and the varied compounds of ethnic loyalties, cultural

[1] *Christian Realism and Political Problems*, Ch. 2.

162

traditions, social hopes, envies and fears which enter into the policies of nations and which lie at the foundation of their political cohesions.'[1]

Therefore America is in danger of being imperialistic, because she is not sufficiently aware of the imperialist tendency inherent in her power. She is in danger of failing to carry her own valid point in the non-Communist world—that Communist power can only be dealt with from a position of strength which forces it to adjust—because she tends to measure the whole world by her moral yardstick. Of Asia Niebuhr writes:

'In our moral pride we think we are a beacon light of freedom to Asia. In our military pride we think we could win the battle against Communism in Asia by military might. The fact is that Asia is a continent in the convulsions of half a dozen revolutions at once. It is a coloured continent, justly resenting the white man's arrogance. It is a continent of quasi-colonial peoples or of nations recently emancipated from colonial rule. The Asian peoples certainly do not understand the perils of Communism. But on the other hand they have no reason to believe that democracy, as we understand it, would help them out of the morass of their poverty.'[2]

The only valid answer to this ironic predicament is an approach to world problems, especially to that of world Communism, which is pragmatic and which frankly recognizes the relativity of our perspective to our interests, preserving 'a decent respect for the opinions of mankind, derived from modest awareness of the limits of our own knowledge and power.' Here Niebuhr backs George F. Kennan in his opposition to John Foster Dulles' foreign policy of 'moral principle'. (*supra* Ch. 1.) It is the knowledge that all human achievements and ideals contain an element of self-assertion over against others, which should keep us modest and humble in our policies and our dealings with other nations, even where the most urgent moral principle is involved, or the greatest danger to be faced. This is why we may not declare a crusade against Communism, however great our responsibility for the power God has granted us to contain it.

'There is, in short, even in a conflict with a foe with whom we have so little in common, the possibility and necessity of living in a dimension of

[1]*The Irony of American History*, p. 36.
[2]Editorial in *C. and S.*, XIII (Spring 1948).

meaning in which the urgencies of the struggle are subordinated to a sense of awe before the vastness of the historical drama in which we are jointly involved; to a sense of modesty about the virtue, wisdom, and power available to us for the resolution of its perplexities; to a sense of contribution about the common human frailties and foibles which lie at the foundation of both the enemy's demonry and our vanities; and to a sense of gratitude for the divine mercies which are promised to those who humble themselves.'[1]

The final area of Niebuhr's contribution to this question, closely related to the above, is his continued realism about historical judgement. Niebuhr does call Christians, in the post-war years, to the primary task of preserving 'our civilization' both from enemies without (Communism) and vanities within. This has for him today the urgency which the socialist revolution had in the 'thirties and the conquest of Nazism in the war period, and his vision is limited by it. But this does not mean that Niebuhr has become another culture-theologian. The fate of American power could well become, in his view, one of the great ironies of history. 'One has the uneasy feeling,' he writes, 'that America as both a powerful nation and as a "virtuous" one is involved in the ironic perils which compound the experience of Babylon and Israel.'[2] It is the faith of the prophets which gives Niebuhr this uneasy feeling, when he looks at the world around him today. Because his countrymen share the liberal and Communist illusion that they are masters of their destiny, it may well be they who bring catastrophe on the world by forcing on it some absolute moral decision in the question of atomic war against compromise with tyranny. 'We have no right to play God to historical destiny,' Niebuhr pleads in relation to atomic policy. 'If we cannot escape the dread possibility of wrecking civilization in the process of defending our civilization, we can at least refrain from the hysteria and vainglory which makes such a possibility inevitable.'[3] This is the temptation which could turn all America's relative virtues into vices, and bring on her and all civilization the judgement of God. There is no escape from this except by faith, which knows of a more ultimate judgement of God, of the workings

[1]*The Irony of American History*, pp. 149–50.
[2]Ibid. p. 138.
[3]Editorial in *C. and S.*, XIII (Spring 1948).

of a Providence beyond our morals and our understanding, by which the pretensions of our goodness are judged and found wanting. In this faith repentance which brings forth charity is born, 'and we are more desperately in need of genuine charity than of more technocratic skills.'[1]

Niebuhr does not extend his thinking to a possible Christian life beyond the debacle of civilization or under Communist dominance. He looks bleakly into this future and reminds us only that 'the mystery of God's sovereignty and mercy transcends the fate of empires and civilizations. He will be exalted, though they perish.' And he exhorts us to 'work while it is yet day, since the night cometh when no man can work.'[2] This is hardly helpful to the encounter with the Communism where Christians are not so fortunately situated as to live in a democratic land. But this dark prospect does not deter Niebuhr from applying his theology of history to the present world crisis in a way which preserves its genuinely prophetic quality when dealing with the fundamental issues. All that will be said in criticism here, rests upon gratitude for this contribution to Christian realism in world politics.

10. ALTERNATIVE TO THE COMMUNIST HOPE

When we turn from power realism to a positive doctrine of social order and strategy for social change, however, Niebuhr's new-found pure pragmatism cannot help but raise the question in the reader's mind: what are its unacknowledged presuppositions? In the light of what more basic reality is Niebuhr able to endure this endless tension in society among its competing vitalities; and whence comes his picture, since he has given up socialism as an expression of historical judgement and hope in our time, of the structure of relatively just order which represents today the concrete will of God for society? This is the point at which Niebuhr, despite the dialectical balance of his theology, and precisely because of the unrelieved involvement in social problems and dilemmas which his theology demands, has become more and more conservative. The

---

[1]*The Irony of American History*, p. 129.
[2]*Christian Realism and Political Problems*, pp. 112 f.

organic development of a pragmatic democratic tradition, above all in Anglo-Saxon lands, has come to replace socialism of the future, as the anchor of his social thought. He refers with admiration to Edmund Burke's confidence in a Divine tactic of history which describes a flexible conservatism as the will of God for society.

But Niebuhr's conservatism is not Burke's. His religion is quite elsewhere than immanent in the tradition of a society where Burke places his. Conservatism, he says, is not more just and moral than liberalism in itself.

'Its virtue consisted chiefly in its ability to gauge factors of power in social and international relations which liberals tended to obscure; and to trust the organic processes of social cohesion rather than the abstract schemes which liberals were inclined to advance. . . . This instinct for the possible only a little advanced beyond the actual, instead of the utopian and ideal which hovers so precariously between the possible and the impossible, may be the consequence of experience and responsibility, to be distinguished from the visions of the irresponsible observer. It may also be the fruit of Christian wisdom which has learned the fragmentariness of all human striving and the measure of egoistic corruption in all human virtue.'[1]

This is what has happened, Niebuhr is convinced, in American society under the New Deal. The Marxist analysis of American society was wrong because the American democracy showed more 'residual health' than the radicals had reckoned—more capacity to adjust interest with interest and power with power.

'Long before the "New Deal" radically changed the climate of American political life the sovereign power of the government had been used to enforce taxation laws which embody social policy as well as revenue necessities; great concentrations of power in industry were broken up by law; necessary monopolies in utilities were brought under public regulation; social welfare, security and health and other values which proved to be outside the operations of a free market were secured by political policy. More recently housing, medicine and social security have become matters of public and political policy. All this has been accomplished on a purely pragmatic basis, without the ideological baggage which European labour carried.'[2]

[1] *Christian Realism and Political Problems*, pp. 68 f.
[2] *The Irony of American History*, p. 86.

This basic satisfaction with the progress of the last few years in Anglo-Saxon lands, this confidence in the method by which it was achieved, and this impression which one gains more and more from Niebuhr's writing in recent years, that America has achieved a relative solution of the problem of justice in her domestic life, is all evidence of conservatism. Yet it has little in common with Burke's reverence for the Divine tactic of history in the corporate life. Niebuhr's reference to Burke does not clarify his case, but obscures it. The Providence Niebuhr believes in, is that which upholds an open society where power is free to balance power, and men are sufficiently practical and humble to know that no cause is absolute.

In spite of this, Niebuhr's anchor is in the wrong place, and limits his insight into the issues which the challenge of Communism presents, precisely because it has turned his radicalism into a conservatism which cannot understand deeply enough the extent to which the modern world has lost its sense even of a residual *justitia originalis*. E. H. Carr, the analyst of Soviet Russia, who as much as any modern intellectual illustrates the subtle fascination which the combination of Communist power and Marxist historical determinism can exert on a man to whom Communism as a system is personally repugnant, puts the matter thus:

'The gravamen of the Marxist revolution is not that it has exposed the failures and shortcomings of western democracy, but that it has called in question the moral authority of the ideals and principles of western democracy by declaring them to be a reflection of the interests of a privileged class. The serious thing about the contemporary revolution is not that Marxism has kindled and inflamed the resentments of the underprivileged against the existing order and helped to make them articulate; the serious thing is that it has undermined the self-confidence of the privileged by sapping their own faith in the sincerity and efficacy of the principles on which their moral authority rested.'[1]

Niebuhr is the great apostle of 'realism', but this kind of relativism is beyond the reach of his ministry. He has never been placed in the position where the whole meaning and direction of his life and his society were called in question by a great new ideological

[1]E. H. Carr, *The Soviet Impact on the Western World* (London, 1946), pp. 96–97.

167

power because of their lack of inner coherence and outer order. Shrewdly pessimistic about human nature as Niebuhr is, one looks in vain through his writings for that understanding of existential despair which is the logical consequence of much of his analysis.

Niebuhr stands in a great tradition of empirical liberalism which for the Anglo-Saxon world is also in the best sense conservatism. He is its finest theological expression and most realistic member. Yet he also allows himself such purely secular nourishment out of this tradition as preserves him from the pangs of an existential despair and confusion which are so common in the world today.

One sees the effect of this in his analysis of Communism. It is so much dominated by the problem of Communism's political power precisely because Niebuhr cannot grasp its inner threat and the measures which this requires. For him Communism is not a temptation in the midst of social and personal chaos, but a threat to a social foundation and personal ethics which he finds sound and good. It is an external political threat which therefore is to be kept within bounds by a balance of power. Niebuhr understands that the problem is different in many other lands: that the Marxist analysis of capitalism still applies to the French situation for example, and that Communism has a perverse appeal as a great powerful all-embracing ideal in countries breaking away from agricultural feudalism. He finds it hard to understand, however, that for such countries the international power balance is not the primary question, nor is even opposition to the threat of Communism *per se*. The primary problem is rather to establish some viable form of social and political order, just enough to prevent civil war by dissatisfied elements, dynamic enough to channel revolutionary changes which are going on, and concerned enough for the effective expansion of the economy to prevent dissatisfied masses from undermining every creative political act.

But the subjective factor is just as important. It is hard for all believers in Niebuhr's type of Christian action of a pragmatic sort, to understand that their 'realism' transported out of an Anglo-Saxon environment sounds to others like ideology. It presupposes so much in the way of stable self-conscious individuals and groups that a chaotic or tyrannical society's members have no point of contact with it. It justifies so much of the Anglo-Saxon way of life that it builds up the authority of the white man. In relation to Communism it tends to presuppose a community of 'free' nations against a tyranny, whereas the perspective of another country sees the danger of two great power colossi—one hard and direct, the other softer and more diffuse to be sure, but neither welcome as dominating power.

Niebuhr appears, in short, something like Hromadka in reverse, in much of his recent political thought. Of his theological transcendence of these perspectives there can be no doubt. He gives them only a relative, pragmatic validity, for the time being, as does Hromadka on his side. Nevertheless one notices the same dependence on the philosophy and practice of social environment, for the concrete interpretation of the command of God for our time, which is so flagrant in the case of Hromadka's relation to a Communist society.

It is not surprising therefore that a theological appreciation of revolution as a fact and challenge of our time, has arisen in circles strongly influenced by Niebuhr's theology, especially in Asia, as an amendment and criticism of it.

'The struggle for and the attainment of political freedom have awakened the hitherto submerged peoples of East Asia to a new sense of dignity and historical mission,' declared the East Asia Conference of the World Council of Churches and the International Missionary Council meeting at Bangkok in 1949. 'These are the basic elements in the revolutionary ferment which are at work in the contemporary revolts and power conflicts in Asia. Ideologies have arisen to interpret this revolution to the common man and to lead him in his search for his destiny. Ideological conflicts are becoming increasingly integral to the political and social life of East Asia.'[1]

On the one hand this revolution is a simple social fact, a churning process of destruction and a new formation. No simple moral judgements can be passed on the breakdown of old patterns of family and community life under the impact of modern education and techniques, or on the expanding capacity of man to control economic realities and natural environment. But the revolution is

[1]Statement of the Bangkok Conference, in *The Ecumenical Review*, III (September, 1950), p. 278.

on the other hand an historical development with a meaning before God. This meaning can be fulfilled, or betrayed. It can be ideologically distorted or understood in the light of Christ's reconciling the world unto himself. Demonic powers are at work corrupting every revolution, yet its fundamental dynamic is as much a part of God's commandment for the world as is government with its social order.

'The Christian then is committed to a spiritual struggle. That is to say, he participates in the world's struggle in the power of the Holy Spirit. His life is hid with Christ, and as such is lived in a new way in this world. In a revolutionary situation this new relationship to the world will have a double aspect. First, since the revolution points to a righteousness which God wills for men but which is not yet openly revealed, the Christian says "yes" to the revolution. Secondly, the Christian is aware that in every dynamic revolution demonic forces are released: he therefore says "no" to these evil forces of the spirit.'[1]

This is a theology for a revolutionary situation. It is easy to see what objections Niebuhr might raise. Is this attribution of a moral meaning to a historical revolution not ideological? It seems to have learned from Tillich's doctrine of the socialist *kairos*, and to be shut off from power realities by the idealistic tendencies in this concept. Does not this historicism dull the edge of a truly pragmatic approach to the problem of balance of power? Yet these are criticisms which presuppose a stable framework on the basis of which to act in society. It is precisely this which is lacking in so much of the world. The same social values which Niebuhr holds must be asserted as future demand, as objects of creative revolutionary action, if they are to be held at all. Their validity as God's command must come from the fact that God's act in history is bringing them forth, not that past experience with judgement and grace has shown them to be essential.

In this sense, these thinkers in terms of revolution state its moral goals:

'The revolutionary claims made by the modern world are these: men's lives are more important than anything else; natural resources, power,

[1]M. M. Thomas and D. McCaughey, *The Christian in the World Struggle* (Geneva, 1951), pp. 38 ff, 49–50.

and wealth should be used for the benefit of everybody; the incentive of all organizations of society, political and economic, should be to further the growth of men and women to find their highest good in true fellowship with one another; and all men should, therefore, have real equality in opportunities for self-development.'[1]

Toward such ends the masses of newly awakened peoples are pressing. They are doing so partly because traditional frameworks of life and security—family, caste, feudal order and the like—are breaking down,' but also because western liberalism, democracy, and Christianity have given these masses a new vision of what man is and may become, and because Marxism has contributed an understanding of the terrible contradictions of feudal and capitalist society, the power conflicts of the economic world, and the importance of organizing powerful groups to bring about change. In this framework Marx's mistakes do not seem as important as they do to Niebuhr, beside the more basic contribution which he makes to understanding the nature of group conflict and ideology. These Christians are Marxists somewhat in the sense that Niebuhr was in the nineteen-thirties: rejecting his utopian claims, and his reduction of all power to economic power, but drawing from him an understanding of the dynamics of revolution *per se*.

In the framework of this revolutionary ferment Communism presents itself both as an appeal and as an betrayer. Communism is appealing because it integrates a new community when old communities are disintegrating. It takes intellectuals isolated in their emancipation from the ancient culture, peasants victimized by the insecurities of an accelerating load of debt, workers uprooted from their villages and thrown into the mass society of an industrial centre, and offers them a new fellowship where their life has meaning and direction. It brings to the chaotic, apparently meaningless course of events an explanation and a hope. It furthermore presents itself as the only truly and thoroughly revolutionary party, capable of carrying through the changes of power which are essential if landlords are to be overthrown and imperialism uprooted. It is the power in this appeal which is, in the eyes of these Christians, the

[1]M. M. Thomas and P. Devanandan (eds.), *Communism and the Social Revolution in India* (Calcutta, 1953), p. 7.

171

main problem to be dealt with in a revolutionary society. Can this social revolution be channelled into paths of social freedom and democracy? Can some other force than Communism prove itself sufficiently powerful and revolutionary to bring about land reform and other urgent social measures quickly enough to prevent the Communists from coming to power?

For despite its appeal Communism is the betrayer of the revolution, as God wills it. Man becomes a means to the ends of a class or an oligarchy. No moral reality, no human freedom, stand over against power politics in the service of the Party and Soviet imperialism. The revolutionary ferment is used by Communists to the detriment of its own goals for these other ends.

The encounter with Communism requires therefore, first, an alternative programme, even a social dogma, which will be recognized as such and therefore not absolutized, for the revolution itself.

'The fact is that we cannot live without some social dogmas to inform the life of society. . . . The important thing is that the dogma should itself be open to criticism, since all men's convictions about why they do certain things are imperfectly formulated and become distorted when worked out in practice. Social democracy cannot avoid having an ideology; but social democrats (especially if they are Christians) will avoid giving to the ideology an absolute character so that it is beyond criticism and correction.'[1]

The name of this dogma, for the churches at Bangkok and for writers whom we have been citing, is 'social democracy'—'a society where freedom, order and justice are dependent on and not destroyed by one another.' More concretely it means a society, in a definition from India, where: (1) Democratic curbs on the power of all groups are maintained in the interests of freedom, and radical social changes can be made non-violently: 'democracy takes power and law equally seriously and seeks to prevent the exercise of arbitrary power by law on the one hand and by political opposition on the other.' (2) The basic economic planning of a welfare state is accepted toward abolition of feudalism, control of the profit motive, full employment and equal social opportunities for all: 'the goal

[1]Thomas and McCaughey, op. cit., p. 67.

172

of a casteless and classless society should be steadily before the Indian people.' (3) Economic and political power will be decentralized by deliberate planning as much as is consistent with the requirements of modern government and industry. (4) Innumerable small groups where personal relations are possible become the carriers of social life and culture: 'the problem of modern democracy is to "find democratic ways of living for little men in big societies".'[1]

In short this is a vision of democratic socialism such as the American Fellowship of Socialist Christians might have espoused in the 'thirties, such as the non-dogmatic socialist parties all over the world are seeking to realize. It is presented here in the uncomplicated direct way, which we have learned in the United States to associate with liberal idealism, and which Niebuhr has taught us to scorn in favour of a more pragmatic, less comprehensive strategy of balancing powers and experimenting with regulative techniques combined with areas of freedom. It may be that many social democrats in India—even Christian ones—are in fact being idealistic about their programme. But this kind of social thinking need not imply liberal idealism, but rather its opposite. Such a concept as social democracy outlined above, in the thinking of the men here cited, is rather a direct response to the Christian faith and hope in the light of revolutionary social conditions which demand more than a few gradual pragmatic adjustments.

'We present then social democracy not as an uneasy compromise between individualism and collectivism but as an genuine way, in its own right reflecting more truly the nature of man's life in society. At this point there is a great need for Christians to enter into ongoing conversation with post-liberal and post-Marxist thinkers who are beginning to feel that only what happens between man and man can be termed really social and human. . . . In doing so our Christian understanding of man will be both sharpened and distorted: the task will never be complete: it will rest on each generation to bear its own witness in its own society to what has been revealed to it of what *is*.'[2]

It is the ability to absorb all of Niebuhr's insights, and yet to

[1]Thomas and Devanandan, op. cit., pp. 58–59.
[2]Thomas and McCaughey, op. cit., p. 68.

speak directly from faith in the risen Christ to the task of cultural and social creation in a revolutionary situation, which marks the improvement which these men have made on Niebuhr's encounter with Communism itself. They have experienced the chaotic relativism, the nihilism of man's predicament, more deeply than Niebuhr. They have laid hold of God the Redeemer more desperately, hence more firmly than he. They have grasped the historical meaning of revolutionary change more fully than his perpetual tension allows, and have spoken to it more clearly. Therefore they have understood Communism in its twofold aspect more deeply—as an appealing faith and as a distorting power woven into the texture of this revolutionary change—and are prepared, as Niebuhr is not, to deal with the post-Communist mood which is now arising in the world.

11. MINISTRY TO THE COMMUNIST

A final criticism remains of Niebuhr's encounter with Communism. It is, as we have seen, a realistic and indispensable guide for holders of power in the western world, responsible for the use of that power in the face of the opposing dangers of atomic war and Communist tyranny. Yet for Christians confronted with Communists as neighbours—whether under their power in a Communist land, or in those countries where Communism represents an appeal and temptation—Niebuhr is of surprisingly little help considering his experience and insight. He is concerned with the history of human effort, pride, contrition and responsibility, tempered by God's relation to it. Yet his emphasis remains curiously humanistic, even when pessimistically so. The personal God who calls and redeems in Christ, leading us to concrete personal relation with him and our neighbour in faith, is rarely brought to the fore.

Therefore the whole question of the Christian's personal ministry to the Communist as a neighbour does not come up. He has no suggestions on the complex problem of the relation between the Communist as a fanatic of his creed and the Communist as human being made by God. He seldom raises for discussion the question of different relations with 'soft' Communists—supporters of the Party from labour, intellectuals etc.—and with 'hard' ones, in the central core of the disciplined Party. Although he has many words about Communism as a secular religious faith, he has almost none about the spiritual problems of the Communist in that faith—his character, discipline, conviction, and moral sense—as problems for the Christian.

' "On the plane of politics, we oppose (the Communist), it is true," writes an Indian Christian. "But in that very protest we should be engaged in a dialogue with the Communist seeking to make clear the relevance of the Christian doctrine of sin and forgiveness. This possibility of communicating the Gospel in the very act of resisting the claims of Communism is not sufficiently recognized by Christian evangelists." '[1]

Niebuhr is such an evangelist. He fails to understand much of the inner dynamic of the Communist movement, and many of the resources, other than political, which are available to the Christian for meeting it.

He is further unhelpful to the Christian without power, because his reference to Christian life and witness in a powerless situation always makes of it a limiting case. There are places, especially in his sermons, where he refers with highest praise to such cases, such as the resistance of the Church, on a purely Biblical basis, to Nazi tyranny in Germany.[2] One magnificent sermon on Christ before Pilate, in which this reference occurs, catches the spirit of a transcendent Christian independence of tyranny, which yet is politically relevant, a powerless witness to the power of God in Christ. Occasional references to the community of Christians as the source of prophetic insight and vocation show through. But on the whole Niebuhr's criticisms of the pretensions of the Church far outweigh his constructive statements about its vocation. The Church as a free community in an unfree society, as a source of truth and love where these are officially distorted, as a point of contact between the power of God and the powerless Christian giving him direction and strength in his witness—these are themes which Niebuhr has not developed, for he remains too much the Christian-in-society to appreciate their full value. His suggestions therefore of the uses of powerlessness and suffering for Christian service and witness lack the positive tone which he could have given

[1]Thomas and Devanandan, op. cit., p. 78.
[2]*Beyond Tragedy*, p. 283.

175

them without any danger of reducing the Cross to a success story. In his own words, 'The only kingdom which can defy and conquer this world is one which is not of this world.' It is in the power of God and not of man which opens the way for Christian action. It is this power which can be trusted when human power fails. Had Niebuhr developed this theme more through all his writing, he might have seen more clearly that Christian encounter with the earthly power of Communism finds its first resource in God's evangelistic commission, to reach the Communist with both truth and love, and only secondly in a strategic resistance to his political power.

5

REVELATION AND IDEOLOGY:
KARL BARTH

(In the light of the influence of his theology on the Christian
encounter with Communism in Europe)

THE right of Karl Barth to take his place in this study at all must
be first established. It rests not on his understanding of Marxist
theory or Communist practice, but on his theological influence
which has encountered Communism second hand, yet so intensely
since the Second World War, that the most significant types of this
encounter in Europe today, especially in Germany, are rooted in
Barthian theology. We must consider Barth therefore in the light
of these encounters which are at least partly fruits of his thinking.
We must ask how far his theology provides an adequate foundation
for the Christian encounter with Communism, as well as examin-
ing his own rather *ad hoc* opinions on the situation behind the Iron
Curtain, or on the East-West conflict. Barth's political opinions are
only one, and not necessarily the most valid, application of his
theology to this problem.

1. BARTH AND SOCIALISM

We find this conviction confirmed when we turn to Barth's encounter with socialism in general and Marxism in particular. Barth
has a socialist background to be sure. One of the influences on his
youth, to whom he pays handsome tribute, was the Zürich Christian socialist Hermann Kutter.[1] During his earliest ministry and up
to the second edition of his *Römerbrief* he numbered himself among
the Christian socialists. His first edition of the *Römerbrief* is shot
through with this socialist hope for mankind against the background of a Platonic-Origenistic dialectic of man's original identity

[1] *Kirchliche Dogmatik* (Munich and Zürich, 1932 ff.), I/1, pp. 75–76.
(Eng. tr., Edinburgh, 1936 ff.)

with God, fall into humanity, and turning to Christ, the absolute spirit of truth and goodness, away from himself.

'Subjectivity reflects itself as "individualism"; salvation "into organic relation with the new humanity which has appeared in Christ", is to "turn away from the curse of individual loneness" (229). It means divine expropriation of "our private possession" (72), yes, even of the "sacrilege (Unheiligkeit) of our individuality" (218). "Individual differences" are only "the surface of our existence" (101). The "kenosis" is nothing else than this "elimination of the personal" (423), and this is the real "revolution" (234). We hear further that this doctrine is that of the truly "spiritual man" (239, 402), indeed of the whole "aristocracy of the Spirit, from Moses to John the Baptist, from Plato to the socialists" (46). These are the truly free and strong spirits, "the superior men who show the way forward", who use their strength however not in "tumultuous individualism", but "as strength to bear the weak" (421). The weak still need "religion, piety," and above all "the churches", even though the last have long been exposed by the strong as "illusory churches" (262). These strong men, since like God Himself, they have left behind all "standpoints which reflect religion, church, school, Judaism, Christianity, morality, or any idealism" (181), will, like God, be patient, and allow that kingdom to grow organically, whose "midwives by God's grace" (188) they are.'[1]

But this was, from the beginning, Christian socialism, not Marxism. Kutter himself was a prophet of Jeremian intensity, who believed the social democrats of his time to be carrying out the promises and purposes of God, but he was in no sense a Marxist. He proclaimed directly the moral necessity behind social democracy, its judgement on a Church which had come to regard its existence as an end in itself, its determined, revolutionary war on the rule of Mammon in the world, on the spirit of the capitalist system and its lust for profit at the expense of the poor. He believed the capitalist system to be doomed because it was a robbery defended by an obsequious morality and religion, and he hailed the social democrats as the only effective consistent force

[1]I have taken this summary of the socialist elements in the first edition of Barth's *Der Römerbrief* (Bern, 1919) from Hans Urs von Balthasar, *Karl Barth: Darstellung und Deutung seiner Theologie*, Olten, Switzerland, 1951, p. 74. The original of this edition of Barth's work was not available.

for bringing about a more Christian social order.[1] But neither he nor Barth so much as touch upon the 'scientific' side of Marxism: its application of Hegelian dialectic to the relations of production, its doctrine of determinism by economics, its revolutionary strategy and tactics. One central theme alone Barth seems to have learned from Marx by way of Kutter: that the system of capitalism is in itself an unjust and spiritually debilitating order of society, which needs the correction of socialism.

This conviction lost its *theological* status when Barth turned from religious socialism to dialectical theology, with the second edition of his *Römerbrief*. This was parallel in a sense to Niebuhr's movement over a longer period of time, from the Social Gospel of his youth to the dialectical theology and ethics of his teaching years, though the function of Marxism in Niebuhr's change is performed for Barth by a more general, more metaphysical sense of the crisis of all humanity before God, as we shall see more fully below. In any case socialism became, for the Barth of the nineteen-twenties and -thirties, primarily a social question no longer, but one of faith and philosophy. He saw it, in the hands of Ragaz, Tillich, and other religious socialists, and in the light of what it had once been for him, as a danger: the danger of secularizing Christ by hyphenating our faith, of identifying our hope with our human efforts to achieve the vision of a just society, of identifying the act of God with our programme and work.[2] So far as Barth deals with social questions

[1]Barth lists *Sie Müssen* (1903), *Gerechtigkeit* (1905) and *Wir Pfarrer* (Leipzig, 1907), as especially prophetic with relation to pre-war social democracy (*Dogmatik* I/1, pp. 75 f.). Of these *They Must, or God and the Social Democracy* (Chicago, 1908) has appeared in English, and gives a fair taste of the moral passion and prophetic hope which Kutter brings to the defence of the Social Democrats. The book breathes a totally different atmosphere from that of Marxism, touching Marxist analysis only in Kutter's scornful *exposé* of the bourgeois weakness of the Christian social reformers who drew their inspiration from Adolf Stoecker and Friedrich Naumann (pp. 43 ff.).

[2]Cf. especially 'The Problem of Ethics Today' and 'The Christian's Place in Society' in *The Word of God and the Word of Man*, tr. by Douglas Horton (London, 1929) (German: *Das Wort Gottes und die Theologie*). It is surprising however, how little space Barth devotes to this question. He disposes of both Tillich and Ragaz, as far as their religious socialism is concerned, in a few lines (*Dogmatik* I/1, p. 76).

at all in these years, we find him bending every effort to achieve, by dialectic, independence of every structure of social action or existence whether conservative or radical, behind which might lurk a philosophy, a hope, a man-centred construct, which could interfere with the free movement of the Word of God to man. This is part, of course, of the general action of his dialectical theology during this time, cutting across every field of philosophy and ethics. Its application to our field is most vividly portrayed in Barth's exegesis of Rom. 12.21-13.7 where he deals with the question of legitimate authority and revolution.[1]

Here we find no such conservatism as was almost instinctive for the Reformers. Barth's socialist background makes him as thorough a revolutionary against the powers that be, as the most ardent Marxist. No more vehement words have been spoken against the pretension of political authority to legitimacy by any Marxist, than those which Barth uses here:

'Order! What is existing order?. . . a new strengthening and defence of men against God; a securing of the normal course of the world against the uneasiness which creeps into it from all sides because its very presuppositions are so dubious; a conspiracy of the far too many against the One. . . . Not the bad quality, not the relative degree of corruption of this order, is called in question by all the accusations which have been hurled at it, from the Book of Revelation to Nietzsche, and from the Anabaptists to the Anarchists; but its existence' (p. 462). . . . 'What legality is not illegal at heart? What authority is not tyranny, precisely in that which makes it authority? This or that deficiency of existing order can only be the occasion for our recognizing that existing order (*das Bestehende*) as such is the evil' (p. 463).

In such words as these we see what has become of Barth the Christian socialist. He has become more fundamentally a rebel against *das Bestehende* than revolutionary socialism could any longer express. It is for him no longer a question of the oppression of one class by another, but of the organized rebellion of man against God, which man expresses in the structures of society, particularly in those which he endows with moral and spiritual

[1]*Der Romerbrief* 2te Auflage (Munich, 1922), pp. 459–75. (Eng. tr. of 6th edition, Oxford, 1930.) Figures in the text at this point refer to page numbers in this section.

authority! Of this rebellion, man's oppression of man is but a manifestation. In this recognition not only Marx, but Nietszche, the Anabaptists, and all who express the most complete rebellion against the power that is, have their point.

The problem however, of the revolutionary is that he does not go far enough. He imagines that he is the subject of freedom. He claims what no man can claim—to be right over against his neighbour. He sets up a new order which is then just as tyrannical as the old. 'The revolutionary is more conquered by evil than the conservative, because with his "No" he places himself so terribly near to God' (p. 464). And so the revolutionary act becomes in fact merely a reaction. It is an attempt to overcome this world's evil with another evil. 'The revolutionary has erred; he meant *the* Revolution, which is the impossible possibility: the forgiveness of sins, and the resurrection of the dead' (p. 464).

Christ the victor is the answer to the evil of *das Bestehende* as such. He demands of us, precisely in the name of *his* revolution, that we should not break through the regulation of the secular authority with our own revolutionary hope and power. Our first obedience must be a negative act, a restraint. The whole is a commentary on Rom. 12.21: 'Be not overcome of evil, but overcome evil with good.' How little this negative obedience justifies the legitimacy of the powers that be, Barth illustrates by pointing out that this command follows that in v. 20 to be kind to our enemies!

This subjection, then, to the powers that be, is the real act of revolution, precisely because it is a pure act of obedience to God and not to those powers. It deprives the existing order of all its ultimate worth and validity. It denies its claim, but without the pathos of a human counter-claim. 'There is no more energetic way to undermine existing order (*das Bestehende*) than to let it prevail without illusion or celebration. State, Church, society, positive law, family, incorporated science, and so on, live from the credulity of men which is ever nourished by "sermons on the battlefield" and ceremonious humbug of all kinds. Take this pathos from them, and they starve the surest way!' (p. 467). Through Christian obedience rulers are deprived of their power. This is the meaning of Paul's statement that 'rulers are not a terror to good conduct but to bad'.

181

When this has been established and stressed as the sole first principle, then Barth is prepared to recognize in the powers of this world a certain value as parables, as 'shadow pictures of the outlines of him who is over against us' (p. 472). The existing order is God's servant in the sense that 'everything given, when it has once been recognized in its pure negativity, begins to shine in the positivity of God who is not a "given".' Then there is place for calm reflection and action which depends only on our relation to God, a 'not doing', for its rightness.

'In place of a cramped revolutionism comes then a calm consideration of right and wrong, calm because it is no longer concerned with final assertions and accusations; a thoughtful reckoning with reality, which has left behind the pride of making war for the Good against the Evil; an honest worldly humanity which knows that the opposition between the Kingdom of God and Antichrist is not at issue every time men try their experiments in state, church, and society, their strange games of chess with, or against, other men. Politics for example, becomes possible from that time on, when it becomes clear that in it one cannot speak of objective law (*Recht*); from that time on when the absolute note disappears from theses and antitheses, in order to make place for a perhaps relatively moderate, or perhaps relatively radical consideration of human possibilities' (p. 472).

This vivid example should make clear the sense in which Barth broke with the socialism of his earlier years, as he broke with all other human absolutes.

'The Christian as witness is a man who flees from the wisdom and folly of this human world to the testimony of God,'[1]

he wrote in the nineteen-thirties, and he explicated this statement by reference to the Christian's social task. It cannot be carried out by religious socialism which so fails to understand the depths of man's misery, but only by placing oneself in prayer and witness under the action of God—'*thy* Kingdom come!' It should also be clear why Barth never has and never could share the kind of illusions which Hromadka (and with somewhat more questionable sincerity the Hungarian Church Press) betrays about the nature of

[1] 'The Christian as a Witness' in *God in Action* (Edinburgh, 1936) (German original: *Der Christ als Zeuge*, address delivered to an International Student Conference, Summer 1934 in Switzerland); pp. 112 f., 124 ff.

the Communist Revolution in the U.S.S.R. The above passages in *Der Römerbrief* were written explicitly with this revolution in mind. On a number of later occasions Barth has referred to the system in the Soviet Union in similar tones of rejection. There is in his thinking none of Hromadka's somewhat romantic fascination with the inevitability of historical movements and revolutions. Although Hromadka would count himself a pupil of Karl Barth, his thinking differs from Barth in the philosophical mark which Marxism has made on it at this point, from which Barth remains completely free, one might even say, too free. For Barth, as we shall see below, has been forced to take a position in relation to Communism by the events of the post-war world. The position bears the marks of being ill-considered, because Barth had previously given far too little thought to Marxist theory and Communist reality in relation to his theology. The name of Marx appears only rarely in the *Kirchliche Dogmatik* and the challenge of his thought is dealt with only once (III/2, pp. 464 f). Lenin, and Communism as a present reality, do not appear at all. Barth's political writing up to 1947 does no better. Below we shall explore the question how adequate Barth's theology is for the understanding of Communism. Here we need only note that his theological perspective on what was and was not worthy of attention and study, seems to have left him uninformed about Communism and unimpressed with Marxism until very recent years.

Despite all this however, Barth retained the mark of Christian socialism on his 'calm, sober and relative' judgements, on moral, political economic, and social questions. It must be made clearer than Barth sometimes makes it, that this concern for social questions was never absent in principle from Barth's thinking or life, despite the common polemic against him in the United States. This polemic rests on a confusion between Barth's denial of *independent validity* over against the action of God to human ideals and programmes, and a denial of their *relative importance* as acts of Christian confession and witness, in the light of God's act of love. Barth himself, especially in his earlier writings, leaves this unclear. The above selection from *Der Römerbrief* represents his undeveloped thought, still wrapped in the swaddling clothes of an extreme dialectic, and lacking a positive centre from which the Christian life might be illumined. We see Barth wrestling, as he does throughout this book, to free himself dialectically from the pretensions involved in every human point of view, yet behind it we see a certain impatience with human creatureliness itself so far as it means being other than God, a *Gegenüber*. The sharply dialectical Barth of these years was clearing the ground for his theology, yet he was (contrary to the common opinion) not yet sufficiently free from a philosophy of yearning for identity with God, and of seeing in the present world only its antithesis—to proceed with the work of massive theological construction. Despite this however, this philosophy, and the extreme use of the dialectic in its service, has proved to be only the swaddling, since discarded. The growing child was Barth's central preoccupation with God's revelation in Christ, which finally allows no philosophy alongside of it, yet finds nothing human irrelevant.

Barth's concern for social questions therefore went underground for a period. It was, as he explained it,[1] a professional question. He believed himself called to be a theologian, not a politician; a line of reasoning understandable in Germany before Hitler where he was working. His return to politics during the Nazi period led to much creative thought on questions of democracy and totalitarianism but it is not until the post-war period that Barth's socialist background once more plays a role in his judgements. This has been to be sure, a subordinate motive; the dominant one being the demand for relative, objective decisions in the field of politics and economics, unmixed with covert ideologies and absolute programmes. Barth could for this reason never be a doctrinaire or 'left wing' socialist in

[1]In *Theologische Existenz Heute* pp. 1–3 (*Theological Existence Today*, tr. R. Birch Hoyle, London, 1933, pp. 9–11). Barth felt himself as one of a group of servants of the Church with complementary vocations—his being basic theology, a task not simply at the beck and call of world events. He felt himself, precisely in this essay, drawn into political controversy however because (1) some of his former pupils were making political applications of this theology which he must repudiate, and because (2) other theologians, the 'German-Christians', were mixing theology with Nazi politics in a way which must be fought. His acceptance of the fact that Nazism is in itself a problem on the theological level, and its effects on his political thought, we shall discuss below.

the sense common in political parlance today. But the background of Kutter shows itself in those few places where, since the war, he has turned his attention to the ethical analysis of western society.[1] We see this in two ways.

1. A moral condemnation of the capitalist system, not for its failure to produce wealth, for its inefficiency or self-destructive tendencies, but for turning man into an instrument of the technological process, for erecting exploitation of man by man, competition not as a stimulating game, but as desperate war for life, the autonomy of capital controlled by the few, and the cultivation of endless lust for profit and material goods, into principles of an economic order. Such a system, says Barth, is evil in its basic structure. That which can be done within it, to modify it—and he is prepared to recognize that capitalists are not as bad as in the days of Marx, nor the system as pure in its inhuman tendencies—is incidental to the basic fact 'that this system not only allows, but demands in principle, that man make a mere instrument, a means to his own ends, of other men with their work. This is the inhumanity, and therefore the injustice of it.'[2]

In such a society human work can only in the exceptional case be truly needful, meaningful work, for the service of the neighbour and God. The evil of it, in Barth's mind, is less the economic oppression of the poor, than the depersonalizing of man. Man becomes an instrument. He is forced into class war, and competitive struggle. His work loses the meaning God has given it, whether he belongs to the exploiting or exploited class. If he is only a worker he has no stake or security in society, save his labour. If he is an employer he is spiritually debilitated by the demand on him to seek profits, to stimulate wants, and by the temptations of irresponsible power. All this is a development of Kutter's polemic against the worship of Mammon, and the false values which moneyed power introduces into society.[3] It is Marxist only in the sense that Barth has accepted,

[1]Briefly in 'Die geistigen Voraussetzungen für den Neuaufbau in der Nachkriegszeit', a lecture given in May, 1945, in *Eine Schweizer Stimme* (Zürich, 1945), pp. 422–3. More extendedly in *Kirchliche Dogmatik III/4*, pp. 609–26 (Zürich, 1951).

[2]*Dogmatik III/4*, p. 623.

[3]Kutter, *They Must, passim.*

as Kutter did earlier, Marx's picture of dehumanizing conflict and exploitation in the economic order—the laws of competitition and class war—not as a problem and factor in every economy, but as an evil specific to capitalism. There is an element of conservatism in this; a certain rebellion against the overwhelming dynamic of the industrial revolution itself; in contrast to the vigorous affirmation of modern society combined with a realistic evaluation of its ethical dilemmas which we find in Reinhold Niebuhr. Barth introduces into this and his other rare discussions of the economic order, a category of moral judgement containing a Marxist, a conservative, and an idealist element which seems to have continued unchanged throughout his whole career, and to be only externally related to his theology.[1]

2. Barth, following Kutter, treats socialism, by which he means Marxist socialism apparently from the context, as a necessary counter-force (*Gegenbewegung*) to the basic injustice of capitalism. Here his refusal to distinguish between socialism in the western sense, and Communism (which he refers to as *Staatssozialismus* and treats in this passage as if it were a straight economic phenomenon), makes these pages sound much like the arguments of

[1]For example, Barth's analysis at this point bears some similarity to the Oxford Conference report on the Economic Order, especially its enumeration of the points where the economic order challenges a Christian understanding of life (Oxford Conference Official Report, *Church, Community and State*, Vol. VIII [London, 1937], pp. 86–92). But the more specific recommendations in this report, and the whole discussion in ecumenical circles of the Christian and economic problems, from Oxford to Evanston, seems to have passed Barth by. There is no discussion in his pages of the concept of a mixed economy, the relative dangers of big business and big government, the place and limits of a private sector in the economy, the problem of effective production versus just distribution, the various degrees of regulation and co-operation which form the spectrum between state and private ownership, the balance of freedom with order and all the other concrete questions which concern Christian ethics in this field. He simply assumes that in spite of modifications, the battle between capitalist and worker describes the economic tension of society today. He fails to consider the effects of the restraint of competition. He confuses the dangerous results of technological society *per se*, with those of the capitalist system. In short Barth makes little contact with the ethical problems of Christians as they actually present themselves in the economic order today.

Bishop Berecsky. Barth admits that a great deal has been done by *Gegenbewegungen* to bring capitalism under control in the last few decades—factory laws, insurance, co-operation with management etc.—'In short, in the course of time, a barrier which is more than merely relative has been set up against the exploitation of the weak by the strong.' He recognizes that 'State Socialism' is beginning(!) to show evidence of using the worker even more as an instrument than capitalism did, so that the injustice continues under other auspices. However, class war still continues among us; and in it, Barth proclaims:

'The command of God, as far as men can and will listen to it, (will) of course be here also a call to counter-movement, to humanity and against its denial in this form or that; and therefore a call to us to take up the cause of the weak against every form which the attack of the strong may take.'[1]

The Church was late in recognizing the injustice of the capitalist system. It is therefore guilty of implication in it.

'We are therefore hardly in a position today, to point a deprecating finger at the signs (which to be sure, are there) that state socialism, which pretends to be conquest of oppression and of the exploitation of man by man, finally only can result in another, if possible crasser, form of this injustice. Whether this be so or not, Christianity has first of all enough to do in understanding disorder in the form which still prevails *here*, in remembering and acting on the command of God over against *this* disorder, in keeping herself to the "left" of *its* representatives i.e. in taking up the cause of those who suffer loss by this disorder, and making it fundamentally her own.'[2]

This does not mean making the programme of the *Gegenbewegung* the programme of the Church. Christians should be best

[1] *Dogmatik* III/4, p. 624. The tone of this paragraph is notably hesitating. 'The files are still open. Here history still has to speak,' and similar qualifying phrases indicate Barth's desire to suspend judgement on the economic system of Soviet Russia itself, as to its humanity or justice. We shall deal with this more fully in a later section, but note here that Barth seems to fear the bad spiritual consequences for the Church in the western world of making a correct ethical-economic judgement on the Soviet system, thereby removing its effectiveness as a goad and judgement on western injustices.

[2] Ibid. pp. 624–5.

equipped to realize that all social reforms are relative and may be corrupt. Even the relative hopes which are necessary to keep us loyal to the *Gegenbewegung* in its immanent opposition to an evil system, to keep us determined to do what is possible in evil conditions against powerful injustice, even these relative hopes depend on the fact that Christ's kingdom has come on earth, though not yet revealed. Barth closes with a positive restatement of the relation of the theme of *Römerbrief* to the theme of his socialism:

'The Christian congregation can and must indeed advocate this or that form of social progress, or even of socialism; always the most helpful form in a particular situation at a particular place and time. Her decisive word however, can never consist in the proclamation of social progress or of socialism; it can only consist in the proclamation of God's revolution against all "ungodliness and wickedness of men" (Rom. 1. 18), which means however precisely the proclamation of his kingdom which has come and is coming.'[1]

Such is Barth's direct encounter with socialism and Marxism, and such is the way his mind runs on social questions. We see throughout the mind of a theologian at work whose direct interest in Marxism, and the ethical problems of the economic world as illumined by Christian thinkers[2] or by the science of economics, is slight indeed, and borrowed from years ago, though the charge is no longer true that his theology cuts him off from social action. Yet Barth remains, in a deeper sense, a contemporary of Karl Marx; a cousin who did not know him, so to speak, but who shared the

[1]Dogmatik III/4, p. 626.
[2]It is, for example, amazing to find in this section no reference to the works of Eduard Heimann, to the economic thinking going on in the German Christian Democratic Union, to the work of Banning, van Biemen, and other representatives of the 'break-through' between socialist and Christian ideologies in Holland, with the repercussions which this has had all over Europe, to Christian thinking in the British Labour Party, or the development of socialist Christianity to a more pragmatic approach, which is dealt with in Chapter IV of this study. Barth seems to be thinking out his ethics here in a vacuum, or with the help only of a few of his theologically congenial friends. (He mentions especially Søe and Bonhoeffer at the beginning of III/4 as helpful writers on ethics.) The result is surprisingly fruitful considering this isolation, but Barth's missed opportunities, and the misunderstanding which they perpetuate, are tragic.

same spiritual ancestors, and the same revolutionary drive against the pretensions and complacency of a bourgeois society. Both men grappled with the challenge to German idealism of revolutionary figures such as Feuerbach. Both were oppressed by the moral self-justification, the ideology, involved in this idealism, whether its exemplar was Hegel or Schleiermacher, and both wrestled with the problem of truth and knowledge until they had established what they believed to be no longer a merely subjective starting point, but one which responded to a reality outside themselves—in Marx's case the dialectical movement of material forces of production, in Barth's the Word of God which calls man in question. In each case this reality was known as an acting reality which claims the allegiance of the total man, cutting off the possibility of meaningful thought or life outside the circle of its action. In each case this action constituted a new community, for Marx the proletariat, for Barth the Church, to which time and history are relative, in the sense that these are dimensions of the purpose and fulfilment of this community. In each case the history of the world beyond them is incidental, and the believer retains a sovereign independence of this world and the problems *it* raises on its own presuppositions. From such parallels we can see the way in which Barth's real challenge to Marx comes not from having learned from him, but in the attempt to present consistently *theological* answers to the same profound reactions—to the *groteske Felsenmelodie* (Marx's description) of Hegel's idealism, to the nihilist despair which grips him who reacts against it, to the complacency of the bourgeois in the face of the dehumanizing situation of modern industry and the superficial this-worldliness of modern culture—which drove Marx to form his system. It would be well therefore, to turn to the resources which Barth's theology provides, for meeting Communism at the points where it makes its basic challenge to Christian thought. We must preface this, however, presumptuous as it may be, with a brief statement of where Barth's central concern does lie —what the principle object of his encounter with the world is— since we have made clear that the whole area of social questions *per se*, including Marxism and all other theory about it, lies only on the periphery of his interest.

2. BARTH'S CENTRAL CONCERN

There are two levels on which we can speak of Barth's encounter: —that with the world and his experience of it which has brought him to his theological position, and that which his theological position itself attempts to express. Barth, Brunner, Tillich, and others of the inter-war circle of crisis theologians, all started in a sense from the same cultural experience. They saw the problem of 'the world' more or less in the same terms, conditioned by the same predecessors. The parallel in this regard between Barth and Tillich is especially striking. The object which concerned both was not, as with Niebuhr, the concrete problems of an underprivileged group in society, nor even, as with Berdyaev, the fate of a culture with its idea, but the more fundamental problem of existential despair, and reaction against idealistic philosophy and theology. Kierkegaard plays a decisive role in this for both men, with his devastating dialectic which so destroys the pretension of human reason. Both are concerned to find a theological answer to the problem raised for the spirit of European culture by the fall of reason before the onslaught of this existential and nihilist (Nietzsche) reaction. Both see here a fundamental crisis of human society but they see it basically expressed in philosophy and theology.

Beyond this point however, the similarity ceases. Tillich remains, throughout his life, the thinker in the boundary situation, a position which Barth regards as still caught in the man-centred circle of thought, whose consequence is still despair. We see Tillich balancing the Power of the Origin against the Unconditional Demand, heteronomy against autonomy, the philosopher's quest and the theologian's testimony. But for Barth the crisis is more radical still: not a boundary situation, in which something infused with divine meaning is threatened with destruction unless by God's new Being, and man's new apprehension of its Unconditional nature, this dynamic which threatens to destroy is brought to fulfilment, but rather a sense of the total wrongness of the human enterprise, of its hopeless destruction, unless from without God comes to us with his grace.

'We are to understand the whole unbearable human situation, espouse it, take it upon ourselves. We are to bend before the doom revealed in the

190

problem of ethics. It is through the unescapable severity of this doom that we come upon the reality of *God*.'[1]

It was Barth's religious experience that *no* human way of thought or action leads us anywhere save to God's judgement, not even—especially not—the way of practical piety or orthodox religious confession. In his early years he employed his dialectical method in the unremitting effort to reduce every human system and plan to its antinomy. In so doing he regarded himself as expressing the message of Paul himself. For it is by God's grace that we see the hopeless abyss of human sin:

'It is because *God himself* and *God alone* lends our life its possibility that it becomes so impossible for us to live. It is because *God* says "Yes" to us that the "No" of our existence is so fundamental and inescapable. It is because the answer to all our questions is *God* and *God's* conduct toward *us*, that the only answers that we can find in terms of our own conduct either change immediately into questions or are otherwise too vast for us. It is because the deathless life of *God* is our portion that the necessity of death reminds us so inexorably of the sinful narrowness of our will to live. *Through* our doom we see therefore what is beyond our doom, God's love; *through* our awareness of sin, forgiveness; *through* death and the end of all things, the beginning of a new and primary life.'[2]

The final human possibility is a *desperatio fiducialis*, a believing despair, in which 'man joyfully gives himself up for lost' because beyond this God waits for him. Yet even this act of dialectical desperation assures nothing and achieves nothing. 'There is no way from us to God—not even a *via negativa*—not even a *via dialectica* nor *paradoxa*.'[3] Everything depends on the act of God's grace and not on ourselves.

This is the negative side of Barth's dialectical method, which expresses his sense of the total crisis in which he stands. We can understand from it why the formulations of the early Marx, so important to Tillich—the doctrine of human self-estrangement, of the proletarian situation, and of the *kairos* of revolutionary socialism

[1]'The Problem of Ethics Today', in *The Word of God and the Word of Man*, p. 168.
[2]Ibid. p. 169.
[3]Ibid. p. 177.

—had so little relevance to Barth. No sense of reverence for tradition, or even for Being itself, impresses him as having religious significance. In this sense he is more radical than Tillich. He shares the fundamental rebellion against what is, which unites the spirits of Marx and Berdyaev. With Marx he shares at least a basic conviction that the wrongness of the world demands a total change, and that the dialectic is the instrument of this revolution, not (as in Hegel) the illumination of an achieved harmony, nor (as with Schleiermacher) merely a condition of creative tension. With Berdyaev, he rebels against Being itself, against that objectification of order and system in thought and life which is one more expression of human sin.

In his attempt to affirm his theological object, however, Barth is unique. For his object is God, alone and unqualified by human needs or questions; God in his sovereign freedom over all human conceptions and from all analogy with the human; God in his self-revelation which is pure act, absolute decision, the source of all possible existence and response of the creature, bringing the creature from death to life. In the sense in which we have used the words in this study Barth tries precisely, in his early years, to eliminate the whole idea of an 'object of encounter'. It is precisely preoccupation with some human problem or situation, precisely the testing of revelation's validity by its relevance thereto (Brunner's 'Other Task of Theology')[1] precisely the treatment of man's capacity for or approach to the Word of God as a serious problem, against which Barth turns all his power. This is the substance of his polemic against Brunner's search for a natural theology which will give the theologian a 'point of contact' (*Anknüpfungspunkt*) with the non-believer. It is God who asks the questions, who searches for man, who in Jesus Christ reveals to us at once our utter lostness and his all-sufficient grace. It is the action of God's grace by which men and society are given their existence and meaning. It is the task of theology not to relate this to some supposedly other Being outside of it, but to bear witness to this movement, this action, this revelation of God in his Word,

[1]The title of an article in *Zwischen den Zeiten*, quoted again in *Natur und Gnade*, the article which evoked Barth's *Nein*.

and to call all men to realize their place within it, which is life.[1]

One could, in short, say that this movement of God toward man, this *Selbstbewegung der Wahrheit is* the object which fills the horizon for the early Barth. Man has no standpoint over against it from which to understand it, not even a theological one. Dialectic is for Barth a means of expressing this movement, which yet cannot be expressed:

'Is ever a single one of my words *the* Word I seek, which I want to speak, out of my great need and hope? Can I then speak in any other way than so that one word cancels out the other?'[2]

Man cannot control God, nor the knowledge of God, the way a scientist controls his relation to that which he investigates. There are no fixed principles by which God's act can be bound. He controls us, and our act can only be a following (*nachvollziehen*) of his act, our thought a response to his, glorifying him precisely through the fact that our word cannot express the mystery of his Word,[3] and that our social orders can only be for us the place where this act and thought of obedience takes place.

Such is the earliest theme in Barth's dialectical theology—one which seems to annihilate the whole question of a subject and an object with its emphasis on God, to the very exclusion of a place for the creature as a *Gegenüber*; and with its dialectically expressed dynamism, to the very exclusion of the question of Being.[4] In his

[1]Cf. *Nein: Antwort an Emil Brunner* (Theologische Existenz Heute, Nr. 14, Munich, 1934), p. 57 ff. English translation of this and Brunner's *Natur und Gnade* in *Natural Theology*, introd. by John Baillie (London, 1947). This theme is of course developed throughout the prolegomena of the *Dogmatik* (1/1 and 1/2).

[2]*Römerbrief*, p. 243.

[3]In a lecture in 1922 he puts this problem with classic simplicity: 'As ministers we ought to speak of God. We are human however and so we cannot speak of God. We ought therefore to recognize both our obligation and our inability and by that very recognition give God the glory' (*The Word of God and the Word of Man*, p. 186).

[4]Hans Urs von Balthasar maintains that the dialectic, unsubordinated to its later Christological object, becomes itself precisely that which it set out to destroy: the absolute human standpoint over against God:

'It is just in its infallibility (as radical fallibility) that it goes against the task imposed on it to speak of God and not of itself. Its "I cannot" is disobedience. As if its relativity itself were something absolute and not something relative!' (p. 92).

recent years, Barth has not surrendered this dynamism, nor has he admitted any other centre of interest than God. But he has expanded his understanding of both in such a way that human concerns and acts begin once more to take their places as objects of interest. The key to this development is Barth's discovery, which by his own admission came only in the 'thirties, of the full meaning for theology of Christ as its centre: the Word of God who was God *and* man.[1]

'In the *Kirchliche Dogmatik*' writes Barth's most penetrating analyst, Hans Urs von Balthasar, 'there takes place imperceptibly but unceasingly the substitution of the central concept "Jesus Christ, God and Man" for the central concept, "Word of God".'[2] 'The Word', Barth came to discover, is only one expression of the fullness of this Christ. God is therefore not only this incomprehensible wholly Other, this 'Unknown One who justifies the godless, who raises the dead and addresses the non-existent as existing; as he in whom one can only believe without hope but toward the hope he will bring.'[3] He is not only a Word spoken into our nothingness, beyond death and all hope, but a God who reveals himself fully as the Father of our Lord Jesus Christ:

'If you ask me where we hear this Word of God, I can only point to himself, who enables us to hear it, and reply with the mighty centre of the Confession, with the second article, that the Word of God's grace in which he meets us is called Jesus Christ, the Son of God, and Son of man, true God and true Man, Immanuel, God with us in this One. Christian faith is meeting with this "Immanuel", the meeting with Jesus Christ and in him with the living Word of God.'[4]

What has happened between these two quotations is the replacement of a purely dialectical, a static dialectical, relation between man's self-destruction in his sin and the act of God's grace, by an analogical understanding of the relation of God and man in the

---

[1]'Parergon' in *Evangelische Theologie* 1948–9, p. 272. Autobiographical report for the years 1928–38 (first published in *The Christian Century*, 1939), p. 272.
[2]Hans Urs von Balthasar, *Karl Barth*, p. 124.
[3]*Römerbrief* p. 65.
[4]*Dogmatics in Outline* (London, 1949), p. 17 (German original: *Dogmatik im Umriss*, Zürich, 1947).

light of Jesus Christ. It is in Christ that man once more discovers what it is to be a creature before God. It is in Christ that Barth discovers that it is good to be a creature, to be an object, a *Gegenüber*[1] to God's grace and not swept into identity with it out of an evil separation.

We must note that Barth sets out here to build up a positive understanding of the relation of man to God and of men to each other, according to a new pattern of thought which breaks completely with the traditional habit of conceiving Being as neutral substance, indeed with the habit of thinking in terms of general categories of human reason at all. There is, for him, no Being which then possesses attributes such as movement, perfection, corruption, and the like. There are no analogies by which we can understand man's being in and from itself in relation to God's being. The whole *Dogmatik* turns on Barth's rejection of the Roman Catholic doctrine of the *analogia entis*, and his attempt to build a genuinely Reformation theology based on revelation alone. The starting point for Barth is not the general category of understanding, but the concrete God who reveals himself in Christ; not a God and men with being and attributes, but an act, an event, which when we see the actor so acting, we presume to presuppose certain things about his being. But in every case it is the act which contains the being and fulfils it: 'God is who he is, in the deed of his Revelation.'[2] God's being *is* event, the event of the birth, death, resurrection and coming again of Jesus Christ. He *is* living God, acting God, and beyond or behind this there is no transcendent depth of Being, no static eternity in which this action and event is contained.

This is the starting point and indicates the method by which Barth develops his theology of the relation between God and man and society. Both the *Ordo Essendi* and the *Ordo Cognoscendi*, the

[1] I use the term *Gegenüber* in the German because it conveys a meaning for which there is no adequate English equivalent. Barth uses *Gegenüber* to describe that being which stands so to speak on its own feet and enters into a relation with the subject, whether the subject be God or man. It is that being the existence of whom is the presupposition of an I-Thou relationship.

[2] *Dogmatik* II/1, p. 293.

195

order of being and the order of knowledge, start with the concrete event, the most concrete event, the one event (*concretissimum*) of God's action in Christ. Being, substantive existence, remains throughout dependent upon action, upon the work of God which creates it as the space, the presupposition of his work of grace. It is like the system of tunnels in a coal mine, never considered in itself or for itself, never an end in itself, but purely the presupposition of that activity which gives the coal mine its meaning and its name. We see this in the doctrine of creation, where Barth defines Creation dynamically: 'a special work, a special moment in the work of God, in which he, on the basis of his own inner will and decision, turns outward.'[1]

Creation is given its glory precisely because it stands so directly in relation to God's plan and will, the beginning of his work *nach aussen* in which he will reveal the glory of his grace. Yet Creation is not independent in its meaning, not a substance in itself, but the first of God's activities. It includes in it the beginning of time. It is the space, or better a kind of model or shell, of the history of the covenant of Grace which will follow from God's activity. It is in a sense dependent on this history for its meaning. No general truths about Being can be drawn from the Creation, but only historical, dynamic truths in the light of God's further activity toward that which he has created, truths about its historical goal in relation to the purposes of God.

It is the person of Christ who gives to this way of thinking that dimension which is usually supplied in natural theology by the *analogia entis* between man and God. It is to him that such words as Event, Grace, and the like, refer. In the Trinity itself there is a genuine *Gegenüber*, a dynamic relation. Christ expresses God's will to hold man in a covenant of Grace, in a true partnership, precisely in the I-Thou relation:

'For just this is . . . the power of the Divine act of sovereign grace: that God does not keep his true being for himself, but waited to make it as such into our human being, and thus to turn us to himself, thus to make new men, thus to take care of keeping the covenant from our side as well, and thus to give us peace with him.'[2]

[1]III/1, p. 44.   [2]IV/1, p. 96.

The man Jesus is first the particular object through whom we know what God's gracious action means, through whom and in whom God makes all men into his covenant partners. He is 'the readiness of man, already included in the readiness of God,'[1] for this covenant relation. This man is *the* man, whom God has elected, who is the only-begotten son of God, who is completely open and ready for God, who is completely and without remainder the man for other men.[2] This man knows the Father as the Father knows him. 'In our flesh God recognizes himself.'[3] This is the relation, the activity of God in its innermost and essential form, complete in itself. This is the concrete *esse* and *cognoscere* from relation to which all other human and historical being and knowledge, the general and the specific, come. But it is precisely the nature of this God, revealed in this relation to himself as Son made flesh, to include and fulfil all that is human, all that belongs to our history, society, and psychology as he has created it, atones (*versöhnt*) and redeems (*erlöst*) it.

'The conduct (*das Verhalten*) of God, in which the faithfulness of the Creator and therefore also the enduring relations (*Verhältnisse*) of the human being which he has created are revealed and recognizable, is quite simply his conduct toward the *Man Jesus;* his election of this man, his becoming and remaining one with him, his revelation, his action, his endurance in him and through him, his love, which is turned toward him, through him to those who believe in him, and finally to the whole creation, his freedom and lordship, which finds in this man their created bearer and representative. He is God, in that he, in his eternal Godhead, himself became this man in his human creatureliness. This, precisely, is God's conduct toward sinful men.'[4]

This is the basis for Barth's concern for the creature of God and his society. It remains both a dynamic interest to which Being is

[1] II/1, p. 167.

[2] Barth underlines the fact that Jesus can in no sense be called the ideal man, the essence of man, or man as he potentially is. This would be illusory Gospel, for we would not be in the least helped by this knowledge. It would amount to one more attempt to save ourselves by approaching God from the side of man. Christ is a concrete man, and the secret of his ability to save lies in the dynamic of his being *for* other men, as the one in whom and through whom God's grace and historical purpose are manifest (II/1, p. 168; cf. III/2, pp. 242 ff.).

[3] II/1, p. 169.   [4] III/2, p. 47.

subordinate (the word *Verhalten* instead of *Verhältnis* in the above quotation is deliberately chosen), and an interest which is peripheral, or rather outgoing from his interest in Christ and what God reveals in his relation to Christ. Before we examine the dynamics of this outgoing, however, we should note how this way of thinking is related to Hegel and Marx. At one point at least, Barth acknowledges the debt of theology to Hegel, in Hegel's reminder that truth can be history, event, and as such not to be perceived except by participation, in obedience to the 'Self-movement of truth', as response to the way in which the truth presents itself in a given moment (*je und je in Aktualität*).[1] Yet it is striking to see the way in which Barth's criticisms of Hegel parallel those of Marx a certain distance on the beginning of their way:

'1. Hegel means the truth for thought, which is presented as the culmination and centre of humanity. But has humanity *this* centre? Has it such a centre at all?'

So Barth, and so far also Marx. From the same criticism of Hegel Marx moved to his doctrine of the class nature of all truth because of the dependence of consciousness upon existence—his doctrine of ideology and class-interested thought—and Barth to his understanding of the way in which human sin destroys all possible avenues to truth from the human side, and disguises by ideologies the fact that it has done so.

'2. Hegel's self-movement of truth is identical with the self-movement of the thinking of the human subject, and with the human subject himself in so far as he is in thought truly himself. The Hegelian doctrine of the Trinity coincides with the basic principle of the Hegelian logic which is at the same time the basic principle of the Hegelian doctrine of man and of life.'[2]

Here we hear parallel tones to the Marx-Engels criticism that Hegel's dialectic of the mind was a mystification, a form of religion which finally justified only the social class interest of the philosopher himself. From here Marx and Engels turned to an inversion of the dialectic, pretending to find in the material, i.e. economic

[1] *Die protestantische Theologie des neunzehnten Jahrhunderts*, p. 372 (English translation in preparation).
[2] Ibid. pp. 374–5.

conditions of his existence in their dynamic relations, the contact with 'man as he really is' which Hegel lacked; while Barth found the 'self-movement' of God toward man to be absolutely primal and discontinuous with that of the human subject—whether as idealist or materialist, in spiritual speculation or empirical investigation—to be known as he sets himself forth.

Barth and Marx were at least parallel therefore in the direction in which they reacted against idealism. Each sought 'the real man' behind all of man's attempts to build, out of his own mind, structures of thought through which to explain himself and justify his (social or individual) *status quo*. Each took from Hegel the insight that truth is historical event, requiring participation and response rather than merely intellectual approval, and tried to apply it more consistently than Hegel to man's response to external historical realities which claim his allegiance. Each used thought and defined Being in the service of his Lord with such consistent revolutionary strategy as to destroy the very ground of common discussion with those of other faiths. Barth's rejection of Brunner in the first pages of *Nein* reminds one of Marx and Engels' *Theses on Feuerbach*. Barth rejects even the negative task of natural theology, even the formulation of his objections to it, because this in itself would imply accepting the frame of reference which natural theology provides, accepting it as an 'independent theme'. 'When one is concerned with real theology, one can only pass by the so-called natural theology, as one passes an abyss into which one should not step if one does not wish to fall.'[1] One does not discuss with the world about its religion, in the hopes of improving it. One proclaims the Gospel to it. One works to change its total orientation in the light of this reality. Here is all the scorn which Marx and Engels poured on the post-Hegelian philosophers culminating in Feuerbach with whose critical propositions they could agree so thoroughly. All these philosophers sought to understand the world. The point, however, is to change it, to change it in the light of a new reality which forces itself upon our consciousness from without. Hegelian philosophy then becomes the 'abyss', and the business of furthering the proletarian revolution, sometimes by

[1]*Nein: Antwort an Emil Brunner*, p. 12.

using philosophy to be sure, becomes the real task of man. To make the parallel more accurate one might liken Brunner to a reformist, a Menshevik, who begins, under the guise of more effective revolution, to seek accommodation with that world of human speculation and the *status quo*, which forms the temptation and the enemy. Barth and Marx are alike in their stern reminder that truth is known only when one is captive to the Object from which it comes, bearing witness to its power breaking into the closed circle of bourgeois (they even use this word in common)[1] existence.

We have, of course, stretched this parallel as far as it will go. Much more of Hegel clings to Marx than to Barth, and much more of 'the philosopher', i.e. one dependent on the action of words on the mind rather than the self in society, clings to Barth than to Marx. But, as we shall see below, the fact that Barth's theology so thoroughly understands and shares the critical, revolutionary moment which informs Marxist Communism, has helped to make its encounter with Communism the more fruitful.

We return then to the question of Barth's object of encounter, to the structure of his concern, first for man, and second for society.

The primary question for one who thinks as Barth does, out from the concrete act of God, is how man as a *Gegenüber* is related to the man Jesus Christ, and so to God. This is the question which Barth seeks to answer with his own version of the doctrine of analogy: not the analogy of being, but the analogy of faith in the area of knowledge, and the analogy of relation in the field of life. This is, to be sure, not a primary question for Barth himself. He explicitly calls it only a *Rückfrage*, an attempt to fill out the answer which in its essence is already given in the fact of the atonement. It is a fact that Jesus Christ has reconciled all men to God, that all men have a part in the new creature which he is. In his most comprehensive treatment of the atonement, to date, the survey of this

[1]Barth, in *Dogmatik* II/1, pp. 157–8, scornfully defines it as the domestication and *'Verharmlosung'* of the Gospel in terms of general culture and education. The essentially revolutionary note of this scorn for the ways of life of ordinary citizens (the word *bürgerlich* in German has a double meaning) continues to inform Barth's social judgements.

doctrine as it will be developed in the forthcoming fourth section of the *Dogmatik*,[1] Barth simply absorbs the question into his contemplation of the fact, using indiscriminately phrases which seem to carry an idealistic, a nominalistic, or a purely poetic meaning. Yet the question is primary for us, because precisely the *manner* in which Barth establishes this relation between the central act of God in Christ and the multifarious acts and structures of human life, is determinative when we seek to answer the question of the effectiveness of his theology in meeting Communism.

Fortunately, therefore, Barth has faced this question for us, and the answer, as we might have surmised, turns on the historical action of God in Christ for men.

'The being of man,' reads the heading of Paragraph 44, 'is the history in which one of God's creatures is elected and called by God, is included in his self-responsibility before God, and in which he shows himself qualified for this call and task.'[2]

The being of man is a history, the history of what Jesus Christ has done. The human nature of Jesus is the same as ours, yet it is different in Jesus from what it is in us, precisely because Jesus was at the same time the Lord of this human nature, the creator God in whom the created nature of man was preserved and realized, brought to its true fruition. It has in Jesus 'another condition (*Stand*), but not another createdness',[3] than our nature. Yet precisely in this condition, which amounts simply to an elucidation of the seemingly contradictory formula of Chalcedon, Christ is the mediator of God to man. He is the man who is at once wholly for God, and wholly for other men. 'In him man is ready for God.'[4] He is the bearer of our flesh. In him our flesh is present when God the Son knows the Father. He carries the sins of our flesh unto death, and so removes the enmity, the judgement of God which lies upon it. We have only to receive what has been done for us. 'It is a matter of the gentle, not loud, mild, not harsh, intimate, not strange, awakening of children in their father's house, to life in this house.'[5]

[1]Cf. the survey in *Dogmatik* IV/1, pp. 83–171. [2]III/2, p. 64.
[3]Ibid. p. 62. [4]II/1, p. 169. [5]IV/1, p. 108.

201

'Our community with God rests on the fact that he and he alone is one with God. He himself is God acting in his person; he himself is the Kingdom of God. He alone is first and truly elected; but elected as the head and Lord of all the elected. We, as elected, are only the members of his body. He alone is at once the receiver and giver of grace.'[1]

We, through the work of the Holy Spirit, participate in the history of Christ's work. Our human nature, our being, is therefore derivative from his human nature. We have it as a loan (*Leihgabe*) through our participation in him. 'Jesus Christ himself takes care that we are in and through him, and not outside of him.'[2] The Holy Spirit sees to it that this inclusion of all men in the work of Christ is not a second, an additional work after his incarnation, but a part of it, by faith:

'Faith means . . . to depend completely on the fact that our temporal existence receives, has, and receives ever anew its truth, not from itself, but only from its relation to what Jesus Christ is and does as our intercessor and mediator in God himself'[3]—

by love, the simple realization by man that he lives already by God's grace in the house of his Father: 'Christian love is first of all, speaking generally, the active human recognition . . . of the love of God. It recognizes this love in following it, copying it, and creating in its image'[4]—
and by hope:

'The world is reconciled with God in Jesus Christ by the fact that in him this promise is given to it by God himself; that in him its own future here and now has sunk into its present; that in the middle of its present it is grasped by its future being, and determined by it.'[5]

Such is a taste of the way in which Barth develops the one mighty theme of all his dogmatic thinking—Jesus Christ, God for man and man for God. The key word through it all one might, with some daring, call the little word 'for'. It is this word and what it means which continually undermines every natural human tendency to relapse into a picture of this whole theological relationship in

[1] III/2, p. 57. [2] II/1, p. 174.
[3] Ibid. p. 178. Cf. IV/I, pp. 98–106.
[4] IV/1, p. 111. [5] Ibid. p. 126.

202

terms of rational categories of being and attributes, in fixed relations. It is this word applied to God in his revelation, to Christ and his work, to man in his created being as he comes to see it in Christ, which throws the whole Divine-human universe into motion. Because this word is basic there can be no abstract categories, not even time itself, as we shall see, with neutral status. Yet more, because this word is basic to the description of God, we cannot think of him as contained within any circle of his own contemplation, as containing any Oneness at rest in his own perfection. That is why the circle of God's knowledge of himself through the flesh can only include the whole world of all that is truly human in its scope. God *is* for man. Finally this is why the human creature can be at once so absolutely *von Gott her*, so completely dependent on God's act for his very existence and response, and at the same time be confirmed, atoned, and fulfilled in his creaturely being *Gott gegenüber*. This 'for-ness' is not a philosophical category. Its background is rather Biblical, and experiential testimony to its validity can come not from the logical mind but only from the responses of faith, hope and love in human life. In these terms we must understand Barth's description of the structure of these responses as *analogia relationis* to God rather than the Scholastic *analogia entis*.

'The analogy between God and Man is, in all simplicity, existence in the relation I-Thou.'[1] With this simple statement Barth puts the essence of his doctrine of the creature as creature. There is no continuity of being between man and God, but there is an analogous relation, a reflection, a response, in the creature, of and to the very dynamism of God's own constitution. This analogy is expressed in the created nature of man as man and wife—not as simply bisexual like all mammals, but in the personal *Gegenüber* of two persons who differ fundamentally and yet are as fundamentally one. This is the *imago dei* in man, 'in the patterns of mutual dependence, fellowship, and simple togetherness of man and wife which happen day by day'.[2] It is rooted in the differentiation of their creation, but it remains the act and gift of God,

[1]III/1, p. 207.
[2]Ibid. p. 219. The created relation of man and wife is developed again in III/2, pp. 344–91, and in III/4, pp. 127–269.

realized in its fullness in the man who was the true image of God, Jesus Christ in relation to the Church. So we have a threefold analogy of relation. God in relation to himself as Father and Son, man as created in relation to his wife, and Christ with his Church, who together form the image of God in its Christological form. We have the central I-Thou relation in God's revealed nature moving outwards in the analogies impelled by his love, like waves over the water when a stone is dropped.[1] The relation of human beings to each other is set by this radiating analogy, and impelled by the dynamic of this love. Thus man stands in a dynamic dependence. He comes by creation from grace, and moves toward God's grace again, yet not in such a way that this movement is a mere restoration of his created position. His existence is bound up with the history of Jesus Christ, destined for the glory of God. His freedom in this relation is the freedom gratefully to respond and partake of what God does for him. Sin, says Barth, is an 'ontological impossibility', though it is of course a fact.[2] His existence is existence in responsibility toward God. It is existence in encounter. As Jesus' humanity is complete co-humanity, so our humanity depends on our fellow man. 'I am, in that you are.'[3]

Such are a few of the essentials of the theology by which Barth expresses God's relation to man, and determines the place of man's life and work as an object of concern. We have in the whole discussion barely touched on the *social* object of Barth's theological interest, for two reasons. It is, in the first place, peripheral for him, and in the second place, still largely to be developed, in the coming volumes of his Section IV—*Die Lehre von der Versöhnung*. Barth himself confesses that he could not deal with the problem of *Der Mensch und die Menschheit*—the problem of individual and community—in the framework of his doctrine of man, 'because I was not sure of the proper theological approach to this question, and

[1]III/2, p. 262 speaks of love as the impelling force, and emphasizes the trinitarian form of the analogy, in which the Holy Spirit is the confirmation and binding power of the relationship. The wave image is my own.

[2]III/2, pp. 83–86. The 'ontological impossibility' of sin is of course not a logical statement. It means that the sinner chooses against his own existence, as does also (p. 162) the godless.

[3]Ibid. p. 299.

therefore not sure how to deal with it.'[1] Some of his thought does appear on this question in III/4 (*Die Nahen und die Fernen*, pp. 320–65), but again more in the nature of fencing off the area of *Volk* and culture from the encroachments of illegitimate theological orders, than of exploring the area itself. There are however certain basic lines of thinking which Barth uses in approaching social questions which can be noted here.

Existence is existence in the I-Thou encounter. Here alone lies the analogous relation to God's activity. As the image of God in Jesus is precisely his radical co-humanity as 'the Man for others', so also human existence is basically personal. The basic unit is two people: 'Note the not unimportant fact that there are always only two people at a time, really an "I" and a "Thou", who look each other in the eye, who therefore can see and be seen by one another.'[2] All human existence in society therefore must be seen basically as personal, of which the relation of man and wife is the parable rooted in the very creation itself. So far as society exists before its Creator therefore, it is the fabric of personal relations of which marriage is the strongest strand. It is the participation of one in another in understanding, help, giving of the self and receiving from another self. There is no place in all this, either for the ideal of the independent individual whose end is the development of his inner creative capacities and powers (the Nietzschian ideal) or for the endowment of groups with personal characteristics. Both group and individual are subordinate to the I-Thou relation. Neither individual capacities nor group characteristics have more than a phenomenological status. They may be for a man 'God's disposition which he will regard, honour, and accept as God's work', but they are not divine orders, not in themselves analogous to God's activity as is the relation of man and wife. They convey in themselves no commandment.

This has a double consequence. On the one hand it leads Barth into a caution over against generalized sociological thinking:

'(In this science) there can fundamentally only be a question of education, and not of the child; only of psychology and not of other people; only

[1] Introduction to Volume III/2, p. viii.
[2] III/2, p. 300.

205

of sociological statistics and not of this or that other person; only a question, as far as I can see, of the general, and not of the particular which alone is valid (*echt*).'[1]

And on the other hand a condemnation of 'Bureaucracy', which needs to be set over against Barth's socialist leanings in balancing his social thought:

'Bureaucracy is the name for that kind of participation of man in his fellow man, where precisely the first step—the step into mutual openness —is lacking. It is lacking because, for the sake of the simplicity of a general picture and a general process, the I-Thou relation is avoided. Bureaucracy is the encounter of blind men with others whom they treat as if also blind. An office is a place where human beings are attended to, managed, and disposed of under certain categories and according to certain plans, principles, and rules.'[2]

On the other hand, this basic view of society leads to an attitude of free responsibility toward those structures of social life in which a man by God's disposing (*Fügung*) finds himself, such as language and therefore culture unit, people (*Volk*), tradition, and geographical neighbourhood (*Raum*). Barth points out at some length the basic difference between this kind of human bond, and that which unites the man and wife, parent and child; for these broader relations, in which, to be sure, God always finds men and in which he calls them, do not belong to the created essence of man himself, but to the secondary developments of world history. One hears of them first in the stories of the Tower of Babel and the lists of the descendants of Noah (Gen. 10–11.9), after we have already had seven chapters of human history preceded by the history of creation itself. These broader relations, between the near and the far, come into being, Barth maintains, only as a consequence of the covenant, as the background against which the history of redemption is to take place. In the *eschaton* they will vanish once again. The main theme of history is that which started in creation and runs through the calling of Abraham to Christ, the theme of God's covenant with man. The history of peoples and of humanity in general is a secondary theme, it is only *mitgemeint*. God's kingdom breaks into the field of this general social history and illumines it,

[1]III/2, p. 301.   [2]Ibid. p. 302.

so that the prophets can speak the Word of God over the nations. But never can an event in this general history, in the field of these general group relations, be in itself an event revealing the kingdom of God. This is reserved for the personal relations which occur in the history of God's covenant itself.

Therefore these group relations are of a different sort than those of the archetype man-wife, parent-child. They are (*a*) reversible, reciprocal, based on a human sameness, not on created differences, (*b*) shifting (*fliessend*), not only in that cultural groups and peoples migrate, but also in that new economic conditions create new groupings, growth in experience changes perspective and the like; (*c*) removable (*aufhebbar*) not only in the *eschaton*, but from time to time in history itself. These groupings, traditions, loyalties in which man is born are God's gifts, his dispensation (*Fügung*) for and in which man is responsible—not to the gifts!—but to God in his covenant in Christ. As an object of God's gracious election man is free over against these conditions of his existence—a pilgrim on the earth. There is not even a general commandment: '*Thou shalt speak thy mother tongue.*'

The significance of this position should not be underestimated. Barth here is giving not only a caution, but also a charter, to free, responsible, and (in a general sense unbound to any philosophical system) empirical ethical thinking in the whole field of ethics, guided only by a determination, as realistic and scientific as may be, of the social conditions at hand, and a Biblical, Christ-centred understanding of the needs of the fellow man. Here he sets himself against all romanticism and idealism about tradition which could distort the efficient relative service of the real man as he stands *uns gegenüber*.[1] Here is a theological prohibition against a

---

[1] III/4, pp. 345–9. Barth has especially in mind, as these pages show, the raising of *Volk* to the status of a theological concept, a crime of which he accuses post-war German theologians, and acquits their nineteenth century forbears, however liberal. This in itself indicates a significant shift in Barth's emphasis, a shift which brings him closer to Anglo-Saxon thinking because his polemic is directed, not against the humane (though unsuccessful) efforts of liberal theologians to combine faith and human understanding, but against a clearly definable attempt to sanctify the profane.

too simply theological ethic, and a plea for responsible openness to changing social conditions, to the developing ecumenical encounter. In all this Barth is not devaluing the history of nations and social groups. He is demythologizing them. In all this he is of one mind and heart with Reinhold Niebuhr.

It is the same when Barth speaks of the relative place of culture and of the sciences. Since, for example, he sees the central concern of theology as the relation of God and man, he places cosmology, in contrast to Tillich, as a peripheral concern and draws the line sharply against attempts, on whatever basis, to integrate scientific, philosophical, and theological factors into one view of the whole natural world. Yet precisely for this reason he finds theology in basic harmony of method with the *exakte Wissenschaften*, though the two are engaged in quite different tasks. These exact sciences (presumably those, such as physics, chemistry, and biology, which seek exact information about the world of nature) are concerned, as are all sciences, with the phenomenology of man and all creation, not with their reality (*Wirklichkeit*). Their source of knowledge is not faith and God's Word, but observation and thought. Yet these sciences parallel theological method in; (*a*) having no world-view of their own, but being bound to a phenomenological interpretation of their object; (*b*) recognizing the centrality of man in the cosmos; (*c*) respecting the existence of earth and heaven, that is, of a realm of observable comprehensible data, and of a realm of reality which is beyond the grasp of human minds and observation (*Wahrnehmung*). This example is typical. It is precisely the sciences and philosophies which know their limits, which do not claim to interpret man and the world in their own light, and which respect the difference between heaven and earth, which have their due place in elucidating the full being of man against the background of creation. These sciences can be instruments for the faithful. They can also, on their own presuppositions, not on those of faith, discover some of the characteristics of human potentiality as a creature of God.

This is, however, only one of Barth's perspectives on the social object—the perspective of creation. An early article on the Church and culture gives us a glimpse of what the other perspectives may become. As culture in the perspective of creation is the original promise given to man of what he should become: 'completeness, unity, wholeness in his sphere as creature, as man, as God is complete and whole in his sphere,'[1] so in the perspective of redemption culture is the law, the command, according to which the redeemed Christian is to exercise his obedience:

'Always the content of the Law is quite simply culture. Always sanctification, being set apart for God, doing the will of God, means as its content being humanized. Humans ought to become *human*, no more, but also no less.'[2]

And finally, from the point of view of salvation (*Erlösung*), that is, the point of view of the Christ who is coming, through whom all things are to be made new, culture is the limit (*die Grenze*) of human life beyond which God stands who fulfils through the resurrection of the dead, in that he makes all things new. So the Church serves culture best when she puts it in this eschatological perspective:

'Not from depreciation of the work of culture, but in highest appreciation of that toward which she sees all cultural work to be aimed. Not from pessimism, but from boundless hope. Not as a spoil-sport, but knowing that art and science, economics and politics, technology and education are really a sport (*Spiel*), a serious sport but still a sport; and that means an activity which in the long run does not have its meaning in its own achievable goals, but in what it means to play that much better and more objectively, because one knows the sport to be a reflection, and not the goal of life itself. It would not hurt our seriousness, if we should make clear to ourselves that it can never be a *final* seriousness, and that God alone has the right and the possibility of being completely serious.'[3]

This concept of *das Spiel*, which we have already met in the *Römerbrief* to describe the political and cultural activities of men, is not a depreciation of earthly life, as this quotation clearly shows. It is rather a way of describing the quality of an existence which God blesses, which provides the background and material for the action of his grace in Jesus Christ for all men, in the time which is

[1]'Kirche und Kultur', in *Die Theologie and Die Kirche* (Munich, 1935), pp. 375–6.
[2]Ibid. p. 380. [3]Ibid. p. 384.

given to it. Here we have a combination of the profoundly revolutionary motif which Barth shares with Marx over against the claims of this world's social order to basic harmony and perfectibility, with an appreciation of the relative place of the creature in creation, dynamically restored in Christ, expressible in all the social relations of this world, which Marx utterly lacked. Marx's eschatology foreshadows that of Barth precisely in its vision of a new heaven and a new earth to be brought in by an outside agent, in which all present relations and activities will receive a new meaning, and therefore a new reality, one incapable of the corruption and misuse which now belongs to their created nature. Barth even parallels Marx in regarding this present world of cultural political, and technical activity (*das Spiel*) as meaningful not in terms of its own ends and goals, but only in terms of the opportunity it affords for activity which anticipates the new world to come. Yet Barth is able to rejoice in creation at the same time, in the light of its redemption. For him sin and evil are not the utter wrongness, the utter slavery of human society in all its relations, in the light of the coming revolution, as for Marx. They are not the source of unending tension in human life, overcome only in the *eschaton*, as with Niebuhr. They are not the demonic corruption of creative possibilities, as with Tillich. They are rather the attempt of the creature to transcend the relativity of his position, the dependence of his very existence on God's gracious act, and become himself judge of right, wrong and truth, his own helper and end, grounded in his own independent being. But this very act of rebellion has been overcome by God in Christ. In him a flood of light has been shed on God's relation to his creature man, so that man need no longer choose his non-being, his death. Barth's affirmation of this world and its structures seems from a point of view outside this faith to be a collection of paradoxes. He values and honours human culture precisely because it is *not* itself continuous with the Divine Being, not even in that paradoxical way which Tillich calls theonomous; but because it is (when it truly *is*) the response in human personal relations to the action of God's grace. He finds the Christian able to be a more sensitive and complete advocate of relative human values because he does not depend on these for the meaning of his life—be they freedom, democracy, justice or peace! He finds the Christian to be a more responsible worker in the world because he is not anxious for the world, its culture, its science, its political order. The Christian who is capable of rejoicing in the opportunities which dictatorship, poverty, prison or death bring for grateful response to God's love, is by this capacity better qualified to appreciate the true meaning and value of wealthier and freer culture and society, and to live responsibly in it. The Christian whose hope is set on the coming of Christ in his kingdom, is freest to see the realities of this world unveiled by radical or conservative illusions, and act accordingly in serving his neighbour.

This is Barth's relation to the social object of his concern. It is also the basic attitude toward society which informs a large number of Christians whose encounter with Communism in the past few years has been far more profound than has Barth's. Yet neither Barth, nor his followers in Germany, East or West, would like to see it labelled only with the name of the Swiss theologian. For it claims to be, basically, nothing but the New Testament attitude toward society, interpreted for our day. This attitude might be briefly described as positive and responsible in the light of Christ's victory over the powers of evil; free and defiant, in the hope of Christ's coming again. Several charges have been brought against it:

A. That it is a theology only for moments of great crisis and absolute witness, not helpful in the relative decisions of daily life, because it does not strongly enough affirm this life's value.

B. That it does not take seriously the problems which beset man in society in his daily responsibility, nor undergird the creators of culture, economic and political policy in the ethical complexities of their tasks.

c. That its emphasis on redemption as the overarching total ontological fact fails to take sin, and the necessity for opposing social evil, seriously enough.

It would perhaps be invidious to point out that these are questions, *mutatis mutandis*, to the New Testament itself. They must nevertheless be answered. We have seen how they are already answered in principle. It will be the task of the coming pages to

211

evaluate the answer in practice, specifically the practice of the Barthian encounter with Communism.

3. THE QUESTION OF IDEOLOGY

Against this background of Barth's own perspective and concern (from which his views on church and state have been omitted because they have been so largely forged in the heat of political controversy from 1933 to date, that they can hardly be defined apart from the critical discussion of these controversies in Chapter VI below)[1] we turn now to the question of the adequacy of his theology to the encounter with Communism. It corresponds fully to Barth's own way of thinking that we come first to the challenge of the Marxist doctrine of ideology and criticism of religion. Unlike Reinhold Niebuhr, whose centre of interest lay in history and social action, Barth has from the beginning, as we have seen, wrestled with the problem of religious knowledge in the light of man's condition. But this is too weak a statement. Unlike Tillich, he has been fairly overwhelmed by the crisis of man's religious knowledge, and has sought with desperate absoluteness the true Object of faith over against man. In this, as we have noted, his passion corresponds to that of Marx, a fact which makes it all the more surprising that only in two places in all of Barth's writings do we find a straightforward encounter with Marx's philosophical position. These, however, form a good basis from which to consider this question. They are a brief consideration of Marx's historical materialism as an aspect of materialism in general, in the framework of the definition of man as soul and body,[2] and an early article on Ludwig Feuerbach.[3] The latter, to be sure, mentions Marx and Engels only once, but it grapples with those essentials of the Marxist criticism of religion which Marx and Engels learned from Feuerbach.

[1]There is of course a Barthian doctrine of the Church *per se*, without the mention of which this section may well have given a lopsided impression. Cf. *Die Theologie und die Kirche*, last four chapters; *Dogmatik* I/2, pars. 19–21 (pp. 505–990); *The Church and the Churches* (London, 1937); *Dogmatik* IV/2, pp. 695–824.

[2]*Dogmatik* III/2, pp. 464–68.

[3]*Die Theologie und die Kirche*, pp. 212–39.

The message of these two passages is basically the same. Although Feuerbach's apotheosis of man (Barth does not bring out the fact that this apotheosis is to be found in the early Marx and Engels—especially with relation to the *Gattungswesen* of man— and finds vigorous expression, all 'science' and 'materialism' to the contrary, in contemporary Soviet literature)[1] is an 'incomparable banality', when one looks at what man really is, in the light of Christ's judgement and grace, it carries unanswerable force over against most of nineteenth century theology. For it was this nineteenth century theology which set the problem: 'whether and how far religion, revelation, and relation to God can be made understandable as a predicate of man.'[2] The attempt to establish the nature of religion, to know God, from human presuppositions led only to the logical conclusion, or at least to the logical question, whether religion were not after all the worship of man in the fullness of his capacities, body and soul, whether God were not 'for man the scrap-book of his highest feelings and thoughts; the book of his heritage, in which he enters the names of his dearest and holiest essences'; or 'the qualities of the genus man (*Gattung*) distributed among men and realizing themselves in the course of history, gathered together in one concept for the use of limited individuals.'[3]

Secondly, and more seriously, however, the materialism of Feuerbach, given power and passion by the Marxist eschatology of class war and classless society, was able to grip the imagination of the socialist working-class because the Church had failed to read the signs of the times and has failed to preach the full Gospel at two important points.

A. She failed to counter, while it was arising, the view of man as a being without a soul, which arose not only in the philosophy of

[1]For Marx see especially *Nationalökonomie und Philosophie*, new edition edited and introduced by Erich Thier (Cologne and Berlin, 1950), pp. 147–51, 180. An example of modern Soviet collectivist humanism is Glatkov, *Zement*.

[2]*Die Theologie und die Kirche*, p. 226.

[3]These are two quotations from Feuerbach—*Das Wesen des Christentums* (p. 132) and *Philosophie der Zukunft* (p. 28)—which Barth uses in his article, op. cit. pp. 221–2.

the nineteenth century, but in the realities of the industrial revolution. Materialism, says Barth,

'. . . lives from that which is not only forced construction in historical materialism, but historically true and real beyond a doubt. It lives from the actual existence of that soulless human form which the nineteenth century so visibly produced.'

The tragedy of Marxism, says Barth, is that it falls victim to this lack of soul, despite its intensely human hope for the day when exploitation will be abolished and a genuine morality will be possible.

'Precisely the determined, the consistent, the orthodox representatives of the Marxism which is bound to this (materialist) connexion, have taken on themselves more and more of this evil spirit of the robot-man.'[1]

But the Church has placed against this materialism only its teaching about the immortality of the soul, its pietistic separation of body from soul which is just as surely 'spiritualized this-worldliness'[2] as materialism is this-worldly in its way.

'For whoever denies the this-worldliness (*Diesseits*) of man, denies the "other-worldliness" of God at least as badly as the usual and much less dangerous denier of "the other world". Christian hope will first earn its name, when it makes materialism and idealism both impossible with one blow.'

This 'blow' is the message of the resurrection of the dead, which proves

'. . . that God's judgement and God's promise concern the whole man, and can therefore neither be affirmed and believed apart from material economic reality, nor can they be denied and pushed aside as ideology in contrast to material economic reality.'[3]

So long as the Church does not revise her doctrine of man from the point of view of *this* eschatological hope; so long as she does not learn that God's promise is given to men in both body and soul, a total blessing and hope; so long as she hides in a body-soul dualism instead of confronting the world with the message of the king-

[1] *Dogmatik* III/2, pp. 466–7.
[2] *Theologie und Kirche*, p. 233 n.
[3] *Dogmatik* III/2, p. 467.

dom of God, she will face the Communists helpless because of her own bad conscience.

B. The Church has failed to understand the nature of the social battle in the nineteenth and into the twentieth century. She has not recognized the way in which philosophies have actually been the tools of battling classes—'scientific' socialism the weapon of a working class's war for liberation, and idealist philosophy the expression of a 'self-glorifying bourgeoisie'.[1] Therefore she reacted only to the surface, the overt, action of this battle, fighting indeed the bourgeois Enlightenment, but only after a whole new world of problems and needs had opened up, and the front was elsewhere. She should have been as quick to point out that the 'God' in whom the bourgeois idealist pretended to believe was as much an idol, as the 'Man' whom Feuerbach put in his place and whom Marx turned into the proletariat. She should have shown both sides in this battle that the only true liberation from idols is knowledge of the true God. Since she did not do so, it was Feuerbach and the Marxists who discovered the ideology behind the Church's idealist theology and bourgeois practice, and God became to them 'a lovely dream', and worse, 'a deliberately sustained presentation of false facts in order to curb the battle for liberation'.[2] The godlessness of the social democrats is a *mene tekel* for the Church.

What then is the Church to do now? What form should her repentance take in order to wash the stain of ideology, hence of incredibility, from her message? Here the Barth of 1926, like the Niebuhr of 1936, reaches out to express an insight implicit, yet far too little explicit, in the theology of both men otherwise. There is no intellectual answer, not even a theological one, which will convince in itself. The first act of a Christian must be to allow himself to be knocked from his earthly standpoint by this criticism:

'to admit to Feuerbach that his explanation of religion is right the whole way, in so far as it refers to religion as the experience of bad and mortal men; even men in high position, even profound thinkers, even the "Christian" religion of these men. (We must) admit that *we* are and remain liars even in our relation to God, who can claim his certainty, his salvation, as grace but only as grace.'[3]

[1] *Theologie und Kirche*, p. 234.   [2] Ibid. p. 235.   [3] Ibid. pp. 238–9.

215

Secondly, the Church must make herself credible once more by an *ethic* which 'will be fundamentally different from the cults of old and new culture forms (*Hypostasen*) and ideologies. Then people will believe that her God also is not an illusion.'[1]

Thus Barth in 1926. One could wish him no finer development than the unfolding of these two insights in interacting parallel : that no formulation of man, not even the finest theological statement, can capture the truth which comes to us by God's grace alone, and that the Christian must prove his dependence on that gracious God (and therefore bear witness to his reality) by the way in which his ethical life, his behaviour in the I-Thou relation, shows another basis than that given by his culture or class. Here the seeds of an adequate Christian encounter with Communism and with the secular world as a whole are contained. Barth however is a theologian more than a man of ethical reflection. The first insight above reflects his central concern. The second, as an essential way of making the Gospel credible, of testing the soundness of the religion we practise, has fallen by the way. This poses for us our problem. For, unlike Niebuhr, Tillich, and Berdyaev, Barth's thought presents itself to us on two levels. We must first ask how adequate a theological answer he gives us, to the problem of ideology presented by Feuerbach, Marx, and the Communist movement. Then we must ask the second question, how adequately he applies this theology to the problem of the Christian's political responsibility, especially in the face of Communism, bearing in mind the question how this ethical practice reflects on the meaning of the theology itself.

When we divide the question in this way, we must start by saying that no one of the theologians with whom we deal in this study, gives as adequate a Christian answer to the intellectual problem raised by the Marxist doctrine of ideology, as does Barth. He goes as far as theological words and thoughts can go in exploring its depths, in searching for the answer which comes in truth from beyond the distortion of human sin, and in protecting that answer from distortion when it encounters human realities. His deepest contribution however has been positive: the attempt to build a Christocentric way of thinking which will contain within

[1] *Theologie und Kirche*, p. 236.

itself its own corrective against ideological distortion, because it will be a true reflection of the act of God in Christ, and not a system itself. We need to look at Barth's answer to the problem of ideology from the point of view of two different human existences, therefore: the negative existence of man in sin, and the positive existence of man in response to the grace of God in Jesus Christ; although it goes without saying that for Barth these are not two existences, but existence itself, and the denial by the creature of his existence. On the negative side, Barth goes further than any other theologian in describing the total way in which existence in sin destroys, scatters into unconnected phenomena, any knowledge which man might have of his own true being or of God apart from Christ's redeeming act. Again his formal resemblance to Marx is evident. Like Marx he rejects utterly any neutrally objective position from which truth, or good and evil, may be known. Like Marx he finds that man can only recognize the truth which is acting dynamically on him, requiring his decision and response. Both men regard the depth of the crisis in which man stands as only visible to the eyes of faith, in the light of revelation. But for Barth this crisis is not primarily social. It does not involve some particular historical form of human living which enslaves man. The revelation is not some new science and the decision of faith not some new programme by which man will bring himself out of his self-estrangement. In Christ every such attempt to give meaning to life from some human perspective—all philosophy, and all natural theology, along with these 'sciences' which are covert philosophies and religions themselves—is revealed as ideological. Ideology is characteristic of man-centred thinking as such, not only of the thought of certain social groups. Man, seeking the meaning of life apart from Christ, is the very type of the ideologue. What he sets up as truth and right, and the system with which he binds it together, can only be a reflection of the negativity (*Nichtigkeit*) of his existence, and of his conflict with other men and God. But because of this, he cannot understand his thought and situation as what they are. There is no escape from this condition from the human side. There is no point of contact in this human being which could make his redemption of a two-sided affair, a matter of

217

co-operation between him and God. Sin is not a characteristic of man which tomorrow may change. Man *is* sinner, in that by his act he violates himself. 'In that his pride is radical and basic, it is also total, and universal. It runs through and determines all his thoughts, words, and works, his whole inner secret life, and all his visible movements and connexions.'[1]

It is characteristic of human pride, the foundation of all human sin, that it seeks to conceal from itself and from others its basic interest; to be as God, to be lord and not servant, to be judge of good and evil, and to be its own helper and support. The ways by which pride does this are many and subtle, and none is more subtle or more dangerous than the way of 'religion', that degeneration of true faith and obedience, where man practises 'what purports to be the raising of his soul to God, the erection and veneration of images of his purported being and essence, . . . the deed of sinful men which leads unfailingly to nothing but really flagrant continuations and confirmations, surpassing one another, of his faithlessness; which leads therefore to nothing but self-contradictions; and in which then the alternatives of doubt, scepticism, or atheism will ever and again break out with new force.'[2]

In all this Barth has shared Karl Marx's rebellious spirit most completely, and has expanded far beyond the narrow limits of Marx's political purposes. He has shared the rebellion also of Feuerbach, Kierkegaard, Nietzsche, and the modern existentialists. Yet their systems as well have proved too man-centred, too much concerned with the subject 'man' and his experience, to express in human thought that reality by which our ideological circle, our enclosure in our own sin and complacency, is broken, and our new being is constituted. This must come from without. This is God made man for us in Jesus Christ. Everything, for Barth, starts here. For this act of God there can be no human preparation; not even the negative one whereby man exposes himself as sinner and hypocrite about his sin. Nothing short of this complete and absolute Object in whom everything begins and whom no human thought or act can qualify, will satisfy as an answer to the question contained in the fact of ideology.

[1]*Dogmatik* IV/1, p. 552.   [2]Ibid. p. 537.

The questions which this raises for Barth's positive theology of existence in grace can be brought most sharply into focus by comparing his answer to the problem of ideology with that of Tillich, who puts—from the perspective of religious socialism more deeply involved in the problems of the movement which Marx originated —the sharpest challenge to Barth's conception of existence in sin and the ideological problems it raises.

Tillich's thought puts first the question whether theology, and in this case Barth's theology with its rejection of all approaches from the 'natural man' to God, can take seriously the proletarian situation out of which Marxist socialism was born and of which it is so acute an expression. We know from the above how Barth would answer this, and we know how inadequately Tillich understood the continuing power of human self-deception which resisted the kind of religious explanation of socialism to itself which he and his colleagues attempted. Barth is certainly right in distinguishing the knowledge of our human predicament, of conflict and meaninglessness and the like, from our knowledge of our sinful nature, and in refusing to regard the former as an avenue to the latter. Yet the question remains one to Barth's construction of a positive theology, whether it enables the Christian believer to understand man in the proletarian situation and relate the Gospel to his condition; whether it moves the Christian to that radical questioning of his own securities and interests in the interest of his disadvantaged neighbour which alone is evidence of his freedom from ideological thinking.

Second, Tillich's thought raises the question whether Barth's theology is capable of taking the relative events of world history seriously enough to bring about not only Christian participation in it, but Christian planning and creativity, Christian activity if need be for revolutionary change, Christian conception and initiation of the new orders for which the times may be ripe. Here again Barth has taken the fact of existence in sin with its ideological consequences more seriously than Tillich, and denied the way out which finds patterns of revealed meaning in culture itself. But the question remains whether his theology of grace, so utterly concentrated on the act of God in Christ's coming once, presence with us now, and coming again, can take world history seriously enough not to

219

be 'indifferent to the special heights and depths' of its process.[1] For a theology, however Biblical, which numbs man's sensitivity to the movements of world history, which detaches his conscience and creative imagination from participation in its processes, remains an ideology of conservative effects.

Thirdly, Tillich, this time directly, accuses Barth of propagating a new form of heteronomy in the name of the sovereignty of God. Translated into terms of our discussion here, Barth, according to his critic, has only succeeded, through his uncompromising purification of theology from all taint of human subjectivity mixed with the Word of God, in setting up a more arbitrary, still human, orthodoxy as final authority. This orthodoxy violates human nature and forces it from without, instead of appealing to man from the depths of his own being as fulfilment. Barth, maintains Tillich, has placed himself in the old tradition of authoritarian religion which had its origins in the patriarchal father-God of the Old Testament who ruled first by arbitrary power and fear over against man.[2] But this kind of religion is in its way an ideology, for it undergirds the pride—however subtly concealed by the content of the faith he arbitrarily flaunts—the aggressions, and the failure in human contact of the religious man. The only way out of the circle of ideological thinking, maintains Tillich, is when man finds in the depths of his own being the Unconditional ground of all Being, which is at once the Power of Being in its fulfilment. God is thus not authority over against us, but this unconditional ground. His relation to us starts in an ontological act of justification and love, and theonomy—that cultural state in which all things are informed with divine meaning without being divine themselves—is the answer to ideology, not some dogmatic or ecclesiastical heteronomy.

[1] Tillich, *The Protestant Era*, p. 44. This criticism comes out of an early German article '*Kairos*', first published in 1922 in the German magazine *Die Tat*. It has in mind only Barth's *Römerbrief* in its second edition, though Tillich's failure to edit these references in the light of Barth's later works before publishing them again in 1948 must be counted as his reaffirmation of them.

[2] This view of authority and its problems, developed generally, and not specifically against Barth, is found among other places in 'Authority and Revelation'—the Dudleian lecture on revealed religion, also delivered in German at the Kirchliche Hochschule, Berlin, July, 1952 and mimeographed by the school.

The valid question to Barth in this attack does not lie in the strength of Tillich's alternative to Barth's doctrine of authority. For we have seen already Tillich's failure to come to grips with that manifestation of evil and sin in this world which takes the form of rebellion against true fulfilment and meaning, and satisfaction with this rebellion. It lies rather in the fact that Tillich voices here the most general criticism of Barth's theology, out of a real concern for the way in which it seems to violate the basic canons of human relations in the intellectual world. The question is real, even to Barth's theology of grace, which indeed Tillich has not even taken into account in his criticism: has Barth cleared the ground of all human approaches to God's revelation, only to erect a 'positivism of revelation',[1] an arbitrary structure of Biblical ideas and dogmas whose design is Barth's and not God's, in its place? Does Barth's positive reconstruction of theology really violate the freedom of man with an arbitrary authority as Tillich maintains?

These questions, taken in reverse order, are the basic questions of this study to each theologian. The first deals with man in society, the second with history, the third directly with knowledge itself. For Barth however, as we have mentioned, the question of ideology is logically first, and the other two are in a sense illustrations of it. Let us turn then to the positive attempt which he makes to develop, from Christ as a centre, and source of all, a truly theological (hence liberated from any human ideological) understanding.

'Fundamentally' wrote Tillich in 1935 '(Barth's) entire theology is contained in the first commandment, "I am the Lord thy God; thou shalt not have any Gods beside me." Every single sentence of his writings can be understood as the application of this notion to a particular phase of the relation between God and the world.'[2] Nothing could more thoroughly mislead us than to take

[1] This phrase originates with Dietrich Bonhoeffer, *Letters and Papers from Prison* (London, 1953; tr. of *Widerstand und Ergebung*), p. 126. Bonhoeffer had at least *Dogmatik* II/1 in mind when writing, and Barth's earnest attempt to take account of this charge and answer it (though he does not mention Bonhoeffer in this connexion by name) is in Vols. III/2 and III/4.

[2] Tillich, 'What's Wrong with Dialectical Theology', in *The Journal of Religion*, XV, 2, April, 1935, p. 129.

this judgement as applying to Barth's theology as we know it to-day. It may surprise Anglo-Saxon readers to realize it, but the problems of Barth's point of view, ever since he has developed his Christocentric position systematically, have not lain in the aloofness of his God from the affairs and problems of men, but rather in the thoroughness with which even creation and transcendence are elucidated from that point where God became man for our redemption. They lie not in Barth's over-consciousness of human sin, but rather in his banishment of sin to the realm of an 'ontological impossibility' of so little weight before the overwhelming power of God's gracious election, so utterly cancelled out and *nichtig*, that one becomes concerned for Barth's realism about human limitations. In his ethic it is more his differences with liberal perfectionism, than his differences with Luther and Calvin which need to be clarified. Niebuhr seems to have sensed this in his post-war polemic against Barth, which might well account for its virulence.[1] Yet Barth has not surrendered the first commandment, nor his absolute 'no' to natural theology. Christ himself is, for him, both the source and affirmation of all that is human, and the guarantee that the human will not usurp the place of God. It is because the act of God which is himself, is so utterly revealed as gracious toward men in Jesus Christ, that it becomes not only perversity but utter folly to seek approaches to God by some other route. It is because the continuity of man's nature is so unbroken by the worst of human rebellion, when we see creation in the light of the gracious purposes of God the Redeemer, that attempts to ground it in some human faculty apart from this gracious redeeming act become so contradictory and perverse. Gradually Barth's earlier negative polemic gives way to so comprehensive and powerful a statement of what God has revealed in Christ, for the fullness of human life, that every other world view must ask itself what truth about this God and his act its own resources could contribute, which would

[1]Brunner also finds Barth's description of sin as an 'ontological impossibility' simply impossible. He is deeply concerned, along with many other critics as well, about Barth's attempt to derive all creation from Christ and to see it only from the angle of redemption, for fear lest redemption then lose its unique significance. Cf. 'The New Barth', *Scottish Journal of Theology*, IV, June, 1951.

not in this light merely show up as darkness. Whether Barth's theology can lead Christians truly out of the ideological self-doubt and bourgeois ineffectiveness where the rise of Marxist socialism and the fact of proletarian living has placed them, into a response to truth itself in their social living, or whether his thought is, as Tillich says, a new heteronomy, the worse for being so 'orthodox', must be decided by the power of positive truth in his doctrine of Christ.

We come once more therefore to the great central theme of Barth's whole work, from the second part of his *Dogmatik* on, a theme so simple that a sentence would state it[1] yet so various, so sensitive and majestic at once in its orchestrations that only a faint echo (and in no sense an outline or synopsis) of them can appear in the limits of this study related to this question. The complete centrality of Christ as the measure and source of all that is human bears on the question of truth and ideology at two main points.

First and fundamentally we find Christ to be, for Barth, the centre of his doctrine of predestination and election, on which he builds all the rest of his positive dogmatic system. If Barth has a thought system, a closed explanation of human reality, its keystone is here.[2] For God is shown to be one who is by his very nature a gracious God, one who in his original decision before all time and creation, turned to man and elected him through his love in Jesus Christ. 'The eternal God of the Bible is the electing God . . . God's

[1] In his *Dogmatics in Outline* Barth suggests the simple words from the Christmas carol: 'Welt ging verloren. Christ ist geboren. Freue, freue Dich, O Christenheit.' On another occasion he is reported to have replied to an inquirer who asked him to give a few of the fundamental principles of his thinking, that he had no principles: 'But one thing I know. Christ lives. All the rest comes from there.'

[2] Von Balthasar finds that Barth's system derives its power, confidence, and emotional appeal from its daring completeness at this point. But he finds that because of this Barth has a *Denkform* (not a philosophical one to be sure) which might be likened to an hour-glass of which Christ is the constricted centre, and God and the creature the two bowls. From God above comes the revelation, and sets, to be sure, a counter-response in action. But both depend on the narrow neck, the most concrete event and person through which all the contact passes, from which all meaning comes (*Karl Barth*, pp. 201–10).

gracious election as the beginning of all things is God's giving of himself by his eternal counsel.'[1]

God decided in all eternity to give himself to covenant and community with man, to his own danger and loss! This is predestination. There is nothing in it of the terrible *decretum absolutum*, the inscrutable arbitrary choice of an unknowable God which imparted a background of fear to the theology of Calvin and Augustine. There is no ground here for that kind of confidence among the elect which sets them apart as a superior, disciplined group, such as were the Puritans; a theological mis-step which led in the direction of that further corruption, the theological self-justification of the successful business class. Precisely because Christ, God's election of man and the man whom God has elected, is the content of God's eternal decision, there is no need to draw on these philosophical presuppositions about a God apart from revelation, presuppositions which because they are not from God himself but about God, from man, so quickly become ideologies in the service of some men against others.

Predestination is, to be sure, double, for Barth—election and rejection (*Erwählung und Verwerfung*). In determining, choosing, creating cosmos, God banned chaos. In giving form to man, God rejected other possibilities of what man might be (which achieved their very being as possibilities, because of God's rejection and not from some eternal fund of possibilities behind God). There are rejected and elected people. Yet who these are and what this means we know only in the light again of Jesus Christ who is the elected man and the rejected man at the same time. In him God has loved and chosen man, chosen man so far that he has sent his Son into rejection to share the rejection which man's sin had brought upon him. God in Christ took this rejection on himself, measured, so to speak, the depth of its chaos, and carried our fate for us. Out of this emerges the election precisely of the rejected. There is really *no* condemnation for those who are in Christ Jesus. And since Christ died for all men, the very possibility of rejection assumes a paradoxical character. It is adherence to a conquered enemy, the attempt to choose that chaos which not only is contrary to one's

[1]*Dogmatik* II/2, pp. 161, 176.

224

nature and being, but which has already been conquered by a gracious God. The Church should not take unbelief too seriously, for there is a reciprocal relation, precisely in God's grace, between the Christian and the godless. Precisely the lie of life without God points to and can only be understood in the light of the suffering and rejection of Christ. Because of Christ the godless can never rekindle the wrath of God against themselves. 'With all their godlessness they can never restore the wrongness, for whose elimination he gave up himself.'[1] They stand under the promise. At the same time they remind the elected of their own godlessness, of the fact that but for Christ they too are lost, and of their vocation precisely as the elect, by analogy with Christ, to carry vicariously the rejection of their brother. Barth works this into a kind of system to the glory of God's grace:

'Therefore the elected and the rejected, despite the greatest dissimilarities, can look only too alike in large areas. Therefore they not only work together, with all their differences of function; they can even in their functions stand in for one another. So intensively are they ordered to one another, so greatly do they condition one another, that the *one* form of Jesus Christ is often more clearly visible in the contrast of the *two* forms of the elected and the rejected, than is their contrast. Precisely in that the electing and calling God divides between them, they can only be so divided that he, God alone, is and remains just over against both and for the benefit of both; never so that anyone would to any extent fall away from his electing and his grace, or be released from his responsibility before God and God's responsibility for him.'[2]

Is this a new system, a system of universal grace and salvation, which might, in spite of everything, be likened to a monistic idealism? Does such a central doctrine as this lead Barth clear away from his early revolutionary dialectic, to a too simple affirmation of all that is, by virtue of God's grace which works through it one way or the other?[3] Barth denies it. God's grace and election come

---

[1]Ibid. p. 388.   [2]Ibid. p. 390.

[3]So von Balthasar: 'Christologische Engführung *ist* Systematik, weil sie ein Schliessen von Türen und (für Gott) möglichen Ausgängen ist. Ist es wahr, dass Christus das Prius der Natur ist, dann ist er auch das Prius der Sünde, dann ist sein Kreuz nicht eigentlich durch die Sünde bedingt, sondern durch seine von Ewigkeit beschlossene Selbstentäusserung, die also solche den Rahmen für die Möglichkeit der Konzession

out of his freedom. There is no law of universal atonement. The whole process which theology here describes is not a logical, rational one, but a free, personal one between God and the creature whom he has chosen. We may not draw logical inferences from it for ourselves; neither that evil is no more because it has been conquered, nor that all men are elected because God does not will that any be lost. Again it is Christ who defines the content of election: the utter grace of God who would be our covenant partner; the gracious judgement of God who bears our condemnation, the consequences of our sin and unbelief, for us and stays with us whether as enemy or friend; the life of thankful response whose content is bearing others' burdens and bringing them the Gospel.

A second point where the centrality of Christ bears on the question of ideology is in the emphasis which Barth lays on the priority of concrete action in relation, over being. First, the concrete alone is real. All mankind lives, as we have heard, from the *Concretissimum* which is the relation within the Trinity itself. The Word of God is one Word which contains all the fullness of reality, and comes concretely and specifically to man. God is not to be understood from a general concept of religion, nor man from a general theory of the human, not even the best and truest theological ideas. Rather the reverse. Yet this is not nominalism, for all wisdom and truth is to be found in God, and the analogy of relation in which he has created human beings is none the less real a reflection of this truth for being dependent on the personal outgoing grace of the Creator and Redeemer.

Second, God *is*, in his revelation, in his act in Jesus Christ. Human being *is* a history. Creation is to be understood in the light of its purposes and direction. The relations between man and

---

des Sündenfalls bildet, aber auch als Klammer um alle mögliche Sünde gelegt ist, so dass mit einer nicht anzufechtenden Notwendigkeit eine letzte Verurteilung des Sünders unmöglich wird. Und der Christ wird angeleitet, sich jubelnd und strahlend auf das Jüngste Gericht zu freuen. . . . Aber redet die Bibel denn so? Sind wir hier nicht hinter den Spiegel geraten, in den wir schauen sollten? Wird nicht hier dem lieben Gott in die Karten geblickt? Ist nicht das Geheimnis aufgeklärt, so gründlich, dass alle existentielle Verkleidung nicht daran hindern kann, dass es hier nach—Aufklärung riecht?' (op. cit., pp. 255–6).

woman, man and fellow man, God and man, are not static formulae but historical, in the light of the destiny they approach, in response to the grace which has formed them. Yet neither in God nor in man is Being lost in a continuum of events. Once again it is Christ in whom the *Gegenüber* is established and confirmed in his being which lives as free creature from God and toward him. In Christ we see the meaning and content of this history, in the communion of man with God.

In all these examples Barth seeks to liberate the real, the concrete human being, as he is before God, in the history where God has chosen him, from the bonds of every generalization and abstraction which would limit his human nature and destiny by merely human ideas. The man who believes is for the first time the truly free and fulfilled man; free to make full use of his understanding, his faculties, and his will. But Barth goes further yet. Jesus Christ was present at the Creation. He is the ground of the created nature of man. 'The ontological determination of man is grounded in the fact that in the midst of all other men, is one of them, the man Jesus.'[1] God's gracious Word made flesh is not only the restoration, the correction, of his erring creation, but the source and ground of creation in the first place. Here we have the union of the order of being and the order of knowing (*die ontische und noetische Ordnung*), Barth's answer to the epistemological problem as a whole. The Creator can be no irrefutable idea, which for all its certainty remains an idea and not a reality. 'We are speaking therefore not of a further supposition of our consciousness, but of a position which comes to us from over against us, and of the knowledge which is based on this and only on this.'[2]

Because God exists as Creator who reveals himself; because God knows himself in Jesus Christ, and all creation and all men in and through Christ; in short because of God's gracious free decision to be for us, we human beings can know of our own existence as coming from him.

'If, taught by God himself, one knows of God and his existence, then one knows along with it of oneself and one's own existence, and of one's surroundings and their existence. . . . In that God first says: "I am!",

[1] III/2, p. 158.   [2] III/1, p. 399.

a man can and may not only repeat: "Yes, Thou art!", but also the other thing: "I am myself, and this is what it means to be me!" [1]

This existence, and the knowledge of it which God has revealed, is not, however, a bare fact, but precisely existence 'as this domain and object of the Covenant, as the being on whom God has bestowed his good pleasure, whom he has made to partake of the overflowing of his own fullness'.[2] It is existence for the sake of, and in the history of, the covenant of God's grace. The content of this existence, God's revelation, is 'the good news that God in his Son is not against him but for him.' This parallelism of being and knowing, and the complete dependence of both on God's gracious act in Christ has, for Barth, two consequences which stand in contrast to one another.

The first is that faith, and only faith, is the way by which man receives and responds to this creation and this revelation. For faith is not a human possibility, a work of man, but is given by the act of God in his revelation, the analogous human decision called forth by God's decision in love toward man. Here and here alone one can speak of a 'point of contact', of a 'divine form' in man.

'Precisely when we understand the divine form (*Gottförmigkeit*) of man which takes place in faith, and the point of contact (*Anknüpfungspunkt*) for the Word of God which is given in it, not as an inherited or acquired characteristic of man, but as the sole work of the present grace of God, there remains for us only the final word: God deals with man in his Word. Because it is man's work by faith, in which God's work happens, therefore man can recognize God's Word. He recognizes in that he is recognized by God.'[3]

Here alone we have contact with Truth, with Reality, in its uncreated source. And in faith we encounter it, not as some eternally true idea or structure, but precisely as the act of a personal God, who grasps us in our historical existence, and calls forth our joyful obedience. Any other knowledge about God than this response by this channel, is abstract and unreal. Faith 'is, in that it becomes an event, a historical, in fact a saving historical (*heilgeschichtliche*) determinate of human existence.'[4] It is being known of God. But to

[1]III/1, p. 400. [2]Ibid. p. 416. [3]I/1, p. 257.
[4]III/3, p. 280. Cf. III/1, p. 400.

know, even as we are known, to have full vision of God's meaning and reality, will be an eschatological experience.

Second, however, precisely because the act of God's grace, coupled with his revelation, is not some magic connexion with the faithful against a dark and unfathomable reality; but rather the source and purpose of all historical being itself, there is constituted by God's creation, a human nature, a relative and derived reality knowable in its phenomena (which are nevertheless truth, in this relative sense) by man even apart from Christ. It is precisely God's grace in Jesus Christ which is the presupposition and limit of this self-knowledge and relative truth, even in the minds of those who do not know him. We are, to be sure, speaking here of relative, derived truth, which is set up by analogy to the uncreated truth which is in the act of God's grace and the relation of his being itself. There is no way from this derived truth upward to the real truth as it is in God. There is no way to build secular insights into human nature, though they may form a pattern of the truth about man as a created being, into a whole which will unlock the secrets of the real man in his destiny under God's election. It is when 'natural' knowledge attempts to construct a way to God, when it is not content to be relative and incomplete, that Barth takes sharp issue with it.

Yet this polemic against ideology, *Weltanschauung*, and natural theology turns out in this context to be the very instrument by which the independence and validity of secular, created truth is preserved, above all from the incursions of theologians! Barth makes this abundantly clear after he has described *die Grundform der Menschlichkeit* as existence in personal encounter, in the give and take, the listening to one another, the helping of and enjoyment of one another—a typical construct of natural ethics, though based on analogy with the co-humanity of Jesus Christ with all men. It is this ethical understanding of created humanity which, Barth maintains, may be known, perhaps better known, by the children of this world, even where there is no question of Christian revelation. Human nature is not destroyed by sin, and sin can never become a kind of second human nature.

'We have not joined in the frequent theological practice of pushing human nature first of all as far down as possible, in order then to place

229

what becomes of man by God's grace more effectively over against it. . . . When we see man in the light of the man Jesus, we must first of all simply let ourselves be told that there is a human nature which has been created as such by God, and which therefore is not evil but right.'[1]

It is *kein ehrliches Spiel* on the part of parsons and theologians to hold up human foibles and failings and perversities as human nature without Christ, in order thereby to present real humanity as only possible under the conditions of faith. The result is only scepticism on the part of the hearers of such a Gospel, who after all are human, and know well from experience how much real humanity there is in the world. The Church itself then becomes the place where man is not encountered and redeemed but misrepresented and alienated.[2]

Christians and non-Christians, therefore, share a common humanity, and, in accordance with the parallel we have already described of being and knowing, a common ability to know this humanity. Christians possess, by virtue of their special relation of faith to the Creator, no special knowledge in this field, save the understanding that the crown and root of humanity lies in no theory, no ideal of man whatever, but in the freedom of the human heart for the fellow man.

[1]III/2, p. 330. The whole of pp. 44 and 45, pp. 64–390 contains continual references to this theme of the continuity of created human nature by God's grace, despite sin, toward redemption.

[2]Ibid. pp. 329–41. This whole theme reflects a prior consideration of it by Dietrich Bonhoeffer in *Letters and Papers*, pp. 156 ff. Bonhoeffer pours his scorn on the religious 'exploitation of human weakness', the attempt to convince a mature world that it is immature, and healthy men that they are sick, thereby finding a point at which one can recommend to them the medicine of faith. 'Man may be a sinner, but by no means common or mean!' Bonhoeffer, in these letters, puts the problem of Christian evangelism more clearly than Barth has done anywhere, yet basically in harmony with Barth's insights: it is to confront a mature world which one respects as such, with Jesus Christ, by sharing the being of Christ in such a world. It is not to justify such a world in its sin, but to recognize that it is the strength and not the weakness of man where sin is to be found. 'Napoleon was not a sinner because he was a bad husband.' It is to recognize that this mature world is not religious in the old sense of dependence. Christ must come in a new way to it, first through those who live in it as 'non-religious Christians, then perhaps, as God gives us insight, through the 'non-religious' reinterpretation of theological concepts'. On this latter point Bonhoeffer believed Barth to have failed.

All this is being said, to be sure, from the perspective of faith and faith alone, from the perspective of response to absolute reality, about a relative and derived reality. The humanity here referred to is only a part, the created part, of the truth about man. It remains for faith alone to preach the Gospel of Christ the redeemer, in the knowledge of whom man understands his destiny as God's covenant partner, the depth of his sin, and his utter dependence on God's grace. Only in Christ can one know what love is, for all the free co-humanity described above is not yet fellowship in love, but only the created presupposition of love.

Nevertheless it is precisely this believer who is called by faith, most unswervingly to preserve the autonomy of that derived, relative truth about the phenomena of nature and human nature, which God has created and which exists as parable and analogy of his absolute truth. For man is created as *ein Gott-vernehmendes Wesen*—a God-hearing or -perceiving entity. The order of being and knowledge are parallel. God reveals himself in that he creates. Therefore *all* men are created as God-perceiving entities. When a man refuses to perceive God, when he turns his attention instead to general perception and abstract thinking divorced from God, this refusal to believe does not abrogate this quality of his nature, but turns it toward idols:

'The perceiving man is in the Bible concretely the sinful man, who as such would like to withdraw above all from God's perception of him, but who, in this desire, opposes his own real nature, and thus acts not reasonably, despite all his presumed wisdom and imagined rationality, but as a fool. He withers himself away, precisely in his reasonable nature. However this does not mean that he can change this nature. It itself then judges and condemns him. It is and remains directed toward God, even when a man refuses to believe it, even when he acts as if this were not so.'[1]

Barth underlines his point. God has created in man no general capacity for observation (*Wahrnehmung*) and thought (*Denken*), the two branches of perception, but only a capacity for perception of himself, which includes all else. This is healthy thinking and observation. Any other form is a '*Defizienzerscheinung*'.

This paradox is drawn as tightly as any in Barth's thinking. And

[1]III/2, pp. 483 ff.

yet we dare not forget his equal emphasis on both sides at once. The man who perceives and thinks in the realm of created nature and human nature, apart from God, does so as a man who has, so to speak, chosen unbelief, and thus he has tried to deny, but in fact has only misdirected, his faith. This is another way of saying that he observes and thinks as an ideologue and a sinner. *Yet* he can observe and think relative truths about human phenomena and those of nature. This perception stands, to be sure, in constant danger of being distorted by the misdirection of his central perception. He may, for instance, become a pure empiricist, denying finally any larger meaning, or a pure rationalist violating the concreteness of human reality. Both would be abstraction from the full task of perception, the one of observation alone, the other of thought alone. Nevertheless this man without faith remains a being who can be reminded with more or less success, of his distortions on this phenomenological level, whose conscience and sense for truth operate here more or less, with whom therefore a common search for relative truth is possible.

This defines the task of the Christian in this realm, of nature and humanity in general. Negatively, the very fact of his perception of the true God in faith, prevents him from imposing the abstractions of his own thought on this realm. This faith, which gives him such certain knowledge of God's grace, becomes daring confidence in his leading rather than certain knowledge, when the believer ventures into the world. It is this faith which tells him that all truth in this realm is phenomenological, that its test and standard in human relations is the welfare of the other human being and the development of human life together. To abandon this concrete response in humility would be to fall back into some form of religious ideology, whether it sought to control all human phenomena in a hierarchical system of grace and nature as in Roman Catholicism, or to stake out, as the Pietists do, a certain area of the human only, as that where religion rules.

Positively the Christian is the guardian of the objectivity and validity of phenomenological truth about humanity and nature, against all ideologies, because he knows more than others of its reliability, and its friendliness to man.

'In view of the absolute trustworthiness of the Creator and based therein, there is a relative trustworthiness also in Creation. . . . Only in faith (based not in the Creation but only in the Creator!) is there this confidence. In faith however there *is* this confidence. . . . It cannot wish to set limits to God. But it acknowledges the limits which God has set for his Creation as such.'[1]

No human law can guarantee this reliability—not even, Barth remarks, the law of contradiction in logic—but only the fact that God is reliable and has made his creation thus and not otherwise. For this reason however it is reliable. We need not think of possibilities, in logic or in human life, which lie beyond reality.

Secondly, the Christian knows that creation is friendly, and that it reflects everywhere like a mirror, the goodness of the Creator:

'If one were a child of one's father, one would recognize his house by many and ever more similarities to him. One would not confuse things by imagining that the house were the father; as if that which can only be a parable (*Gleichnis*) were the thing itself. One would hear everywhere the echo as an echo; and one would feel oneself in the middle of all that happens in this creation, not strange, but at home.'[2]

Therefore the Christian is called to be simply and truly human in a relative and practical way, objective, relative, realistic in his thinking, and perceptively helpful in his actions toward other men. He above all is free for this because he has no need to depend on human systems—of philosophy, or of politics—for the meaning of life. He can give proper weight to the abstractions of philosophy or of the social sciences, without falling into the temptation of the man without faith, to make reality and system of these abstractions. Theological anthropology

'. . . presupposes, then, that the real man is recognizable and has been recognized in the light of the Word and the revelation of God. It sees and understands, then, the phenomena which are recognizable to it in the form of simple human self-understanding, in the light of this Light. Thus it sees more modestly, less metaphysically, but for just this reason more exactly, more sharply, and more completely.'[3]

The Christian above all, because of Christ, can keep the real

[1]II/1, p. 603.   [2]III/3, p. 58.   [3]III/2, p. 241.

human being, and no ideal, conservative or revolutionary, which violates that human being, before his eyes.

Finally, the Christian is kept from turning his very theology into another philosophy, by the fact that he knows himself dependent on the historical act of God in Christ, and not on imparted wisdom. Man, as redeemed sinner, is not, even in faith, participant in all the mysteries of God. His 'certain knowledge', all the reasonableness of his faith, is still broken in his theology and his life as a believer. Therefore his theology must be fundamentally a report of what God has done for him, *Erzählung* (recounting), not a system of knowledge. It must tell a story of God's acts, which place man before the decision of obedience. But in no sense is this an 'explanation' of God. Theology remains, so to speak, the thought side of the act of response and obedience, whose source and completion is in God alone.[1]

Such are the lines of Barth's attempt to liberate the Christian faith once and for all, from the charge that it is one more ideology. When the reader of Barth steps back for a moment from the shadow of these bold and massive volumes to see the picture of their message whole, three reactions come to mind.

1.

The first of these is, that Karl Barth has made his case, as far as human words can make it, and theology can express it. He has produced a theology so completely dominated by its object, Jesus Christ, God and man, that whatever other criticisms may be brought against it, it cannot be accused of being one more reflection of and cover for human interests. Starting with the paradox in the Chalcedonian creed[2] Barth develops all his thinking in rigorous response to Christ alone, regardless of the claims which reason, ideals, principles, or any other inner consistency or drive of human life make in their own right upon him. No one is more conscious than he of the danger of ideology which lurks on every side of this enterprise. No one is more concerned to make his thought in no sense an explanatory system, but a reference to the mystery of Christ in whom the fullness of human life is bound up; in no sense

[1]III/3, pp. 332 ff.   [2]II/1, pp. 138, 152 f. *et al.*

234

a law for human life, but a pointing to the act of God's grace which calls forth free human response and decision.

But Barth does more. Precisely his most original presentations of the themes of Christian faith give us, sometimes for the first time in history, a clear understanding of the way in which Christ himself can be the reality which breaks through all human ideology. This was, indeed, the major task he set himself. He fulfilled it in a series of bold theological ventures, so radical toward customary habits of human thought, that generations to come will be called on to test and interpret them. Let us summarize those few of them which have a place in our study here:

A. The derivation of all reality, both act and being, from the central relation between God the Father, Son and Holy Spirit, and the description of this reality in all its relations in terms of God's historical act which is at once the basis of being and knowing, in Christ God for man and man for God. In this starting point, and in the analogy of relation which is built on it, Barth places the I-Thou relation at the very basis of reality. He eliminates generalized concepts, the abstractions of philosophy and ethics by which the relation between man and God, and between man and other men, are usually described, in favour of response to the concrete event of God's revelation which is his act. There is no more room in this thinking for the seed beds of ideology: the problem of being in itself and its attributes; the question of the structure of the Good in itself, or the Created Good, especially in society, apart from God's historical acts in redemption and salvation; the question of the meaning of change; and the question of the relation of human knowledge to human decision and act. Being becomes an attribute of the history of God's gracious acts: *esse sequitur operari*, Barth suggests, reversing the Scholastic formula.[1] It is like a tool, defined by the highest fulfilment of its purposes, not by its substance. The Good becomes what God has done and is doing in the fullness of Christ for men—a person in relation to us; only by way of commentary a commandment, and never a system or order. Change becomes not only history, but God's history; the time God has for us; the history of the covenant, accompanied—like a shadow to be

[1] II/1, p. 90.

235

accepted but not submitted to—by 'world history'. Human knowledge and decision become aspects of human response, dominated not by a system of principles, but by responsible relation to the other human being in the response of both to God, in whose relation to his Son this human relation is included, and to which it is analogous.

It was Karl Marx who flung down the gauntlet to theology on these points, for he thought on formally similar lines. For him being is material in dialectical conflict and motion, which for human being means the relations of production; the Good is response to the requirements of history in the light of its coming judgement and fulfilment in the classless society; change is the science of dialectics which carries in it the grace of certain victory until that time; human knowledge and act are one in the service of the demands of the revolutionary cause. Both Tillich and Berdyaev, though deeply impressed with this challenge, have in each case, like Marx himself, fallen back on an ideal picture of reality which violates the fullness of human historical life. Tillich's has been, so to speak, the philosopher's ideology, so convinced of the power of immanent spiritual being to interpret the ultimate concern of the world to itself, as to fail to come to grips with Communist reality. Berdyaev has carried a rebel personalist idealism to the point where freedom and an ideal communion in the spirit seem to consume creation and love in their fire. Yet Barth shares and develops fundamental insights which belong to both men. The concern for human freedom, which they both shared so passionately, finds itself again in Barth's unremitting fight against any other authority in thought or life, save that of a gracious God. Their existential concern to find true meaning in decision and action, becomes in Barth's theology an interpretation of the Trinity itself in its *Selbstkundgebung*. Tillich's search for a justification which reaches more deeply into man's being than any possibility of his doubt or sin (and parallel to it his search for a theonomous culture) is reflected over and over again in the way in which Barth describes the victory of Christ over the powers of evil, and the calling of the Church. And finally Berdyaev's Promethean rebellion against being, against creation itself and history in the realm of 'objectivization', in the name of a

236

transcendent communion of the spirit which should transform it—
that questionable theology which made him so acute an interpreter
of the Russian revolution—we find taken up in all the intensity of its
revolutionary fervour and depth, into Barth's rejection of the
analogia entis, the *Schöpfungsordnungen*, and historical science with
its object *Weltgeschichte*. Barth's theology has been tempered in the
fire of a rebellion against this world as thorough as Marx's or
Berdyaev's, resulting in a freedom from the world in the very act
of affirming it in Christ, more complete than either.

These thoughts however, lead us to the next points in our
summary.

B. The unqualified way in which Barth finds grace, electing and
redeeming grace such as is revealed in Jesus Christ, to be the
ground of creation, and the meaning of all history. 'It is not the
least of Karl Barth's services,' writes Otto Weber, that he has
closed the circle of creatureliness and salvation (*Geschöpflichkeit und
Heil*) so securely.'[1] Von Balthasar finds this massive doctrine of
election by grace also to be the centre, the victorious power, but
also the systematizing danger of Barth's theology.[2] Whether
inspired or dangerous, however, there is no doubt that the trium-
phant march of electing grace through the whole of Barth's dogmatics focuses the whole of human life on response to Jesus Christ
in a way unique in the history of theology. There have been liberal
theologians who have been as much enthralled by the nothingness
of sin beside the power of the love of God. As we shall see,
Barth errs in many of his ethical judgements in the direction of a
naïveté about the subtleties of sin in human behaviour which
parallels liberalism. But Barth is in no sense liberal precisely because
the whole of his thought rests on God's election, God's redeeming
grace, and in no sense on the capacities of a human nature from
within itself to know God or its own destiny; wholly on God's act,
and not at all on the harmonies of nature. The whole of Barth's
doctrine of grace is an attempt to bring out the Gospel, the dynamic
story of God's personal concern for man, his decision from all
eternity to seek partnership with man, his creation of man for this

[1]Otto Weber, *Karl Barth's Church Dogmatics* (London, 1953).
[2]Von Balthasar, *Karl Barth*, p. 200 and pp. 253 ff.

end, his bearing of man's rebellion and self-destruction, and thus his conquest of evil. Finally man responds to this history by the praise of his Maker and Redeemer and analogous action in relation to his fellow man until the day of final fulfilment. This is to be a positive alternative to any need, be it conservative or liberal, for importing structures of human thought to explain God's act or commandment. For when this importation happens, in the name of a sound doctrine of Creation over against Redemption, in order to take proper account of sin and the need for its control, in order to rescue the righteousness of God from being inundated by his grace, or perhaps, as with liberals, to prove the capacity of men to fulfil the law of love, the result is a theological system which limits man's understanding of his fellow man, and which tends to justify one group of men over against another. We have seen this demonstrated in the case of Emil Brunner, whose orders of creation based on Biblical sources and reason have led to a kind of idealism about the communal relations inherent in Swiss society, and to the subsumption of Communism under a principle of evil, 'totalitarianism', which fails to grasp the human reality which Communism is. Barth could also raise a question however to Reinhold Niebuhr's use of empiricism in thought and pragmatism in social ethics, as unideological methods. For each of these presupposes a more basic stable order. Is not Niebuhr thrown back into dependence on the truths and goodness in his own cultural background—which appears so vividly as ideological to those who have not shared this background—because he cannot share Barth's unqualified conviction about the victory of Christ and the all-creating grace of God?

Barth's doctrine of election, and his treatment of evil and sin in the light of it, remain his most vulnerable theological point. This study cannot discuss the general question as to whether such an absolutely Christological doctrine of being and revelation is in general admissible. We must say however that Barth has successfully raised one question for all other theologians, concerning the ideological nature of their thought. Can any theology successfully avoid justifying one group of men against another, and do full justice to the variety and concreteness of human relations, if it defines God the creator and lawgiver, love, justice, the relations of

Church and State, and above all sin and the means of its control, otherwise than by the light which Christ sheds upon them?

c. Barth and Reinhold Niebuhr are at one in the manner in which they affirm the relative goodness of human reason, and human life in society, on its own level and in its own time. To be sure they approach this task from different angles—Barth from a doctrine of utter grace against the background of utter crisis, Niebuhr from his struggles against social injustice and the ideologies which justify it. But both men are concerned in the same way to liberate science from the shackles of all world views for its relative task of elucidating the realities of human life in a relative way, helpful to human action. Both find in philosophies and sciences, and in the thought and behaviour of social groups and ordinary men, a dialectical struggle between a basic sense for humanity and respect for the mysteries of ultimate truth, and the distortions and conflicts which come from placing human systems and interests on a level with God. Both share, on the other hand, a critical attitude toward the claims of religious groups and dogmas to dominate culture and society with their own ideologies. Both men stand over against the desire of Brunner to lay down theologically derived laws and ideals for society; the tendency of Hromadka to find the hand of God in the movement of world history; Berdyaev's idealistic demands on and mystic hopes for culture; and Tillich's mixture of theology and history in the concepts of *kairos* and theonomy. Both men, finally, affirm the Christian's responsible involvement in the world in basically the same terms—sober, self-critical, pragmatic (the word can be used of Barth as well) co-operation with fellow men for the best possible service of the general welfare, keeping a strong guard against every sacrifice of concrete men to an idea, a system, or one social group's interest.

There are of course differences. They are fundamentally differences in emphasis. Barth finds in the relativity of culture and society—in its dependence on grace, in the freedom of revelation from it, in the transcendence of the Church over it and in the hope of an *eschaton* when all things will be made new—the necessary freedom and perspective for the Christian. Only thus oriented, can he avoid anxiety for the world, dependence on it, commitment with more than just relative responsible judgement and action, to one of its structures. Barth seeks a kind of responsibility in the world which can be exercised with equal gratitude to God in any society, bond or free. In this mood and emphasis, based on his theology of grace, he differs from Niebuhr, and could well question Niebuhr, at two points.

First, is there not, in Niebuhr's mind, a confusion about natural theology? Niebuhr flaunts his acceptance of a relative natural law, and the capacity of natural man for understanding his relativity and sin.[1] Yet there is still for Niebuhr a basic discontinuity between this and God's revelation. There is ideology whereby man covers his sin from himself and justifies it to others. There is no natural truth for him which is incorruptible and no aspect of man unqualifiedly good. He is repeatedly critical of Brunner's undialectical ethics out of creation and law.[2] Grace must create its own point of contact with man in Niebuhr's thought as well as in Barth's; and this is not altered by the fact that man from the fullness of his being recognizes this grace as his own redemption afterward, according to both men. Is not the real difference between the two men a difference about the manner of Christ's revelation, and the balance between his conquest of evil and the persistence of that evil, rather than about revelation and natural knowledge itself?[3]

[1]Cf. *The Children of Light and the Children of Darkness*, pp. 69–79; *The Nature and Destiny of Man*, Vol. II, pp. 263 ff.

[2]Niebuhr's main point (*Nature and Destiny of Man*, Vol. II, pp. 195 ff.) is that Brunner follows the traditional Lutheran separation of Law from Gospel to such an extent that Law becomes a thing of only negative value in itself, capable only of order and without moral tension toward a higher and more imaginative justice. Hence Brunner becomes a conservative, dignifying the *Schöpfungsordnungen* with more divine sanction than any 'natural' order deserves, and isolating love from its task as leaven. Barth has criticized the *Schöpfungsordnungen* from the same point of view, with relation to the pride of human knowledge involved in them. His attempt to put Gospel before Law (II/2 § 36, pp. 564–611) and his recent political writings run in the same direction as Niebuhr. The latter is compelled to admit in a later book (*Faith and History*, p. 220) that Barth is doing a better job of social ethics than Brunner, when he compares Brunner's *Gerechtigkeit* with Barth's *Christengemeinde und Bürgergemeinde*.

[3]Niebuhr develops his theory of the relation of general to special revelation, which he equates with natural and specially revealed knowledge of God, in *The Nature and Destiny of Man*, Vol. I, Ch. 5. His point with

Secondly, is life in joyful response to God's grace, as Barth describes it, really irresponsible toward the seriousness of human problems and responsibilities, an aeroplane view of life, as Niebuhr charges? Is it really responsible toward even the most serious problems of society and man, not to live from a grace which is victorious over them? Does not the danger always lurk that the fellow man, who may live with different problems, or see the same ones in the light of other factors, may become an enemy, not because of history's inevitable tragedy, but because one has oneself taken one's own conviction more seriously than God allows? To pose the question, what policy the non-Communist world should adopt toward Soviet Russia from the perspective of the United States, Korea, India, and Colombia will make this question con-

---

relation to knowledge, which he later directs specifically against Barth, is that the human mind tends on the one hand to erect finite centres of meaning as absolute, and on the other to reach out toward mystical absolutes which are empty of meaning, to which, however, the category of sin does not apply. Revelation must therefore engage in a conversation with the natural man, using his natural tendency to reach beyond himself and his interests, against his sin, as a point of contact for the Gospel, and for responsible living. He accuses Barth: (*a*) of ethical relativism leading to a social policy for the catacombs and not for responsible living in the relativities of daily life; (*b*) of epistemological positivism which, without commerce with other cultural disciplines, ends in an allegorical literalism about the Bible unrelated to any real meanings or real history; (*c*) of an arbitrary doctrine of grace which refuses to see the coherences which are present in natural man's capacity for justice and sense of absolute or ultimate meaning. To this must be said:

1. Niebuhr does not seem sufficiently to understand, or perhaps he does not sufficiently trust, his own faith, and the extent to which it is a faith based on revelation alone. His natural theology, accompanied by his brilliant dialectical insight into its pretensions and limits, is 'natural' only by his own definition. It would not be recognized as such by most other defenders of natural knowledge's ability to lead us to God. There may be a difference of opinion between Barth and Niebuhr about the nature of mysticism, but Niebuhr depends on mysticism for revealed truth as little as does Barth, while Barth engages (cf. III/2) in the same kind of dialectical appreciation and criticism of non-Christian understanding as does Niebuhr.

2. Niebuhr's charges against Barth are every one of them wrong. Niebuhr has had to imagine a caricature of Barth in order to place himself in the middle between him and Aquinas. Niebuhr completely fails to

crete. In such a world as ours, Barth's way of affirming human responsibility may prove more adequate than Niebuhr's.

D. Barth remains throughout the crisis theologian. This note must be remembered in order to keep his doctrine of electing grace in perspective, as *grace* and not as nature. Barth shares with Niebuhr, and with Berdyaev (excepting the mystic nature of his ideal for Russia), that sharply radical approach to the structures of human society and thought to which Marx first challenged the world. That rebellion against 'Legitimacy' which we found in the *Römerbrief* continues today in the character of Barth's freedom over against tradition and earthly authority, a freedom which brings much of his thought closer to Anglo-Saxon thinking than to that of Germany. He draws the line and declares a conflict whenever he

---

grasp the inclusive, affirming nature of Barth's Christological doctrine of grace: that in Christ created humanity is fulfilled, not arbitrarily limited and refined; that because of this the Christian naturally rejoices at all the positive insights which are produced about man apart from Christ. When Barth attributes these to the working of God's grace in creation he refers not to some arbitrary irrational force working in the darkness, but to the ground of all creation and the source of all reason. Barth furthermore cannot be accused of refusing conversation with secular sciences and culture. On the contrary he seeks to lay a foundation for this conversation on which the Christian will not for ever be threatening the autonomy of the secular thinker by leading him to his boundaries and pointing out inadequacies which demand his importing theological premises into his work. This can only be done, however, without surrendering the autonomy of faith and theology as well, if theology deals with another realm of reality than the secular science, and says 'No' to science's and culture's incursions into that realm. Niebuhr and Barth are most deeply alike in their genuine *theological* engagement in the world in just this sense.

3. Niebuhr remains different from Barth in the *balance* of his thinking and the areas which he feels it important to define and explore. Whole areas of detail which are helpful to the Christian in the task of apologetics and ethical action, are present in his thought and missing in Barth. Barth on the other hand seeks to clarify the mysteries of God's gracious act itself, the meaning of faith itself, and the relations of men in the light of it, an occupation which Niebuhr regards with a kind of holy fear, lest the believer on these heights slip into the most disastrous of all pride. Each is, understandably, somewhat annoyed at the other's preoccupation. But this writer ventures the prediction that future generations will overrule Niebuhr's attempt to set himself apart from Barth's theology, even if this means that some of Niebuhr's own theological ideas must be redefined.

finds an attempt, especially in Christian disguise, to give information about the meaning and destiny of human life, or to demand an unqualified allegiance, other than in Christ; wherever, in short, he sees the danger of an ideology. His positive development of the doctrines of man, and of ethics in family and group relations, have sought in detail to sift out the human relations involved and to free them from each fetter which an abstract morality or a false allegiance (to *Volk*, language, traditions about birth control etc.) might place upon them.

2.

Barth has made his case, as a theology free of ideology. And yet one has the feeling that he has made it only because Christ has made it for him, much as Marx made his case in the nineteenth century because the development of the relations of production in early capitalism made it for him. The comparison is perhaps belittling. Yet for the sake of a different perspective we must carry it further. For Barth has carried the same kind of criticism and assertion into theology, which Marx used in founding his scientific socialism. Its basis is not to take up the challenge of the outsider, but rather to reorient the whole of the believer's thought and will so completely around the new object that he will be unable to think except within the circle of its dominance. This is, for Barth, to think theologically, for Marx, to think dialectically. This thought does not submit itself to outside standards of logic or description of reality, though it may use insights borrowed from without. It is wholly captive to the task of describing the action of the object. So also decision, action, response to the environment, is determined only by obedience to the object, and by the light shed from there on the world around.

For Marx, of course, the object was a pseudo-science of social salvation, the ideology of the proletariat, and a destructive illusion. For Barth the object is the gracious God revealed in Jesus Christ, and we who are Christians must grant him that no less than a total surrender to that Object will really meet the challenge which the anti-faith of Marxist Communism presents. Barth is right in making this claim on our whole mind and action in the name of Jesus Christ. He convicts most of us of living, in fact, in two conflicting

worlds, to both of which we give allegiance; of having two conflicting ways of thought and of feeling righteous about the doubts
which arise from the conflicts. We do in fact find ourselves torn in
human allegiances, for we love our families, our communities, and
our traditions not only for Christ's sake but in themselves, or rather
for our sakes. The question remains however, is it *possible* so to
believe and give ourselves, so to think exclusively in the freedom
which Christ gives, in practice? Can any other man successfully
present us with this challenge? Barth has come as near to this
success as any theologian since Paul. Yet we are left with questions,
questions which we believe to be theological in Barth's sense of the
word, yet they cast doubt on the success of the very enterprise to
which he has called himself and us.

A. Is not the ethical indicative of the redeemed man, the claim
that we only know creation and our fall from it in sin, in the light
of our redemption and the reduction of sin to a kind of impossible
possibility, a concealment of our real position as men before God?
It will not have escaped the reader that Barth falls into a kind of
ontological confusion when he speaks of sin and what it does to
human being. He is so concerned to present to us the drama of
God's grace in every stage of creation and history, that he cannot
grant that sin and evil *are.* They remain rather in the realm of
rejected possibility. Yet in that realm they still partake of a
shadowy, and sometimes only too substantial, personality, power,
in short, being. Man's being cannot be destroyed by sin, though
man can rebel against his being and attempt its destruction. Yet
man *is* sinner in his sin. The sin is not accidental but essential to
him. It is not merely the lack of something. Christ must bring him
—Barth uses Tillich's word—a new being.

This is partly a reflection of Barth's sovereign independence of
philosophical consistency. As if Being were anything in and of itself,
apart from the action of God whose instrument it is! But it is partly
the confusion resulting from Barth's attempt to maintain the utter
grace of Divine sovereignty and the utter sovereignty of Divine
grace. In short, it is the confusion about sin and evil resulting from
Barth's exclusive concentration on Christ. How does Barth's
Christocentric doctrine of election work out in the heart of the

believer? Does this confusion continue there? Is the human response to the word of this complete grace only joy, repentance, gratitude and love for the neighbour; or is it, as Niebuhr suspects, slackened ethical tension, less responsibility for the neighbour, and failure any longer to understand the depth of his problems and suffering? What happens to the believer when he reads the marvellous way in which God weaves the destinies of the elected and the rejected together for good, even for the good of the rejected? Only rejoicing in the mercies of God, or also a kind of sovereign indifference to the relative distinctions of good and evil in politics and society?

In other words, is it possible to say with Barth, that our very knowledge of God begins with the victory of redemption? Are we worthy of the freedom this gives us? Or is the experience of moral struggle and suffering under the law not necessary, to make us duly sensitive to our fellow men and duly responsible moral agents, before the final word of forgiveness and redemption is spoken over our efforts?[1]

B. Is Barth's absolute division between relative, phenomenological truth about humanity and absolute truth about God and man, sufficient protection of the dignity of relative truth, including its power to compel moral decision, against the absolutists of faith? This again is a question of what happens to the believer who reads Barth and accepts what he says. It again is a question whether the believer is worthy of the freedom—this time the freedom from principles of truth and goodness—which Barth claims for him in Christ. What happens when he is liberated from the very need for explaining and justifying his faith, and from the requirement of ethical behaviour according to principles? A greater appreciation of

[1]Cf. not only Niebuhr, but also Dietrich Bonhoeffer, *Letters and Papers from Prison*, p. 79; 'It is only when one knows the ineffability of the Name of God that one can utter the name of Jesus Christ. It is only when one loves life and the world so much that without them everything would be gone, that one can believe in the resurrection and a new world. It is only when one submits to the law that one can speak of grace, and only when one sees the anger and wrath of God hanging like grim realities over the head of one's enemies that one can know something of what it means to love and forgive them. I don't think it is Christian to want to get to the New Testament too soon and too directly.'

all truth wherever found? A more sensitive ethical insight? Or the erection of a new law of his own in both these areas, an orthodoxy bearing the name of Barth?

3.

These are questions for which Barth can provide no further theological answers. Theologically he has challenged us, as far as words can go, with the answer to ideological thinking—the free grace of God in Jesus Christ. Yet in the light of our questions we must differ with Barth at one fundamental point. No theology is justified by itself. It is not an independent science, but a part of the actual response of man to God's revelation, a reflection on that response which becomes true or false according to the way it operates in the apologetic and the ethical situations in which Christians find themselves. This need not violate Barth's basic premise; for no other standard for the Christian's decision need be present than his knowledge of what God has done for him and his world in Jesus Christ. But it is here, in the quality of an ethical decision, and in personal contact with an unbeliever, where the validity of Barth's, or any other, theology is truly tested for its power to liberate the believer from ideology.

It might be well therefore to conclude this chapter with an application of Barth's theology to political ideology in practice, by one of his followers, Helmut Gollwitzer. Gollwitzer comes out of the German Confessing Church struggle with Nazism, and left-wing socialist politics. He was convinced, as he went into a Russian prison in 1945, that the collapse of Nazism was the sign for a new appraisal of Russian Communism, an openness to new possibilities which history might have opened up in and through this hitherto closed but nevertheless culture-building ideological system.[1] His

[1]Helmut Gollwitzer, *Und führen wohin Du nicht willst* (Munich, 1951), pp. 126–33; English translation, *Unwilling Journey* (London, 1953), pp. 117–23. This whole book contains a Christian response to the Communist challenge in a fullness of experience and reflection on it, which one is at a loss to capture in a formal study, or to divide under headings. The reader is urged to read the whole book as illustrative of all the points in this chapter, or, if he prefers, to read it for its own sake instead of this chapter!

entire experience in Russian camps was one long attempt at openness to the Communist based on Christian freedom from the prejudices of another ideology. He finds that the Marxist challenge to the Church hits the mark at two points:

A. The Church was incapable, in the nineteenth century, of grasping the true significance of the rise of the proletariat, because of its long heritage, going back to Constantine, of association with earthly power. Christianity had helped to create and maintain, through its responsibilities in education and the formation of culture, the whole structure of 'the West'.

'Out of this unexpected reward from the world (the Constantinian conversion) grew not only new responsibilities for the Church which she could not avoid, but also the price she was forced to pay, in having to make peace from her side with the world. She renounced largely her task as the great disturber, the creator of unrest, the prophetic advocate of the lowly and the oppressed; she sanctified the existing order. Thus she became incapable of recognizing her new task.'[1]

So it was Marx and Engels who were able to see the world from the proletarian standpoint, and to discover in this new perspective the emptiness of bourgeois idealism, and the problematic character of the whole Christian cultural structure of tradition. It should have been clear to Christians as well, had they followed the way of their Lord into a proletarian existence.[2]

B. Marxism shows up the degree to which Christianity has adapted itself to a contradiction of its basic faith, in the faith of the Enlightenment. This part of the bourgeois state of *das christliche Abendland*—its faith in scientific reason and the infinite capacities of the natural man—has been drawn out to its logical consequences, made absolute, and turned against the Christian faith. Thus the opposition is one of faith, and therefore irreconcilable. But Christians will not be able to make this clear as long as their defence of their faith is based on reference to this same scientific reason and natural man, and to the bourgeois society which he has built.

[1]'Christentum und Marxismus', in the magazine *Unterwegs*, 1951, Heft 1, p. 10.
[2]Gollwitzer draws heavily on Dirks, 'Marxismus in christlicher Sicht'. See pp. 104 n., 105–7.

Gollwitzer strikes unique notes in this analysis: his appreciation of what it means to call Communism another faith, and his sense of continuing responsibility for the culture and structure of the West, even after they have been stripped of every ideological pretension, simply because this culture is serviceable to human beings, especially in comparison to Communism. Therefore his development of Christian witness in freedom from ideology toward Communism, bears a somewhat different tone from that of Barth himself.

A. The Christian is basically free from both of the great world powers today. He serves neither fundamentally, but only his new master, who has ransomed him from all other lords. No compulsion of self-interest, fear, or lesser loyalty can determine him. 'A Christian', Gollwitzer defines simply, 'is a slave who belongs to someone else.'

B. The Christian cannot allow that any conflict in this world is absolute, in the light of the fact that the one great antithesis— between the sinner and God—has been overcome by Christ's reconciliation.

'What can all the other antitheses that surround him be then? They are *either* (especially when they are absolute antitheses) antitheses of unredeemed humanity, seething in the hatred of their own religions and ideologies, their own nationalisms, and so on. As such they are none other than different forms in which unredeemed man pretends to be righteous, crusades of self-idolization and self-redemption. . . . *Or* they are antitheses which, in spite of his reconciliation, Christ has allowed to continue, just as he let the old world continue after his resurrection, and which are present, even in the Church. . . . They have been rendered harmless. The cleavage is no longer final; it can no longer prevent brotherhood—on the contrary it kindles brotherhood.'[1]

To be sure these antitheses remain real, and the Christian does not simply stand above them. He lives *in* the West or *in* the East. Gollwitzer explicitly disavows the implicit political neutralism in Barth's way of repudiating political ideologies. But the friend-foe attitude is no longer his standard for action. 'The antithesis never

[1]'Der Christ zwischen Ost und West' in *Evangelische Theologie*, October, 1950; tr., *The Christian between East and West* (Ecumenical Study Document, World Council of Churches, Geneva, 1951), p. 2.

cancels out the common features; the Christian does not lose sight of his fellow man by calling him his "enemy".'[1] Hence the Christian is able to see these relative antitheses judiciously and without illusions. He refuses to endow them with 'an obscure cloud of moralism'.

c. The Christian takes as his task a realistic reconciliation: a reconciliation which does not underestimate the conflict or the enemy, in this case Communism with its strategy, yet does not cease from the task of struggle for peace which involves the conversion of the enemy, not his defeat.

D. The Christian seeks the welfare of the city, in East or West. Gollwitzer however, draws out of this responsibility not only an opposition to ideologies and defence plans, but also the possibility of a responsible resistance to tyranny under certain circumstances, and responsibility for defence of the relative values and of the opportunity to engage in more positive acts of reconstruction and service in the West.

It is Gollwitzer, therefore, out of his experience with the ideological problems of both the Communist and non-Communist worlds, who brings us closer than even Barth himself, to the experience of Christians in Eastern Germany.[2] Here the problem of ideological conflict is central for the Christian—even more central than the problem posed by the police state as such. For Communism presents itself here in such unmistakable terms as a religion of salvation (*Heilslehre*), claiming the whole allegiance of man, as we shall describe in more detail below, that the critical problem of

---

[1] Ibid. p. 4.

[2] It must not be overlooked that the men whose writings are here quoted are one and all Lutherans by confessional background, and that their theology shows the influence not only of Luther, but of other teachers as well as Barth. I take the liberty here of describing their ideas as an extension and critique of Barth's own because his thought has so permeated the church circles to which these men belong. Not only his political but also his theological leadership during the Nazi time and before mean that certain basic attitudes, e.g. that toward natural theology and revelation, toward Christology, and toward ideology, which he has formulated, are shared by all of them, over against, for example, the more strictly 'confessional' Lutheran theology of the Erlangen school.

daily life for the Christian becomes that of thinking as a Christian in a world where every source of information is served to him with the demand that he take a stand with relation to it, based on presuppositions which are alien to his faith. Here he is no longer confronted with the appeal to his bad conscience as a religious ideologue alone, but with this appeal as part of a total onslaught on his mind, against which he must fight for his existence in any sort of independent thought or decision.

Yet precisely here Barth's insights have borne their richest fruits. For those who have learned from him find not only a Communist ideology in this situation, but also a confusion of other ideologies, bred of resentment and reaction against oppression. Elements of German nationalism—in its old imperial, or its Nazi form—of religious and political conservatism, and even of revolutionary idealism combine in one loose union around the two poles of hatred of the present government to the point of complete inner emigration, and hope for the day of 'liberation'. This ideology may express itself in acts of occasional terror and sabotage, or in that extra degree of subservience to the government which comes from its lively and totally futuristic eschatology: hope for the day when the armies of the West will march.[1] This ideology they find they must also resist as Christians, the more vigorously because it is the greater temptation of the two. It is not only a cultural substitute for response to and faith in God's victory in Christ, but it is at once irresponsible in its attitude toward human beings, and finally unstable. It is based—the very definition of religion in Feuerbach—on the projection of human wish-dreams into reality.

The end product of this is nihilism, a state of mind as hard to describe as it is real. It is that disillusion with all questions of truth and lie, right and wrong, which has resulted from too frequent deception of the human spirit by one ideology after another. It is scepticism over against every human value and human being, which combines an inner loneliness and withdrawal, with an outward

[1] For a Christian expression of this general point of view see Hans Köhler, *Zur geistigen und seelischen Situation der Menschen in der Sowjetzone* (Bonner Berichte—Bundesministerium für gesamtdeutsche Fragen, Bonn, 1952).

conformity to whatever power is at hand. One eastern writer regards Communism 'only as an extreme attempt to ban and drive out nihilism by (a movement) under the same atheistic and nihilistic stigma.'[1] And many an example could illustrate the fact that one of the basic spiritual problems among Communists as well as among the people as a whole, is not the wrong faith, but this nihilistic lack of faith which covers a broken conscience and lost spirit with conformity to the power of the time. Here we have the counterpart in life of that final rebellion, that final despair, which Barth sensed in Nietzsche and existentialism, and which he tried to meet by finding this very scepticism toward all human enterprise both expressed and answered in the Word of God. Analysis of the East German situation brings out some of the earlier more dialectical themes of Barth's theology.

The Christian answer however draws more on the later Christocentric Barth. There is, to follow the writer we have quoted above, no way out of this ideological dilemma in the development of a Christian world view. Pietistic abandonment of the world to the evil in it is impossible not only because of Communist criticism but because 'doubt rises again and again in our own selves, out of the depths of our natural existence'.[2]

The Christian who tries to emigrate out of the world realizes that he carries the world in himself, even while he leaves the outside world to the victory of ideological powers. The attempt to reject in principle every attack on Christianity, to make of it a body of knowledge and practice to be defended whole and at every point, is equally useless. It rests on a secret lack of faith: the fear that one criticism taken seriously would shatter faith itself and that one concession of power or privilege by the Church would shatter its power and the power of God. But on the other side, to adopt simply the standards of criticism which the Marxist accuser himself presents, to attempt to prove by adaptation, by 'progressive' Christianity, that Christianity is harmonious with a Communist society,

[1] Günter Jacob, *Das Licht scheint in der Finsternis* (Stuttgart, 1954), p. 68. Dr Jacob is General Superintendent of the Church in East Brandenburg, Soviet Zone.
[2] Ibid. p. 48.

is also hopeless and suicidal.[1] It has its notorious predecessors in the 'German-Christians' of Nazi times and the alliance of throne and altar in the nineteenth century.

There remains only one possibility:

'We Christians will have to listen seriously to the reproaches and accusations which the public prosecutors of different systems and worldviews continually hold before us, to hear therein the question, how far we all share the guilt that such distortions of our Christian existence can be publicly propounded. . . . Finally all the accusing speeches of all the public prosecutors pale before that accusation which the Christian congregation perceives ever again from its own message. Before the Biblical message we Christians all stand with final seriousness as the accused; as those who ever and again obscure and distort the illuminating power of this message by the guilt of our theoretical falsification of Christian truth and our practical failure as Christians.'[2]

Christ alone is the real accuser. By him and him alone the Christian is finally questioned and all the Communist questions refer to his. So the dialogue between Christians and Communists must go on, but in Christ who seeks out both Christian and Communist in his grace. The nihilist finds his spirit met and overcome in the condemned and rejected Christ, who is yet God and Lord.

[1]The fate of 'progressive' Christianity is so pitiful in East Germany as to create wonder at its relative success in Hungary, Czechoslovakia, and China. Not only did the Communist-dominated Eastern Christian Democratic Union fail to capture more than 2 per cent of the pastors, it has had its line of propaganda specifically counteracted from above and has lost some of its most active leaders by arrest and condemnation. Its main ideological effort was *Christlicher Realismus*, a series of twenty-two theses and the supporting speeches, which repudiated Marxist materialism, but recognized a tradition of social revolution, going from Jesus to Marx and Lenin and the present day national front, in the struggle against imperialism and opposition to its aggressions. Two pamphlets however have appeared since, translated from the Russian, which completely contradict this line: Kolonitzki, *Kommunistische und religiöse Moral* and P. Pawjolkin, *Der religiöse Aberglaube und seine Schädlichkeit* (Berlin, 1954). Both have been circulated independently of the C.D.U. Both emphasize the absolute incompatibility of Christian faith and Communism doctrine, and point out the task of Communists to work for the elimination of superstition. Both have been made study material in Communist youth groups.

[2]Jacob, op. cit., p. 56.

'The Christian today can only be a Christian who goes through the fire zones of our day, through the crater of nihilism and through the explosions of Communism; overcoming them in himself in the light of Jesus Christ. As the Christian of the New Testament was a Christ-conquered Jew or a Christ-conquered Gentile, so the Christian today can only be a Christ-conquered Nihilist or a Christ-conquered Communist.'[1]

Therefore the Christian is first of all open to the fellow human being who is a Communist, out of his very freedom from fear of his ideological attack:

'Our freedom' writes another Christian out of the same background,

'consists of the fact that we love our brother here and now, that we offer him truth, time, and much understanding, even when our openness delivers us into his hands and we have no more control over the possible results. We show how bound we are when we take the Marxist uniform of the Communist propagandists too seriously, instead of speaking to them from the beginning in the certainty that here God is sending his children, who bear his image and for whom Christ died, into our house.'[2]

'We stand in conversation with the Communists as human beings,' another has put it, 'on the basis of the "No" which we say to their ideology.' It is precisely this 'No' which creates a genuine encounter by removing the Christian from the field of the Communist's manipulation. It stands together with openness for the man himself. The implications of this encounter, and its results, we come to below.

Secondly, the Christian becomes, in an ideologized society, the custodian of direct, factual, un-ideologized truth and human relations:

'The Church orders men to one another in such a way that their activity remains activity among men who are all under the judgement of God. She knows of God's love to man, and through it she becomes a living community of free men to whom God has granted and secured justice and honour by his love. The Gospel makes these men in their

[1]Jacob, op. cit., p. 63.
[2]Quoted from 'Christian Witness in East Germany' (Anonymous), in *Christianity and Crisis*, 25th May, 1954, p. 68.

public responsibility free for the courage to see with their eyes, to hear with their ears, to judge objectively and to use their own understanding.'[1]

Here the same theme which Gollwitzer develops in different ways in the West, appears in the East against its special background. It is not easy to maintain this witness in the face of a total ideology. An ideology threatens constructive work. 'When the ideologist builds a road, it serves first of all not its reasonable purpose. Its first use is to increase the convincing power of the Idea.'[2] It also threatens the worker who does not accept the idea. 'We live,' writes the author we are quoting, 'from the inconsistencies of the ideology.'[3] Yet in some ways the East German Christian sees himself less threatened, or less tempted, by ideological thinking than his western compatriot. One exhortation put it thus:

' "Little children, keep yourselves from idols" warns the first epistle of John. Our idols are all too recognizable to be able to falsify our faith or teachings (although they are dangerous enough for our temptable flesh, for our honour and goods, for our freedom and life). Your idols are far more dangerous. They are, if I mistake not, loved, honoured, and respected to a large degree within Christendom itself. All of these idols, really all of them, lie here among us in dust and ashes (although for them we have new ones). All that we once trusted and relied on, that we loved and valued, that we grew up in and never wanted to leave; all of this failed to hold in the time of temptation. And this time did not first come over us in 1945. One doesn't die for the idol of liberal democracy; one doesn't even suffer for it! Still less for "Christianity"; and for a Christian culture least of all. Where have the once holy ideas among us, of truthfulness, free opinion, legality, gone to? The Communist acid has dissolved them all, and shown that life in this bourgeois-liberal-Christian atmosphere of the nineteenth century is already undermined and inwardly finished, even when it goes on a while outwardly.'[4]

The Christian therefore must bear witness to a sober factual truth and human relation which is free of the structure of inherited

[1]Martin Fischer, *Die öffentliche Verantwortung des Christen Heute* (Berlin, 1952). The lecture was delivered at the Synod of the Evangelical Church in Germany in Elbingerode (Soviet Zone), October, 1952.

[2]Ibid. p. 21.

[3]Ibid. p. 22.

[4]Gottlieb Zonesius, 'Die armen Verwandten' in *Unterwegs*, 1952, Heft 4, p. 201.

cultural ideals, even while he seeks to reaffirm some of the values of that tradition independently of it. In teaching and learning his subject free of the Marx-Leninist framework, in bearing witness to the duty of justice even in courts where justice has disappeared, in advocating, at risk, the cause of reasonable production and human relations on the farm and in industry against the almighty Plan— in such acts as these the Christian is called to pursue his unideological calling and witness, and thus to commend his faith in such a Communist society as Eastern Germany. It is a witness which owes much to the background of Barth's theology.

It is also both an extension and a correction of Barth's theology into the heat of the encounter with Communism. It is an extension and intensification of his attempt to free the Word of God from every human *Weltanschauung*. It becomes a matter of life and death to the Church in a Communist land to be able to speak and understand in a way which falls into the patterns of no political ideology, whether Communist, or anti-Communist. But this witness is also a correction of Barth, for the centre of its emphasis is on the problem of encounter, the problem of apologetics and ethics, rather than on theology itself. The churchmen in East Germany whom we have quoted, and those of their circle, are, in their way, even more critical of ideological thinking than is Barth himself, and more suspicious of the ideological elements which may lie in all thinking, on that level where the Christian lives, works, and encounters others in society. 'I would like,' writes one, 'to indicate everything which provides the background for our decisions by the *terminus technicus* "western thinking and feeling".' He meant by that the whole tradition through which the Gospel had been applied in his background, to daily life. His thinking cannot help but be influenced by a compound of Barth's polemic against natural theology and the Communist questions to the Church as to whether it is in reality a 'tool of western imperialism'. For him the concepts, freedom, democracy, 'Christianity', Antichrist, true and false religion, and even conscience, have become of questionable content. He sees them misused by both Communist and anti-Communist. His thinking tends to lack that joyful abandon with which Barth can call Christians to co-operate with other men in discovering the relative truth about humanity, can develop a series of practical proposals for the policy of a democratic state out of his theological responsibility,[1] and inform the Christian that not only is he free from all other *Weltenschauungen*, but he has no need of one for himself, to guide his service in the world.[2] These ideas are good and right, but the problems arise when they are applied. What can a Christian say to the farmer, or how can he act as a farmer toward Communist land reform, so that he knows his actions to be a pure application of the good news of the Gospel to the task of living with the neighbour, and not tainted by ideological elements out of his feudal or bourgeois past? How can he answer Communist ideas about education, economics or politics without setting forth a 'Christian world view' and giving way to the pride of absolutizing his partial perspective? In each concrete decision the question becomes acute for him, how far he is witnessing to the Gospel, and how far to something ideological; how far he points in his actions toward the victory of Christ's love, and how far he perpetuates human divisions. Here is where the helpfulness of the answer to ideological thinking, which Barth has worked out so well in theory, is tested in practice.

[1]Cf. *Christengemeinde und Burgergemeinde* (Zürich, 1946), pp. 15 ff. Tr. in *Against the Stream* (London, 1954), pp. 34 ff.

[2]*Dogmatik*, III/3, pp. 64 f.

6

HISTORY AND POLITICS:
BARTH AND HIS CRITICS

W E must ask, therefore, in this chapter, how Barth applies his theological insight to the problems of society at those points where Marxism presents its challenge. The question of history is the dynamic of this application, and the question of politics (for, as we have seen, Barth has little to say about economics) is its static, relational aspect.

1. CHRISTIAN ESCHATOLOGY: THEORY AND PRACTICE

The challenge which Marx presented to other views of history was the challenge of a radical dynamic which changes society— a revolutionary eschatology for a revolutionary world. For him the movement of history was an inevitable and a redemptive force, the source of hope. It was directly linked to a strategy for combatting present social evil, guiding change in society, and forming culture in a society whose ties with the past have been broken. To all of this Barth's thought presents the same kind of formal parallel which we have already seen.

But Barth is confronted with a formidable array of theological critics as well as Marx. Tillich, as we have seen, finds Barth indifferent to the heights and depths of the historical process, because the latter will grant to world history no divine meaning of its own save in the light of God's act toward man in Christ—the *Bundesgeschichte*. He finds in Barth's refusal to accept the idea of a secondary *kairos*, and of theonomous periods, in his projection of the *Bundesgeschichte* and the *Weltgeschichte* more or less on parallel if interacting lines toward the *eschaton*, an indifference to culture and history which cannot be meaningful or creative. In the other direction Hromadka offers to Barth the picture of a line of God's history and of world history which cross, and occasionally run for a while together, even though they have each their own destinies, meanings and dynamics. He proposes the idea that the Christian shall say 'Yes' to a piece of world history, the downfall of the bourgeoisie and the rise of Communist power, in these temporary terms, on the basis of a theology which claims to follow Barth's. Niebuhr accuses Barth of having taken up this option, of being so indiscriminately enamoured of redemption that the tensions of relative responsibility no longer weigh on him, allowing him to accept the most flagrant injustice as a witness to the grace of God, so long as that injustice does not present itself in terms of Christian faith itself.

All of these concern the relation which Barth establishes between *Heilsgeschichte* or *Bundesgeschichte*, and *Weltgeschichte*. It would be well to set forth as briefly as may be, therefore, how Barth conceives of both.

A. Barth's difference with Tillich is the most fundamental, for it roots in a basically different understanding of the concepts 'time' and 'eternity' themselves. The basis of all Barth's thinking about history is contained in his conviction that these concepts must be defined, not according to some abstract standard satisfying to the human reason, but with relation to the primary concrete reality, God. From this perspective Barth denies from the start that eternity, God's eternity, is timeless, or in negation of time. On the contrary,

'The eternity of God is, like his unity and constancy, determined by his freedom. It is the sovereignty and majesty of his love, in so far as this love lasts for ever and is itself everlastingness.'[1]

Eternity is the formal principle of God's freedom itself, just as time is the formal principle of his activity reaching outward. It is the form in which God's relation to his Son, and in him to all mankind, is expressed. God is everlasting. Time has no power over him. But he is so precisely as love, as the God who in the determination of his grace is *for* man. His unity includes manifoldness. His permanence (*Beständigkeit*) includes movement—the movement of his love. His Trinity which includes all his purpose and activity is expressed in calling him eternal. Eternity is therefore not a concept restricted by logic, but defined by God in his freedom

[1]*Kirchliche Dogmatik*, II/1, p. 685.

and love. It is quite legitimate to speak of 'eternal time' as God's time, of *reine Dauer* which includes, indeed is in a sense the pre-existence of, the elements of created time.

Eternity, therefore, includes all time. 'The eternity of God is itself beginning, process, and end.'[1] Here again eternity cannot be the negation of time. The eternity of God is the source of all that begins, carries on, and ends; and begins, carries on, and ends in it. The fact that in God beginning, continuity, and end, are held together without division, does not mean in any sense that they are negated. We see Barth's insistence that an Aristotelian Unmoved Mover, a static pure Actuality, apart from gracious activity, is not the Christian God, again emphasized. God *is* for man, so God *is* time for man, 'just as surely as his revelation, Jesus Christ, is truly he himself.'[2]

B. This gives a different status to created time, than that which it holds in most theology and philosophy. Barth distinguishes it sharply from 'our time' or fallen, lost time, thus carrying his rejection of natural theology into the very concept of time itself. Created time is the time of God's revelation, the time which he has for man, and which he gives us. It is the form of our creatureliness, just as eternity is the form of his freedom. It is the limit of man only in the sense that it is the delineation, the determination of man as creature. This limitation gives him being. Created time is the form in which man has fellowship with God, the form of history. It is the form of existence in which things happen one after the other in a lineal development from past, to present, to future. Creation therefore is the basis (*Grund*) of time, but also occurs in time. It is (Barth takes issue here with Augustine) temporal in its *Setzung*. It has past, as well as present and future, from the beginning, precisely as relative created time which is analogous to God's eternal time.

'Precisely his eternity however reveals itself in the act of creation as his readiness for time, as pre-temporal, as (over or) with time, as post-temporal, and so as the source of time, the absolute, the ultimate time. And so this, his revelation, is the act of creation together with the development of the creature and the beginning of time. It occurs not outside of, but in the new space which it itself sets.'[3]

[1]II/1, p. 689.   [2]Ibid. p. 690.   [3]III/1, p. 76.

259

Created time is therefore historical time, the time of the history of man as God determines it. History, for its part, is

'the continuum of events in which God makes, carries through, and brings to its goal this, his Covenant with man; and so makes true in the realm of the creature what he has decided for himself from all eternity. It is the continuum of events for whose sake God has patience with his creature and gives him time with his creation; time whose content is these events, and which is "fulfilled" and thus made ripe for its end by their conclusion.'[1]

This *is* history, in Barth's view. There is no other history which is not *Heilsgeschichte*. There is no other content to time which does not derive its meaning from the covenant relation which God establishes with man and carries through. As we have already seen that man's being is itself a history, the history of his relation with God in the covenant, and so dynamic and concrete, not general or abstract, so here we see that history is the story of God's grace in this covenant with man. There is no history of man as such, in independence of this. There is no history of nature apart from this grace, although there is a realm of nature apart from the realm of grace.

'The secret of all that happens in the world is the eternally preceding decision of God. That is the saving event (*Heilsgeschehen*) which is the goal of all other events in the world. For its sake all the rest must happen: that this decision of God which precedes all and therefore the divine election of man must become visible and effective in man's existence as elected; in the form of the spoken and heard Word of God, in the form of the people of Israel and the Church, in the form of the calling, justification, sanctification, and glorification of man, and in the form of man's love and hope.'[2]

c. Nevertheless there is such a thing as 'our time'—time from the perspective of human beings thinking in their sin, without reference to God. There is such a thing as *Historie* as distinct from *Geschichte*—history from the point of view of this same humanity without God. Both of these illustrate the ambiguous sense of the word 'is' which we have already noticed in Barth when he deals with sin and evil! It would perhaps clarify the thought to say, with

[1]III/1, p. 63.   [2]II/2, p. 203.

260

Barth, that this is not objective time and objective history at all. It is a subjective form, and a subjective illusion about the dynamics of content, from the perspective of autonomous man. It is abstract time and abstract history, conceived apart from the concrete act of God's sovereign grace which alone gives them meaning.

'It is the time whose flow has become a curse. It is the time in which there is no real present, and therefore no real past or future; no middle and therefore no beginning and no end, or beginning and end only as the form of appearance of a middle which is really the One and the Whole, and therefore not real time in any case.'[1]

It is time and history that have been riddles and vexations for the philosophers from time immemorial. From the point of view of God's revelation it is lost time, the time of lost men, unfulfilled time. Its past is a time of regrets, of lost memories, of reminders that all good things end, of shadows which we would like to keep but cannot. Its future is problematic, filled with the certainty of death and the probability that our plans, our hopes, will be disappointed. So our present, which should be most real, disappears between past and future, becomes a moment of ephemeral anxiety for good things lost and hopes that may never come to pass.[2] The same in parallel is true of *Historie*. It is the science of *Weltgeschichte*, 'a history of the world grounded in and determined through and through by its ignoring and rejecting of the will, the word, and the work of God.'[3]

Barth's rejection of this world history is as strong as Berdyaev's, and is expressed most vigorously in his most recent work. World history is determined by human pride. All its movements, beginnings, endings and new beginnings are enclosed in one great disobedience toward God. They stand under his judgement, his 'No', which is his 'Yes', his act of grace, toward the poor sinners who perpetrate this history and are its victims. Historical science therefore, eliminating as it does all evidence from Revelation itself and dealing only with generalizations about human actions as subjects of history, can only trace the shadow of this 'No'. In so far as it does

[1]III/1, p. 78. [2]III/2, pp. 617–26. [3]IV/1, p. 563.

more than this it falls into one *Weltanschauung* or another, or borrows secretly from theological sources.

D. All of this is background for explaining why our normal concepts of time and history are incapable of explaining the form or content of the real historical acts of God, either in Creation, or in the coming of Jesus Christ. Creation comes to us in the form of a tale (*Sage*) because no historical concepts could embrace pure history which it is. It is in this sense 'unhistorical' history (*unhistorische Geschichte*). But, Barth adds immediately, 'the whole of history (*Geschichte*) is also unhistorical and can only be reported unhistorically, in that God's creation continues in it, so that the whole of history in all its movements, relations, and forms, always has an aspect to it which is immediately set by God.'[1]

Yet Jesus Christ is at one and the same time *historisch* and *geschichtlich*. There is a part of his time on earth which cannot be verified by historical science, which 'will always be understood and labelled by the thought form and language of present-day science as "tale" or "legend".'[2] Yet it is precisely the meaning of God's redemption in Christ, that he took our lost, our hopeless time upon himself; that he entered and played a role in our world history as a part of his taking God's rejection of human sin, and the fate of the rejected sinner on himself.

In Christ God creates time for us; restores, normalizes, and heals the created time which we had spoiled and lost. This lifetime of Jesus, although it belongs to our lost 'historical' time, becomes new time, 'the time of the Lord of time. It is, in contrast to our time, controlled, and precisely therein truly fulfilled time.'[3] In the life of Jesus, and most especially, according to Barth, in those forty days of fulfilled time when the risen Christ walked on earth after the Resurrection, we see all the fullness of time, the full content of history. 'Real time is primarily the lifetime of Jesus Christ.'[4] From this high point the Christian looks forward and back over history and understands its meaning. Easter was a prism through which the apostles and the Church saw Jesus in all his relations to them: present, past and future.[5] Easter is the event by which all

[1]III/1, pp. 84–5. [2]IV/1, p. 370. [3]I/2, p. 57. [4]III/1, p. 82.
[5]III/2, p. 530.

other events and times are mastered, relativized, and illumined.[1] It would be well for us to look forward and back from this vantage point, to see the way in which Barth relates human and divine events in the light of it.

E. Looking figuratively backward toward creation and God's rule over human events in general, we discover it to have been, before Christ, a time of expectation, to which the whole Old Testament bears witness,[2] and a time in which God, far from abandoning his world to itself outside the covenant, governed and still governs world history by his judgement and grace, wrath and mercy, to the end that it shall serve and reflect, however imperfectly, his history of gracious dealing with men.

Here we must make a distinction, which Barth implies but does not explicate, between *Weltgeschichte* and *Weltgeschehen*. *Weltgeschehen* is that which happens in the world of God's creatures. It is the objective reality of the events which make up the history of man on earth, his life cycle, his attempts to set up order, his sinful destruction of order, his relations to his neighbour, and the rest. *Weltgeschichte*, on the other hand, refers not to these events as such, which lie in the hand of God, but to these events in so far as man himself is their subject, sees himself as their creator, and endows them with meaning of his own. The same distinction might be made with relation to time. God did not, Barth points out, create the concept 'time' on the fourth day, but the stars, and by derivation the clocks and calendars, by which man could measure.[3] Man brought forth the abstraction, and imagined himself, so thinking and measuring, the master of time.

Das Weltgeschehen then, is not at odds with grace and *Heilsgeschichte*:

'This is God's faithfulness, that he orders creaturely events (*Geschehen*) under his Lordship into and under the event of the covenant and the grace of his salvation, and lets them serve it; that he adds them to the coming of his kingdom, in which the whole reality which is different from himself gains its historical substance, and lets them have a part in this coming.'[4]

[1]III/2, pp. 546–7. [2]I/2, pp. 77 ff. [3]III/1, p. 77. [4]III/3, p. 47.

This is, in itself, a work of God's grace, the work by which he creates and maintains the outer basis (*äusseren Grund*) of the history of his covenant. It must be a continual work because the creature is free over against God. Often he seems less in control than the powers of human effort or natural chance.

'What man has before his eyes in this case is simply the fullness and confusion of creaturely events which, in itself and as such, cannot be identified with the happening of the will of God, as surely as the creature is not God.'[1]

Yet the believer who seeks the work of God revealed in Christ through all this is no dreamer. 'He stands and acts in the reality of the world objectively in that he knows he has to do with God himself in all its developments.'[2] He knows, and finds it carried out in world events, that they have the character of a mirror, a tarnished, obscure mirror, but nevertheless a reflection, of the true history of God's covenant with man. He sees that the sovereignty of *this* God is manifest in that which he judges as well as that which he finds good, in and through human rebellion as well as human service.

Therefore human activity is a tool which God has made useful in history and chooses to use. Therefore worldly events have 'constitutive meaning for the events of the history of the Covenant'.[3] Barth differentiates this doctrine of Providence and of world events from two others:

I. From all pessimistic and optimistic *Weltanschauungen* which attempt to trace a pattern of meaning in history from some human point of view, even a theological one. Either these end by giving some part of history its own meaning over against God and therefore over against other men, or, as with Marx, they give it a negative meaning in very rebellion against it, consigning it to the rule of an alien law.[4]

II. From a Christian doctrine of parallelism between world history and God's redemption, whereby Creation would only be the state of man's existence until he was reached by God's saving grace, without that grace making use of creaturely activity as such.[5]

[1]III/3, p. 51. [2]Ibid. [3]Ibid. p. 62. [4]IV/1, p. 564. [5]III/3, p. 45.

F. It is the look forward from Easter, however, which comes closest to our question, for it brings us to our point in history. Here, for Barth, everything depends on the central lordship of Jesus Christ, fulfilled history in those forty days, hence object of remembrance, and yet 'a being which is subject to no passing away, and which needs no becoming,'[1] and so a present Lord, and one who is to come, whom our lives are filled with expecting. In contrast to his earlier pure eschatology, Barth gives special emphasis to none of these three aspects of Christ's historical being. The New Testament, he claims, is not consistently eschatological. It is only consistently Christological. We stand in the light of the great event by which history was given a new start, or rather restored to its created purpose.

'In the death of Jesus Christ God justified sinful man by restoring human dignity in the Person of his Son and by restoring law between man and man by accepting man as his child. This is the great change from which the world of today derives.'[2]

In Christ the time of the unreconciled man, 'our time' as Barth called it, has been overcome and brought to an end. Even though it lingers because of God's patience Christ has become its limit. Such concepts of its future as this time and this world history may develop are illusory. This is the great reality which is prior to all human decision and all history which follows it. It does not depend on human decision of faith; it is not a subjective time and history with the believer standing in an everlasting tension *simul justus et peccator* in the point of crisis. In contrast to Niebuhr Barth proclaims:

'Our sin is past, our righteousness comes. God says "Yes" to our righteousness, in that he says "No" to our sin. Only with this destiny, only with this preponderance, only in this decision are we both at once: righteous and sinners.'[3]

Neither does it depend on the history of world events, but rather brings to them its meaning:

[1]I/2, p. 127.
[2]From *Christliche Gemeinde im Wechsel der Staatsordnungen*, a lecture given in Budapest, Hungary, in 1948 and published in a book of the same name (Zurich, 1948). Tr. in *Against the Stream*, p. 78.
[3]*Kirchliche Dogmat k* II/1, p. 707.

'We may call this great change quite simply Jesus Christ in the two-fold aspect of his death on the Cross and his coming again in glory, as made known in his resurrection. The Christian Church knows that not only itself but the whole world exists in the time between these two events; between the action God has already taken and the action he has still to take for man through his only Son. Political changes, along with all other changes, take place in this time between. They are significant for the Christian Church because they take place in this framework. The beginning and goal of what we call world history is at all events the history of God's salvation of man.'[1]

Christ therefore is now the full content of our time, past, present and future. He is our past, in that the fulfilled time, the years one to thirty, the time of his life on earth and especially after his resurrection, give meaning and content to all history. His saving act in taking the creature's negation into himself re-established the life of the creature—the life of world events, of the laws of common sense, of nature, and of the useful service of the creature to the covenant fellowship of God and man—but relativized it, purged it of its own 'time', its own 'history' and its own ideological delusions of grandeur.

He is our present, this present between the Ascension and his coming again, in which the old, already conquered and negated history and time are allowed to continue for a while. This is the time of God's patience, time for our repentance.

'The time of faith and not yet the time of seeing. Not a time of blindness but a time of seeing in a mirror. Not a time of darkness or lack of knowledge but a time of veiling. Not a lost time, but a time of testing.'[2]

It is therefore the time of the Church, of preaching and sacrament, whereby the knowledge of God's grace and Christ's lordship is both proclaimed to the world and lived in the community of fellow men bound together by the Holy Spirit. It is at the same time the time of political orders, designed to secure the common life against chaos by a system of balance between freedoms and community control, regulated by law, the time, in short, of relative justice under God's providence.

[1]*Against the Stream*, loc. cit.
[2]Ibid. p. 80.

The dynamics of our present is, for Barth, the dynamics of redemption. This shows itself in the history of the Church, which Barth describes as constituted and sustained by an event (*Ereignis*) —the event of Christ's redeeming action, calling the congregation together through preaching and sacrament.[1] The ontology of the Church is determined by this history and mission to the world:

'The real Church lives in the fellowship of the Holy Spirit, i.e. from the knowledge that the Kingdom of God has come, in prayer for the revelation of his Glory and therefore for the commission to tell all men that God was, is and will be for them all.'[2]

The very victory of Jesus Christ, the fact that he was man for all men, precludes the Church's being an end in itself, a being for itself. It exists in the knowledge that 'God so loved the world', and its inner life in that knowledge, its life of faith, obedience, and prayer[3] is directed toward partaking of and bearing witness to that love. The Church would not be the Church if it did not depend wholly and completely on the calling act of Jesus Christ and not on any absolute order, or worldly definition. It would not be the Church however if it were not wholly in the world and for the world in its confession of faith, political guardianship, and service of the neighbour, bearing witness not to itself, but to Christ. At this point Barth is extreme in asserting the functional, the dynamic and open nature of the Church. Von Balthasar finds him to be of all theologians the most open to the world, and finds it hard to see how in his theology the Church can be defined clearly at all over against the world.[4] Newbigin on the other hand complains that Barth

[1]Barth's most succinct presentation, which is also incidentally his most extreme one, of his doctrine of the Church is 'The Church: Living Congregation of the Lord Jesus Christ', in *The Universal Church in God's Design*, Amsterdam Assembly Series (London, 1948), Vol. I, pp. 67–76. In this essay he says bluntly that the Biblical view of the Church tends in the direction of congregational polity, and refuses to allow any real authority to a synod or a church hierarchy over a congregation.

[2]From 'The Real Church', a lecture given on the same visit to Hungary. *Against the Stream*, p. 71.

[3]*Kirchliche Dogmatik*, III/3, pp. 279–321.

[4]Von Balthasar, *Karl Barth: Darstellung und Deutung seiner Theologie*, pp. 257–8.

forgets the nature of the Church as an organic and ordered community, dissolving it into a series of 'events', of preaching and of witness.[1] It is certain that Barth however places the Church, the congregation of believers, for this period in history, in the very centre of his thinking. His whole dogmatics is *Kirchliche Dogmatik* designed to instruct and guide the Church for our time. Yet he could inscribe von Balthasar's criticism on his flag. The test of true faith, of the existence of a congregation, is the nature of its confessing Christ to the world, a confession which at times must be quite concretely political. This is the crisis in which the Church lives, a crisis parallel to that in the life of the Christian, confronted in his life with many *kairoi* which call for his decision; a decision which is not a matter of indifference but takes on the quality of life and death, of choice for or against God, in the situation concerned.[2] There is no protection for the being of the Church against such crises and such temptations. Any 'Church' may cease to be the Church when this confession fails, when it does not allow itself to be ever reformed and renewed by the work of Christ toward the world. Yet the security of the Church lies in the fact that Christ is faithful when we are unfaithful, and that he does not leave himself without witness in the world, that he can create and recreate the congregation.

The state also stands under the dynamics of redemption in this age. At this point Barth's fundamental thinking is yet to be expressed in the disciplined continuity of the *Dogmatik* itself, and his utterances in the heat of political controversy present us with a sharp paradox. Over this paradox stands indeed one fundamental belief. The outcome of the struggle with the powers of evil in this world has been decided in Christ. He is Lord in our time, even though his lordship be hidden from the world and known only in faith and hope. In our time there can arise no incarnations of the devil in political or any other form, no demonic states, no antichrists of power and ideology. This is true whether we speak of Hitler,[3]

---

[1]Lesslie Newbigin, *The Household of God* (London, 1953), p. 49.
[2]*Kirchliche Dogmatik*, III/2, p. 641.
[3]'Des Christen Wehr und Waffen' a lecture given in Bern in 1940. *Eine Schweizer Stimme* (Zurich, 1945), pp. 141 f.

or of present day Communism.[1] Therefore the Christian may not use apocalyptic terms in describing political conflicts in our time. He may not think in terms of absolute enmity, of a Christian crusade against the powers of evil, but only of the relative, sober, human protection and service of his fellow man, perhaps against a human enemy. Barth is prepared to recognize that, according to Scripture, the antichrist will come at the end of history. For this battle the Christian must prepare himself, with the weapons of the Spirit described in Eph. 6. But just for this reason he need not and must not stake all his hopes and fears on a present battle in this time.

The direct implications to be drawn from this fact form one side of the paradox. The Christian must not allow himself to be distracted by changes in political order, or by the relative struggles for power in history, from the primary task of proclaiming the reconciliation of man and God in Christ. His political decisions will be objective, aiming in the direction of freeing men from fear of their enemies, reconciliation of worldly antitheses of power, and peace. He will seek in, behind, and through the most unjust state and the most violent political changes, what God in his judgement and grace may have had in mind. He will always act positively, in service and witness, to God's 'Yes' to man, not in condemnation, as the possessor of a superior truth and morality. So Barth speaks consistently with relation to the encounter with Communism as we shall see in more detail below. But he laid the groundwork for it in the picture which he drew of the relation between Pilate, the type of the earthly state, and Christ, in the midst of the Nazi period. Pilate belongs to the second Article of the Creed, to the order of Redemption, because it is the positive function of the state to be just, to preserve the outward temporary order balanced with freedom in which the divine justification can be preached. Pilate did not do this. His was an unjust political power. Yet in this very injustice he was made to serve the purposes of divine justification. 'Even at the moment when Pilate (still in the garb of justice! and in the exercise of the power given him by God) allowed injustice to run its course, he was the human created instrument of that justification

[1]In answer to questions on the aforementioned lecture in Budapest in 1948. *Against the Stream*, pp. 94 ff.

of sinful man that was completed once for all time through that very crucifixion.'[1] Thus the state, even the unjust one, cannot escape the rule of God's gracious Providence, or the role assigned to it in God's redeeming act.

'Even if the State betrays its divine calling it will nevertheless be constrained to fulfil its function to guarantee the freedom of the Church, even if in a quite different way! The "honour" which the State owes to the Church will then consist in the suffering of the followers of Christ, described in the First Epistle of Peter: and the punishment of evildoers will then consist in the fact that the glory of this suffering will be witheld from them.'[2]

This is one side of the paradox. The other side lies in the fact that nothing which Barth says about the victory of Christ in this age, prevents him from declaring crises in political history, crises which are determined not by questions of justice and injustice directly, but by the pretension of earthly political structures to claim an authority over men which belongs only to God, and by the temptation they offer to Christians to identify their faith with an earthly system or ideology. These crises lose nothing of their absolute quality from the fact of Christ's redemption which stands over the whole of our time. At one point Barth sees in these present struggles the seeds, the fruit of which will be apparent in the final struggle of the Judgement Day:

'Such conflicts and decisions as those of the present war would not press us so; we would not have to fight so bitterly for our lives and for those things which are worth more than life—honour, a little justice, order and freedom in the world—as we must today (despite the relativity of these good things and the questionableness of our enterprise); if the world were not destined by its end to be a place where temporary human conflicts and decisions show themselves, in which the terrible danger, but also the wonderful triumph, of the messianic war of the day of judgement announces itself.'[3]

Despite what he knows about the relativity, the questionableness, of all such human enterprise, the Christian is under certain

[1] From *Rechtfertigung und Recht*, reprinted in *Eine Schweizer Stimme*, p. 21. Tr. *Church and State* (London, 1939), p. 16.
[2] Ibid. p. 54 (German original p. 40).
[3] *Eine Schweizer Stimme*, p. 140.

circumstances called to proclaim his 'No' to an earthly enemy and fight him, to proclaim this 'No' furthermore in the form of carrying out his confession as a Christian (*Vollzug des Bekenntnisses*) in such a way that he makes a binding claim for it. He is called to 'divide the spirits' (*die Geister scheiden*) of men according to whether they join his confession at this point or not, to challenge the validity of their faith by their political decision. This he did specifically in calling the Church to oppose National Socialism:

'The fact that (the call to oppose Nazism) is not recognized as true by all does not release those who have recognized it as true, from bearing witness to it united with their confession of Jesus Christ as true and thus as binding. If they are erring or false witnesses, then it is the job of those who speak against them to bring forth a similar counter-witness. . . . Not that they keep themselves free to have another opinion . . . but the confession of their *other faith* we would like to hear from them.'[1]

But he reiterated the same principle in general terms in one of his most recent writings:

'As he looks at the backgrounds of the two sets of arguments the Christian confronts the mystery of history and of his own life, in the conflict between the God who rules the world, and the chaos that resists him. This is a case where it becomes impossible to say "Perhaps—or perhaps not". He has to listen to God's commandment; he has to choose aright not only between a better and a worse, but in accordance with his Christian faith ("in proportion to his faith": Rom.12.6) and therefore, in the meaning of Deuteronomy, he has to choose between life and death, God and idols. In the midst of problems of reason and evaluation, the Christian faces the problem of obedience. Since (and the salvation of his soul is at stake!) he can only do justice to the problem in one absolutely definite direction and can answer it in one way only and in no other, he finds himself called and constrained to make a concrete political decision and to stand by his decision, to defend it publicly and to summon other Christians (and non-Christians) at all costs to make the same decision (since God, known or unknown, is the God of them all).'[2]

The Christian must make such a confession not every day with

[1] *Eine Schweizer Stimme*, pp. 104, 106. From 'Die Kirche und die politische Frage von Heute', 1938; Eng. tr., *The Church and the Political Problem of Our Day* (London, 1939).
[2] *Against the Stream*, p. 154. From *Politische Entscheidung in der Einheit des Glaubens* (Theologische Existenz Heute, N.F. 34, Munich, 1952).

271

relation to every question, but with relation to fundamental questions where he discerns a spirit at work in a train of arguments or a policy, which is basically at odds with the Holy Spirit. So wrote Barth in 1952 with the battle of his friends against the rearmament of Germany in the back of his mind. But his one personal example of political confession, that against National Socialism, is more specific. He called the Church to opposition as Church to Nazism because: (a) It claimed not only to be a political experiment, but also a *religiöse Heilsanstalt*. It claimed love and total allegiance such as man can only give to God. (b) It was, as such 'the total dictatorship, the very principle of dictatorship, which not only embraces and determines man and men in their wholeness of body and soul, but takes away their humanity; which not only limits and orders human freedom, but annihilates it.' (c) It was therefore the 'fundamentally anti-Christian counter-Church', the 'demonic counter-picture' under a man-god, a false Messiah. (d) It was the 'fundamental dissolution of the just state'. It was not only a bad political authority. It was 'as a political experiment one single destruction of all order, all justice, all freedom, and therein of all authority itself.'[1] It is in short no state at all, except in so far as it includes within itself the remnants of non-Nazi function and organization. It is 'anarchy tempered by tyranny' and vice versa. Such a state, if we may generalize on Barth's specific description, demands the Christian's basic opposition as an act of his Christian confession. It is like what the Turks were for Luther, a menace under a false prophet. Christian prayers and actions should aim at its destruction, and not at peace with it. Christians should be confident in such a battle that they are defending 'the concern of the Christian Church' when they fight to preserve a just (*rechte*) state against the onslaught of these modern Turks. So wrote Barth to Professor Hromadka in the Sudeten crisis of 1938.[2] And—how unfortunate to be a great man all of whose letters are preserved and later laid to one's account!—in a letter to Holland in the same year we have this pinnacle of our paradox expressed:

[1] *Eine Schweizer Stimme*, pp. 80 ff. Here is Barth's classic description of Nazism and his condemnation of it as a system.

[2] 'Brief an Professor Hromadka in Prague 1938', ibid. pp. 57–8.

'Dictatorship is the unconcealed rule of conscious and planned injustice and unfreedom. Dictatorship is as such a threat to true peace. In the age of dictatorships the Church must demand and approve in all lands which are not yet ruled by it, the will to a just peace and the preparedness to defend it. She must, for the sake of the Gospel and by proclaiming the Gospel, call the democratic state to be a *strong* state at all costs, even at the cost of suffering and destruction; a state which will order a halt to dictatorships on its borders with every means. And the Church must say to its members for the sake of the Gospel and by proclaiming it, that there is something which is worse than dying or killing: the willing affirmation of the shameful rule of the Antichrist.'[1]

There is no escaping the paradox we have here described, throughout Barth's thinking. We have seen it in the tension between his polemic against natural theology as if the fate of the world depended on the sharp clarity by which revelation were divided from human approaches to God, and the all-conquering and all affirming movement of grace in the world through Jesus Christ. We see it here in Barth's treatment of a political struggle as a historical crisis in which the spiritual life and death of man, and the existence of the Church are involved, over against his theological confidence in the power of the redeeming Christ over and through all political orders and disorders, just and unjust states, which relieves us human beings of the illusion that we are fighting absolute battles against the forces of evil, and frees us for relative, responsible participation in the positive tasks of order, justice, service and witness. Before taking up this paradox critically, however, we have one more aspect of Barth's doctrine of history to set forth.

G. Christ is our future. This means that there is no Last Judgement in general:

'For Jesus Christ really comes from heaven as he who sits at the right hand of God, therefore as the Risen One, therefore as the Revealer of the reconciliation accomplished in him, therefore as he who has accomplished this reconciliation, and therefore in fact as the Judge who anticipated the judgement for us and through whose punishment we are righteous. Dare we forget that and cancel it out in favour of an abstract divine, or rather all-too-human, figure of a judge?'[2]

[1]'Brief an eine Vertreterin des Vereins "Kirche und Frieden" in Holland 1938', ibid. p. 64.
[2]*Credo* (tr. London, 1936), pp. 123–4.

Hope is nothing but remembrance of Christ, remembrance of those forty days of fulfilled time, turned at an angle of 180 degrees. It is hope based on the knowledge that this Christ is 'with us, unto the end of the world', that our reconciliation with God in him is already accomplished, and the only question on which we will be judged is whether or not we have truly lived out our faith in God's compassion, whether we have believed with our lives, that our sins are completely borne by him. The Christian hope is not looking forward to something which is 'not yet', something which could therefore perhaps 'never' come to pass. It is confidence in the fulfilment of him who already is, whose reign has begun:

'So his resurrection and his parousia are for us two events, for him however only one. His resurrection is the anticipation of his parousia, as his parousia is the fulfilment of his resurrection.'[1]

That Christ is our future is hope for the world, primarily indeed for the world. Indeed the Christians are called, through their hope, to be the *Platzhalter* (place-holders) and *Stellvertreter* (substitutes) for the world which does not yet believe. But the object of God's act is the world itself. The Church is a community of this age, not of the age to come.

'The object of the promise, and the hope in which the Christian community has its eternal goal, consists, according to the unmistakable assertion of the New Testament, not in an eternal Church but in the *polis* built by God and coming down from heaven to earth, and the nations shall walk in the light of it and the kings of the earth will bring their glory and honour into it (Rev. 21.2,24)—it consists in a heavenly *politeuma* (Phil. 3.20)—in the *basileia* of God—in the judgement of the King on the throne of his glory (Matt. 25.31 f.).'[2]

The Church can give no higher honour to the state, says Barth, than to see in it a parable (*Gleichnis*) of this heavenly kingdom, and to challenge it with the responsibility of establishing, in this relative, temporary and external sphere of its activity, that righteousness which is in some way analogous to this future fulfilment.

That Christ is our future, finally, does not exclude temporary

[1]*Kirchliche Dogmatik*, III/2, p. 588.
[2]*Against the Stream*, p. 19. From *Christengemeinde und Bürgergemeinde*.

hopes, or the fulfilment of our life in the present, but rather includes them. The larger hope of the Christian is of course set on the fulfilment of all things in Christ, the coming of the kingdom. In this hope he is at once patient and alert. This hope sheds a sober clear light on each event in history, giving the proper balance of participation and restraint, free from false apocalypses, to his actions. But the Christian may also hope for smaller temporary signs of the working of the grace of God in history today and tomorrow.

'The promised future is not only that of the day of the Lord at the end of all days. Rather, just because the latter is the end and goal of all days, the former is also the nearest day—today or tomorrow. Also in this respect no division is possible for the Christian hope. Rather the one measures the other.'[1]

Barth is the sworn enemy of historical teleology in general. Yet such statements as this remind us that once again what was thrown out when it rested on a philosophical basis may reappear in a theological context. One can, Barth admits, in correcting his earlier totally futuristic eschatology, speak of a teleological direction of world events under God's providence. The believer (of course only the Christian believer, and he sometimes in ways quite other than his unbelieving neighbour) can find signs of this gracious providence working toward redemption in ways we have already described. This, says Barth, must be balanced against the Reformers' too exclusive emphasis on *Vorzeitlichkeit* (pretemporality) and his own earlier too great emphasis on *Nachzeitlichkeit* (post-temporality).[2] It is not surprising then to see him speaking in connexion with economic ethics[3] of the inevitability of provisional hopes in social policy.

Such are the dynamics of Barth's application of theology to the world about him. When we look at it whole, we are confronted with a curious discontinuity which, as we shall see even more clearly below, is the real question to Barth's thought when we look at it from the angle we have chosen. It is the discontinuity, which sometimes becomes a conflict, between the direction in which his theology

[1] *Kirchliche Dogmatik*, IV/1, p. 131.
[2] II/1, p. 715. [3] III/4, p. 626.

leads us, in dealing with social questions, and the direction in which he himself moves when he enters this field. Let us look at the two sides of this discontinuity more closely.

1.

One of Barth's profoundest contributions to the whole Christian encounter with Communism, is to have given Christians a new theological perspective (or is it the old, the Biblical perspective, defined for the first time with relation to modern rationalist and dialectical idealist aberrations?) on time and eternity, which in truth circumvents the Marxist-Idealist antithesis. It is no accident that he turns to Augustine both for background and for criticism, because it was Augustine who performed a similar task for the classical world. Yet the task is different today. The concept of linear time, history with a beginning and an end moving in some way forward, and informed with a purpose, originally a Christian insight, has become the leading secular presupposition. It is this time, to which Hegel sought to give meaning by his categories of dialectical movement, whose ideal synthesis bore so close a resemblance to the Prussian state. This is the time which nineteenth-century liberals informed with a progressive development through liberty for both the selfish and unselfish impulses of the individual man, to an ever greater harmony of the interests of all. This is the history, the cruelty of whose face in both these seemingly beneficent expressions Karl Marx saw from a proletarian perspective; and which he therefore condemned as 'pre-history', the history of class struggles, the time of human self-estrangement. Yet this is the history in which Communism finally remains caught in the very act of trying to escape from it. The proletarian revolution does not usher in a new time, or a new history, but only a return to the old liberal-progressive view, superimposed on the inverted dialectical idealist view, carried through the stage of one more revolution. Yet the Communist attempt to maintain a new time as an article of faith endows these old errors with a new, demonic force. Barth meets this Marxist rebellion against 'our time' in three stages:

A. First, he takes the Marxist rebellion against the tyranny of history seriously, more seriously than any other theologian except

Berdyaev, although the earlier Niebuhr must certainly be associated with this rebellion. What we have already said about Barth's revolutionary attitude toward unredeemed thought and existence and thinking as a whole applies with equal force here. Like Marx he exposed the self-justifying, the conservative nature of all attempts to find meaning in 'our time'. Like Marx, indeed more acutely than Marx, he sensed the inhumanity of all philosophies of history in general: their tendency to make of concrete human beings pawns in a general process, and to set one group of men, in self-righteous crusade for its own interest, against another. Like Marx he proclaimed the inner contradiction—in his language *die Nichtigkeit*— of this earthly history with all its pretensions to meaning, and the victory of a new time and history, which is the restoration of original time but on a higher and more creative level. This has liberated those who have learned from him, to face Communist changes without feeling that the meaning of history is being destroyed by them, and without dependence on remaining shreds of an old culture, supposedly Christian. Barth's radicalism at this point contrasts significantly with Niebuhr. Niebuhr indeed expresses precisely this kind of prophetic freedom from philosophies of history in some of his sermons and throughout his writings in many places. Yet Niebuhr seems to regard Barth's attempt to formulate distinctly theological concepts of time and history, as in itself irresponsible toward philosophy and science.[1] The result is that Niebuhr's radicalism is always specific, against particular injustices and particular illusions within society, combined with a general anxious sense that in a way beyond which we cannot see, God's judgement may lie over the whole. His appropriation of Marx, as we have seen, never comprehended the depth and completeness of Marx's revolutionary protest against 'our time' itself, and the 'natural theologies of history' by which it was made meaningful, be these Hegelian dialectics, Thomist Aristotelianism, liberal progress theory, or pietist views on eternal life. Barth's theological boldness, on the other hand, becomes convincing precisely where Niebuhr's dialectical insight reaches its limit: at the point where men find themselves spiritually in the proletarian

[1]Niebuhr, *Christian Realism and Political Problems*, pp. 185 ff.

situation; when their rebellion against historical forces is no longer specific and limited, but general. At the same time Barth becomes convincing where Tillich reaches his limit, when the proletarian no longer stands in inner spiritual contact with the philosopher who seeks to interpret his situation to him and lead him beyond it. For in the last analysis Barth's view of history does not lead man to depend on his ability to interpret a revolutionary situation to himself or others, even theologically. It leads him to action, as Marx also leads his followers, on the plane of history itself out of the radical freedom of response to the Lord who defines history in his terms.

B. Barth and Marx set each a concrete Lord of history over against all philosophies and explanations of history. Each bases his doctrine of history on the action of a redeemer who does not depend on the immanent laws of the historical process, even partially, but arises in the midst of these old laws as a mighty contradiction to them, a concrete historical victor and saviour already at work toward the day of fulfilment. The fact that Marx claimed the adjective 'scientific' for his view of history does not change this fact. The immanent laws his science pretended to discover were present in the presuppositions with which he worked—those of dialectical idealism turned upside down to form the pattern of an intra-historical eschatology for a revolutionary movement. 'Science' for Marx meant not general laws, but escape from them to the concrete; movement from the perspective of the experimental observer to the perspective of the participant. Both Barth and Marx are *prophets* of *redemption*, with emphasis on both these words. In this lies the secret of their dynamic radicalism. This is why it is foolish to say of Barth, as does Tillich, that he is indifferent to the special heights and depths of history, because he does not admit the historical possibility of a theonomous culture. The patterns of redeemed time catch up and transform all of 'our time' giving to each stage a significance more real than Tillich's *kairos* doctrine was able to impart even to the socialist movement, because this significance is not beholden to philosophical justification.

In this radicalism of redemption, however, Barth leaves Marx behind. For Marx's trinity—the dialectical movements of economic history, self-redeemed man in the proletarian class, and the strategy of revolution-cum-socialist construction—achieves only a grotesque shadow of its purpose which was the discovery and fulfilment of concrete historical man. Barth could agree thoroughly with Niebuhr's thesis (though Barth has never felt called to analyse Marxism *per se*) that Marxism is informed by a false eschatology which subordinates the human being to an abstract system where the few dominate the many; that precisely its pretension to be redemptive—its 'hard utopianism'—is its danger. But where Niebuhr answers this danger only with his dialectical pragmatism in tension between absolute good and relative choice until the end of history, Barth presents a dynamic of redemption in history which can understand the fullness of the revolution of our time. For Barth takes the full measure both of Marxist rebellion and of Marxist hope. His opposition to Marxism is that of the discoverer of true grace in history toward those who have simulated this grace, for lack of it. He catches up the revolution, metaphysical, as well as social, into his concept of God's time and ours, but finds, in the personal concrete human relations which express God's historical activity, an endlessly radical and creative source of reconstruction.

To put this in another way: the paradox which we found in Barth's actual writings, between the lordship of Christ and historical crisis, need not be, and was not intended to be, a contradiction. Skilfully handled it becomes rather a forceps with two prongs designed to probe and grasp the concrete historical will of God. On the one side we need treat no conflict in history with anxious pride, as if the victory of God depended on us. God is not so dependent on his creatures, that our acts of disobedience or of foolishness bring him into inner insecurity or risk the failure of his gracious purposes with us. We dare not consign any state, social condition, or human relation to a hell beyond the reach of his providential use to the ends of redemption. On the other hand our life and death is involved in whether or not we take this concrete present seriously as participants in God's act. It is the very meaning of our existence as objects of his love to bear witness to this act, discerning the true and false spirits at work in the world, bearing our responsibility for our neighbour. From the one side comes freedom from illusion and anxiety, for that sober objectivity which alone can discern truth in human relations. From the other comes that inner participation, the critical urgency of love, which alone can give this truth expression. From the one comes humility, reconciliation, and the willingness to accept another man beyond all differences or enmity. From the other comes that critical responsibility for bearing witness to the truth which alone can give these reconciling virtues form. Thus Gollwitzer (p. 249 above) speaks of realistic reconciliation, consistent with the Christian's witness to the reality of that which he must defend from the Communists, knowing the unreliability of Communist strategy, yet refusing to absolutize the conflict. Thus in Eastern Germany the confidence that even there the trend of events is in God's hands, liberates the believer, not to escape from the Communist society, but to act independently within it, to the point of speaking the truth in love to ideological enemies:

'This man who is so completely without religion . . . , has a sensitive ear for the voice of the living God, who is the commander, judge and rescuer of all. What happens in his encounters with Christians and pastors, quiet and hidden though it is, is the most important event of our days. Because here it becomes clear that there is no counter-power against the Gospel when it is clearly spoken, and that these estranged fanatics who seem to be at some quite different point, stand in fact on the threshold of faith. Much, much closer to it than townsmen and farmers as long as they lived undisturbed. The divine sword smashes tirelessly, even today, the ideological armour. If only all Christians would take it in their hand! "Christianity" has shown itself to have failed hopelessly, but the Word of the Lord who has come and is coming strides forward without pause, and will triumph even in the defeats and failures of his messengers.'[1]

This example could be multiplied to bear witness to the same pattern. The professor who in faith maintains the objectivity of his teaching and his responsibility for the personal development of his students; the lawyer who consistently reminds the Communist court of standards of justice which it has lost; the student who speaks openly to his Communist colleague truths both of faith and politics; all these and hundreds more illustrate the application of Barth's paradox to creative Christian encounter with Communism.

[1]Johannes Hamel, 'Pfarrer in der Ostzone' in *Die neue Furche*, June, 1951, p. 663.

For all are free in Christ to see and hold the truth, and compelled, at the crisis of their lives, by love for the neighbour, even the Communist, to bear witness to it. All are impelled by that realistic reconciliation of which Gollwitzer spoke—a resistance for the sake of the one resisted.

c. Barth thirdly meets the Marxist eschatology not just with criticism, but with a genuine eschatology, whose centre is not some coming state of affairs, but Christ himself. As in his whole theology it is this Christocentricity which makes his point of view unique. In this his eschatology differs even from that of Berdyaev who retains strong idealistic tones even though he bases his hopes on personal relations between subjects. Though Barth does not overstress the Christ who is to come, eschatological expectation nevertheless holds his Christology together and preserves its historical dynamic. It is a guarantee against its relapse into an idealism of redemption. And in the encounter of those who have learned from him with Communism it plays a decisive role.

'It is not sufficient' writes H. D. Wendland in West Germany, 'to "reject" the Communist hope and its social forms of appearance, and to demonstrate with theological pre-judgements that it is "erroneous doctrine". Rather, the Christendom of the whole earth is called and commanded by the hope of Communist man as never before, to ask itself what it hopes; whether it still hopes anything; or whether perhaps it has not degraded Christ to a man of the past and given itself up to hopelessness.'[1]

Not in any picture of a Christian world-view, whether present or to come, but in the *Ethos der handelnden Kirche* which expresses its hope in Christ in the quality of its freedom and the realism of its love, in its own community life and its work for social change, will the Communist hope be countered. This is work with a future emphasis because precisely the Church has bound its social ethic to forms of society which the industrial revolution has outmoded, while all the other modern historical faiths—progress, idealism, democracy etc.—are crumbling.

[1]H. D. Wendland, 'Christliche und kommunistische Hoffnung', in *Marxismusstudien* (Tübingen, 1954), p. 236.

'If Christendom is turned toward (the Kingdom of God), it combines the humility which recognizes that no future society can be the Kingdom, with the certainty of that coming victory which gives it power to do the deeds of love, and to fight for social orders of justice and freedom.'[1]

But the test of this eschatology in practice is in East Germany.[2] There life depends on hope, for it is the only answer to the question of the meaning of a time of privation and revolution. The Communists themselves live on hope. Wendland speaks from deep experience when he claims that the driving force in Communism is still today its Chiliasm.[3] For them also the present is a time of trial. The masses of anti-Communist people, especially the middle classes of city and country, also live on hope—that the old order will be restored and their Zone 'liberated'. They hope that meanwhile they may succeed in upholding a bit of that order in their own families, in their professions and circles of friends. Over against both of these stands the Christian hope, as Barth has expressed it for us.

It is a hope, first of all, which releases the Christian from responsibility for the total political and social strategy with relation to Communist power. In this it takes issue with Hromadka, and with the implications which suggest themselves from Niebuhr's thought, for the same reason. Hromadka calls the Christian to total responsibility within the Communist social and political order. He denounces as irresponsible the failure to play one's part thus in the movements of world history. But he overestimates the breadth of a Christian's responsibility. For him hope seems to lie in these historical movements. Actually the breadth of Christian responsibility does not exceed the area which the believer can oversee, and where his choice is significant. He can love the neighbour whom he can see and trust God for the movements of history.

[1]Wendland, op. cit., p. 243.
[2]For two straight theological expressions of eschatology of East German origin see Propst Hildebrand—'Wie sehen wir in die Zukunft?' in *Wählt das Leben* (Bericht des vierten evangelischen Kirchentages, Stuttgart, 1952) and Hamel 'Der vergessene Glaubensartikel von der Wiederkunft Christi' (*Kirchentagsbericht*, 1954).
[3]Wendland, op. cit., p. 226. Cf. Gollwitzer, *Und führen wohin Du nicht willst*, pp. 140-3 (*Unwilling Journey*, pp. 129-32).

Niebuhr's thought would seem also to imply that the Christian bears responsibility for a 'politically relevant' decision, i.e. for a decision which would have a direct influence on the balance of political power, which in a Communist land could only mean some form of active resistance. Such would be the logical conclusion of his approach to the Communist encounter primarily in terms of power struggle, and such is the tendency of a Niebuhrian concept of historical tension in political decision. But the East German is not placed where *any* political choice of this kind could lead anywhere but to disaster, whether for or against his Communist masters. By standards of worldly calculation his situation is hopeless at the moment. There is no over-all strategy possible, but only the small strategies of daily living and witnessing in the space left one in which to move. In this situation, knowing the world to be expecting its Lord is release from anxiety and despair.

Second, it is a hope which gives a positive place to suffering and judgement. It is the suffering Christ who is Lord of the world, and the way of hope may lead through suffering. 'The people now in prison are harbingers of spring' wrote Martin Fischer in the midst of the church struggle of 1953.[1] But judgement too plays a role. Every traditional way of life and social institution is called in question, and the Christian hopes for a new world to come upon the judgement of God over this one. He differs from the restorer and defender of the old order in that he can discern *this* judgement— for instance in land reform—and can accept from the hand of God the opportunities for witness and service which the new situation brings, without falling into Communist analyses and hopes. He can see in prison, in persecution, in poverty and insecurity, the promises of God, and can grasp them for his own. At least one pastor, recently released from prison, left his cell with regret because he had found a new parish there among his fellow prisoners. To hope in a coming kingdom which will be new, is to recognize what God is doing in a revolutionary time, and to act creatively in it.

[1]*Das Zeugnis der Verhafteten* (Berlin, 1953), tr. by Marie Jeanne de Haller as *The Witness of the Imprisoned* (World Student Christian Federation, 1953).

Third, this hope in the fulfilment of God's promises gives the Christian a freedom over against the hopes which arise out of non-theological calculations, either to accept them with gratitude to God, or to live without them. 'I thank God I have no provisional hopes,' said a student in the author's hearing. 'When I stand on the platform in a mass meeting of the Free German Youth to answer charges, I don't want to hope any more that I may be able to finish my course of study, or even that I may survive that meeting. I only hope that I may speak the truth and bear witness to the lordship and coming of Christ.' This is the experience of most Christians who face such crises. Only the most illusionless realism—there is only a small percentage of possibility that things may work out well—and the most exclusive hope in Christ, avails then. On the other hand the believer who is alert discovers that signs of Christ's lordship and coming multiply even in a totalitarian state. The change in Russian policy in Germany, especially toward the Church, in June 1953 was generally accepted by the Church as such a sign. As a sign it might be temporary. 'Our breathing space' was a common description of it. He who depends on the sign instead of on the Christ behind it, sets his hope on appearances and is bound to false hope. Yet it is a simple act of faith for the Christian to analyse his world, even though totalitarian, from the point of view that Christ is its future as well as its present lord. As an example of this, a pastor writes:

'Where people take their place in this self-movement of the Gospel, there opens, usually by surprise, a door by which they can get on in their earthly life. To be sure this door is only visible, most of the time, at the last moment. One must have enough faith to run against a doorless wall up to the last centimetre, in the certain hope that God who leads one in this way will not allow his people to break their heads. A professor seeks students for assistance in his research, a paid job. "Please," he says, "send me Christians. They are the only ones I can rely on." Several were helped thus on their way. An assistant is the only one who discusses with reason and facts, in the compulsory weekly Marxist training courses for assistants. The other 70 keep still or make fun of it. In private they say to him: "Why do you expose yourself? You can't get anywhere in any case." One day he was suspended. Why was he so careless? The case was heard before the local union officials. With some anxiety he defended his position. Result: a few days later he was reinstated. To be sure—for how long? But all 70 greeted him respectfully and warmly. Often this is how people begin a little to praise their Father in Heaven, because they see good works which point to him. And out of this, as a by-product, comes a bit more room for honest work in a profession. In this case also some room was gained for free science and scholarship; if only more people would move with conviction into this room!'[1]

2.

Such is the contribution of Barth's doctrine of history to the encounter with Communism. Significantly, the application of his theology has been made by others. For it is at the point of his application of his own insights to historical decision that we must raise questions. Although the forceps we have described above have been delicately wielded by others, Barth himself seems remarkably clumsy in their use, and, one might add, remarkably lacking in humility about this clumsiness. In strong contrast to his breadth and sensitivity of insight into the movements of philosophy and culture, which make his answer to the problem of ideology so convincing in application, he remains in the fields which form the backbone of history—politics, economics and the other social sciences— rather unsubtle and limited. This in itself would not be an objection if his own participation in these fields did not continually ignore this limitation, bringing theology directly to bear on historical decision in a way which confuses both. Let us illustrate:

A. The status which Barth gives to natural science as a relative and useful tool of Christian understanding is clear. The status which he gives to the social sciences is less so. On the one hand (pp. 230 ff. above) Barth's doctrine of the existence of man by God's grace, gives place for both social sciences and a science of history, which would, so far as genuinely relative and empirical, illuminate the meaning of *Menschlichkeit*. Yet Barth seems less averse to a doctrine of natural morality than he does to the positive development of these descriptive sciences of human relations! To historical science he assigns the sole function of giving the chronicle of human rebellion, though there is evidence that he treats it with

[1]'Gottes geliebte Ostzone' in the *Schweizerische Evangelische Pressedienst*, March, 1951, pp. 5–6.

285

somewhat more respect in relation to the doctrine of creation[1] and in describing the world-historical constants which are in a sense signs of God's history.[2] In the social sciences he is a constant pleader for objectivity and sobriety, for direct understanding of the human realities, unobscured by any ideologies. Yet he himself rushes into political and economic judgements armed only with theological insight and a limited experience, ignoring (at least from the evidence of his published writings) the vast body of social scientific literature, some of it standard for Christian understanding in these fields, which might enlighten him as to the actual human situation he confronts. We find him in the same speech pleading for a new age of sober enlightenment in the next few years, in which men will be free to use their own intelligence, free from the bonds which propaganda and ideology set on it; and then pronouncing a sweeping judgement to the effect that 'what was called freedom in the European Age has now collapsed'.[3] It is certain Barth would not treat other fields of learning so cavalierly. He defines the border between theology and science in his doctrine of creation, but does not cross it. His appreciation of philosophy has already been described. But Niebuhr's criticism, that the man who campaigns so vigorously against ideologies operates himself with ideologies in reaching political decisions, has a certain validity.[4]

[1]The following quotation, though ambiguous to this writer, would seem to indicate a fairly positive attitude toward *Historie* on its own level, especially when followed as it is by an explanation of the way in which the story of Creation is *unhistorisch* in distinction from the events of which there are human witnesses (*Dogmatik* III/1, pp. 84 ff.) : 'Historie, d.h. die dem Menschen zugängliche, weil übersehbare, weil ihm wahrnehmbare und für ihn begreifbare Geschichte ist *objektiv:* kreatürliche Geschichte im Zusammenhang mit anderer kreatürlicher Geschichte—ein Geschehen, vor dem und neben dem es auch noch anderes, prinzipiell gleichartiges Geschehen gibt, mit dem sich jenes vergleichen, mit dem es sich zu einem Bilde zusammenordnen lässt. Und so ist Historie *subjektiv:* das Bild solchen kreatürlichen Geschehens in seinem kreatürlichen Zusammenhang.'
[2]III/3, pp. 225–70.
[3]'Modern Youth: Its Inheritance and its Responsibilities', speech given during Barth's trip to Hungary. *Against the Stream*, pp. 60–61.
[4]Cf. Niebuhr's review of Barth's *Against the Stream*, in *Christianity and Society*, 4th quarter 1954.

The word 'ideology' is probably too strong. Rather Barth seems to have left an empty space in his thought between his theological insight and political and social reality; a space from which he continually excludes, for he suspects them of ideology or the pride of human self-dependence, the analyses and programmes of the social scientists and the politicians. Into this empty space comes then the overflow from his knowledge of culture in general, his generalizations on very limited personal experience in the politics of Germany and Switzerland, and information and judgements from friends whose theology he trusts.

B. The result of this is confusion and ineptitude in Barth's theology of politics, where he faces the difficult decisions which Christians must make in crisis situations. This confusion extends to history when we compare, not only Barth's different tone in describing the historical importance of Nazism and Communism, but the difference during the Nazi period itself. Barth's declaration of total war on the Nazis as the incarnation of tyranny and anarchy, in 'Die Kirche und die politische Frage von Heute', is a humanly understandable reaction to the inhuman revolution of nihilism which was then going on. But the picture of historical crisis which Barth here conjured up, his demand that the Christian confess his faith directly in political decision at this point, and judge the faith of others by their decision, his use of the words *dämonisch, grundsätzliche Auflösung des rechten Staates,* 'Antichrist' and the like, leave the reader confused about the very nature of this redeemed time in which, according to the deeper lines of his theology set forth in *Rechtfertigung und Recht* (1938), we live. In the same year, Barth manipulated both prongs of his forceps, but he never brought them together. The problem was only shifted to his eschatology when, two years later, he referred to the war against Nazism as a foreshadowing of the final war with the Antichrist. This relativized his earlier hyperbole about the conflict, to be sure, but it raised a question he has not yet answered about the significance of that final warfare for our encounter with such forces today as for instance Communism. Direct quotation could be lifted from this anti-Nazi polemic and applied with equal validity to a description of Communist government today, with the same consequences for Christian action. Yet Barth feels called to say almost exactly opposite things to this situation:

'Let me remind you . . . we shall not meet a perfect Christian state until the day of judgement, nor the devil's state either. We shall be always moving between the two. And so, even if the State begins to show signs of the beast from the abyss, as Christians we shall not immediately clutch at the *ultima ratio*: Yes or No—consent or martyrdom. Just because we are Christians we shall be free to wait a little and give ourselves time to examine the whole situation in detail.'[1]

From this advice, typical of that given to the Hungarians in 1948, the element of crisis, confession and decision, the warning against the dissolution of the state itself through tyranny and anarchy, is quite missing. One could grant Barth's contention that the Nazi and Communist situations are quite different for Christians and require different advice, if there were in his thought some analysis of their similarities and differences, some more rounded picture of the problem of Christian responsibility in each. As it is one is inclined to question (*a*) whether Barth's application of theology to politics in either case is valid, (*b*) whether in politics, Barth does not select from his theology to ground opinions reached by other means.

c. Barth's field of greatest knowledge and interest, as a Christian in the world, is culture and philosophy, where ideas and attitudes are the fundamental moral factors. This leads him in a number of cases to misjudge social and political problems, where attitudes and lines of thought are indeed important, but where the final moral fact is the deed itself, the way in which the neighbour is in fact treated or the state in fact organized. One sees this in the development of Barth's opposition to Nazism, which started on the simple issue of the freedom of the Church itself, and the purity of its teaching against the 'German-Christian' heresy. It was not until he could see that the basic problem was the false religion of Nazism itself, from which all its inhumanities came, that he moved into total opposition. Then, to be sure, the inhuman acts of this government—the persecution of the Jews, its perpetration of aggression and the like—played their full part in this opposition. Yet Barth's retro-

[1]From the question period in Budapest 1948. *Against the Stream*, p. 98.

spect on this conflict is also interesting. It stresses, almost equally with the evil of Nazism itself, the danger of its *temptation* for good people of bourgeois background, even Christians. It is this temptation, he maintains, which is absent in relation to the Communist dictatorship today, so putting it in quite a different light. There is no 'definite spiritual crisis' which endangers men's souls. Communism is no temptation for the Christian. Barth seems to find the outspoken atheism, the open profession of a creed and programme with which we disagree, almost as something good for Christians, like a hard wind. The fact that people suffer injustice, privation, imprisonment and death, or even the forcing of their minds, is less important for him than whether their spirits meet the challenges before them in a Christian way. He seems to be suspicious of the too direct human reaction to injustice because of the bourgeois conception of rights, justice, and freedom it may imply; because of the cultural or personal self-justification it may express.

Yet all this is only one side of Barth—the side which he applies to the discernment of political crises. There is another side —the simple natural co-humanity of man through the grace of God —which he sets at the heart of all reasonable social thought and action, and which implies as well a perception of inhumanity and its dangers, in deed, not only in thought. From his own doctrine of man, Barth should know that the real crises which man faces in his dealings with his fellow men are direct questions of moral action, and that there is no simple derivation of bad moral acts from bad ideology. From his doctrine of God's grace in Christ he should know that a political organization or programme is not to be judged by the human spirit or ideology which informs it alone, but by what, in God's providence or in defiance thereof, it is actually doing to concrete human beings.

D. We come to the summarizing point of this criticism. The basic problem in Barth's application of his doctrine of history to recent political history is that he has been far too simple, too sweeping, in identifying the point where the Christian faces the crisis of obedience or rebellion, life or death, confession or denial of his faith, in political life. Human self-justification is more subtle and human decision is more complex—without being for that reason more relative, or less of a crisis—than Barth takes account of. So for example one searches Barth's writing of the time in vain for any help on the problem of Christian responsibility for the Nazi as a person, the pastoral problem of his help and conversion, beyond the general statements about church and state in *Rechtfertigung und Recht*. One looks in vain for any recognition that there was still, even under the Nazis and through their administration, a solid core of uncorrupted state service. One fails to find any recognition that different positions in society required different kinds and degrees of resistance to the Nazi corruption. Indeed Barth was most violently intolerant of variations at this point![1] In short Barth neglected a whole side of his theology in this situation—the side which speaks of the victory of the grace of God and refuses to allow us therefore to absolutize the conflict with our enemy, to cut ourselves off from ministry to him as a human being, or to forget to be sober and realistic in our appraisal of social facts. Had he not neglected this basic theological insight, he would have made more use of objective sociological and political analysis of the complexities of the Third Reich, instead of merely blasting it with (by his own standards!) questionably used theological terms. Without losing sight of the crisis in which Nazism as such placed the Christian, he might have helped believers to locate the point of decision for themselves more accurately. He might have uncovered not one, but a complex of ideologies and spiritual temptations which bore on the problem of political witness.

All this applies as well to Barth's approach to Communism and the politics of the western world in the post-war period. This brings us, however, to our final section.

2. THE STRUCTURE OF CHRISTIAN SOCIAL RESPONSIBILITY: POLITICS AND COMMUNISM

We must take a step back at this point to clarify Barth's approach to social questions as a whole, which underlies his politics. We have seen that he grants to social groups no status as sources of of God's commandment, no theological meaning of their own

[1] Cf. his polemic in the case of Eugen Gerstenmaier. *Kirchenblatt für die reformierte Schweiz*, 1946.

(pp. 206–8 above). We have described the two sides of his understanding of historical action: confidence in the victory of redemption and the sense of crisis and decision over against false spirits. The structure of Christian social responsibility, of the relation between Church and state, must always be understood as historically dynamic, never endowed with a moral or social being of its own, apart from this history:

'Just for this reason (the Church) can neither give itself to a strange politics nor inaugurate her own ecclesiastical politics, perhaps that of a Christian party. She can only, over against all human politics—to be sure in a deeply participating, positive "over against"—refer to God's politics, which is no system, but sovereign, hidden action.'[1]

Despite this however there is a structure of Christian responsibility in Barth's thinking, and there are continuing relations between Church and state. They find their origin in Barth's attempt, starting in the Nazi period, to break through the conservative Lutheran 'two-kingdoms' division of this world from the Church, the realm of law from the realm of Gospel, to make way for a more positive and Biblical doctrine of the Christian in society. This received its full formulation in the chapter of his *Dogmatik* which immediately followed that on God's election.[2] Here Barth regards the whole of human responsibility, the whole of ethics, as a consequence of God's gift of grace: 'God makes man responsible precisely in that he makes himself responsible for man. It is ruling grace which is commanding grace.'[3]

The Law is the form of the Gospel therefore. It is the way in which the being which we have through that which Jesus Christ has done for us is expressed. It is the consequence of God's gift, and of his continual giving. There is, therefore, no general commandment of God, not even the ten commandments; there is no permanent moral law. There is only the Commander who has given us our full humanity in Christ, and so commands us concretely as covenant partners responsible to him in his work. Commandment is historical event, the realization of God's gracious election.

[1]*Kirchliche Dogmatik*, III/4, p. 587.
[2]II/2; Ch. 8 of the whole work: 'Gottes Gebot'.
[3]Ibid. p. 567.

'Man does not belong to himself. . . . Because Jesus Christ as true God and true man is the beginning of all the ways and works of God, man is, whether he knows it and wills it or not, bound to God and confronted with God, brought under the order of his will, word, and commandment, destined to realize his existence as God's covenant partner. In that he is a man, he is measured, as a matter of objective fact, by this, his destiny, and is asked to realize it. This is his responsibility.'[1]

Nevertheless there is a constancy, a continuity, in the Divine commanding, which Barth does not hesitate to call an *Ordnung*; and, in relation to that part of the Divine commanding which relates especially to his action toward us as Creator, a *Schöpfungsordnung* (order of Creation). He thoroughly differentiates this concept, however, from Brunner's idea of it, in that he refuses to give it the status of a principle or law, existing alongside of God's grace and known to some degree by the perception of natural law. This order is rather 'spheres of divine commanding and human activity, in which the God who is gracious to man in Jesus Christ, commands also as Creator.'[2] These are spheres (*Bereiche*) in which man is called to freedom in an area of life, not structures to which man, because of his sin, must submit. 'The commandment of God sets men free. The commandment of God allows. Thus, and only thus, does it command.'[3] The comandment of God basically tells us what we *may* do, because we are freed by his gracious calling and sacrifice; and what we *need no longer* do, because we are no longer imprisoned by Adam's sin, no longer in a condition where such deeds would seem to fulfil us.

We are now in a position to return to Barth's view of politics and, in this context, to his view of the encounter with Communist politics. The basic structure of political life is, for Barth, as we have seen it foreshadowed in his view of history, the *Gegenüber* of the two *Bundesordnungen* (orders of the covenant) which belong to the sphere of redemption: church and state, or, as Barth's more developed thinking names them: *Christengemeinde* and *Bürgergemeinde*.[4] Of these two *Gemeinden* the Church has a certain priority. Its meaning is the common life of the people in the Holy Spirit, in

[1]II/2, p. 713.   [2]III/4, p. 49.   [3]II/2, p. 650.
[4]'The Christian Community and the Civil Community', in *Against the Stream*; for definition of the two communities see pp. 15 ff.

obedience to the Word of God through faith, hope, and love, and in the preaching of this Word, in word and deed, to all the world. It is therefore an universal community without limits or competition with other communities. It is a seeing community which knows of God's gracious purpose for the civil community of all men, in a way to which the civil community as such is blind. The very purpose of the civil community is

'the safeguarding of both the external, relative and provisional freedom of the individuals and the external and relative peace of their community, and to that extent the safeguarding of the external, relative and provisional humanity of their life both as individuals and as a community.'[1]

And it does this in order to give man time to hear the Gospel of his justification, 'time for repentance, time for faith'. The just state safeguards the freedom to preach justification.

Yet the state is also an order of redemption, 'not a product of sin but one of the constants of Divine Providence'.[2] Through the state God sets limits on the capacity of sinful men to destroy their time and common life. In an earlier work influenced by the passion of the Nazi conflict Barth hazards the exegesis of Rom. 13, that political power is one of the angelic powers, the *exousiai* (Rom. 13.1), whose function and meaning is to serve Jesus Christ and his work, though it has a relatively independent substance. It can become demonic, by denying its true function, by enslaving itself to a false conception of its own autonomy, but it cannot escape the service of Christ in one way or another.[3] This idea, however, though it remains in his thought in revised form,[4] is less important than his later concept of the *Bürgergemeinde*, a human community. More indicative of Barth's mature thinking is his post-war picture of the state as a parable or sign[5] of the heavenly kingdom which is the goal and hope of the whole world under God's redemption, 'capable of reflecting indirectly the truth and reality which constitute the

[1]*Against the Stream*, p. 16.   [2]Ibid. p. 21.
[3]*Church and State*, pp. 23 ff. (Tr. of *Rechtfertigung und Recht*).
[4]*Dogmatik*, III/3, p. 535.
[5]Gollwitzer prefers to use the concept *Zeichen* from Barth's earlier *Römerbrief* at this point rather than Barth's words 'Gleichnis, Entsprechung, Analogon zu dem in der Kirche geglaubten und von der Kirche

Christian community'[1] because it forms the outer circle of the world's existence in grace, concentric with the Church. Not that the State can become the Kingdom of God. It is an order which God uses in a world not yet redeemed, where the rule of Christ is still hidden. Yet just in this sense the Church, and it alone, can fully recognize its goodness.

'The benefaction which it acknowledges consists in the external, relative and provisional sanctification of the unhallowed world which is brought about by the existence of political power and order.'[2]

Thus the relation between the two communities is so defined that the Church bears a special responsibility, out of its special relation to the truth in Christ, for the independent functioning of the state. Not that the Church can evolve, out of her own knowledge of revelation, the Christian form of a state. The Church is herself too much bedevilled with the very political problems which beset the state on a larger scale, to set herself up as the dispenser of that revelation, to which she was made to be only a witness. The image of concentric circles must be placed in a third dimension to be rightly understood. The centre of the Church is outside itself, like the centre of a beam of light. The outer and inner brilliance of this light both depend utterly on the source, the grace of a living God, and in no sense does the periphery have its source and meaning in the inner circle. Rather both have their meaning and centre only in Christ. The Christian is 'subject to the powers that be' in the sense that he carries with the rest of the world joint responsibility for the civil order.

'The Christian community participates—on the basis of and by belief in the divine Revelation—in the human search for the best form, for the most fitting system of political organization.'[3]

---

verkündigten Reich Gottes', *Christengemeinde und Bürgergemeinde*, p. 28, § 14; *Against the Stream*, p. 32.

Barth does not mean any similarity between the state and the Kingdom of God, out of the natural being of the state, but rather an analogical consequence of the action of God's grace. *Die christliche Gemeinde in der politischen Welt* (Tübingen, 1954), p. 38.

[1]*Against the Stream*, p. 33.   [2]Ibid. p. 22.   [3]Ibid. p. 25.

Once again we find revelation guiding the Christian past all ideologies, even 'Christian' ones, of what a social order should be, to free and practical thinking about the service of the fellow man. Precisely this is the Church's first duty toward the state: to pray for it, to remind it of its responsibility to God thereby, by whose gracious act justice is defined, and to seek in all the 'natural, profane and secular tasks and problems' with which the civil community is confronted, those choices and policies which provide most nearly that

'. . . the active grace of God, as revealed from heaven, should be reflected in the earthly material of the external, relative and provisional actions and modes of action of the political community.'[1]

The Church therefore will not allow any concept, not even the 'democratic' one, to stand for the Christian idea of a state, even though, as we shall see below, Barth considers a democratic structure of participation in the state most nearly expressive of the New Testament. It will not measure a state by the respect which that state pays to the Church's privileges and freedom, nor demand a special place in the state.

'It can accompany every political system. But it cannot serve strange gods. It cannot therefore ally itself with any political system, old or new, for better or for worse, just as it cannot oppose any system unconditionally. It can offer absolute and abstract obedience or resistance to none but to each only the relative concrete obedience or resistance which it is commanded to offer by the Word of God.'[2]

This Barth declared in Hungary with a Communist state before him. We have seen that he said quite different things about resistance to the Nazi state. This quotation nevertheless represents the basic line of his thought. His sweeping rejection of *bestehende Ordnung* which we found in the *Römerbrief* (pp. 180–2 above) has been superseded by his discovery of that Christ-centred providence to which the state belongs.

It continues however, as a kind of antithesis in his thought. The very fact that the state is itself without revelation, that it is

[1] *Against the Stream*, p. 34.
[2] From 'The Christian Community in the Midst of Political Change', lecture delivered in Budapest, 1948, *Against the Stream*, p. 86.

'graceless', that it can know of itself only law which then is a law of its own making, places it in constant danger, gives it a constant tendency toward injustice. The state indeed has been ordained to exercise force, fear, and threat:

'Where it is only a matter of creating time and freedom for the proclamation and recognition of grace; only a matter of making the common life of men possible under the precondition that their lives (against the grace of God) are graceless; there grace itself must take on and uphold the form of a graceless order.'[1]

It is a temporary order, Barth urges in this context, and the Christian by his submission to (participation in) it bears witness to this temporary character. But it is constantly tempted to claim more than this. Every state, he says in a recent writing, although what it *is* in the sight of God, is defined in Rom. 13, in fact moves between this and the beast from the abyss described in Rev. 13. There can be in history no totally demonic state; always some remnant of Providential order clings to the worst tyranny. But there can be in history no ideal state either, by which Barth means one which corresponds to the description which Rom. 13 gives! Rom. 13 therefore is a statement of the *exousia* which is given to the state by God's grace, not an empirical description of human government.

'On the basis of this command ("Let every person be subject to the governing authorities") the Christian sees reality as it is, and may feel some cause for fear when he remembers that the beast from the abyss is waiting at the end of the inclined plane on which the state may find itself.'[2]

Precisely here, in a state blind to revelation and without grace by its very nature, a 'neutral, pagan, ignorant state' which 'knows nothing of the kingdom of God', a state authoritarian by habit, keeping order by force and fear, a state constantly on the inclined plane toward tyranny and anarchy; here the Church becomes above all the true support and servant of the state, reminding it of the

[1]*Kirchliche Dogmatik*, II/2, p. 806. Here, in 1942, Barth presents a new exegesis of Rom. 12 and 13 which can be considered to supersede that in the *Römerbrief*, when coupled with that in *Rechtfertigung und Recht*.

[2]From the answers to questions in Budapest 1948. *Against the Stream*, p. 96.

true function which God has given it. The Church does this by the quality of its submission, in prayer for the state, in its preaching, which includes prophetic criticism, and in its active service, to the end that the state shall be a true or just state. 'Be subject to (hupotassesthai)' means not blind submission, but to respect an authority as his office demands. This respect will be given, however, even when the bearer of the office is unworthy of it. It will be expressed on occasion in the Christian's submission to injustice at the hands of the state, a submission which however will at the same time be priestly:

'Christians will render unto Caesar the things that are Caesar's, i.e. whatever is his due, not as a good or a bad Caesar, but simply as Caesar; the right which is his, even if he turns that right to wrong. . . . But the fact also remains unalterable that Christians must render unto God the things which are God's. . . . Thus the "subjection" required of Christians can *not* mean that they accept and take upon themselves responsibility for those intentions and undertakings of the state which directly or indirectly are aimed against the freedom of the Christian message. Of course it must be understood that even then the "subjection" will not cease. But their subjection, their respect for the power of the state to which they continue to give what they owe, will consist in becoming its victims, who in their concrete action will not accept any responsibility, who cannot inwardly co-operate.'[1]

'All this will be done' Barth concludes, 'not *against* the state, but as the Church's service *for* the state!' This word applies to all that he says about the unjust state. Christians would be enemies of a state if they did *not* resist when that state threatened their Christian freedom. 'If the state has perverted its God-given authority it cannot be honoured better than by this criticism which is due to it in all circumstances.' This is a natural extension of intercessory prayer for the state. It is 'defending the state against the state'.[2] The state lives from this intercession by the Church, whether it knows it or not.

'It is just (the Christians) who have the objectivity which is necessary to take part in these things, the openness and the courage which are necessary to distinguish between state order and all the forms of disorder which hide themselves in the garment of state order. It is just they who

[1]*Church and State*, pp. 67–68.   [2]Ibid. pp. 69–71.

297

always understand Caesar better than he understands himself, and know better how to give him what is his, than he knows himself how to demand it.'[1]

Prayer and preaching require service. The Christian cannot submit to the state without willing it positively, and he can only will it as a just state, not as a 'Pilate state'. This will requires action. This action will not simply be the suffering 'No' which the Christian must say to the state which demands love, inward spiritual allegiance from him. It may mean revolutionary resistance to the state:

'Can we pray that the state shall preserve us, and that it may continue to do so as a just state, or that it will again become a just state, and not at the same time pledge ourselves personally, both in thought and action, in order that this may happen; without sharing the earnest desire of the Scottish Confession, saying with it: "Vitae bonorum adesse, tyrannidem opprimere, ab infirmioribus vim improborum defendere"; thus without in certain cases like Zwingli reckoning that we may have to "overthrow with God" those rulers who do not follow the lines laid down by Christ?'[2]

Thus the Christian's relation to the unjust state. In the extreme case Barth comes indeed to the possibility of revolution and resistance against the state for the sake of the state. But nowhere do we see that call to total opposition, that confession in crisis, which characterizes his polemical writings against Nazism. Even revolution becomes an instrument of that freedom in which Divine Grace calls the Christian to 'seek the welfare of the city' by upholding the true state.

When we turn to Barth's positive suggestions for political ethics, this lack of crisis is all the more apparent. He starts from the proposition that 'the direction and line of Christian political decision, judgement, choice, desire, and participation is based on the capacity and need of politics to be a parable' of the kingdom of God.[3] Later, in answer to a question in Hungary, he defines the true, the just state more fully:

[1]*Kirchliche Dogmatik*, II/2, p. 808.
[2]*Church and State*, pp. 79–80.
[3]*Christengemeinde und Bürgergemeinde*, p. 28. My own translation. The translation of *Gleichnis* as 'allegory' in the published English version is a mistake (*Against the Stream*, p. 32).

'A state is an attempt undertaken by men to organize the outward life of man with the intention of preventing individual encroachments on the rights of the whole community and at the same time encroachments of the community on the rights of individuals. The order set up is guaranteed by force, . . . but . . . must be supported by the free responsibility of its members. . . . A proper state will be one in which the concepts of order, freedom, community, power, responsibility are balanced in equal proportions, where none of these elements is made an absolute dominating all the others.'[1]

The central concern of the Christian however is not any of these concepts as such, but the concrete human being. 'Right itself becomes wrong when it is allowed to rule as an abstract form . . . man has not to serve causes; causes have to serve man.'[2] The process of discovering what political structure and action best serves the outward security and welfare of man, is one where the Church can only think by suggestive analogy, it can only give direction, with more or less authority depending on the situation. It can do no more than helpfully define certain areas along the borderline between Church and state, and give by the example of its own congregational life, some picture of what the life of the civil community ought to be. In this phase of his thinking Barth wanders so far from his crisis thinking that he sounds almost like a liberal pragmatist because of Redemption.

Some of these directions and analogies, however, Barth considers fairly compelling. One of the most basic of these is the constitutional, democratic state. In spite of the fact that the New Testament knew only an authoritarian government, to interpret subjection in terms of active participation and to base the state on the free responsibility of citizens is, he believes, a legitimate extension of New Testament thinking. Though no particular democracy is Christian,

'There is no reason . . . why it should be overlooked or denied that Christian choices and purposes in politics tend on the whole towards the form of state, which, if it is not actually realized in the so-called "democracies", is at any rate more or less honestly clearly intended and desired. . . . There certainly is an affinity between the Christian community and the civil communities of free peoples.'[3]

[1]*Against the Stream*, p. 95.   [2]Ibid. p. 35.
[3]Ibid. p. 44. Cf. *Church and State*, pp. 78–80.

Other concrete suggestions fill out this picture of a democratic state. It must be constitutional—affording equal protection of the laws to all as a bulwark against both tyranny and anarchy. It must seek to redress the disadvantage which the economic system places on the poor. It must grant freedom in the spheres of family, education, art, science, religion, and culture, and safeguard that freedom by law. It will separate the powers of government to provide checks and balances. It will practise open diplomacy and seek the widest international co-operation. It will subordinate power to service. All these suggestions, rooted in the Swiss experience, were aimed directly at the Germany of 1946, where the lectures from which they are taken were delivered. They were designed as suggestions for German reconstruction, in line with previous suggestions which Barth made in the later war years.[1] As such they are examples of ideal thinking applied in a relative and suggestive way to a concrete situation.

With this we have also defined the lines of political thinking which Barth applies also to the Communist society in Hungary, the only concrete situation in which he has attempted to advise Christians in their encounter with Communism. He presupposes, in all this advice, the sovereign freedom of the Christian from every political ideology, including Communism. Where theology demands it, he takes sharp issue with Communist doctrine, as for example with relation to the possibility of a stateless society, or the necessity of joining a party. He calls the Church to repentance and renewal in the face of a new society, but by her own standards and in her own freedom. Here is no confusion of Christian repentance with Communist self-criticism. But withal, Barth's attitude toward the Communist state and revolution in Hungary is deeply positive, despite the dangers he recognizes. One might almost call it benevolent. In sharp contrast to his attitude toward Nazism he finds Communism at least a system which has made a serious attempt to solve the social problem which the West has neglected. He concedes that Communism is godless, but contends that it does not offer a temptation for Christians as did Nazism:

[1]Cf. *Eine Schweizer Stimme*, pp. 334, 371, 414 *et al.*

'Communism, as distinguished from Nazism, has not done, and by its nature cannot do one thing: it has never made the slightest attempt to reinterpret or to falsify Christianity, or to shroud itself in a Christian garment. It has never committed the basic crime of the Nazis, the removal and replacement of the real Christ by a national Jesus, and it has never committed the crime of anti-Semitism. There is nothing of the false prophet about it.'[1]

He attributes Communism's brutality and despotism to Russia rather than to the ideology.

Against the background of such perspectives as these on the facts of Communist doctrine and practice, Barth is able to see in the political change which came about in Hungary a reminder of that one great change toward which the world moves and which has already occurred in Christ. In the meantime

'The Christian Church will certainly not omit to see in such changes a new offer of the divine provision for all men. When one political system, the work of men's hands, collapses to make way for another, it means at least that the work of divine patience and wisdom is not yet completed. Once again, a limit has been set to some abuse of law and freedom, of community and power. A new political system means that men have been allowed a new chance to order their common life differently, and, possibly better. . . . It is impossible to see how the Christian Church could refuse to be prepared to take a hopeful interest in such an event at any rate as a matter of principle.'[2]

He calls the Church therefore to examine herself, the Scripture, and society to find out why, in God's providence, this change took place, and if the Church herself is denied privilege and attacked, to ask what failure in herself has brought on this judgement rather than insisting on her prerogatives. Finally he advises the Hungarians not to take any stand on principle, but to make their contribution to a revolutionary age by calm, impartial judgement on concrete cases where the welfare of man is involved, by concrete suggestions for the next step in politics, and thus, by participation, criticism, or resistance ('even in the best state Christians will never be able to express their gratitude for God's gift and ordinance

[1]Cf. 'Die Kirche zwischen Ost und West', in *Unterwegs*, June, 1949, pp. 25–26. Tr. in *Against the Stream*, pp. 139–40.
[2]*Against the Stream*, p. 84.

except in the form of serious opposition'[1]) from time to time as the situation calls for it. Since the Church's task is to preach the Gospel of grace, it can never 'defend or proclaim—or even attack—abstract norms, ideals, historical laws and socio-political ideologies as such'. It can only take up particular political circumstances. Barth deprecates the idea that we are confronted, in Communism, with a totalitarian force whose dangers to human spiritual and bodily freedom require in themselves constant vigilance and warning. He is more concerned about the danger of anxiety, fear, and hate in the face of Communist pressure.

All of this runs parallel to Barth's neutralist attitude toward the problem of western defence against Communism. His central positive point is that Christians in the West owe the godless Communist East, not a crusade, not an aggressive vaunting of our superior religion, justice and wisdom, but the Word of the Cross through which we also allow ourselves to be renewed. The primary task of western society is reconstruction, so that the Communist criticism will have not the slightest moral foothold because of the inhumanity of our social system. The primary task of the Church is self-renewal so that Communist atheism will be deprived of the substance which our culture-Christianity has given it. Barth inveighs against the whole concept of a Christian West as a battle cry—as if the Church could be identified with one political power group, so that the line of good and evil ran along the Iron Curtain. He rejects the idea that Christians should say the same things about the East-West conflict, that most of the western world is also saying. He feels that this involves a process of self-justification in the West; the proclamation of the Gospel in politics should always speak first the word of repentance to the Christian. It should go 'against the stream' of human righteousness.

Therefore, Barth believes, the Church belongs between East and West, seeking in all ways to preach the Gospel of reconciliation in Christ to both; seeking all practical ways toward reconstruction and peace; seeking, especially in the West, to liberate men from the terrible fear which grips them at the thought of Communist power. This is the theological-ethical argument which he makes in *The*

[1] *Against the Stream*, p. 81.

Church Between East and West. But Barth does not stop with this. He lines up the ideology of Communism in its criticism of the west against the 'ideology' of the west in its criticism of Communism, and more or less equates them. He treats America on one side as an ideological imperialism of the same order as Russia on the other. He defines the present world conflict as a pure power struggle between these two, and as such as a conflict in which the Church has no interest whatever. He calls the Church to seek a third way between these warring ideological powers, a way which will offer a third way also to Europe, between East and West.

It is in connexion with this third way, as explicated by Niemöller, Heinemann and their friends in relation to German rearmament, that, curiously enough, the crisis and confessional element of Barth's political thinking re-emerges. Not against Communism, but against Adenauer and his conception of the defence of a Christian Europe, the Christian is called to declare his binding 'No', to point out the evil spirit at work, and even call the unity of the Church in question by its response to this political confession. Barth, to be sure, does not limit crisis and confession to this question. He only cites Niemöller and Heinemann as the lone contemporary examples of the kind of political decision a Christian must make, and associates himself with their witness. He declares it to be the task of prophets to add up the rational arguments in the case of alternative political possibilities, and then to discern the spirits moving in each line of political action. On this his political confession as a Christian will be based. Because he has found a clear call to Christian obedience in one political decision he will not hesitate to declare it a *status confessionis* and not just a question of degree (*Ermessensfrage*) on which Christians can amicably differ. Thus he challenges other Christians to take seriously the question of their political obedience, and either to join him, or bear convincing witness in the same sense over against him. This is dangerous, says Barth, but it is necessary, for the only unity worth anything in evangelical Christianity is the dynamic unity of the confessing congregation. At the same time the prophet himself must be aware of the difficulty and danger of his witness as well as its necessity. He must be at once a witness to the Old Testament severity and commitment, which includes sober and convincing common sense, and New Testament freedom and joy.

'If political decisions in the unity of faith are to occur at all, they can become a reality only when they take place on the extremely narrow frontier that divides the world from the Kingdom of God: where common sense speaks the language of the Holy Spirit, and the Holy Spirit the language of common sense.'[1]

This is the structure of Barth's theology of politics itself, and of his attempt to apply his thought to political decision in the post-war world, in the face of its division into (from the European perspective) East and West. In it we see reflected on the most practical level both the strengths and weaknesses of this thought in the encounter with Communism, whose roots and development we have already traced.

1.

Despite all the ineptitude of Barth's own thought in the field of social and political decision, it must be recognized that it is he who fundamentally has liberated European Protestant theology both from bondage to one political ideology (whether bourgeois liberal or socialist) and from the sterile, basically escapist division of life into the two kingdoms of grace and law. He has done more than any other theologian in the tradition of the Reformation to open the way for a Christian dynamic in political life which made a Christian encounter with Communism possible at all. This is said with due regard for the contribution of Paul Tillich and the religious socialists in pointing out the religious and prophetic qualities in the socialist movement, and for their deeper involvement in and understanding of Marxism. It was nevertheless Barth who provided the theological elements of the encounter where it most fruitfully takes place today in Europe: the elements of Christological understanding of the state, a free direct approach to human beings and their welfare, and knowledge of the crisis of Christian obedience in the political sphere.

[1]'Political Decision in the Unity of Faith', in *Against the Stream*, p. 160.

A. Barth's Christological understanding of the state, as an order of Redemption alongside of, though outside, the Church, carries into politics the revolutionary yet positive quality which we have already seen in Barth's Christ-centred thinking in general. Against conservative Lutheran political doctrine, and to a certain extent against Brunner, it breaks the habit of negative thinking about the state in Protestant Christian circles of Reformation heritage, without falling into the opposite tendency of liberal idealism. Here once again, as in all the rest of Barth's theology, we have Marx's revolutionary impulse to society taken with final seriousness, and yet we see the Communist ideal of socialist construction outbid by the reality of redemption. The intrinsically conservative tendency which we have already seen to lie in such attempts as Brunner's to build knowledge of a political order and ethic on the purely 'sustaining grace' of God, has no place in this way of thinking. The old Lutheran tendency to set up a double ethic: one for the realm of the state where God's law rules for the control of sin, and another for the realm of the Church where grace rules for man's redemption, is for Barth anathema, not because like the liberals he is more cheerful about human natural possibilities, but because like Marx he repudiates the concealed self-justification, the political irresponsibility which roots in satisfaction with the *status quo* (or, as in some circles in Nazi Germany and again in Communist Germany today, in fear for the consequences a Christian witness would bring, in flight to the security of an ecclesiastical haven), which this ethic implies. In the face of Christ's work there can be no political order justified by less than its service to the end of man's redemption, however external this service may be, or created by less than the grace of a loving God. The Christian is therefore free from the world in Barth's thought, to be for the world as Christ is for the world. He has expressed more successfully than any other theologian in this study, the way in which the Christian is a radical toward every political system and loyalty, more consistently radical than the Communist himself; and at the same time more positive, more constructive than any idealist, in affirming and discovering the true service of the state.

B. The second element of Barth's political thinking—the free

approach to the knowledge and service of one's fellow man—brings
Barth closest to the Anglo-Saxon tradition in Christian ethics. We
have seen how the way is open here for all the empirical data of
human experience, and how all universal laws are subordinated to
man's direct free response to the act and love of God. Here again it
is Barth's contribution to have given the concept *Menschlichkeit* a
new meaning and content by referring it so completely to the
Mitmenschlichkeit of Christ. It is hard for Anglo-Saxons to understand the degree to which the very concept of the human had been
confused in Europe, first by the absolutes of the Enlightenment,
then by Hegelian idealism, then by Marx and Communism, Hitler
and Nazism, Nietzsche, and existentialism. It is Barth who has
done more than any other great thinker of the European continent
in recent years, to restore to man his freedom to encounter his
fellow man without the distorted perspectives of this or that conception of man; not even depending on a Christian ideal of humanity, but seeing him as he is, as God has made him and as Christ
died for him. Barthian theology therefore has contributed everywhere in Europe toward breaking down ideological politics in
favour of a more pragmatic and practical approach to the problems
of state.[1]

c. Thirdly, Barth's return to the note of crisis and confession in
politics is a necessary balance to the other elements we have mentioned, and an approach to the analytical realism of Reinhold
Niebuhr. Niebuhr, significantly, was at pains to agree when, in

[1]We see this especially in Holland, where both Protestants and
Catholics have long had their particular parties and ideologies and
Barth's theological opponent is orthodox Calvinism. We see it also in
Germany where the influence of the Confessing Church from the days of
the Nazis has prevented the regrowth of a political party of Evangelical-
Conservative background such as was the old Deutsche Nationale Volkspartei, and has at one and the same time contributed to the unideological
realism of the Christian Democratic Union, preventing it from
becoming once again a Catholic party, and to reconcilation of the Evangelical Church with the Social Democrats. Even the unfortunate political
adventures of Gustav Heinemann, including his formation of a 'Gesamtdeutsche Volkspartei', have been based not on the injection of a new
ideology into the political scene, but on the attempt to give popular expression to a particular policy, which Heinemann feels is being ignored
by the major parties because of their *weltanschauliche* tendencies.

1938, Barth first proclaimed the idea of a confessional witness in political questions to bear which was binding on the whole Church.[1] Judging from what he then wrote, Niebuhr would certainly agree in general today with Barth's formulation of the challenging nature of Christian obedience in political decision and the dynamic nature of the Church to which it contributes. Whatever may be said about the ineptitude with which Barth applies this insight, it remains true that in political questions not only technical factors but also spirits are involved, which must be proved, and which give the Christian decision in politics a moral urgency which binds and challenges the whole Church.

Of all these points, the most illuminating example in practice is the encounter of the Evangelical Church with Communism in Eastern Germany. In the words of a speaker before a recent synod, which, although not directly Christological, express strongly the spirit of Barth:

'Political authority (*Obrigkeit*, Greek *exousiai*—authorized powers, Rom. 13.1) is, and remains, an *institutum dei*, even when it does not respect God's commands. God will either force it to, or destroy it. To be sure the same God who binds us to the *Obrigkeit* makes us free over against it. But a "No" to concrete enterprises of the *Obrigkeit* must always be based on a "Yes" to its function. . . . I take part in the given task of the *Obrigkeit* by recognizing the function which God has given it. For the sake of this function itself I shall have to offer resistance in certain circumstances; only so can I do God's will. For the *Obrigkeit* is mysteriously dependent on the second table of the ten commandments. No *Obrigkeit* can stand, which basically and systematically breaks the commandments. It depends then on the good works of those who fulfil the commandments. It is then openly forced by God for the sake of its very existence, to pass by, so to speak, its ideology, and take up factual work and responsible order.'[2]

[1]Cf. Niebuhr's comment on Barth's political battle cry against Nazism, 'Die Kirche und die politische Frage von Heute' (*Eine Schweizer Stimme*, pp. 69–107):

'We have insisted that we have no right to declare that only socialistic political convictions are compatible with the Christian faith, but that we have both the right and the duty to insist that they are binding upon us and that they are organically related to the Christian faith; and that we have the right and the duty to challenge those who do not agree with us to validate their political convictions in the light of their faith.' *Radical Religion*, Spring 1939, p. 4.

[2]Martin Fischer, *Die öffentliche Verantwortung des Christen heute*, pp. 26–7.

This means first, that, following Barth's more general re-interpretation of *hupotassesthai* in Rom. 13.1 rather than his specific attitude toward the Nazi state, the Christian cannot abstractly or on principle reject the authority of any state, even the most illegal. The concept of legality by which the western world attempts to deny the existence of the 'German Democratic Republic' in Eastern Germany has no place as such in Christian thinking. When confronted with a state, such as the Communist state is, which claims the total allegiance of its citizens, and rules not according to the will of God or the needs of man but according to the plan of an ideology, the Christian has first to recognize that despite itself this state, in God's providence, exercises some of the functions of ordered government. The Christian first of all therefore addresses such a state, as a citizen who expects justice and order from it, and who respects its officials for the function they should be fulfilling as servants of God. This is why apparently fruitless Church protests against injustices and ideological pressure continue to be sent to the State. This is why, during the persecution in early 1953, the Church fought every case of those arrested for religious activity, through the courts in full form, and negotiated daily with the highest authorities for their release, though both these forms of activity were without prospects from the beginning. This is the basis on which every Christian where he happens to be, can appeal to the government official nearest him (in that official's own truest interest, in honest well-wishing and without the secret hope that he will shortly be served up with his deserts), to cut the corners of his ideological training, in the interest of simple justice and humanity.

This means secondly, however, that the Christians' recognition of the *Obrigkeit* is always relative and functional, never total. 'The Christian Church will dispute the right of any government at any time to demand unconditional obedience,'[1] declares the Administration

[1] Cf. 'Für die Möglichkeit eines echten und hilfreichen Gespräches. Stellungnahme der evangelischen Kirchenleitung der Kirchenprovinz Sachsen zur Weltfriedensbewegung, zur Politik der Regierung und zum Verhältnis Kirche und Staat.' A statement given to the Minister-President of the Province, 11th December, 1950. Published in *Hat die Kirche geschwiegen?* das öffentliche Wort der evangelischen Kirche aus den Jahren 1945–54 (Berlin, 1954), pp. 77–89.

of the Church in the Province of Saxony in reply to the state's objection to one of its protests against election pressures. On this basis the Church in East Germany has resisted with all its power especially the state's pressure on the minds of youth and other citizens. Basing itself on the fifth thesis of the Barmen Declaration, which Barth also makes a cornerstone of his political thought,[1] the Saxon Church continues:

'As long as the government tries to force on the whole population a materialist world view, and to form the whole of public life according to the principles of this world view, the difficulties in the mutual relations between Church and state will not cease, but will rather sharpen as long as the Church remains true to her confession and her mission.'[2]

It is not the materialistic world view as such but the total nature of the claim which it forces on the educational system, on the various mass organizations, and on the media of public communication, which these churchmen see as the issue. The issue however is always concrete: as concrete as the need of the neighbour himself.

[1]As quoted in the above document, this thesis reads:
'Fürchtet Gott, ehret den König!' (I Peter 2.17) 'Die Schrift sagt uns, dass der Staat nach göttlicher Anordnung die Aufgabe habe, in der noch nicht erlösten Welt, in der auch die Kirche steht, nach dem Mass menschlicher Einsicht und menschlichen Vermögens unter Androhung und Ausübung von Gewalt für Recht, und Frieden zu sorgen. Die Kirche erkennt in Dank und Ehrfurcht gegen Gott die Wohltat dieser seiner Anordnung an. Sie erinnert an Gottes Reich, an Gottes Gebot, und Gerechtigkeit und damit an die Verantwortung der Regierenden und Regierten. Sie vertraut und gehorcht der Kraft des Wortes, durch das Gott alle Dinge trägt.'
'Wir verwerfen die falsche Lehre, als solle und könne der Staat über seinen besonderen Auftrag hinaus die einzige und totale Ordnung menschlichen Lebens werden und also auch die Bestimmung der Kirche erfüllen.'
'Wir verwerfen die falsche Lehre, als solle und könne sich die Kirche über ihren besonderen Auftrag hinaus staatliche Art, staatliche Aufgaben und staatliche Würde aneignen und damit selbst zu einem Organ des Staates werden.' Op. cit. p. 84. Karl Barth quotes the same article at the end of his *Christengemeinde und Bürgergemeinde* (§36), and claims to have done nothing more in his whole essay than to have expounded its meaning. *Against the Stream*, p. 50.
[2]*Hat die Kirche geschwiegen?* pp. 84–85.

It is not a general declaration of ideological war which we read here but the Church's warning that her pastoral concern for the welfare of concrete human beings will constantly bring conflicts with the state on this issue, where it comes to a head, in local schools, in youth organizations, in factories, farms, and polling booths, and perhaps also in prison. Always however not the social principle, but justice to the human being is the issue, which is the true function of the state. Not the pros and cons of land reform as a technical economic measure but the fate of the farmer in the process of land reform;[1] not socialism *versus* private enterprise, but the freedom and security of the worker in each[2]—these and many others are illustrations of the direct approach to human beings in politics which is the strength of this Christian witness in the face of an ideology which tries to distort or hide these human realities.

Thirdly, the Christian finds himself in human solidarity with the oppressed, the poor, and the suffering. He stands on their side, as God does, over against the oppressing powers, and warns these powers of the judgement of God in the resentment and resistance of their victims. This significance in rebellion and revolution, which Barth, like Hromadka and Berecsky, applies to the Communist conquest of power, applies in Eastern Germany in reverse. So it was, in relation to the demonstrations of 17th June, 1953, that the

[1]Cf. Erich Hoffman, 'Bleibt das Dorf?' in *Wählt das Leben* (Stuttgart, 1952), pp. 449–56. Also from the same author—*Der soziologisch-ökonomische Umschichtungsprozess auf dem Dorfe* (Berlin, 1951). Prof. Hoffman is Professor of Agricultural Economy in Halle, East Germany. He points out that socialized and private forms of agricultural life must supplement each other today in order to re-establish that organic community which is the will of God for rural life, and which has been destroyed not first and only by Communist collectivization, but by bourgeois conceptions of absolute private property. He calls the Church to become the community centre from which this organic health will again radiate into the community as a whole.

[2]Cf. Lothar Kreyssig, 'Wem gehört der Betrieb?' in *Wählt das Leben*, pp. 370–80. Expanded in *Betrieb und Feierabend*, Heft 7 in Schriftenreihe *Kirche im Volk* (published by the Evangelical Church in the Rheinland, 1952) pp. 30–50. Kreyssig, a member of the administration of the Evangelical Church of the Province of Saxony, points out the place of responsible administration of such property as is given to man, in the interest of the welfare of other men, in the face of materialism in both East and West.

Church took every occasion to declare its solidarity with the suffering of the workers who rose up, to protest against the draconian measures with which the demonstrations were suppressed, and to call injustice by its name. This does not mean however that the Christian shares the illusions or the hatred of these victims, or that he can make the strategy of their revolution unqualifiedly his own. The church bells did not ring to call people into the street, and pastors have repeatedly had to speak out against a spirit of hatred and revenge. 'If the Russians withdrew', said one church leader recently, 'the first task of the Christians would be to rush to the market place to save the Communists from the mob.' *They* would then suddenly be the oppressed who were yesterday the oppressors.

Finally, the possibility of revolution is not completely eliminated, as it is in Lutheran orthodoxy, though it is treated with great reserve because it so easily becomes a mythology in its own right. The question must be put to every revolutionary plan whether it serves 'the welfare of the city' (Jer. 29.7): whether it stands a positive chance of producing more justice and order than it destroys. This demands realistic power calculations which are not on a different level from meditation on the Word of God, but, as in Barth's thought as well, belong to it. Here we see the clearest example of Barth's doctrine of crisis in political decision, in the encounter with Communism. Responsible Christian leaders have almost unanimously opposed revolutionary activity in the present situation of the East Zone of Germany, for three main reasons: (*a*) The people are not fitted in spirit or tradition for guerilla warfare. Their strengths lie in other forms of resistance and independence. The country, furthermore, is geographically and politically not suitable for such warfare. (*b*) Russian power is now such that there is no reasonable hope of achieving independence of it by violent resistance, unless this resistance precipitates total war. (*c*) Participation in underground resistance movements wastes the lives of young idealists whose courage is desperately needed at other points, and it disintegrates the character of participants, because the negative impulses of terror, hate, revenge, lies, and espionage—as counterweapons against the same evils of

311

Communism—so predominate. These are arguments of the reason. But they add up to a perception of the *status confessionis* in this matter. Most Christians reject underground resistance and the total rejection of the East German social order, which feeds it, as a false spirit, just as is Communism on the other side. This however is not a matter of unchanging moral principles. It is Christian witness which makes a binding claim for validity in a particular historical and social situation.

2.

This is the use which has been made of Barth's insight, or parallel insights, in East Germany. Barth himself however, fails precisely in that synthesis of his three theological elements which would give his political judgement depth and validity. At different times we find different aspects stressed. Toward Swiss democracy both during and after the war we find a kind of suggestive idealism, based on a firm conviction that the Swiss Comradeship of the Oath (*die Schweizerische Eidgenossenschaft*—official title of the Swiss state) sets forth a kind of order which Europe has lost and must find again, a kind of just state which reflects, in its appointed way, the Gospel of Jesus Christ which has been preached to the whole West, and the grace of God in and through it. In this framework Barth can be prophetically sharp, pointing out the way in which the Swiss may lose this gift, or mildly suggestive.[1] Toward the Nazi state, as we have seen, his attitude was one of total war, for he found here a false spirit at work which placed man in a crisis over against it, and demanded his confession. Toward the Communist state his attitude is one of the greatest possible freedom for a pragmatic approach to concrete problems, partly in reaction to a false spirit which he detects in the attempts to draw the ideological issue too sharply in the West. In each case a different element of his theology predominates. In no case does he adequately relate them to produce a fully convincing political ethic. In one situation we are confronted

[1]'Im Namen Gottes des Allmächtigen!', a lecture delivered in Switzerland in 1941. In *Eine Schweizer Stimme*, pp. 209–32. Cf. *Christengemeinde und Bürgergemeinde, passim.*

with an unmodified declaration of crisis and *status confessionis* against the political demons of our day, and in another we find counsel to wait, reserve judgement, and remember that God's grace rules even the demons. And we find this arbitrary selection from different theological emphases for different political situations justified by appeal to Christian freedom in response to Christ!

'The Church . . . preserves its freedom to judge each new event afresh. If yesterday it travelled along one path, it is not bound to keep to the same path today. If yesterday it spoke from its position of responsibility, then today it should be silent if in this position it considers silence to be the better course.'[1]

However justified this polemic may be against Brunner's attempt to subsume the whole Communist issue under the heading of 'totalitarianism' in order to treat it as an instance of this universal, Barth is still covering with these words his own failure to integrate his theology of politics. It is here that he fails to meet the challenge of Reinhold Niebuhr. Niebuhr's concentration on the facts of human political experience themselves, and his theology of continuing tension between love and law in political decision, compel him to take the realities of human social experience in all their complexity with a seriousness which Barth's theology allows, to be sure, but does not compel. Niebuhr's doctrine of sin and grace operates in each analysis and decision to produce greater political realism than Barth. He balances more accurately the demonic and creative forces at work. He is more aware of the balance between relativity (and sin) and confessional urgency in concrete decisions. He is, in short, without falling into any pattern of natural law, more acutely aware than Barth, of the ways of God with human structures of power, order, and justice, precisely because, or so it seems, of his refusal to place the whole political process from the beginning under the order of Redemption. Barth seems, because of his doctrine of all-embracing grace, to neglect his responsibility for that difficult empirical analysis of real human relations, most especially in politics, which the Christian, just because of his

[1]From Barth's reply to Emil Brunner's question to his attitude in the Hungarian situation. *Against the Stream*, p. 114.

faith, should take more seriously than all others. His movement from theology to political decision is for ever beset by over-simplification of the political issues and by blindness to some of the factors involved, not less when he speaks of freedom than when he speaks of crisis or of the structure of the just state. He is reported once to have said that only two things were really interesting: the Bible, and the concrete human being, in his history and his society. Yet this deceptive truth betrays him; for the concrete human being is not easily understood, without careful examination of all the supposedly 'uninteresting' body of secular political, economic, sociological analysis which, so far as it is relative and empirical, helps the Christian to define his *Menschlichkeit*.

Yet Barth and Niebuhr are not so far apart, even in politics, as the reader of the religious press might suppose. There is no reason why Niebuhr's political wisdom cannot be used to complete and improve Barth's theology, because there is a basic similarity, though a difference of emphasis, in the theology with which the two men approach political questions. That which Niebuhr calls relative natural law, the natural conscience of man, and calls on to provide the background of justice in history, is closer to Barth's doctrine of gracious providence in the state, than to any Catholic or liberal doctrine of natural law. In the final analysis it is just as dependent on Christ for its existence. Outside this it has only a dialectical existence, with no clear sphere of its own. It is Christ, the law of love, who gives all other justice and law its relative validity and its limitation, for Niebuhr and, expressed in other words, for Barth. Secondly, Barth's doctrine of freedom for the direct encounter with human need in politics has its almost exact parallel in Niebuhr's pragmatism. Both declare war on the distortions which political ideologies bring into the problems of human relations. Thirdly, Barth's doctrine of crisis and confession calls forth a responsive chord in the urgency with which Niebuhr approaches all political problems. All Niebuhr's strategic thinking and all his realism about the balance and use of power in politics have not diminished in the least his solidarity with Barth in opposing the kind of *Realpolitik* in which everything is relative, an *Ermessensfrage*, and no political Christian witness is possible.

There is therefore no reason why Niebuhr cannot be called upon to draw together Barth's disjointed theology of politics at two central points.

A. Niebuhr can remind Barth, as Barth from his own theological presuppositions should know, that the action of the grace of God in giving form to political justice, and the action of powers of evil in turning political order to the ends of human power, are more subtle in their interaction than can be grasped by applying one or the other concept alone to any given situation. The spirits behind a given policy may be not one but many, both evil and good. This is certainly true of the issue in which Barth sees the confessional crisis today—that of German rearmament. The reference of the whole proposal to the false ideology of a western 'Christian culture' is far too simple a diagnosis of the spiritual temptations and dangers involved both in favouring and opposing it. Barth's own basic reason for opposition—that militarism is a disease of the German spirit which will destroy its new start in healthy life, defeating any possible good which a German army might bring to the security of the West—is equally a single-minded judgement which belongs in the category of understandable emotion rather than shrewd analysis.[1] Other spirits are at work in this situation: fear, which Barth finds to be the dominant mood of the West, over against the Communist threat, expresses itself not only in a more bitter and warlike anti-Communism, but also in silent resignation toward the probable coming of Communism, in the mood of *ohne mich* and in the very neutralism of which Barth is an exponent. Irresponsibility and distrust toward the only constructive moves which Europe has made since the war in the direction of economic co-operation, political unity, and a reasonable common defence—an irresponsibility with its roots in wounded nationalism, in party politics, and in private or group interest—has guided opposition to German rearmament more than genuine concern for its spiritual effects. In short, Barth, and his friends in west Germany of this political persuasion, have failed to identify the complex of crises in which political man in Germany stands, over against the Communist pressure, because they have operated too simply in their analysis with Barth's doctrine

[1]Cf. Letter to the Editor of *Unterwegs* in *Unterwegs*, 1950, Heft 5.

of crisis and confession, not balancing it with his more positive understanding of the grace of God in the state.

The same is equally true in reverse. Barth's neutralism, an extension of his idea of the meaning of Swiss democracy for Europe as a whole, though he presents it as a political mission of the Church, is based on a simple refusal to face the facts of power politics as they relate to the various more or less dangerous ideologies which have power in their hands. In other words we have, in his well-known pamphlet *The Church Between East and West*, an emphasis on construction of such a state of justice with such open humility that the element of truth in the Communist charge against us will be removed; which utterly ignores the whole problem of the crisis in which we are placed by the actual powers which confront us, and with whom we have to deal. He calls the Church to lead Europe in abjuring altogether the conflict between Russia and America because it is supposedly nothing but a power conflict between two ideological powers. Yet he offers no guidance beyond moral exhortation to Europeans as to how they shall organize their economy in this area 'between East and West', or deal with the power cross-currents in their midst. And the only answer he offers to the problem of common defence is a plea for no partisanship, for a reconciling attitude toward the East, and the statement that 'if we are concerned with reconstruction in the West, then we need have no fear of the East.'[1]

Barth has yet to develop his systematic doctrine of the state. When he does so, he would do well to learn in detail from Niebuhr how the appreciation of that justice which God in his grace has placed in every political order and in the conscience of men, interacts at every point with the sinful organization of power for human ends, ideologized or otherwise, so that once again knowledge of grace and knowledge of crisis must act as two prongs of a forceps to probe each political reality.

B. Niebuhr can remind Barth also that the freedom which man has in Christ is a freedom from the distortions of pride and self-interest and from the ideologies which cover them, to see the neighbour as he is, in the social reality which stands under God's

[1]*Against the Stream*, p. 144.

gracious providence. It is therefore a freedom which affirms human experience, and, so far as it is relative and objective, human thinking about that experience, by virtue of its standard and source in Christ. This is a freedom which is in no sense a substitute for the careful understanding of the social and political situation in which the Christian has to act, but frees the Christian for this understanding. 'The Christian ethic goes through the whole world of morality, tests everything and retains the best.' wrote Barth in a recent lecture.[1] His own theology bears witness against the Adviser to the Hungarians who proclaimed the Christian's freedom from all programmes and principles as a principle and programme in itself. 'Christian politics are bound to seem strange, incalculable, and surprising in the eyes of the world—otherwise they would not be Christian.'[2] This delight in an irresponsible and arbitrary kind of freedom—this unhappiness unless he is going 'against the stream' —is one side of Barth's personality. It expresses itself in his claim for the Church of the right to withdraw altogether from participation in political life if the 'time' does not suit her for speaking and acting; a position completely inconsistent with his more basic teaching about the continuing political responsibility of the Church. It expresses itself in his words to Brunner quoted above which imply that 'isms and systems can be ignored because they are no part of historical reality—a verbal gesture which again flouts the main lines of his dogmatic thinking (Cf. III/2 on existentialism *et al.*) by absolutizing one point in it. It expresses itself most seriously however in that which Barth neglects in his thinking; the vast body of secular thinking about political realities and political responsibilities in which Christians as well as non-Christians have recorded the actual interaction of the grace of God with the sin of man in the life of the state. Again and again one sees the narrow base of Barth's experience in this realm—the Christian socialism of his youth, with its lasting anti-bourgeois prejudice, the overwhelming impact which the Nazi revolution made on him, and the life of a thoughtful citizen of the Swiss Comradeship of the Oath—being

[1]'Die christliche Ethik', in *Zwei Vortrage* (Theologische Existenz Heute, Neue Folge, Nr. 3, Munich, 1946).
[2]*Against the Stream*, p. 92.

made the basis of political and economic judgements much too broad for such a base to carry, because Barth has not felt compelled by his theology to participate more widely in the political experience of mankind. Here is where Niebuhr's deeper and wider participation in politics, out of the same Christian freedom, corrects and completes the narrow arbitrariness which too often characterizes Barth's expression of this freedom.

Another corrector, who is also a follower, of Barth at this point is Helmut Gollwitzer. Gollwitzer is concerned at all costs to maintain the fullness of the dialectic between appreciation of and participation in the whole of political life, and the claim of Christ over it all. This includes, in his mind, the recognition that every act of political justice, even when by a non-Christian, is for the sake of Christ, and that the Christian is the witness to this fact, and its guarantor:

'Especially the experiences of the last decades can only be truly understood from this angle. Was there, is there any action of Christians over against the totalitarian powers, any protest against Hitler, any refusal of obedience to Stalin . . . that was not done (even when the doer was not theologically clear about it) finally for the sake of Christ, in obedience to him whom one must obey more than man, and as witness to his lordship and salvation? When a hunted Jew was hidden, when a man was ordered to denounce another and refused, when it came to accusing the conscience of an official, Christians found themselves in unforgettable community with non-Christians, humanists, socialists and others who often shamed them by their readiness to take their part. But whereas these others thought it was merely a question of human rights, or of natural law, Christians knew . . . that it was a question in these deeds of God's right to man; of the fact that this hunted man is the property of Jesus Christ, and that that official must be called away from his slavery to idols for the service of Jesus Christ. Only from this did these actions receive their unqualified rightness, with which one could reassure oneself in those police hearings where one was subjected to moral attacks which were so hard to withstand.'[1]

From the perspective of this degree of participation in the common life, Gollwitzer finds a more satisfying synthesis of Providence and crisis, than Barth has been able to achieve. Every Christian decision in politics involves both the absolute of hearing and obeying God's word, and the relative of thinking through technical

[1]Gollwitzer, *Die Christliche Gemeinde in der politischen Welt* (Tübingen, 1954), pp. 36–37.

questions (*Ermessensfragen*). But the crisis, the *status confessionis*, relates not to the particular policy which the technical reason works out in detail, but to the relation between this line of technical thinking and the act of listening to and obeying the commandment of God which is its cause. Therefore particular political decisions may not be erected into confessional absolutes on which *die Geister sich zu scheiden haben*. The Christian in politics has the more subtle task of testing the spirits which different people and groups show in relating the commandment of God to their practical reason, to see which of them under what circumstances do and do not confess that Jesus Christ is Lord.

Gollwitzer concludes with a plea for an area of Christian thinking between the theological commandment itself and political policy in practice, in which the Church or a prophetic group can give, not binding exegeses of the commandments, but *Weisungen* for political life which move out beyond the existing lines of political and theological order to suggest the lines of a new more creative human society, or to revitalize forgotten truths and values. Gollwitzer attributes this idea to Barth, and Barth indeed develops *Weisungen* for German society in the early post-war period, as we have seen above. But Gollwitzer himself is responsible for liberating this concept from the shackles of a too absolute crisis thinking, and giving it proper dignity as a creative ethical force. He has opened the way, by this synthesis of Barth's elements, for a theology of politics which is both confessional, in the sense that the Christian's witness carries the conviction and power of his *Gehorsamsgewissheit*, and creative, by suggesting to a world in revolution new forms of its social life.

3.

We turn finally to a criticism of Barth in the light of Gollwitzer, which will make the foregoing more concrete. In the last analysis the weakness of Karl Barth himself in the encounter with Communism lies in the fact that, like Tillich's, the encounter of his whole life has been primarily not with concrete persons and their problems, but with philosophical systems and movements of culture. His encounter with these has, to be sure, been quite different from

319

Tillich's. His sense of reality has been so determined by Biblical revelation, above all by the central figure of Christ that, like Moses, he has more than anyone else helped to lead theology out of the wilderness of philosophy to its own promised land which is the dealing of God with concrete men. His participation in the life of the Church in Germany and Switzerland is, unlike Tillich's, very real. The concrete persons and problems which arise in this circle are actively present to him, a fact which helps to explain the range and sensitivity of his teaching in the ethics of marriage and the family. But still Barth's thinking, despite all its exaltation of the concrete, finds it difficult to break through to the concrete. Despite all his affirmation of the world in Christ, he shows himself strangely insensitive to the world in practice. Despite all the theoretical urgency of truth and love toward the neighbour in Christ, one misses ever again that urgency of practical concern which would complete and validate it. Nowhere is this more evident than in Barth's failure to grasp the real human problems involved in the encounter with Communism.

One has the impression that Barth approaches the encounter with Communism as a warrior who has already fought many campaigns and whose thought is so thoroughly moulded by these issues of the past, that he sees in the Communist problem only the old conflicts once again. He has fought his life long for a clear response to the Word of God against the temptations of Christian cultures and politics. It has been his glory to be Christ's revolutionary. It is not surprising therefore to see him imposing this primary conflict on the Hungarian situation once more, and reacting strongly against any alliance with the culture-Christians of the West against the Communist menace. It is natural that he should push Communism to the peripheral role of a healthy challenge and reminder to us of our own inhumanity, materialism, and man-centred religion. But this is a clear example of the way in which an ideological issue blinds Barth to the problems and temptations of the human spirit in a Communist situation. Contrary to the deepest insights of his own theology Barth is here bound by his opposition to culture-Christianity. He is not free to see it as only one, at the moment not the major one, of the spiritual issues involved.

Any reader of Gollwitzer's Russian diary *Unwilling Journey*, and anyone who deals with Christians in Eastern Germany can point out, quite in the spirit of the theology which Barth teaches, the issues which he has neglected. He fails completely to measure the force of Communist ideological pressure through schools, mass organizations, training camps and the like, in the service of the total claim which the state makes on the lives of its citizens. To be sure he has said much in Hitler's time about the Christian's 'No' to a state which demands inward allegiance and love,[1] and about the demonic nature of a state which claims total allegiance and goodness.[2] He has repeated these principles under questioning in Hungary, yet he seems dismayed and doubtful about their application to the Communist state as a whole. He is undoubtedly right in opposing those western thinkers such as Brunner who dispose of the Communist state and movement by interpreting it as the logical unfolding of an evil ideology. But his refusal to acknowledge the force which this secular religion actually has over human lives and spirits, leads him to neglect the temptations and struggles of real people—school children, students, workers, farmers, intellectuals, and all who must daily decide how much they may sacrifice in order to tell some degree of the truth—and to talk past them. He falls at this point into an unintended justification of Hromadka and Berecsky by concentrating on the secondary problem (which is of course still a real problem) of the Christian's freedom from the religious culture, with its security and congeniality, of his past.[3]

[1]*Church and State*, p. 77.
[2]'Die Kirche und die Politische Frage von Heute', *Eine Schweizer Stimme*, p. 85.
[3]As a corollary of this, one is also impressed with the way in which Barth ignores the whole spiritual problem raised by the pressure of the state in its system of espionage, into which it presses as many citizens as possible, and which certainly must have presented an acute problem in his visit to Hungary for instance. His judgements on that country seem blithely unaware of the problem of false information, of the distrust and hypocrisy by which even some Christians would find it necessary to protect themselves against others who were identified with state power; and perhaps even against the distinguished Swiss visitor who showed so little acumen as to identify himself with those others. Cf. Gollwitzer, *Unwilling Journey*, especially pp. 170–3, 191, 193, for a more penetrating insight into this problem in a Communist society.

This justification is unintended, as is clearly indicated by his letter to Berecsky in 1951. Barth took him to task for a eulogistic attitude toward the Communist government of Hungary which seemed almost to identify it with a second source of revelation, and warned him of the similarity between his thinking and that of the 'German-Christians' in Nazi times. This letter was published without Barth's permission. Only he knows how many others there are which would redress the balance of his public influence if they were known. Yet here again it is the warrior, rather than the man of spiritual insight, who draws the issue.

Barth is a lifelong warrior, though the conflict is submerged and subordinate, against bourgeois capitalism as well. The socialist strain in his thinking comes up despite his repudiation of socialism as an ideology, whenever questions of politics and economics are to the fore. This again hinders his insight into the human problems of the Christian encounter with Communism, this time on the level of economics and politics, for Barth cannot distinguish clearly enough between Communism as a system of total power and Communism as a radical form of socialism. His statements that Communism has evolved a constructive idea, however brutal, for the solution of the social problem, his general statements about the values and opportunities in political changes in Hungary, and the attitude they reflect, simply fail to make contact with the dilemma of actual Christians confronted with the demands of the total plan, threatened with collectivization which involves not only loss of property but of freedom, trying to weigh their responsibility as producers of goods and services to their neighbour, against the way in which these goods and services are being regimented not for the neighbour but for the state.

Barth is, thirdly, a warrior, dating from 1938, against Nazism, which means against a wild brutal messianic political power destructive of all reasonable order, delighting in persecution, linked with a great nation's nationalism, which yet was capable of casting a spell over good bourgeois people, and even Christians, presenting itself in the garb of 'positive Christianity', and developing an induced current within Christian circles prepared to rewrite the Bible and Christian history and give place to a new revelation.

Contact with this product of a western nation was such a shock, that he cannot believe Communist power, based on a careful theory, inspired by a utopia, attractive to intellectuals and idealists of Barth's own sort, disciplined in its structure, to be in any way comparable. It is the potential Nazi resurgence in any form on our western soil, which is for Barth the international enemy, lurking in a new German army, in the hearts of unrepentant Germans, in Spain, in the drive of American capitalism, and so on. But once again he is prevented by his polemic from seeing the human issues in the encounter, this time with the power of the Communist movement in the world. There is of course a difference between Communism and Nazism, which makes both Brunner's and Niebuhr's transfers from one to the other too simple. The difference, at the crucial point of their attitude toward human beings, is illustrated most effectively by Gollwitzer[1] in describing the way in which the inhumanity of Communism is utopian, not simply cynical. It is a disregard for human life in particular in the interest of humanity, of the plan; 'a bloodless cruelty', not the satisfaction of brutal impulses and emotions. And it may have as its obverse the most surprising demonstration of concern for humanity in some circumstances. There is a 'moral pathos' in Communism which Nazism lacks,[2] a reflection of the fact that it is not, as was Nazism, a nihilistic rebellion against Christian faith and morals itself, but a secular corruption of these, at once more dangerous in its self-righteousness, and more admirable in many of its fruits.

When this has been said, however, Barth disregards the fact that the danger which these two systems present to concrete human beings, in their attempt to organize and maintain any reasonably just political life, is indeed comparable. Whereas toward Nazism he required first the absolute 'No' of active opposition, prayer for its removal, rejection of its power claims and the like, and then within the framework of this, the development of a constructive political alternative, his response to Communism is rather the reverse: concentration on social construction and repentance for

[1]Gollwitzer, *Unwilling Journey*, pp. 99–108.
[2]Gollwitzer, 'Christentum und Marxismus', in *Unterwegs*, 1951, Heft 1, p. 18.

the evils of which Communism has reminded us, in the hopes that this will so take the edge off the conflict that the 'No' of resistance and opposition will either not be necessary, or necessary only in a few concrete cases. In this he forgets that Communism is not only judgement on the West, but also, parallel to Nazism despite the differences, a power system whose ideology provides no inner checks on its domination. He forgets those millions who must say 'No' to this power first in order to gain any room or hope for political construction. He forgets that from the perspective of Christians in East Germany, Communism is a more refined, more thorough, and more heartless version of Nazism precisely because of the inexorable force of its ideology, so that here also any constructive witness to the Communists must be based on a 'No' to their attempts to involve one in their form of 'social activity', Party membership and the like.

In all these ways Barth as a person is unfree in his encounter with Communism, bound by conflicts of the past which are only secondary conflicts today. His own attitude toward Communism lacks insight because he fails to understand it *sui generis*, as a movement with its own spirit, dynamic, and problems. But this lack of insight is an example of his lack of political acumen as a whole, illustrated in the disjointed way in which he applies his theology to different political phenomena. In this area of human life Barth remains, to this day, something of a stranger. The vast variety of human data, the vicarious participation in human political experience which is open to him, he has not taken up, despite the fact that he has recognized its pressing importance. He remains here the theologian, in the sense that he contents himself far too often with the somewhat insensitive statement and application of theological propositions lubricated with polemic. Yet this failure accurately to analyse and relevantly to speak to human problems on the political level cannot help but raise questions about Barth's theology itself, especially when that theology proclaims so powerfully that in Christ and because of his work *nihil humanum mihi alienum est*. It is therefore the contribution of Gollwitzer, and of the experience of East German Christians on whom we have drawn in this chapter, to demonstrate another application of Barth's theology to politics,

324

than he himself has given. In these men we see how all that is human can in fact be understood and cultivated in the political realm when we know the state, as Barth teaches us to know it, in a threefold manner as *Ordo Redemptoris*, as a place of man's free response to God's grace, and as the place of critical encounter with spirits and powers other than the Holy Spirit.

7

CHRISTIAN ENCOUNTER WITH
COMMUNISM: A CONCLUSION

IF one conviction has accompanied the whole of this inquiry, it is that which makes 'Christian' the adjective, and 'encounter' the noun, in our title over against Communism. Both Christianity and Communism are living movements. Each, to be sure, has a theory, a system of doctrine, but neither is this alone. It is in the encounter of these movements that God acts. It is this act which theology exists to illumine, thereby helping, not dominating, the Christian in the concrete business of obedience and witness. Our conclusion therefore can do no better than to bring this encounter itself more clearly into view, as illumined by the theologies which have gone before.

1. THE FORM OF REVOLUTION AND RESISTANCE
What is the encounter with Communism? Where does it take place and in what form? What Christian resources are helpful in clarifying this? To this series of questions we must give a frankly two-sided answer, for Communism presents itself differently to different groups of people, for all its sameness of basic theory and strategy.

A. The world meets Communism as a *revolutionary power* corresponding to a revolutionary age. Many of the powers which have revolutionized the life of man in the last century, to be sure—the powers of industrialization and imperialism for example—would be labelled conservative today. It is not the Communists' doing that throughout the world with a few exceptions people by the hundred millions are being uprooted from their traditional customs, homes, ways of making a living, and ways of worship, to be thrust into a new pattern of life with new opportunities, yet with great insecurity and without the depth of meaning which they found in the old. It is not the Communists' doing that new powers, in the hands of hitherto obscure people and classes, now dominate the social scene, or that new philosophies have arisen to guide them. But Communism has met this situation as one of the very few, if not the only thoroughly organized and thoroughly revolutionary force in it. In this consists its appeal. We see it on two levels:

(i) We see it among men of practice—especially among farmers and workers, who find in the Communist Party in many countries the only political force with which they have contact and which seems to be representing their interests. The problem which presents itself to the peasants of India for example is not that of political principle, or even of political freedom, but economic security against the growing pressures of urban manufacturing economy and the centralization of land ownership in absentee hands. For those who have begun to catch a new vision of what is possible in the modern world this grows to the demand for broader opportunity, and a fuller human life. The appeal of Communism to these people lies in its ability to reach their level of concern and give expression to it. Self-sacrificing Communists, largely from other classes, to be sure, live with and organize these people, teaching them, by personal example and confidence, by simple slogans and promises, the fundamentals of the Communist programme. But this programme itself appeals because the Communist Party proves itself to be the one political power which does not compromise with the *status quo*; and which promises to carry through reforms quickly and with force if necessary. This is not necessarily a positive appeal. For many a peasant or worker in such a land, the Communist ideology may be alien and bitter medicine, and the Communists repugnant. His innate shrewdness may even suspect that all is not so revolutionary or so full of promise as appears on the surface, even with these devoted fanatics. Yet even then it may present the appeal of inevitability. It may appear as the only party or organization with the power and inner discipline to bring order in a country out of chaos.

(ii) We see it among men of theory—notably the uprooted intellectuals or half-intellectuals of changing societies. Here another factor mixes with the general rebellion against injustice and insecurity which they share with most of the population: the rebellion

327

of the mind against old standards of truth and right, against old allegiances and communities, and the search for some new working philosophy around which to form their lives. Arnold Toynbee was right that the proletariat in a given society is definable in spiritual terms even more than in economic ones. The classic example which he cited of Alcibiades' betrayal of Athens for Sparta has repeated itself by the thousand today, and Communism has been the largest recipient of these wanderers.

Its appeal to them may be positive and idealistic. Many Chinese intellectuals, even Christians, found in the Communist movement that integrated philosophy of life and hope for society as a whole which was for them an answer to the hopeless chaos, both political and moral, of the Kuomintang. They compared the inner moral discipline and the devoted spirit of the Communist Party favourably even with that of the Christian Church. Most Chinese intellectuals were spiritual revolutionaries before they were Communists. They had already rejected the Confucian tradition of their forefathers, which had proved so artificial and so impotent. They were already seeking a new form for China's life, out of the West, which however would also express their independence over against western power and domination. They sought an integration of the broken and meaningless pieces of culture around them, western and Chinese, into a wholly new pattern which would give their own lives meaning. This is what they found in Communism. The Communists proved themselves the only group able to resist the pressure of old family loyalties, of big Shanghai money, and personal ambition. They proved the only force able to reform the life of the village and control it. They offered the only integration between theory and practice, and the only effective leadership of the revolution which was already in progress. In the light of this, the dangers inherent in dictatorship and dependence on Moscow seemed small by comparison, and fear of these dangers took on the aspect of a suspicious threat to China's only hope.

But this appeal can also have a negative side which is equally convincing; an appeal to the nihilist who cannot for ever live sceptical of all truth, meaning, and value. The conversion of the nihilist from extreme individualism to the service of a fierce and narrow political creed,' writes Michael Polanyi, 'is the turning point of the European revolution.' Marxism, he maintains, became the heir and continuation of the Enlightenment at a time when faith in rational moral values and the rational nature of man had crumbled.

'(These Nihilists) acquired a sense of righteousness, which in a paradoxical manner was fiercely intensified by the mechanical framework in which it was set. . . . Their moral aspirations found an outlet in the scientific prediction of a perfect society. Here was set out a scientific utopia relying for its fulfilment only on violence. Nihilists could accept, and would eagerly embrace, such a prophecy, which required from its disciples no other belief than that in the force of bodily appetites and yet at the same time satisfied their most extravagant moral hopes. . . . There emerged the modern fanatic, armoured with impenetrable scepticism.'[1]

Polanyi is one of a group of polemical analysts who make human beings conform too much to their patterns of thought,[2] but at this point he brings into sharp focus one aspect of the Communist psychological appeal, and helps to explain how it is that in the western world men become Communists for moral reasons, despite open eyes about the brutality and personal subjection it involves. In a world where every culture, every expression of reason and value, has turned out to be the ideology of some group against another, where nothing is sure and nothing sincere, a doctrine arises which takes full account of all this, and offers a science based on it. Then it couples this science with an effective programme for making the world over, and a community which offers meaningful activity and comradeship in return for personal surrender. Despair, loneliness, and the Christian conscience, are the three motives for joining the Communist movement which R. H. S. Crossman finds in the six men who tell their stories in *The God that Failed*. There was despair of all efforts to work out the meaning of life in freedom. There was loneliness where no communities of men were to be trusted any longer. But there was, as E. H. Carr has also emphasized,[3] a sense of guilt about this very condition:

[1]Michael Polanyi, *The Logic of Liberty* (London, 1951), p. 105.
[2]Another example of this kind of typological analysis of Communism is Jules Monnerot, *Le Sociologie du Communisme* (Paris, 1949); 1st and 3rd parts translated as *The Sociology of Communism* (London, 1953).
[3]In *The Soviet Impact on the Western World*. See above, p. 167.

'The intellectual, though he may have abandoned orthodox Christianity, felt its prickings far more acutely than many of his unreflective churchgoing neighbours. He was at least aware of the unfairness of the status and privileges which he enjoyed, whether by reason of race or class or education. The emotional appeal of Communism lay precisely in the sacrifices—both material and spiritual—which it demanded of the convert.'[1]

For such people Communism did not have to measure up to a previously held moral or scientific standard. It did not have to prove itself in benefits for the people. Enough that it was thoroughly revolutionary toward all the pretensions of the 'bourgeois' world, exposing all its hypocrisies and selfishness, and that it presented itself as the organized force whose triumph, for 'scientific materialist' reasons, seemed inevitable.

Such is the encounter with Communism of those who see it primarily as a revolutionary force, perhaps the only organizing force corresponding to the revolution in which they stand.

But the encounter between Communism and Christian faith takes place, in most parts of the world today, in the framework of a revolutionary situation which is broader than Communism; broader, in fact, than any system of politics and philosophy, Christian or otherwise, which might be set against it. In this revolution Communism and the Christian Gospel are unflinchingly dynamic factors. This they share in common over against almost every other spirit at work there. The Christian Gospel yields nothing to Communism in its realism about the relation of ruling social power, philosophy and culture, to group interest; in its self-identification with the proletarian situation; in the fullness of its love and hope for man, both body and soul; or in its thorough identification of truth with response to the neighbour, its unity of theory with practice. These are insights which have made Communism revolutionary in our time because they have been borrowed from much older themes in the Bible itself, for all their 'scientific' and 'materialist' clothing. They have made it convincing because they have appealed to a human conscience which was made for response to a gracious God, whether schooled, as in the West, by centuries of

[1]R. H. S. Crossman (ed.), *The God that Failed* (London, 1950), p. 11.

hearing the Gospel, or, as in the East, by a more hidden Providence. The Church and the Communist Party share at least this, that they are each, by virtue of their basic belief, movable ships on the stream of the revolutionary change of our day, and not rocks in its way, or debris choking it. The first requirement of an effective Christian encounter with Communism is to recognize this common factor as one which is God-given. The very existence of this Communism as a revolutionary force, its very appeal which we have described above, is a judgement on Christians, 'a bill for our neglects', in Gollwitzer's words. This is why the Christian cannot write off the Communist movement for its materialism or for its brutality, for its errors in theory and inhumanity in practice. No merely polemical encounter is adequate or convincing. Rather the Christian must search this power which grew from Karl Marx first with the question: What moments of judgement and prophecy does it contain? What must Christians learn from it about their own witness on the tide of this revolutionary upheaval of our day?

This is why, in the first place, that Christian study of the younger Marx, which we have described as owing a certain impetus to Tillich but going beyond him, is so important. Here the prophetic impulse in the whole Marxist movement is uncovered at its roots. In the younger Marx we discover a rebel and a self-made proletarian who has not yet learned to disguise his direct motivation in the technical language of economics and materialist 'science'. It is the shame of the Christian Church, as Walter Dirks points out, that Karl Marx found no Christian before him when he took the radical step of looking at the world from a consistently proletarian point of view in those early days of capitalism. It is the disgrace of Christian theology that Marx found in it, not the Gospel of good news to the whole man, body and soul, especially to the humble and the poor, not the promise of the coming of an already risen and ruling Christ, but only the division of body from spirit, the hope of a spiritual eternal life, and the neglect or the sanctification of the material arrangements of this world. At a time when a genuine encounter with Marxism (and with the Engels whose burning indignation at *The Condition of the Working Classes in England* bound him close to Marx) might have been possible for Christians, there was no encounter, because no Christian prophet was there to challenge the bourgeois culture-Christianity of his day with that thoroughness which might have forced Marx and Engels into conversation with him. The opportunity passed. Today, as Dirks makes clear, Christians are painfully learning the lessons from their Bibles and from events which, had they known them in that day a century ago, might have turned Marxism in its infancy into other channels.

'His suspicion of ideology, against which Christians have defended themselves for a century shoulder to shoulder with bourgeois idealists, we ratify today in the name of the truth of Christ.'[1]

But it is worth while to learn these lessons, and to ask ourselves still, what Biblical insight, what better obedience, would have equipped Christians in that day to encounter the young Marx and Engels creatively. For this encounter continues still, as the reality behind that other encounter with the strategy, tactics and hardened ideology of Communism as a self-conscious world power. The Christian need not give way before the fact that no amount of freedom from the class interests and ideologies of bourgeois society in his social thought and action will convince the Communist that he is genuinely a free man. It is God who demands this freedom from the world in the name of Christ, having used Marxism to remind Christians of what it means. The Christian need not be discouraged from accepting the revolution of our time as a whole, because the Communists would label his acceptance false. He need not draw back from affirming the fullness of humanity in Christ's name, both body and soul, because the Communists will label his doctrine idealist in any case. He need not shrink from bearing witness to the Truth who is a Lord and saviour, demanding not the affirmation of certain statements or the observance of certain principles, but obedience and faith, because the Communist of today cannot see the relevance of such a challenge. For behind this revolution, this chaotic changing existence designated by the word 'proletarian', but in which we all share somewhat if only by fear of the hydrogen bomb, lies a reality in control. Christians and Communists differ about this reality. In the words of Dirks 'the

[1]Walter Dirks, 'Marxismus in christlicher Sicht', in *Die Frankfurter Hefte*, February, 1947.

human society fulfilling itself dialectically' confronts 'the Father God whose children we are.' The issue between them will never be resolved by setting doctrine against doctrine. But it will break down into fruitful encounter when Christians begin to live and think before God, as those who have learned, from Marxism and from elsewhere, not least from their Bibles, what it means to be in a proletarian situation as his children. It is the great service of Nicholas Berdyaev to have blazed the trail of this kind of thinking, despite all that must be said against his theology. It was he who first put the fact of revolution into a Christian perspective, and pointed to the dynamic implications of Christian freedom in personal community. Karl Barth's radically Christocentric doctrine of knowledge also leads the way, as does Reinhold Niebuhr's realism about the play of power and interest in society.

When this has been said, however, it implies as well the other side. Communism is a betrayal of the revolution in which the world is engaged, as has been recognized most clearly of all in India where that revolution is most acute. In time it reveals these colours, because its hope is in an earthly utopia being built in the Soviet Union, and not in Christ who judges and redeems all time. The proletarian finds himself being used for the ends of the Party's strategy, rather than being himself the object of concern. The ideal of an achieved socialist society is used to cover continued exploitation, and the hope of a classless society becomes opium for the people. In short, the vices against which Marx rebelled return in new clothing because this revolutionary power was not revolutionary enough to subject its own ideals and power to the very proletariat it claimed to lead. The world is confronted with a growing 'post-Communist mood' today among the very dispossessed and homeless people—both in body and in mind—whom we have described as the proletariat, and for whom Communism has had its greatest appeal.

This post-Communist mood is a new opportunity for the Christian: a far greater one than the intoxicating power of a great idealism in earlier days. For that intoxicating power came from an illegitimate mixture of real rebellion against injustice with absolute certainty that an ideal society was at hand, at the end of the struggle. Against this Christians could offer no counter-hope of the same ideological certainty. But in the sobriety, the disillusion, and perhaps the despair of fallen hopes, the Christian can speak again about the real needs of real people. To this encounter we turn next.

B. The world meets Communism as a *tyrannous power*, more thorough-going in its claims on human life than any dictatorship in history, because it combines absolute political power with a religious type of claim to authority, infallibility, and destiny. This must be understood against the background of its appeal as a revolutionary force. The quality of its tyranny and the intensity of its claim come from its pretension to be *the* expression of the revolution of our time, and its fulfilment. And this same pretension gives a total quality, an absolute intensity, to the experience of those who have suffered under this tyranny or have broken with its hold on their allegiance.

This is the encounter of resistance to Communism's total claim and power, which implies the search for an alternative ground on which to stand. It is, as surely as revolutionary repentance such as we described above, also an element in any full response to Communism as a whole. It is wrong to attribute this resistance, as Hromadka does systematically, and Barth tends to do, to nostalgia for the cultural privileges of a bourgeois society. The German workers who rose in 1953 and the Hungarians in 1956, to protest their unfreedom and miserable conditions, were not inspired by some bourgeois ideology, nor was their demonstration part of some anti-Communist political strategy. The stubborn tenacity of the private farmer in Eastern Europe against all the force of collectivization is not due simply to defence of privilege and property. The myriad subterfuges—corruption, slow-downs, false reports and the like—by which the Russian protects himself against the state's system of control and planning are not set in the framework of any other world view whatever. In every one of these cases and countless others, we have to do with the elementary resistance of human beings to this powerful ideology which is threatening their humanity itself. Simple things are here at stake, like the right to a few hours of private time, to a few private thoughts and a few trusted friends with which to share them; the right to family life, and the right to use one's vocational skills responsibly in the service of one's neighbour. Every person caught in the mill of the Communist educational programme learns quickly that to maintain any integrity of character requires spiritual resistance to the combination of persuasion and force which works on them there. Every liberal of the popular front days has learned that the integrity of radical causes themselves depends on keeping them free of Communist influence. All this is basic human experience with Communism. Its truth is only more dramatized in Communism's system of secret police and forced labour. No Christian encounter which ignores these things or fails in resistance to them, can be called a true encounter with Communism. We have seen this to be the moment of truth in Emil Brunner's demand for a basic 'No' to Communism. There is a reality in the experience of slave labourers, subject satellite peoples, and refugees, which cannot be ignored.

But within this resistance to Communism's uniquely inclusive tyranny there arises as serious a problem for the Christian encounter, as that of distinguishing God's providence from Communist theory and practice in the revolution among the 'progressives'. It is the problem of distinguishing human resistance—resistance for the sake of fellow men, resistance as obedience to truth in love, and so, whether the resister would so express it or not, as obedience to God rather than to man—from resistance as a total passion, which seeks to express the power of some conquering ideology over against the Communist claim. This is the problem, posed above all by the intellectuals who have broken with Communism, of the search for an alternative ground on which the resister may stand, and a power from which he may draw. This yearning after some mighty counter-force is well nigh universal in ex-Communist literature. It may express itself in the haunting regrets of the humanist, such as Richard Wright,

'I knew in my heart that I should never be able to write that way again, should never be able to feel with that simple sharpness about life, should never again express such passionate hope, should never again make so total a commitment of faith.'[1]

[1] *The God that Failed*, p. 166.

It may take the form of fanatic devotion to some other total system of faith and philosophy and discipline, such as the Roman Catholic Church, or even some fascist movement, as Ignazio Silone, himself one of the freest of all ex-Communists reminds us.[1] It may speak to us in the sharp words of total war and hatred:

'The Church must become a fighter. . . . Never before has mankind stood in such a decisive struggle of life, and before such an alternative: freedom or slavery; Christian civilization or a life which is worse than war, catastrophes and death.'[2]

Or it may speak to us in the eloquent appeal of a Whittaker Chambers to American civilization to recover a faith in God and freedom which will prevail against 'man's second oldest faith' whose promise the serpent whispered in the Garden of Eden— 'the vision of man without God'.

Christian theology, so far as it is not Roman Catholic or the expression of some other sectarian unity, stands peculiarly helpless over against the demands of this kind of anti-Communism, and peculiarly tempted by it. A few, whom we have mentioned in the first chapter of this study, have yielded to this temptation, to throw the aura of divine blessing around some power or some culture of the non-Communist world, and to interpret the whole of modern civilization in terms of the struggle of this good with the Communist evil. Every Christian thinker is more or less tempted to seek to provide in theology and in the Church the kind of absolute security, power of idea, authority and discipline in action which will appeal to the ex-Communist or the victim of Communism as the conqueror of Communism.

But there is no authority in the Bible for this. It is the temptation to turn resistance which is obedience to God into resistance which is the instrument of the human will to power. It is no accident that with the single exception of the Quaker Chambers we have no record of dramatic conversions from Communism to Protestant Christianity. The Christian theologian stands before the victim and

[1] *The God that Failed*, p. 118.
[2] A. Vööbus, *Communism's Challenge to Christianity* (Watford, 1950), p. 90.

fugitive of Communism as one who must deny him the very thing he wants most of all—another absolute human authority, another ideology, membership in another conquering movement. For precisely this desire is the sickness of his resistance of Communism, and not that resistance itself. The Christian resists the total claims of Communist power and ideology because, in Helmut Gollwitzer's words, 'he is a slave, who belongs to another'. But this prior obedience to Christ is a response to reigning reality, not the promotion of a cause. The Christian resists as the witness to Christ the reconciler, as one who points the Communist to the reality beyond his distortions of truth and breaches of justice, who is a personal Lord, and who forgives and saves, and thus commands. The Christian resists for the sake of the tyrant as well as for the sake of his victim; he resists as one whose soul is never possessed by a *state* of resistance. He resists within the framework of God's act of reconciliation, and as witness to it; as one for whom the friend-foe antithesis is no longer the dominant factor, and as one for whom total powers and ideologies are no longer necessary, even to ward off others, on this earth. This is the freedom in resistance which numerous Christians from Germany's East Zone, and above all Gollwitzer, have defined for the Christian world most clearly. We have found it foreshadowed in Berdyaev's attitude toward events in Soviet Russia, despite its frequent confusion with the mysticism of the Russian idea. This is not surprising, for we are dealing here with a theme most poetically expressed in one of Berdyaev's favourite sources of inspiration: the freedom of man in Christ before even the spiritual tyrannies and temptations of this world, expressed in Dostoievski's legend of Christ confronting the Grand Inquisitor.

We shall see more fully below what these two sides of the spiritual encounter with Communism mean in practice. First, however, we turn to the question of a theology adequate to the Christian-Communist encounter in the forms we have seen it take.

2. THEOLOGY IN A MATURE WORLD

Let us make one point explicit as we turn to this question. There is no theology which in itself is adequate to deal with Communism, and there is no encounter with Communism which by itself embraces the whole of the problem it presents to the Christian faith and life. For the Christian encounter with Communism is set in the more basic framework of the confrontation of Christ with the world.

We have learned about the world directly in this study, that it is a world in revolution, and that it was Marx's prophetic function to have given this revolution its most radical and consistent expression in the secular world. To this we must add another statement about the world, no less implicit in our study, though less expressed. The world has come of age in organizational, rational, and technical competence. Vast areas which once were left to the operation of natural forces are now under human control, and man is surrounded by an organizational network which demands his time and concentration, which presents immediate reality to him. This means however that the world has become non-religious, in the sense that 'God is no longer necessary as a working hypothesis, whether in morals, politics, or science'.[1] That realm of nature which used to be beyond human understanding and control, with which, therefore, one could only establish a creative relation by means of this hypothesis 'God', is now more and more being conquered by reason and technique. But more important, that realm of inward experience of the soul, where the life of piety used to take place, that realm of conscience, of salvation, of eternal life, of communion with a transcendent Being beyond the bounds of this earth, has faded into the background of men's consciousness. It seems no longer important. There is no time for it. Men are too busy serving their neighbours or themselves with their technical reason, solving the relative immediate problems of their own or the common life, to worry about supposedly ultimate problems. The world has become mature in that it has dispensed with metaphysics, including religious metaphysics, and conducts its life on the basis of its own relative principles and knowledge, as if God did not exist. It does not fall into some counter-religion in doing this, but remains relative, realistic, and problem-solving.

That the world is in this state is reflected in the testimony of most of our theologians in this study, whatever attitude they take

[1]Dietrich Bonhoeffer, *Letters and Papers from Prison*, p. 163.

toward it. Only Josef Hromadka and to a certain extent the pro-Communist Christians of Hungary and China interpret the whole revolution in our times, whether its bourgeois western or its Communist eastern phase, exclusively as a religious phenomenon. Only these see the issue purely in terms of spiritual disintegration in the West, and the rise of a new spirit expressing a new class in the East. Brunner analyses in some detail the growth of this secular world, independent of dependence on God, with something akin to horror. For him the destruction of the religious dimension leads straight to the false antithesis of individual and society, which destroys the true picture of person in community and is the source of the inhumanity of both modern *laissez-faire* capitalism, and that epitome of social evil, Communist totalitarianism.

On the other side Tillich, Niebuhr, and Barth, each in his way, affirm this secular maturity of the word, and try to come to grips with it alongside of the fact of revolution. Tillich finds autonomy to be a legitimate historical condition of the spirit, a protest of being and freedom against a religious attempt to violate them, as well as the attempt of finite forms to live without relation to the depths of Being itself. It is a preparation for, as well as antithesis to, the sacramental filling of finite history with transcendent meaning which is theonomy. Barth, as we have seen, is the most radical of all theologians in his rejection of every attempt to build up, from the world's self-understanding, any world view, any ideology of religious value containing truths about man's destiny and the meaning of his life. Yet he does this in order to show how God in Christ upholds and reconciles the world in the relative realities of its secular life. And Niebuhr betrays, in every line of his thought and action, his concern that the Christian never separate himself from the area of relativity and responsible decision, in which the rest of the world must live, even if that means postponing full confidence in the power of Christ's resurrection to the end of history.

The last two of these men are especially important, for it is they who more than all the others have turned Christian attention to the relative problems of human living apart from every total programme or ideology. But neither of them recognizes with the clarity of a man who was a student of both, Dietrich Bonhoeffer, the extent to which this mature secular world is a reality, proof both against attempts (such as Niebuhr's) to build contacts and need for revelation out of the dialectical encounter between moral reason and practical choices, and against the best reorientation of theological concepts, which remains in the realm of words (such as Barth's). It is to Bonhoeffer that we owe the insight that the maturity of this organized, technical world, within the limits of its own relative problem-solving concerns, is a fact of God's providence in our time before which revolutionary impulses and Christian apologetics alike must show the respect which reality sooner or later demands of everyone. His thought therefore will help synthesize an adequate theological approach to Communism, though his own encounter was with another challenge. Let us look at our problem in the light of his insight.

This mature world as Bonhoeffer sees it is not an ideal state, nor even a stable system. Revolutionary change might almost be called its dynamics, and it might be called the attitude and relation appropriate to that change. Characteristic of this coming of age has been the replacement, one by one, of eternal absolute bonds and truths with relative human ones, and the gradual shift from dependence on divine activity to independent human effort. Science and ethics alike have founded themselves on principles which would be true, in the words Bonhoeffer quotes from Grotius, *etsi deus non daretur*. This does not mean, however, as Christian apologists are so quick to claim, that these principles necessarily become gods themselves. It is precisely in the nature of the secular world's maturity that it is able to endure the relativity of its status, its independence of all ultimates, the possible doubt which might overthrow all of its principles and hypotheses. It is adapted to the job of practical living in a changing world where the central realities are human organization and activity. It resists all attempts to push that world back into dependence on some ideology, true or false, religious or secular, as a violation of its encounter with the immediate realities before it.

There is, to be sure, an element in the revolution of our time which runs counter to this autonomy and relativity: the element which we called the spiritual revolution, as distinct from the economic one, the longing of culturally uprooted intellectuals for a new total framework of meaning. It is characteristic of such a world as we have described that it contains this instability, this threat to itself, in its very dynamic. We see this clash most clearly in the figure of Karl Marx himself. Marx was, on one side, the most vigorous proponent of an autonomous secular world where man rules nature by knowing its science. His polemic against idealism included every kind and sort of thought which cut men off from the business of acting in the world. It was conducted in the faith that ideas are validated by their usefulness in guiding action and producing results. In this he was a spokesman for a whole tradition of activists and technicians who have carried the industrial revolution forward. It was quite natural that he should celebrate the historical inevitability, even the power and glory, of the capitalist development of the world, and expect to build his socialist society on its technical achievements. There is a sense in which his claim to be nothing but the consciousness of the proletarian class in action, is the final challenge to every 'religious' and 'metaphysical' world view, as Barth and Bonhoeffer use these terms. It can no longer be answered by a better theory, but only by a counter-demonstration in society itself.

On the other side however, Marx is, as we have seen already, the most consistent revolutionary challenger of the self-sufficiency of this mature and technological world. He speaks not only for the powers of secular autonomy who are asserting their control over nature and society but—and this is the paradox in which lies his power—for the victims of this changing world as well: for the proletariat of body and soul, oppressed and captivated at the same time by the rapid pace of change, and the organized power of modern technology. He and the movement he founded brought home to the mature secular world that its basic principles are not only relative: they are corrupt. They not only are subject to correction as wider interests become known. They solve problems in the interest of some against the interests of others. What were proclaimed as the laws of morals and economics, expressing either the general moral feeling or the general utility of mankind, turn out under Marxist scrutiny to be expressions of the ideology of the liberal businessman's interests. The impact of Marxist revolutionary politics and ideology has kept the secular world mindful that it is more tempted than it realized to absolutize principles which are formally only working hypotheses, above all in ethics, politics and economics; and that it is more enamoured than it knew of false religions which give security to some against the onslaught of others.

Marxism has done all this more effectively on the whole than Christianity. For Marxism has taken its place within the framework of this world of autonomous human problem-solving, and has launched its revolution from there. Its words spoke to the bad conscience of this world; a conscience which, to be sure, is a child of the Christian conscience, but which in this context can be defined as the embarrassment of discovering that one has been untrue to the basic rules of relativity and practicality in one's principles and conduct. The secular world recognized, when Marxism dramatized it, how its economics had absolutized middle class business interests, because its own concept of science opposed such absolutes. Individualistic ethics fell likewise because the Marxists could point out how little they covered the practical welfare of real people in an industrial society. And Marxism's actions gathered the discontented of this society to the form of protest this society most respects —a counter-movement designed to prove itself also in the solution of the problems of the common life, a 'science' to be tested by its results. Against all this Christianity could avail little by calling men back to a religious ideology. To be sure this religious ideology has insights which the autonomous secular world has forgotten. Realities such as death and the state of the inner life of man are its legitimate sphere. But these appeal to the mature secular world as borderline problems, not as central tasks.

Finally, however, Marxism is itself an ideology, a metaphysic.[1] It becomes the apologist for one great social system against others, an idealism of the socialist society. Its 'science' takes as its object not the workings of a capitalist society but the requirements in strategy and tactics of Soviet power. The circle of theory and

[1]D. M. Mackinnon, *Christian Faith and Communist Faith* (London, 1953), pp. 229 ff. Mackinnon points out that Marxism is the metaphysics which has a special appeal for man in revolt.

practice operates here, and no longer between hypothesis (moral or scientific) and the needs and hopes of concrete human beings. Communism stands in an ambiguous relation to the autonomous secular world today. On the one hand its revolutionary force is not yet spent. Wherever in this world man has been called out of a state of dependence on religious and natural forces to the control of his environment, and this control has then been hindered or has moved too slowly, Communism wins its converts. Wherever the powers of this secular world begin to clothe themselves with more absolute authority than their service to the general welfare warrants, whether this authority be religious as with many conservative parties in Christian, Moslem, and Hindu lands, or like much American propaganda, clothed in the language of economic 'science' itself, Communism shows itself still to be their most consistent challenger. Yet on the other hand this secular world, sobered and made more aware of the relativity of all social ethics to group interest, more modest in organizational pretension and more willing to compromise power conflicts, all because of what it has learned from its encounter with this Communist revolutionary challenge—this secular world still must face the problems of social organization and social change without the positive help of Communism, indeed over against its hindrance and opposition, and disillusioned in many cases by the failure of its promise.

Where in this picture is Christian theology? Let us put the prior question, where is Christ in such a world as this? Bonhoeffer's answer combines the adequacy of Niebuhr and Barth. Christ reveals to us God's love, God's being and act, in the middle of this secular mature world, upholding it by his Providence in its relativity, its uncertainty, its temptation, reconciling it to himself out of its sin and rebellion. Reality is not to be found on the boundaries of this world, in those questions which it cannot answer and for which it therefore calls on the hypothesis God, nor in those failures and conflicts which it cannot resolve which drive it in despair to call on some transcendent help. It is not some explanation of the relations between a divine and a human realm. It is the reality of God who has come into this world in Jesus Christ, and the reality of this world as so loved by God.

343

'The reality of God discloses itself only by setting me entirely in the reality of the world; but there I find the reality of the world, already always sustained, accepted, and reconciled in the reality of God.'[1]

This is what Bonhoeffer means by the non-religious nature of Christian faith. In a few notes at the end of his life, intended to be the prospectus for a book, he compresses the essence of what this encounter with the world involves:

'Encounter with Jesus Christ. Experience that here a reversal of all human existence is found, in that Jesus exists only as "the Man for others". This "being for others" of Jesus, is the experience of transcendence! Out of the freedom from himself, out of his "being-for-others" unto death, springs his omnipotence, omniscience, and omnipresence. Faith is participation in this being of Jesus (incarnation, cross, resurrection).'[2]

Jesus was the man-for-others. He was powerless, a servant, who suffered because he carried our sins. This was the revelation of God.

'Man's religiosity makes him look in his distress to the power of God in the world; he uses God as a *Deus ex machina*. The Bible however directs him to the powerlessness and suffering of God; only a suffering God can help. To this extent we may say that the process we have described by which the world came of age was an abandonment of a false conception of God, and a clearing of the decks for the God of the Bible who conquers power and space in the world by his weakness. This must be the starting point for our "worldly" interpretation.'

The Christian therefore is called to be a man, 'not a *homo religiosus* but a man pure and simple, just as Jesus was a man, compared with John the Baptist'. He is called to 'share the being of Christ in the world', which means in the fullest sense to love the world, to be a part of it, to share its problems, its joys, its decisions, its successes and failures, its powers and its helplessness—to know all its melodies to the full as counterpoint to the *cantus firmus* of his love as one who watches with Christ in Gethsemane, who shares his being for others unto death.

[1]Dietrich Bonhoeffer, *Ethics* (London, 1955), p. 61. In this and the following quotations this writer has taken the liberty of revising the translation to bring out the force of the German original.
[2]This and the immediately following quotations from Bonhoeffer, *Letters and Papers from Prison*, pp. 179, 164, 168, 131.

This is the encounter with the secular, the mature world to which the Christian is called. It will probably not first of all be an encounter of words at all, but the encounter of participation in common life. It involves the profoundest form of affirmation of that world in all the variety of its expressions—the affirmation which knows that it is being carried by the reconciling grace of God. And it involves the deepest kind of freedom from that world, even revolutionary impact upon it; the freedom which knows that no extension of the world but only God's action toward and in it, through the life, death and resurrection of Christ, is its reality. All this however the Christian will first of all live, both personally and in community, trying to find at each point in the common life of the world by prayer and action that reality, that form of service which is its truth. Thus he will commend himself to his colleagues in this world until it is given him so to express the Word of God in human words, that his colleagues no longer take it for a 'religious' violation of the integrity of their life and experience. With this let us turn to the three themes of the theological encounter with Marxism as we have dealt with them throughout this study.

A. *Ideology and the needs of the neighbour*

In the final analysis, the challenge of the Marxist doctrine of ideology and criticism of religion is put to us by the whole mature world itself. In the long run Marxism has betrayed the proletarian situation in whose name it has spoken so prophetically. In the long run the 'ideology-unveiling character of the proletarian situation' (Tillich) has proved more real than even the Marxist ideology. But only a small portion of those disillusioned with Communism have taken refuge once again in religion. In Germany (presumably in other Communist lands as well) one notices that, although hatred is as ubiquitous a mood as fear and tends to possess the soul, yet the development of this into a full-fledged ideology of resistance, idealizing the western world, or the world of the past, and living for the day of liberation, tends to be limited to the older generations and to the middle classes; those groups which themselves have never felt the proletarian situation until the Communists themselves forced them into it. The youth and the workers are realistic, in some cases disillusioned, opponents of Communism, but their distrust of western ideologies and propaganda is almost as great. The post-Communist proletariat, whether spiritual or practical, is suspicious of all 'spiritual homes', of all ideals and principles and eternal truths. The relative, the practical, and the problem-solving, whether toward technical success or human welfare, is its medium.

In this, if our analysis is correct, it comes closest to the same mood and outlook among many of the modern holders and wielders of power: the technician and scientist, especially in physics whose responsibility both in theory and practice has been so intensified and broadened by the fact of atomic power; the industrialist and business man who has been forced by the interdependence of the modern world to give up his ideology and think more generally and pragmatically about the use and development of production; and the statesmen, to whom the solution of relative problems in the relations of states to each other is more important than any ideal. Such men as these have, to be sure, come out of another background on the whole; the background of a liberal confidence in human nature and reason. Yet there is to-day something of the proletarian mood in each of them which has broken that liberal confidence without throwing them back on to any other faith. The technical, the problem-solving, relative reason remains focused on more immediate problems of providing some sort of order, some sort of solution to the problems of common life against the threat of chaos, but without the illusion that any such order or any such reason is itself a 'spiritual home'.

It is such a world as this, mature in its relativity and secularism, whether proletarian or (in a chastened and responsible sense) bourgeois, which finally puts the question of ideology to Christian theology. How can the Christian answer it?

Not by the attempt to establish any direct continuity between the relative thinking of this mature world about itself, and Christian revelation. This very attempt is itself ideological, even if it proceeds by way of antithesis. The world may be impressed with the epistemological boundaries of its science and the relativity of all its truths, and some from this world may come to Christianity with the question what basic revealed truth can bring order and absolute security to human thought. The world may be afraid of the chaos into which morality has fallen by the clash of power and interest, afraid even more of the raging of systems of truth and morals such as Communism which proclaim themselves absolute. Some from this world may come to Christianity for the finally authoritative moral law. But these very questions are ideological. They stipulate beforehand what Christian revelation shall reveal. They test it by its success in bringing security and order into the world they have already more or less defined. We have seen how in this study, one theologian after another has lost sight of some important aspect of human reality, has become, in some cases, the apologist of some social group, because he has accepted this kind of continuity. Brunner's orders of creation, and his idealism about Christian civilization blind him to the human realities in the whole proletarian situation and the Communist movement. Berdyaev's thought fails to come to grips with the constructive aspects of human social life because his acute understanding of revolution struggles continually with his desire to see even this in terms of a vast spiritual drama which gives a central place to Russia's divine destiny and the ideal of personalist socialism, a non-formalized communion of the spirit. Tillich is in some ways the most acute of all those who have tried to bring the world into a religious context. He would lead the world to its boundaries by interpreting to it its ultimate concern, in whatever field that might lie, as religious. He would show to socialism its own depth of being, its own *kairos*, by participation in it as a Christian. But finally Tillich's own concept of Being, that undoubtable ultimate Unconditioned, proves to be a highly philosophical and abstract ideology, which fails to come to grips with the facts of a Communist world which rejects his 'religious' ministry.

In short, the world itself, the world of human realities in all their relative interaction with one another, rejects all these attempts, and guards itself instinctively against their pretensions with the weapons either of indifference or the ever-present question *cui bono* —whose interests are being served? It is not the function of the Christian to undermine the world's maturity, or the degree of integrity it succeeds in maintaining, but rather to support it in that integrity, against every attempt to violate its relativity and practicality with systems of ultimate doctrine or ideal culture. 'Trust your own understanding' Karl Barth quoted Kant to the youth of the church in Hungary and was surprised at the ovation he received. It was a healthy word and a healthy response in a Communist situation where every pressure is toward bringing the truths of one's own understanding and experience into conformity with Marx-Leninism. Here the Church cannot say: 'Organize your understanding according to such and such an alternative world-view.' It must say to the mature world: trust your own understanding where it gives you immediate and concrete experience of your own interests and welfare, where it brings you into constant contact with your neighbour and forces you to reflect on your relation to him and order your life accordingly, where it gives you direct knowledge of what is trustworthy and untrustworthy, admirable and execrable, in your neighbour, and in yourself, where it conveys to you concrete scientific or technical knowledge, such as a professional has of his profession, a craftsman of his craft, a farmer of conditions of good productivity, a lawyer of sound law, and the like. Trust this experience and insight in the business of living with your neighbour and adjusting your life to his, your power to his power, your interest to his interest, precisely because you know how relative it is, how little it has to do with absolute truth and value, how often it must be readjusted in the light of new neighbours and new powers, and how quickly it disintegrates when you make it the bulwark of your own security. Guard this relative, problem-solving understanding against every temptation to enslave it to any total system of meaning and culture, to any distorting passions such as hatred or fear, and go about the task of living with your neighbour in sober realism distorted neither by ideals nor by reaction.

The heart of this answer to the problem of ideology lies in the Christian's life being a complete response to the fact that God so loved the world—this world which we have described above—that he sent his Son into the centre of it, into the midst of the network of man's relation to his neighbour. God has become, both actively and passively, our neighbour.

The Christian is called to confront the world with this Christ, in that he shares the being of Christ in the common life of neighbour with neighbour, with all its complex and relative problems. This is and remains a confrontation, never merely an identification. It cannot in our day take the form primarily of preaching theological formulas and insights. It may not take the form of words at all, but of participation in common responsibilities, common conditions of life and common thought, with the world, but with the difference of one who knows that the reality of this world's human relations is the reality of Christ's relation to it. This may result in surer allegiance to empirical fact when others are tempted by an ideology. It may mean the contribution of certain human insights where the world has not seen them. When Helmut Gollwitzer analyses the reasons for Christian gratitude for western society, and defines the grounds and limits of its defence and cultivation, such a confrontation has taken place. When Reinhold Niebuhr, deep in strategic thinking about a responsible American policy toward Communist power, includes in his thinking the danger that our cause may be lost because we over-estimate our relative righteousness, we have another example. When a professor of economics in East Germany maintains the integrity and discipline of his thought and the centrality of concrete human relations in the face of all Marx-Leninist pressures to make him conform to Communist analysis and ideals for humanity, this professor may be doing no more than might be expected of any good economist. But his work is a confrontation of the world with Christ when, because of his response to the truth in him, he sees and maintains this line when his secular colleagues have long since abandoned it.

All this might have been said by Karl Barth, and we have indeed recorded our belief that his theology is the answer to the Communist charge of ideology against religion, as far as words can go in forming this answer. Within the framework of this theological confrontation, however, there remains the question raised by Reinhold Niebuhr. Niebuhr is mistaken in his belief that in order to take the empirical thinking of this world about itself seriously enough, it must be given the status of natural theology.

His own theology is more truly a confrontation with the world, more exclusively based on revelation, than he realizes. But just for this reason the question of emphasis which he raises with Barth points to the need for a continuing dialogue between these two theologies if a truly effective answer to the problem of ideology in theology itself is to be given. The difference lies in the relative importance given to a New Testament and an Old Testament encounter with the world. Niebuhr faces the world more like an Old Testament prophet than Barth. His confrontation is not for that reason less theological, but the emphasis lies on God's blessing and judgement over the life of man in all its variety and fullness, above all, its social fullness. Barth's experience of overwhelming grace allows in theory for all of this. All that is human reappears in his theology under the sign of grace. He is in no sense an apostle of salvation out of this world, but rather of the reconciliation of the world in Christ. But just this manner of world-affirmation, as we have seen, leads Barth in practice to a curious indifference to much that is truly human, especially when this human reality takes the form of complex social responsibilities and relationships. One dimension of Christ himself seems in Barth's theology to be understressed—the dimension of the Christ to whom the whole of the Old Testament was presupposed, and who could weep over the city of Jerusalem.

This is the emphasis which Niebuhr provides and will not allow us to forget. Barth in some ways knows too exclusively the Christ who is the companion and saviour of the proletarian. Niebuhr knows the God who is the companion and the judge of the men who carry responsibility for the political and economic life of this world. Each emphasis tends to be ideological despite itself without the correction of the other. Finally the freedom from the world which only life in the light of the victory of God's grace in the resurrection can give, is the only power which will enable men responsibly involved in their own societies, as Niebuhr is, truly to take account of the life and experience of those in quite another environment; let us say that of India, China, East Europe or Russia. Finally only this removes that anxiety for the fate of one's own society which is the enemy of true responsibility and insight. But it is equally true that without the Old Testament dimension of Christ, the Christian may be tempted to oversimplify the world as God loves it, forgetting the fullness and balance of that responsibility and love to which he is called toward all things human.

B. *Philosophy of History and the Lord of History*

When we turn to history the same pattern expresses itself in another dimension. The Marxist challenge is its uncompromising statement of the theme of human self-estrangement in modern society in terms of historical judgement on it, and its organization of the only unflinchingly revolutionary political action against it in the non-Communist world. This has indeed been turned into a pseudo-scientific system in the effort to impart to it the force of objective inevitability. 'The tragedy of Marxism,' writes Alasdair MacIntyre, 'is that it wished to combine the scope of metaphysics with the certainty of natural sciences'.[1] Still, Communism is the nemesis of all philosophies of history in our mature world, because it has presented a philosophy of history which claims to be simply a response to the forces which are actually moving history, and a means by which they can be known and controlled. It shifts the whole scene of battle from the world of ideas to the world of human struggles, and the whole world in its maturity has recognized this as the real issue. No other philosophy of history but only life lived in response to different realities which control history avails here. It is the place of theology therefore to point to these realities.

This is the great contribution, as we have already pointed out, of Karl Barth. In making of time and history themselves not independent categories dependent on some supposedly rational structure of human logic and experience, but descriptive categories

[1]Alasdair MacIntyre, *Marxism, an Interpretation* (London, 1953), p. 71. In an excellent summary of Marx's pre-materialist work, *National-ökonomie und Philosophie* (1843), MacIntyre points out that the prophetic-moral critique of capitalism which has given Communism its force, is clearer and more telling before it is overlaid with scientific pretensions in the later *Deutsche Ideologie* (1845) and *Capital*. One might add that the post-Communist worker in a Communist land stands just about where Marx described the worker as standing in this early work.

of that which God is doing among men in Jesus Christ, Barth is the emancipator of history from the shackles of conservatism and vested interest such as always cling to these rational structures. He is at the same time its most uncompromising prophet of hope. He is, as we have seen, parallel to Marx in the secular world, the thinker in theology who points Christians beyond thought, in their faith, to response to and hope in a concrete Lord of history. No theology which does less than this, no theology which compounds this with some explanation of history in terms of a God who is other than the father of Jesus Christ, is adequate to face the Communist challenge in the dynamics of history.

When this has been said, however, we must recognize again that Barth with his overwhelming emphasis on the freedom in history which the victory of God's grace gives over against the strategies and responsibilities of historical power and culture, is the theologian of the proletariat and the revolutionary. We have seen his difficulty in co-ordinating the crisis of historical decision with his confidence in the victory of grace, and in coming to grips with the relative responsibilities of historical action where both crisis and grace are involved. This is Niebuhr's objection to him. It is put more effectively by Dietrich Bonhoeffer. Bonhoeffer was by nature and background a responsible member of the bourgeoisie. None of the flamboyant delight which Barth takes in going 'against the stream' of the politics and culture around him is found in his writings. Loving participation in all the ethical and spiritual richness of Prussian tradition was the expression of his life.

'The urban middle class culture', he wrote to his godchild, 'embodied in the home of your mother's parents (his brother's home) stands for pride in public service, intellectual achievement and leadership, a deep-rooted sense of duty towards a noble heritage and cultural tradition. This will give you, even before you are aware of it, a way of thinking and acting which you will never lose without being untrue to yourself.'[1]

He recognized the depth of the revolution through which the world was passing, in the breakdown of his society which had led

[1]This and the immediately following quotations from Bonhoeffer, *Letters and Papers*, pp. 134–5, 61, 65, 135.

to Nazism. 'Our generation can no longer expect as yours could,' he wrote to his parents, 'a life which finds full scope in professional and private activities, and thus achieves perfection and poise. And to make matters worse, we have the example of your life still before our eyes, which makes us painfully aware of the fragmentariness of our own.' His whole rejection of an apologetic 'religious' approach to the 'mature world' reflected his understanding of how far the language and culture, the values and faith, of his own beloved background had become meaningless in the proletarian situation of today. But in all of this there is none of the radical dialectic by which Barth directs his polemic against every form of emotional or theological attachment to tradition, then to admit these things with joyful affirmation under the aegis of Christ's redemptive work. Perhaps this is because Barth after all was able to remain a theoretical proletarian, fighting a sweeping theological revolution when all the while the solid ground of Swiss tradition remained under his feet. Bonhoeffer knew in experience what it is to lose a heritage in the earthly sense. When he speaks of action in crisis, and when in the supreme crisis of his life he acted, responsibility for the purging and renewing of that heritage is in his mind. When he speaks of the victory of the forgiveness of sins he speaks of a *Letztes* (last thing) alongside of which *das Vorletzte* (what is before the last) of 'humanity and goodness' continues as preparation even though the way may lead to the *Letzte* through judgement and destruction. When he hopes, his hopes express themselves in terms of 'a rehabilitation of middle-class life as we have known it in our own families', or in the words to his godchild:

'By the time you are grown up the old country parsonage and the old town villa will belong to a vanished world. But the old spirit will still be there, and will assume new forms, after a time of neglect and weakness.'

Theologically expressed, Bonhoeffer is as much as Barth a theologian of revelation for whom Christ is goal and source of all history. But for him the Old Testament dimension—with its all-embracing concept of God's blessing, its unmistakably direct relation between God and the world in every aspect of its life, and above all its historical hope for Israel's redemption, beyond all

God's struggles with her sin—fills out the picture for those who love and share the tradition of a great society, who regard its shame and glory as their own, and who die a little with it, when it falls to the revolution.

Such are the realities of history. The Christian's response, however, is not preaching but life, in the midst of the relativities, the power and technical realities of world history. Finally the Christian will give evidence to the world of the lordship of Christ by the constructive, the culture-forming qualities of his hope over against that of the Communist. This is not a question of political parties, of labour unions, of agricultural co-operatives, of schools or art forms bearing the label 'Christian' or controlled by the Church, but rather the contrary. The Christian will commend his Lord's coming as the goal of history by the free courage of his service to the welfare of the state or of its victims, when no other hope will move men to do the things everyone knows are right and necessary. He will commend it by the sensitivity of his insight and love for all that is human when all other hopes favour one group against another. He will commend it by the realism of his responsibility in making choices among power alternatives with all the risks it involves, yet not becoming dependent on any earthly power. He will commend it by the way in which he uses both the freedom under grace which Barth taught him, and the disciplined loving use of the heritage which is part of himself, which he has learned from Bonhoeffer. His combination of these may be very different under different circumstances, and in different temperaments. In India, against the background of a pagan culture, and a revolutionary movement fired with high idealism and pressure for rapid change, the Christian emphasis may well be on the support, or perhaps the creation, of new forms which this rapid change may take. Everything may here depend on whether the Christian hope is sufficiently urgent and immediate, spurring the believer to invention and promotion of social forms. In the Communist lands of Eastern Europe, on the other hand, the Christian hope may show itself in the simple confidence with which men continue to serve their neighbours in patterns they know and trust, in spite of all the threats of Communist collectivism and all the temptations of passive resistance.

c. Humanist Ideals and Christian Co-humanity

When we come to the sociology of man, it becomes clearest of all that the Marxist challenge is an intensification and distortion of the challenge which the whole mature secular world presents to the Christian—the challenge of collectivist humanism. This challenge is first of all negative. It is Marxism which has most consistently exposed the errors of individualism, and has brought home most vigorously the determination of man's actions by his economic interests and his social position. Gradually a chastened secular world, after generations of illusion on this point, is learning the Marxist lesson about the collective nature of human life and reactions. But it is more important today as a positive challenge—the challenge of a disciplined body of believers bound together under one authority, one doctrine and one purpose, which shows itself capable of organizing whole societies wherever no other organizing power is able to resist it. To be sure, here as at other points Communism has proved to be one more violation of the maturity of the secular world. Its collectivist humanism may be only a heightened form of the bourgeois liberal view of man. Its economic determinism may have only dramatized the contradiction inherent in liberalism's combination of abstract economic theory with individual freedom. But in the long run the secular world has been forced beyond both individualism and collectivist humanism, without turning back to religion for a definition of man and society. In those lands where the plight of the masses is miserable, and getting more insecure as the economy shifts to urban centres, especially if these masses have some vision before them of what human life might become, there Communism's humanism and effective organization still may be confused with human need and fulfilment itself. Against the background of Confucian views of man and a land which had never known political or cultural freedom many a Chinese intellectual made this easy transfer. In those lands on the other hand where statesmen and economists labour to produce some kind of order which will sufficiently satisfy all parties, so that Communism may not take power over the resulting chaos of conflicting powers, the problems have long outgrown all doctrines of man in their attempt to come to grips with the concretely human. And in those lands where Communism is in control, the struggle for some shred of human life, apart from the all-embracing system of thought and government, also becomes too concrete to ask for a doctrine. It seeks rather a community and contact with greater reality. Both the vitality of Communist humanism—in the devoted discipline of its adherents and the social realism of its politics—and the mood of the secular world which has learned from and rejected the Marxist challenge, put to Christians the same question: what other socially creative reality is there, than that which the Communists offer?

The question, drawing on all that we have so far said, can be put in a Christian form: how can the Christian confront the political and economic world, not with any Christian ideal, commandment, or programme, but with Christ, so that those engaged in this world may better see and more freely serve the concrete needs of men in all their variety and complexity?

This is first of all a question of that other social reality, the Church. We would be untrue to our whole thesis in this study if we made of the Church a place of refuge, another world alongside of the world about which we have been speaking. It is, paradoxically, the Communist Party itself which has reminded us, by the very nature of its inner discipline, at once so exclusive and so entirely devoted to changing the world, of what a Church must be and to what it must be devoted. Once again with Barth, and with the New Testament, we must say first of all that God was in Christ reconciling *the world* unto himself. The world as a whole is the object of God's grace, with all that is human in it, including the state, the civil community. The Church is the community which knows this and lives from it by faith, in love and hope. The Church receives the Word of God and passes it on to the world. It is called to be in its own life and work a witness to God's promise for the world which in Christ's reconciliation he has already begun to fulfil. The Church in short exists for the world. Here is where the Christian answer to Communist humanism and Communist collectivism begins. Here two strikingly different, yet parallel communities face each other—the Christian Church and the Communist Party, each by its very essence a witness to the world, each claiming to be the channel by which the world may see the Truth in whose hands its true fulfilment and destiny lies.

'The task', writes Alasdair MacIntyre, 'is to create a form of community which will exemplify the pattern of the Gospel and which will be enabled to renew continually its repentance for its conformity to the patterns of human sin. . . . First (the dilemmas of this community) will have to be solved in the practice of Christian living rather than in theory. Secondly, it must attempt to combine in its practice politics and compassion. Thirdly, there is only one hope in which this attempt is possible. In the last analysis the difference between a Marxist world and a Christian lies in the fact that in a fully Marxist world prayer would be impossible. The true Christian community will be one of poverty and of prayer.'[1]

This is the Church as God intends it and as it must become if the challenge of Communism or indeed post-Communism in the community life of man is to be met. It is not the Church as it exists today. From the world over, even from mission fields, comes evidence that Protestant Christianity in fact is the religion of the middle-class bourgeoisie. Cases where congregations are made up of the proletariat are so exceptional as to prove the rule. They become cases for special study and admiration. Barth is much too blithe in his assumption that the Christian community can preach the word of God directly, changing only the form of its theology, and not be misunderstood because of what it is as a community, or even more because of what it is not. For the Church has become alienated first from the real community forms of the proletariat, no less the post-Communist proletariat of a Communist land than the Marxist or labour union proletariat of the past and present; and second from the chastened and realistic bourgeoisie itself in its search for answers to the relative and immediate problems of its order and survival. It has become on the whole a community which has appropriated for itself a part of the world, a 'religious' sphere of experiences and practices, or sometimes, in the effort to be open to the world, a part of the sphere of people's leisure time activities in general. It has forgotten its witness in and to the common life of the world itself. 'Paradoxically,' writes MacIntyre, 'it is the contemporary study of Marxism which perhaps brings most clearly

[1] *Marxism, an Interpretation*, pp. 121–2.

357

out what the classical methods of meditation have to say to us about the "dark night of the soul." It is a "dark night", an *ascesis* of poverty and questioning, which must renew our politics.'

Therefore Bonhoeffer is right in calling first for a 'hidden discipline' (*Arkandisziplin*), a renewal of the community of believers in prayer, study and the discipline of Christian life in the world, so that it may become in itself a living witness before it attempts too much to speak to the world.

'During these years the Church has fought for self-preservation as though it were an end in itself, and has thereby lost its chance to speak a word of reconciliation to mankind and the world at large. So our traditional language must perforce become powerless and remain silent, and our Christianity today will be confined to praying for and doing right by our fellow men. Christian thinking, speaking and organization must be reborn out of this praying and this action. . . . "The path of the righteous is a shining light, that shineth more and more unto the perfect day" (Proverbs 4.18).[1]

When this has been said, however, there remains the reality of Christ in the world, whether or not the Christians fail in their corporate witness to his work. Even in the face of the weakness of the Church, the Christian is called to respond in his political and economic decisions to this reality. Once again, with Karl Barth, we must recognize that this reality is dynamic and redemptive in politics too. The state is the outer condition of redemption, preserving man in his humanity, freedom and peace, restraining sin, as a parable of the righteousness of God, reflected in human justice. As such it looks toward the future, though only so far as Christians operate in it and understand its purpose, for the state itself is blind to its purpose before God. So the Christian meets the Communist in politics with the same double mandate as elsewhere;

A. He will not be afraid to confess his faith by seeking new political and economic forms more adequate to human need for security and freedom, nor to proclaim the urgency of these, their judgement on the *status quo*, in the name of Christ the companion of the proletarian.

B. Nevertheless he will uphold precisely that relative, realistic,

[1]Bonhoeffer, *Letters and Papers*, pp. 140–1.

problem-solving approach of practical men so far as this is directed to serving the concrete needs of human beings for order, honest administration, impartial law, productive and yet well distributed economy, and that balance of powers and interests which will minimize exploitation, tyranny, and inequality. He will defend this concrete realism against every attempt, Communist, capitalist, or Christian, to subject the state, the economic order, or human needs, to some world view, some set of abstract moral principles, some ideal conceived out of the experience of one kind of society, or the interest of one class of men. And, since no one group of men in any society can comprehend the fullness of God's judgement or the ways of his justice in that society or in the larger society of an interdependent world, the Christian will be foremost in seeking correction by those with other social experience and interest than his own.

3. THE GATEWAY TO ACTION

We close with the gateway to action, in which all of our theologians stand. It is our final task to point out from here the lines over the whole landscape of Christian life and thought in daily encounter with Communist reality, which show the creative influence of the theology we have examined. We shall do so by looking at four areas of strategy and practice: (a) The encounter with Communist power; (b) the encounter of creative alternatives in different forms of society; (c) the renewal of the Church in the face of Communism; and (d) the personal encounter of the Christian with the Communist.

A. Power

The question of containing Communist power is not simply an extension of the spiritual problem of resistance in love, although this is its presupposition. We have here to do with the practical problem which confronts every responsible statesman and citizen in the western world: how can we defend ourselves from the dynamic power of Communist intentions and influence, without provoking either war or inner social and moral breakdown? This is by analogy the problem of every organization faced with Communist infiltration in the west, and it has its parallels even behind the Iron Curtain. It is basically the question of the responsible use of power by Christians, so far as it is given them.

There is no section of the whole field we are surveying where passions run higher than here. One need only mention such questions as Indian 'neutralism', or German rearmament. The world's greatest theologians seem to lose perspective easily in politics. Yet under the surface a surprising consensus reigns precisely here.

1. Practically all of our theologians agree that the Christian bears a relative but real responsibility for the political and social health, including the reform and the defence, of the non-Communist society of which he is a part. This responsibility is relative, as Gollwitzer, applying here the insights of Barth's *Dogmatik*, points out, in that it does not inhere in our relation to any state of which we happen to be citizens. It depends on our understanding of the will of God for that state, our gratitude for the gifts of God in our society, and the opportunities to reform it.

'By opposing the East's domination of the West, we are indeed affirming the West. But we are only affirming it by affirming the gifts which it has received through God's patience. We are not condoning our own misuse of these gifts. We are not condoning the West altogether, not the West as it is. We do not wish the West to remain in its present state. As Christians we should unmercifully criticize the West as it is; but this criticism will not lead us any nearer to the East, nor recommend to us the "communist" totalitarian East as a solution. That is why we cannot agree without discrimination to use any means, or to accept any allies, for the defence of the West. That is why, in spite of our criticism of the East, we shall not join the ranks of fascism, nor use it as a means of defending ourselves.'[1]

The responsibility for defending the West against Communist power is relative. There may come a time when the Christian must speak as Jeremiah did to Judah, pronouncing the Communists as God's judgement against whom defence is sin. No defence may destroy from within the very gifts of God which are being defended. But the responsibility for defence is none the less real. It is defence of an area of freedom to build a just state, of the opportunity to change society according to the will of God, defence of that balance of power with power, ideology with ideology, which we have

[1]Helmut Gollwitzer, *The Christian Between East and West*.

achieved in order that the true needs of men may be seen and served more clearly, and more justly.

Thus Gollwitzer's statement of the point. But it is echoed elsewhere almost universally, no matter what opinions of immediate policy may be. So a group of Indian Christians, supporting Nehru's policies on the whole, recognizes Communism as the fate which may befall India if non-Communist forces fail to recognize and lead the revolution, yet as a force from which every non-Communist political group must defend itself, and with which the otherwise normal process of co-operation is impossible.[1] But still more impressive is the parallel thinking on this point, obscured though it is by different language and frame of reference, between Gollwitzer, and such an American realist about foreign policy as George F. Kennan.

Kennan is a Christian by faith, but a confessed secularist and relativist in international politics. For the abstract moral standard in international politics, he substitutes the encounter of self-respecting nations each of which can be assumed to have legitimate interests, and a moral character of its own. Where this encounter fails, as with Soviet Russia, he advocates not ideological conflict, but the containment of its power, combined with the careful inducement over a long period of time of that enlightened realism about itself, which it now lacks, but which it must one day recognize.

Kennan's realistic relativism in foreign policy is a part of the well nigh universal insight of the Church in relation to the problem of Communist power at two points:

(i) He repudiates moralism in foreign policy in the name of a genuine Christian humility about American moral pretensions, much as he believes that the values of his American heritage are worth defending. As such he is in line with Reinhold Niebuhr who has warned us that the danger to America in the post-war world is that our relative righteousness over against a Communist opponent may be suddenly turned into an absolute unrighteousness, if we are not aware of the sinful qualities even in the best of human goodness. He agrees with Gollwitzer's refusal to allow that there are any longer any absolute antitheses between political systems and

[1]Cf. *Communism and the Social Revolution in India*; see above p. 171.

cultures, and even with Karl Barth's call for a sober service of direct human needs in politics unconfused by allegiance to ideals of a 'Christian culture'.

(ii) He repudiates the illusion of any nation's or coalition's absolute power or responsibility for the containment of Communist power or its dissolution. 'We must be gardeners and not mechanics in our approach to world affairs.'

'We must come to think of the development of international life as an organic and not a mechanical process. We must realize that we did not create the forces by which this process operates. We must learn to take these forces for what they are and to induce them to work with us and for us by influencing the environmental stimuli to which they are subjected, but to do this gently and patiently, with understanding and sympathy, not trying to force growth by mechanical means, not tearing the plants up by the roots when they fail to behave as we wish them to. . . . We do not need to insist, as the Communists do, that change in the camp of *our* adversaries can come about only by violence. Our concept of the possibility of improvement in the condition of mankind is not predicated, as is that of the Communists, on the employment of violence as a means to its realization. If our outlook on life is, as we believe it to be, more closely attuned to the real nature of man than that of our Communist adversaries, then we can afford to be patient and even, occasionally, to suffer reverses, placing our confidence in the longer and deeper working of history.'[1]

This again parallels Niebuhr's theological attack on the same illusion of American omnipotence. It is an expression of that vocational attitude toward social responsibility, within the framework of the primary act of God, which underlies the political attitudes of Barth and Gollwitzer.

2. There is fairly general consensus among the representative thinkers of Christendom, that the power threat of Communism is both a military one and an ideological one; the former a threat from without, the latter a temptation and danger from within, capitalizing on our weaknesses and our failures both morally and socially. The threat to us from our own failures, however, is by general agreement the most basic. The primary task of the non-Communist world is to radiate that kind of health and mutual respect in its politics and economics, which cannot help but influence

[1]*The Realities of American Foreign Policy* (London, 1954), pp. 93–94.

362

the world behind the Iron Curtain. The task of military defence is secondary to this and must never be allowed to override it. Once again Kennan puts the point:

'Now what the in-between countries are looking to us for is not to be taught how to combat Communism—however much we may think they need to learn about it—but rather for positive and imaginative suggestions as to how the peaceful future of the world might be shaped and how our own vast economic strength in particular might be so adjusted to the lives of other peoples as to permit a fruitful and mutually profitable interchange, without leading to relationships of political dependence and coercion. . . . All the subject peoples within the Communist orbit . . . know that their chances of liberation will be best if we Americans are able to develop positive and constructive purposes that serve to place the negative, destructive purposes of Communism in the shadows where they belong.

'In the larger sense, therefore, it may be said that the problem of world Communism is one of those problems which can be dealt with effectively only if you learn to look away from it, not in the sense that you take no precautionary measures with regard to it, but in the sense that you do not permit it to preoccupy your thoughts and your vision but rather insist on the right to proceed with your positive undertakings in spite of it.'[1]

These sentiments are echoed by Karl Barth, although he would wince at having to admit the basic rejection of co-operation with Communism as a system which is implied. They undergird both sides of the European debate on German rearmament, if one substitutes western Europe for America. And they are basic to the Indian Christian encounter with Communism which owes so much to Niebuhr. There is implied in this, as well, a doctrine of 'liberation' which does not depend on enmity, propaganda, war, or revolutionary act, but rather on the influence of example, the attraction to others of what we are to ourselves. Who knows what changes of spirit, leadership, or policy, what concessions and moderations, this may eventually bring about?

Such, we submit, is a generally agreed form of the Christian encounter with the realities of Communist power, except on those right and left wings where Christians speak either as advocates of a Communist or an anti-Communist power bloc. Differences

[1] *The Realities of American Foreign Policy*, pp. 101–2.

continue, to be sure, on questions of tactics, and in the close interdependence of this world they generate no little heat. But they are differences largely in the evaluation of the forces actually at work in a given situation, differences of judgement on political tactics, not differences in the strategy of dealing with Communist power itself. Here Barth is most certainly wrong in seeing a concrete decision on German rearmament as the point at which the spirits divide and the Christian confession is at stake. But Niebuhr is equally wrong in discovering withdrawal from the power problem in Barth's position 'between East and West'. Here, and in the case of conflicts on the question of defence which come up with Asian Christians, judgements are at issue on the relative importance of Communism as a threat from outside and a threat from within due to chaos and injustice at home; and on the relative danger of anti-Communist ideologies, American or otherwise, to wise and peaceful firmness toward the Communists.

B. *Alternatives*

This leads us to our second question closely related to the power problem: the question of creative alternatives to Communist power and order. This is the question, central in ecumenical thinking of the post-war years, of responsible society. 'Responsible society' is a concept. The Amsterdam Assembly of the World Council of Churches defined it as a society 'where freedom is the freedom of men who acknowledge responsibility to justice and public order, and where those who hold political authority or economic power are responsible for its exercise to God and to the people whose welfare is affected by it.' The Evanston Assembly added:

'Responsible society is not an alternative social or political system, but a criterion by which we judge all existing social orders and at the same time a standard to guide us in the specific choices we have to make. Christians are called to live responsibly, to live in response to God's act of redemption in Christ, in any society, even within the most unfavourable social structures.'[1]

[1]Report of Section III, 'Responsible Society in a World Perspective', of the Evanston Assembly of the World Council of Churches (London, 1955). The points which follow below are taken from this report unless otherwise indicated.

But the term is a concept to end all idealistic thinking in Christian social ethics. This has been clearly shown in the last few years of ecumenical study and discussion around it. In the Evanston report on 'Responsible Society in a World Perspective' three large sections of the world were acknowledged in which Christian social responsibility takes quite different forms. 'Responsible society' has become a charter for frankly plural approaches to social problems, which yet question and converse with one another. Let us compare these with relation to our subject:

(a) Characteristic of thought and action about responsible society in the industrialized countries of western Europe and America has been:

(i) A vigorous rejection of thought about society in terms of general concepts, notably capitalism and socialism, and of premature moralizing about social principles in favour of a clear picture of economic and political facts which provide technical alternatives for a solution of human problems. In the place of these general concepts has come the acceptance of some form of mixed economy, leaving it an open question what the economy shall be called or at what points concretely it should be state controlled, co-operatively run, or left in private hands.

(ii) Development of a number of dialectical criteria: the need for efficient production *versus* the need for fair distribution, decentralized responsibility in state and industry *versus* efficient management, farmers' interests *versus* those of the consumer, and the like, for the determination of just and responsible social action.

(iii) In Europe a campaign for viable forms of economic and political co-operation at the expense of absolute national sovereignty, and against the nationalistic spirit. This, although not reflected in official ecumenical pronouncements, is the principal expression of responsibility among Protestant statesmen on the European continent, in the face of the challenge of Communist domination in eastern Europe. At the same time it is coupled with rejection of an ideal concept of 'Christian Europe'.[1]

[1]Cf. W. A. Visser 't Hooft, 'Can Europe be Defended?' in *European Issues,* 18th February, 1953, published by the Committee on the Christian Responsibility for European Co-operation, Geneva 17, Switzerland.

(iv) In the United States and to a lesser extent in other capital exporting nations, recognition of the dangers of wealth to the spirit, and of an economy geared to ever expanding material wants. Recognition further of the special, critical responsibility of these nations to give such aid, and support such policies, as will contribute to the social health and construction of less developed lands.

(v) Recognition that the state is basic 'trustee for society as a whole' in matters of conflicting interests, and yet that the state itself is the servant and not the master of justice and the public welfare. It must itself be relative and changeable, respecting other forms of association and human freedom.

(vi) Recognition that 'justice is dynamic and its forms must vary to meet changing needs. Those who seek it should be made sensitive by love to discover such needs where they have been neglected.'

In short, this ecumenical wisdom against the background of a relatively stable older society contains all the elements which we have described as being essential in the Christian's response to Christ's rule over society, a dynamic concept of justice defined only by love's insight into human need, support of a relative problem-solving approach to these needs unhampered by ideologies, affirmation of a positive function for the state, and recognition of the urgency of creative response to God's will, in terms of the judgement of God which threatens failure so to respond; a judgement whose name in Europe, and in the world of the underdeveloped nations, is Communism. This ecumenical wisdom is wiser on the whole than any of our theologians. It is wiser even than Niebuhr (who would doubtless subscribe to most of its findings), because it includes the contributions and challenge of men less impressed than he with the wisdom of a pragmatic tradition, or more inclined, on the basis of European experience, still to call themselves socialists. The mixture of these elements, however, is conditioned by the strong experience all these highly developed countries have of a highly valued order and tradition, however thoroughly the ideological pretensions of this tradition may be repudiated. The reform and improvement of the given social order is the object of Christian responsibility.

(*b*) A different experience, which stands in tension with this more stable world, is that of economically underdeveloped countries, above all of Asia, where the primary social fact is revolutionary discontinuity of order and tradition. In this context responsible society takes on different forms:

(i) Strong emphasis on the definition and creation of new forms and concepts which will guide and stimulate the social revolution in directions other than Communist. Definition of the basic rights of man, of (in India) a 'classless and casteless society' or of 'democratic socialism' as goals towards which to work and as definitions of the inherent dynamic of the revolution itself, becomes relatively more important where a basic sense for what true human need and personality is, is developing and changing. The ability to put in positive terms what the lordship of Christ means for new vistas of human opportunity and social development becomes as important as the freedom of technical pragmatic reason to define concrete possibilities.

(ii) Definition of just and responsible social action in terms of reforms which must be achieved as rapidly as possible if extremes of right or left collectivism are to be avoided. In each of them the dialectic of the more stable societies is present but is overshadowed by the more immediate task of achieving the form of a new society at all. The Evanston Report mentions: the development of strong and active political institutions capable of bringing about change in the teeth of opposition, yet free enough to be subject to influence and change; radical land reform, coupled with the development of new forms of rural economy and community; planned industrialization combined with welfare provisions for workers and their families; and population control.

(iii) Almost exclusive concentration on the problem of expanding the economy, eliminating unjust distribution and exploitation and building strong but moderate government at home, as an answer to Communism, often to the extent of compromising with Communist power politics on the world scene, or leaving defence against it to others because of the internal strain, both economic and spiritual, which preoccupation with such defence would mean.

(iv) Concern as much lest society fall into the hands of a

totalitarian right as a totalitarian left, for the totalitarian right would be in most cases the attempt to force on a nation the pattern of an outgrown ideology in the interest of one exploiting class. This force replaces one of the partners in the discussion about responsible society in the west—responsible conservatism.

(c) We turn thirdly to a land behind the Iron Curtain, to the social responsibility of Christians under Communist control. Here we must be more specific, speaking in examples rather than in principles. As we have seen above, this responsibility is, in sharp contrast to both of the other areas, limited in a Communist state, to specific places where the Christian has some ability, some vocation, or meets some occasion which makes his use of it a meaningful thing. The assumption of total responsibility for the whole direction of society is here a temptation and not a call for the Christian. We have seen the idealistic errors to which it has led Hromadka, the Hungarian and the Chinese Christian pro-Communists on one side. We have described the ideological character of an attitude of total resistance, whether active or passive. We turn here to two specific illustrations from East Germany, of what it means that the state is in God's hands in spite of the Communists, so that the very force of political and economic reality ever and again turns up tasks for the Christian, wherever the Communists may put him.

(i) The problem of the farm illustrates the whole of economic life, caught in the inexorable process of socialization by means of 'class warfare' officially sponsored and forced. Behind it we must bear in mind the predicament of the people both in body and in spirit. The 'production co-operative' on the land, like the 'Workers' and Peasants' Faculty' at the university, and the 'people's owned industry', is the nemesis of German society in its old forms. The farmer looks at it with horror as the end of that last bit of life's meaning and freedom which he has been struggling to maintain for himself and his family. In this predicament the Church must help him to act.

In this situation two words at once come from the statements of Church leadership, from pastors in their counselling, and from farmers who try to help other farmers to find their way. They are equally important and belong together.

The first is comfort and encouragement for the farmer who struggles to keep control of his land and his freedom against all odds. Like the workers' demonstration of June 17th, 1953, the resistance of the farmers over the past decade to collectivization is an elementary cry for justice against an oppressor. It comes out of the depths of the realities of peasant life, out of the farmer's attachment to, pride in, and responsibility for his land, out of the primitive self-consciousness of his being. It corresponds to the basic facts of agriculture, which cannot be collectivized and industrialized without violence to its essence. Even in Russia this peasant self-consciousness persists. The farmer does not become a proletarian so long as he still has a garden and an animal. There is no doubt that the collective farm in the hands of Communist power, is an instrument of ideological control and not simply, or even primarily, of increased productive efficiency. The farmer therein becomes materially dependent on the state in every way. Even his family life loses its unity and privacy. His creative relation to the soil is broken.

Therefore the farmer can know that he is doing the will of God in defending the freedom of his farm as long as possible. His silent suffering resistance to collectivization, his heroic struggle to plant and harvest his fields, to deliver impossible quotas in the face of hampering regulations and the absence of help and machinery, is his divine service. But precisely because it is his divine service, the promise and grace of God hallow it. This is the answer to his despair, and to his temptation to suicide or to total resignation. In the face of the fact that he may never see the harvest in his barns, he must plant his fields. It seems almost impossible that at the end of the year he will still be a free man on his own farm. In many cases he must indulge in all manner of black market deals and other chicanery in order to get the machine parts and the seed and fodder which he needs to produce at all. This adds to the insecurity and fear in which he lives. The crucial question for the farmer is not his social action, but his faith.

The second word requires this faith even more than the first. It is the word of disillusioning realism. Unless Communism changes its basic character, or loses its control, agricultural collectivization will come, and the private farmer is doomed. The farmer must reckon with this fact. He must learn to accept it when it comes, out of the hand of God. He must be ready then to accept new tasks with which to praise and serve him, out of the semi-slavery of a 'production co-operative'. The rule of Christ, the facts of agriculture, and the need of his neighbour for food, do not cease with the end of private farming. The farmer in the production co-operative must seek other ways than before to serve his neighbour, and to witness to the rule of God over agriculture. It may be he who has the courage to challenge the party functionary on the basis of his technical knowledge, and to save the whole farm from a disastrous loss of harvest. It may be he who saves an animal from bureaucratic neglect by working overtime himself. There will be countless opportunities to break the bonds of fear and mistrust in a Communist-controlled farm, with acts of love.

Finally, if this Christian farmer is of especially fruitful spirit, he may reflect on his condition, and find in it in fact a judgement of God. Did the free private farmer in Germany ever accept his position as a gift of the grace of God? Did he recognize his private property in land as limited by the rights of others? Did he give up part of his land to help resettle the refugee from the East in 1945? There is still no effective land reform in West Germany today. Was not the whole conception of unlimited private property in land a consequence of false individualism and irresponsibility toward God and other men? What of the black market in agricultural goods before 1947? Was not the moral and spiritual fibre of the farmer's resistance to socialization weakened by these things? This is, to be sure, not the right pastoral word to the free farmer fighting with his back to the wall. But it is reality which no farmer dare forget, for his chance may come again. The 'production co-operative' as a form of agricultural life, may be freed from its dependence on central planning and its function as a school of Communist ideology some day, even though it has become a permanent feature of the East German agricultural system. Once in fact, in mid-1953, there were the elements of a new chance for the farmer. Private farms were restored to those who claimed them back. Central planning was relaxed. The campaign to eliminate the large farmer stopped and even tried to reverse itself. The natural reaction to this change was suspicion; weariness with the uncertainty of a government which can persecute one day and reward the next. The Christian however, can see also quite different forces at work in such a change: the grace of God who has given a new opportunity to work and achieve what he will so long as the respite lasts. In this spirit a farmer from East Germany wrote on the occasion of this change:

'Here in the East we will have to see whether we are sober and clever enough to take up the near, the next jobs before us, to give up false hopes for a "miracle" or a total rescue, and stand, each of us responsibly, in his place.'[1]

(ii) Let us take, secondly, the still sharper example of Christian responsibility toward the law. The law is a somewhat anomalous term to use here, to be sure. It is meant to indicate the whole fearful apparatus of police, open and secret, courts, prisons, torture and brainwashing, and labour camps out in Siberia. The citizen encounters it daily in the ubiquitous espionage system, hears of it regularly in the disappearance of acquaintances, in reports of trials and heavy sentences meted out for vague offences. What can the Christian do about it?

First, he can look at it for what it is, and thereby rob it of much of its terror. The Christian knows by faith that no system of spying can be as all-knowing as the *Staatssicherheitsdienst* (SSD—East German secret police) claims to be. He knows by experience if he has been imprisoned by the SSD how stupid these police actually are about the Church, its structure and beliefs, and how little they care about actual facts in their accusations and investigations. He knows by faith that no place on earth, not even a Siberian labour camp, is beyond the care of God and the opportunity to serve and praise him.[2] He knows from experience that the arrests of the secret police are to a large extent arbitrary, according to the needs of a larger plan—now for the elimination of hotel owners on the Baltic Sea, now for the intimidation of the Church etc.—and not

[1]'Kommt Zurück', in *Unterwegs*, 1953, Heft 3, p. 179.
[2]Cf. Gollwitzer's *Unwilling Journey*, which is one long commentary on this faith.

directly dependent on the activities of the arrested. He knows by faith that secret policemen, spies and informers, inquisitors and their ilk are human beings, often themselves in great spiritual need, and he approaches them as such. He learns from this experience that fearlessness combined with human respect for the other person is the best protection possible when one falls among such people.

When all this is done the apparatus remains a terrible thing, bringing fear and insecurity with it. But fear is one of its weapons, and multiplies its effectiveness. To overcome and banish this fear is the first responsibility of the Christian.

Second, the Christian can bear witness to justice and truth in the face of its absence. This is the attitude which the Church has taken in the case of its arrested workers and in all other cases where it has had to do with the secret police and the courts. Each legal step has been taken with full earnestness, even when hopeless. Each trial gave an opportunity for defence and therefore for witness to the true nature of the case. Every case was duly appealed. This however, is only the framework for a Christian lawyer. He has before him, in all probability, a 'People's judge', poorly and politically trained. He probably knows more about the law than the judge. He certainly knows more about justice. This very courtroom situation gives him an opportunity to reach the judge and jury as human beings, to appeal to their conscience, and to place the whole Church on the bench next to the defendant for these functionaries to see. One such lawyer experiences every so often a judge who apologizes to him in private for the sentence he has given.

Finally, there is a field of responsibility for a Christian, if need be, in prison. There are other people in prison—political offenders, often of high intelligence and idealism, ordinary people who have been caught in the meshes of the secret police, and criminals. There is no more needy field of pastoral work than here. It is where some of the finest people behind the Iron Curtain live. It is simply the extreme case for Christian life everywhere in Communist lands.

These are three different pictures of responsible society in answer to the challenge of Communism from three different social situations. They form however a continuum and not a trichotomy.

None of them is sufficient unto its own situation without the other. Reinhold Niebuhr sitting in the ante-room of the United States Department of State, M. M. Thomas wrestling with the problems of Communist-tinged youth in India, and Helmut Gollwitzer in a Siberian prison camp, need to learn from each other and question each other, each from the insights which his own situation has given him into the total task of Christian encounter with the world of which Communism today forms such a major part. No Christian theologian may rest content that he has discovered the proper response to Communism only for one section of Christendom. The industrial West needs to heed the question inherent in the very nature of the Asian revolutionary situation, whether its security and wealth is not more critically under judgement than it realizes, and whether there is not a covert self-justification aggravating the ideological conflict, in many of its most cherished social principles and strategies in the cold war. The Asian revolutionary on the other hand needs the sober technical practicality of western industrial experience and knowledge of the possible, with its inherent question to his urgency and idealistic desire to solve man's problems in the mass. The whole non-Communist world needs to ask itself in the light of the East German experience how far its responsibility for the world is truly born out of freedom from the world, from the sharing of Christ's being in the world rather than from dependence on the world's securities and ideals. It needs to be reminded from that quarter that there can be worse things for the world as God loves it, than even its fall to Communism, and that even beyond that pale there is Christian responsibility. At the same time Christians behind the Iron Curtain need examples of what Christian responsibility is in a non-totalitarian society, where Christians bear broader responsibility for helping to mould and reform the structures of economic and political life. They need illustrations of Christian realism in facing and solving difficult human problems and injustices, in order to strengthen their own imagination and insight into what social truth and justice are. The conversation therefore must continue, toward deeper mutual understanding, to that point where each Christian can bring the insights of his own experience to relevant questioning and appreciation of his brother out of another situation, and where each bears the other concretely, in terms of his real strengths, needs, and temptations, in intercessory prayer.

c. *Renewal*

We come to the question of the renewal of the Church in the face of Communism. Here we cannot spread out such a comparison as was possible with responsible society. There is, to be frank, too little evidence in the non-Communist world of renewal and reform of church life itself in the face of the whole challenge of Marxism expressed in the labour movements and political parties of the last century, for us to speak as we could in a general way above, of an ecumenical consensus in thought and action. It will be better therefore to turn directly to one example, that of the Evangelical Church in Eastern Germany, which offers some suggestion of what this reform might be like. We do not present here a sociological survey. No responsible leader in this Church would deny that its real situation is defined in MacIntyre's words, 'an *ascesis* of poverty and questioning', and that the signs here described are nothing but signs of what might one day be the renewal of the Church, were the Church to take them from the hands of its prophets and saints, and make them its own. Nevertheless in God's eyes the Church lives in the witness of its prophets and saints. As such we speak of it.

The Church in East Germany has been prepared for this witness by the Communist state itself. Its old position of authority and influence is being systematically undermined. Religious education in the schools is no longer a matter of course. The state practically no longer offers its machinery for the collection of church taxes. Church membership and activity is a handicap in seeking work or advancement, and Christian convictions may be dangerous where they thwart the line of official propaganda. In other words the Church is being thrown back upon the power of its own spiritual life as a community, for its stability and influence.

This is its burden and its opportunity. The very existence of the Church as a living community is first of all its witness. Willy-nilly it becomes the only institution allowed to exist that is not controlled by the total ideology. All the broken pieces of the other ideologies of the past come to it as pastoral problems: the old aristocrat longing for Kaiser Wilhelm; the professional man whose world of high and objective standards is crumbling; the farmer who believed in his land and the work of his hands; the old Nazi; the worker with his socialism; and even, occasionally, the disillusioned old Communist. All these people the Church must lead into a community in which all that is truly human in that ideal from which they have heretofore lived, is valued and purged from its dependence on an ideology. And it must help them to live creatively, strengthened in this community, in a society where the very structures which give life meaning seem to be lost. It must, if it can, save them from suicide, from cynical resignation, and, except in extreme and special cases, from flight to the west.

The Church cannot, by law, seek new forms of activity to do this. It is not free to hold meetings of a general nature, or to organize activities as it will. Everything depends on how the given opportunities are used.

Is the pastor a man who shares the sufferings of the people who come to him? There is a pastor in East Germany (more than one let us hope) who does not hesitate to share with others the perplexities which face him in his pastoral counselling. A youth came to him and asked whether he should yield to the threats and pressures which were pushing him into the army. The answer would seem an easy one. The East German army is an ideological weapon of Communism. It aims to instil a 'glowing hate' in its soldiers against the 'imperialist war-mongers' of the west. 'But can I,' asked the pastor, who himself is not in this danger, 'tell this boy to go to prison, perhaps to death? Am I not sacrificing him to something abstract, though I may call it "the witness of the Church"? And a girl came to him and confessed that she had joined the SED (*Sozialistische Einheitspartei Deutschlands*—the East German Communist party) to keep her job, and now can no longer come to church because 'I have to lie all the time'. What can a pastor say? The Church is his security and profession. What does it cost him to tell the truth?

So this boy and this girl find in the pastor's study none of the ready answers for which they might have hoped. No laws are laid down. Instead there sits a man as perplexed and repentant as they themselves. Together they seek out what the forgiveness of their sins by God's grace in Jesus Christ, might mean for their lives.

A few days later the boy stood up for cross-questioning before a board of Communists, to answer for his refusal. And at the end of an hour of loaded questions, threats and false insinuations the frustrated chairman turned to him and demanded: 'Where did you get your answers? Did the pastor give them to you?' And the girl, on the pastor's advice, continued to go to church. Just because she was so caught, he had told her, she needed more the comfort of the word of God and the fellowship of the congregation. One day she suddenly reached a decision. She resigned from the SED, before six party functionaries. 'Think what will happen to you', they said. 'You are completely dependent on your salary.' And her answer: 'Because I was afraid for myself, I came to you. Because God has made me free from myself, I'm leaving now.'

'That is,' wrote the pastor, 'the greatest miracle, that Christ can, will and does so draw men to himself, that they become free from themselves, go their way in his forgiveness with joy, though they can only see the way a yard ahead.'

Does the pastor pray in public for prisoners, and the victims of injustice? Does his Bible study and exposition reveal the direct relevance of Biblical theme to the problems of the world around him? There are Bible study groups in East Germany in which the atmosphere is electric with expectation of help for each day's encounter with the Communist world. And in one town the public prosecutor found it necessary more to berate the pastor for his intercessory prayer for the prisoner, than to accuse the prisoner himself.

But even more depends on the congregation than on the pastor. Does it support the pastor in his counselling and spiritual life? 'Essentially,' writes one man out of first-hand experience, 'pastoral care in the congregation is practised not only by the pastor, but from layman to layman, as was also the case in the primitive Church and as ought also to be the case in any normal Christian congregation.'

Does the congregation seek informal ways of meeting in groups of friends, encounters when possible with non-Christians, and even with Communists? Such relatively intimate meetings are the most effective single way in which the Christian community spreads its atmosphere of neighbourly love, of mutual trust, and of fearlessness in the face of possible espionage with its evil consequences, abroad into the larger community.

Does the congregation have a programme of mutual help and charity for those in need? There is at least one congregation in the Zone which defeats the Communist attempt to manipulate wages according to political reliability through a regular system of relief for the less fortunate.

What is the attitude of the congregation toward lapsers, of whom there were many, especially among youth, during the pressures of early 1953, and toward those who come to it from without? Can it combine discipline here with love?

And finally, how effectively does the congregation carry each member spiritually in its prayer, in mutual help and counsel, if need be in mutual criticism? The Communist model and parody of this kind of community is always before the Christian, pressing directly on his life. What is the Christian alternative?

"The congregation', writes a pastor from his own experience, 'with its service and its common life, is the area in which there are opportunities available for mutual admonition and comfort. It might be compared with the air in which alone one can breathe. This becomes quite clear on the occasion of the regular elections to the presbyterium (we call it *Vertrauenskreis*—the "trusted group"). The whole group of those who attend Bible study meetings nominates candidates. Then the retiring *Vertrauenskreis* examines these nominations and has searching conversations with the candidates. Then the old presbyterium attempts to draw up a list of candidates. Finally a meeting of the congregation is called and the suggestions, filled out by any nominations it makes, are discussed in detail and a decision is made. What spiritual discipline is necessary in order to speak in a group of over a hundred members (that was the number this time) of matters which become very personal, about the gifts and manner of life of the candidates! And in this, one voice carries as much weight as the majority. . . . It would be difficult to estimate whether many people in these very election meetings are not led to see with special clarity that in the congregation of Jesus no other lord and no other

377

standard rules than he, the Lord himself, who also determines the way in which, in the congregation, people and gifts are sought and found for service, and office-bearers are commissioned.'[1]

Of such stuff is the inner life of a renewed congregation made. The simplest virtues underlie it. 'Why do you go to church?' a Communist functionary asked a country elder. 'Three reasons,' replied the elder. 'In church I am treated as a human being. In church I don't need to be afraid. And in church I hear a free word spoken, and it makes me free.' But these are so fundamental because they are not easy. In a society honeycombed with informers, a community where the members can trust one another shows a special quality in the faith by which it lives. In a society where all meetings are compulsory, a community which meets voluntarily and despite pressure, gives direct witness to the reality of its Object of faith. The free word, simply the truth spoken in love, whether from the pulpit or from member to member, or to someone outside, is based on this and is its crown.

There remains a word to say about the public witness of the Church. It takes first of all the form of the creative use of powerlessness; precisely that lack of any protection against the power of the state which reflects the position of Christ before Pilate. It is the behaviour of Christians in this position which often makes the profoundest impression on the Communist world, so that out of it springs the most surprising creative and reconciling power. What can I do, gentlemen?' replied a school principal to a committee of the Free German Youth (FDJ) who blamed him for not having a more 'progressive' student body. 'Seventy per cent of my students are Christians.' 'We have to give up our attempt to infiltrate that Christian group,' admits an SED leader. 'They all come back to us Christians.' All over the Zone the Church, in the imagination of the Communist functionary, is a powerful mass organization, whose secret means of holding and disciplining its members they cannot quite fathom. One is reminded of the Jews in Thessalonica who accused Paul and Silas: 'These men who have turned the world upside down have come here also.'

[1] Johannes Hamel, 'The Pastoral Care of Students', in *The Student World*, 1st Quarter 1954, pp. 57–8.

378

The story of the girl who left the SED has a sequel which belongs here. Shortly after her interview with the commission, a functionary came to her and said: 'That was unbelievably courageous, what you did. We need people like you. The riff-raff and the opportunists we'll shake off some day in any case. Can't you decide anyway to become a Marxist?' And as the decision on her job came due, word was given from headquarters: 'This woman must be allowed to stay. She has shown unusual character.'

This example could be multiplied at least by hundreds. A mass meeting of the FDJ, called to demand the expulsion from school of a student who refused to declare he hated Adenauer, is brought to silence by one Christian who rises and explains (with his heart in his mouth) that the student's standpoint is based on the Christian commandment of love which allows no exceptions. The meeting closes without a decision. The state allows a harmless Church assembly to take place in hopes of using its propaganda value and perhaps infiltrating it, and it discovers that hundreds of thousands stream there from all corners of the country, that every attempt to infiltrate the meetings fails, that hymns instead of party songs are heard on the street, and that the whole people drinks deep of a new hope and independence which lasts into the following months. This is the kind of power which grows from powerlessness. Nowhere was it more dramatically illustrated than in the events of June 10th, 1958 and immediately following, when the government gave to a church it had been persecuting every concession which it demanded in the effort to restore the confidence and good will among the people which a new policy demanded. So also after the demonstrations of the 17th June, a bishop went to warn a Russian general not to ruin every hope of winning the people by brutal reprisals. And the general replied: 'You know the mind of the people. Why haven't you come to me before?' Such results are temporary. Their political weight is problematical. But they indicate an opportunity for the Church which continues through all policy changes because it is inherent in the very nature of the Christian-Communist encounter itself.

Finally, on the other side, the Church has a certain responsibility for the public power and influence it still exercises in a traditionally

379

Christian land. Even in the Soviet Zone 90 per cent of the people are baptized, 70 pér cent volunteer their children for religious instruction, including even Communist Party members. The idea of a *Volkskirche* is firmly entrenched in the popular mind. Yet there is, by common agreement, nothing sacred about this idea in a time when the fact behind it is gradually dissolving. State financial support, the ownership of land, the right to give religious instruction in the public schools, all of which are signs of the *Volkskirche*, do not belong to the essential freedoms and rights of the Church. Nor do proprietorship of social welfare institutions and other evidences of worldly influence and power. Essential to the Church is that it be a missionary movement which, in the life and death of its institutions, praises its Lord.

Yet this very repentance and renewal under the Word of God strengthens the Church to resist the pressures of a Communist state. This is where the German conviction differs from that of Hromadka and those Hungarians who accept Communist patterns for their Christian repentance. The Communist conception of the essence of the Church is its liturgical service. The Communist attack on the Church may use arguments which appeal to a general socialist conscience—objection to state support for example—but its purpose is the reduction of the Church as a whole to its liturgical expression.

Therefore the Church's influence in society, a matter of indifference in itself, becomes a point of witness in this situation. The Church continues to claim state support, seeks at the same time to be independent of it, and grants no conditions in return for it. The Church holds on to its lands, though these have become a liability instead of a source of income. These lands have in some cases become the only centres where mutual confidence is still possible in agriculture, centres of Christian community in the midst of socialization. The Church has refused to register its meetings, conferences, or synods with the police, and seeks to carry out its full programme in the face of every threat or pressure short of actual police intervention—all this not for the sake of its own prestige but for the sake of the area of freedom thus created, in which all people can breathe and be spiritually nourished. Traditional positions gain new meanings even while Christians strive for inner freedom from dependence on them. They are not perfect, but at the moment they are God's given earthly instruments, offering a certain relative freedom from Communist control.

D. *Ministry*

We come to the final area of practice in the Christian-Communist encounter—the personal encounter between the Christian as a man and the Communist as a man. This is not usually the direct encounter which the Christian may have with the adherent of almost any other faith which is not his own. It is conditioned by all that has been said so far. It is falsified by the hardened ideological casing through which the Communist encounters all reality, and by the ideology which he may in all sincerity attribute to us. It is distorted by his purposes with relation to us and by the resistance we must offer to them. It is made more difficult by the responsibility we have to use our power to protect our neighbour against him, and maintain social health in spite of him. But the Communist himself has personal problems. One may be suspicious of the lurid light which ex-communist literature sheds on this, written as it is from the perspective of a more complete break with the system in mind and spirit than is possible for one still in the midst of it. But at least it is certain that most Communists face the problem of violating personal trust, and sacrificing people whom they know, for the sake of their broader allegiance to the socialist society and Party discipline. The vision of the *Pietà* which so tortured Rubashov in Koestler's *Darkness at Noon*, casting doubt on his whole conviction that the goal was worth this discipline, is an ever-repeated experience. Related to this is the problem of truth and falsehood in an ideological atmosphere, and the issue of personal sincerity. Related too is the whole question of faith in the Soviet system as a whole and its destiny, *versus* the cynicism and corruption which sets in as a reaction to the realities of Communist life. Encounter with the Communist as a person involves finding ways to break through the barrier of his strategy toward us, his ideological blindness about us and the world, and his fear of facing himself—except in the image of a Party adherent—to the human being beneath, whose problems

381

are not so different from what ours would be in his condition.

Our theologians have had surprisingly little to say on this subject. One cannot escape the impression that for none of the principals in our study, has this encounter been a matter of personal attention or experience. One says this with hesitation. Karl Barth has, since the war, shown great openness toward Communist contacts and at the same time great freedom over against them. But we have seen how Barth's concern with other kinds of people, in other sorts of dilemmas, prevents him from penetrating to a genuine personal encounter, however genial, and at the same time outspoken, his meetings may have been.

It is those Christians who have been forced by circumstances and led by sound theological insight into personal contact with Communists, who have most to teach us here, whether their theology, as in India, is largely learned from Niebuhr and the Anglo-Saxon world, or, as in Germany, from Barth. Most of their wisdom is not to be found in writing, and the myriad forms of possible contact are yet to be studied and set down. Yet four guiding thoughts suggest themselves, each illustrated by actual events. It would be well to close our study with them.

(i) The Communist's approach to the Christian only breaks down into real personal encounter, when the Christian can break through the propagandist purpose, the intention to manipulate him, with which the Communist first comes. This intention is almost always present. It may be the intention of the interrogator in prison toward the prisoner, the intention of the informer to trick his victim into a statement which can be used against him, or simply the intention of the propagandist sent to get a signature on a petition or attendance at a meeting. In any case the Christian can only disarm this insincere encounter by not acting as he is expected to act—above all not with insincerity himself, born of fear and distrust of his opponent.

'Our freedom consists in the fact that we love our brother here and now; that we offer him truth, time, and much understanding, even when our openness delivers us into his hand, and we have no more control over the possible results. We show how bound we are when we take the Marxist uniform of the Communist propagandists too seriously, instead of speaking to them from the beginning in the certainty that here God is sending his children, who bear his image and for whom Christ died, into our house. We have rejoiced that at last people have come to us, who (and this is an experience which has surprised us ourselves) put, in the course of the discussion, a genuine question about the reality of God. Certainly these discussions went quite otherwise than these people expected. But still there was a requirement: that Christians listened much, showed a real understanding of Marxism, and held to the hope that God's Word smashes rocks like a hammer, and that God wills to help all men, even the powerful.'[1]

(ii) The Communist believes, as a Christian also believes, but he does not recognize his Marx-Leninism as a commitment of faith. It is the great contribution of the Christian in personal encounter with the Communist to drive the question back to the question of faith, and to point out thereby the choice of faith which the Communist has made in contrast to the Christian. This in itself is a ministry to the Communist, for his certainty and his blindness rests partly on obscuring the fact that he has made this choice.

'Two of them sit opposite me: an old Communist and a young one. I must absolutely go to vote in a plebiscite "for peace", and they have been sent to talk me into it. . . . The usual peace phonograph record laid on for pastors sounds forth. When they finish I begin to ask questions about the real meaning of their fight for peace according to the writings of Lenin. We agree very quickly. By peace they mean not just any sort of peace between nations, but peace in the classless society, which will be achieved by revolution, by the overthrow of capitalist powers, and by the dictatorship of the proletariat.

' "So this plebiscite in which you want my vote 'for peace' also depends inseparably on faith in the truth of Lenin's 'scientific socialism'?"

' "Yes, sir!"

' "But you see, I don't have this faith."

'It is almost breathtaking to see how the two of them react to this unexpected conclusion. They look at me aghast.

' "What then, takes the place of this faith for you?"

'And now begins a three hour conversation about obedience to God's law, about the reality of God, about our sinful hearts, and the Church.

' "How can God be real, if he is not material? Only material is real.'

'I answer with the counter-question whether the love which he and his wife have for each other is real, and whether it is material which he can

[1]'Christian Witness in East Germany', in *Christianity and Crisis*, Vol. XIII, 25th May, 1953, p. 68.

prove by test and measurement. We agree then, that his concept of reality doesn't even suffice to explain human beings and their relation to each other. He thinks it over, and puts to me the surprising question:

' "But suppose I deny that love and trust between two people are realities?"

' "Then," said I, "I am sorry for you in your marriage."

'With this the human being in him breaks through: "You're right. Life would be a nightmare then."

'I show him then that the whole of Marxism gives no answer to the question, what the death of a human being really is, and that therefore it cannot answer the question what a man is. Because we only exist as men who die. Here lurks the real evil in our lives, with which Marxism offers no help. In parting the young functionary, a fine young married worker, says to me:

' "Herr Pastor, I'll tell you frankly, this was my first encounter with the Church. You have told me things that concern me deeply. May I come to you again and hear about Christianity?" '[1]

(iii) There are Communist devotees of different types, from the unthinking fanatic to the sensitive idealist. Far more study must be given to their variety and the ministry appropriate to each.

'If we ask ourselves,' writes Helmut Gollwitzer after describing two such encounters in detail,

'. . . how it comes about that in the face of the same facts some grew enthusiastic about (Stalinism) and some were frightened away from it, then the answer is contained in these two sentences: "You must look at it dialectically", and "You have no idea what good things the future has in store." Anyone wishing to understand why Communism has had treacherous and unwilling followers as well as faithful and enthusiastic partisans must understand these two sentences. These phrases are of course the outcome of blind faith, although the Communists like to think they are the outcome of reason and knowledge. "Seeing dialectically" helps them to resist the temptation to see things as they really are; it is the buffer which absorbs the shock of disappointment. Thus they manage to dispose of everything which conflicts with their wishful thinking in such a way that there is no longer any danger.'[2]

One discovers, however, in contact with the idealists, that many are by no means unaware of the evils of the Soviet system, the corruptions

[1]'Conversations with Marxists' in *Presbyterian Life*, July, 1954.

[2]Gollwitzer, *Unwilling Journey*, p. 140. This quotation is in the context of the author's description of several personal encounters with Communists of this sort, pp. 132–43.

of the movement toward a classless society, and all the other atten-
dant evils which are our reasons for rejecting Communism. There
are many who bear these things on their hearts and give themselves as much to their elimination as to the justification of their
faith in Communism in spite of them. For these, faith in the dialectical process of history according to the pattern of Communist
promises, becomes the kingpin of Communism, the eschatological
consolation and motivation by which they live. At this point, when
it is reached, a frank and searching encounter between Christian
and Communist, centred on the question of hope, is often possible.

(iv) The Communist longs for human values which are not available in his Party and society: for mutual trust between friends, for
respect as a person, for sincerity in thought, and for a place to un-
burden his often tortured sense of guilt. In short, like every human
being, he longs for the fellowship of Christian love. Even at great
risk, it is one of the greatest Christian contributions to the whole
encounter with Communism, to offer him this.

'And then we experienced that here and there a few of us began to talk
to half and full Marxists with love. With love—that means undiplomatic-
ally, in all frankness and freedom, yet not self-righteously or moralistic-
ally. And almost everywhere where that happened, we saw that the evil
spirits stole away and the sea became still. In the place of their dialectically grounded desire to liquidate us (for the moment only rhetorically)
came human respect, then the assurance that they wouldn't do us any
harm because we were "good honest people" whom one protects and
defends. Then, here and there, something quite different occurred. Suddenly the mask which looks so deceivingly like the real face fell, and
revealed a helpless man who sinks under his load of sin and guilt, and who
clings to the Christian who has treated him with a bit of love, who hasn't
lied to him like the others.'[1]

The Christian stands in the gateway to action whenever he
meets the Communist. He stands there naked and unarmed. We
must act toward Communists. There is no escape, for we are
through Christ the neighbours both of them and of their victims.
But we must act as men who have no true philosophy to set against
the false one, no right morality to judge the wrong one, no solving

[1]'Gottes geliebte Ostzone', in the *Schweizerische evangelische Pressedienst*, March, 1951, p. 5.

system of social order for the world. Behind the forces which have built up Communism we perceive the judgement of God on all systems of thought and life which are ours. It is the Christ of the Bible who convicts the Christian of making his religion an ideology. It is the powerlessness of the Son of God which makes power for us such a problem, and the poverty of his servanthood which so questions our sovereign prosperity. It is our calling as Christians to share and demonstrate the work of a Redeemer who is so completely there for others, which strips us of our good conscience and takes our weapons when we defend our own culture, nation, or even religion. Yet it is just this for-ness, of Christ the companion and helper of men unto his death, which prevents us from withdrawing from the responsible use of the power and wealth we have been given.

This is the place where the boundless opportunity for Christian encounter with Communism begins. Communism's fate is neither in its own hands nor in ours. The power we use to contain it will be relatively useful at best. 'Except the Lord keep the city, the watchman waketh but in vain.' Yet as Christians we can commend the power given to us to God's purposes and not our own; it may be that one day the Communist will sense this new direction and control.

The answer to the endless battle of one ideology against another lies not in our truth or our morality but in the work of a saving God toward us all. 'I am the way, the truth and the life; no man cometh to the Father but by me.' Justice and human welfare depend neither on the preserving of great social orders from the past nor on the creation of revolutionary ideals in the future, but on obedient participation in God's concern for our neighbour each day and year. 'Hate the evil, love the good, and establish justice in the gate; it may be that the Lord, the God of hosts may be gracious to the remnant of Joseph.' Here and there, when the Communist senses that across from him stands a perplexed and repentant man, not out to overcome him however great his power and responsibility in the non-Communist world, he himself may begin to reveal the perplexities and guilt which beset him. Here and there he may reach out for friendship and, tacitly, for help;

for his power is to him also a danger and burden, and his answers for society have long begun to mock him. Then it is that all the 'answers to Communism' in all the books and journals of the West, will become event in the encounter between Christian and Communist, event in the life of the Communist himself. The result will not be a victory for the 'Christian' West. But it will mean that these men called Communists will move once more out of their ideological fortress into the road where we all are walking despite the problems, insecurities, and the many conflicts of our interests which beset the way. The theologian's task is to help the Christian to guide the Communist back to the road which is the world. But only the Christian's humble but confident journey itself, with whatever charges and burdens may be given him to carry, only his realistic concern for neighbours at cost to himself, can convince the unbeliever that the Lord and guide of the journey is the servant son of God who bore the cross.

INDEXES

INDEX OF SUBJECTS

Fellowship of Socialist Christians. See Socialism, Christian, American.
Freedom, Christian and political, 36, 72, 106, 112, 116, 142, 144, 149,
    227, 245, 248, 253, 280, 284, 300, 306, 316–18, 332, 345, 382–3

Genesis 10–11.9, 206
German rearmament, 303, 315, 363–4
German reconstruction, 300
German Social Democracy, 96–104
Germany, Eastern, 10, 249–56, 280, 307–12, 337, 345–6, 368–74,
    374–81
God—acts of, 12, 18, 191–5, 234, 235
    —Commandment and will of, 34, 366
    —faith in, 28, 33 f., 193, 202, 228–31
    —forgiveness of, 86, 376
    —grace of, 36, 85, 87, 106, 137, 143, 151, 152, 222–6, 228, 237,
        241–3, 264, 350, 371, 376
    —judgement of, 55, 61, 85, 115, 131, 147, 148, 151, 164, 366, 370
    —knowledge of, 193, 227. See also Knowledge, theory and limits of.
    —sovereignty of, 61, 150, 220

History—Barth's view of, 219, 257–90, 351–2
    —Berdyaev's view of, 111–2
    —Bonhoeffer's view of, 352–4
    —Brunner's view of, 38–9
    —Hromadka's view of, 63, 65–7
    —Marxist view of, 22, 93, 276 f., 351
    —Niebuhr's view of, 148–53
    —Tillich's view of, 78–84
Holy Spirit, 39, 170, 272, 304
Hope—Christian, 194, 202, 214, 273–6, 281–5, 354
    —Communist and Christian compared, 59–60, 94 f., 148, 165–74
Humanism, 12, 24, 82, 87–90, 355
Hungary—43, 55–6, 62, 68–71, 76, 288, 295, 301, 322, 339. See also
    Berecsky and Peter.

Idealism, 39, 93, 106, 160. German, 189.
Ideology—problem of, 139–48, 158, 168, 216–56, 341–2, 345–51
    —Marxist, 19 f., 37 f., 71, 75, 121, 122, 141, 321, 342–3
    —religious, 22 f., 92 f., 212–6. See also Religion.
Imperialism, 126, 163, 172
India, 171–3, 175, 327, 333, 361, 367, 373
Individualism, 32, 39, 68, 126, 137, 152, 355

Justice, 79, 131, 136–7, 144, 149, 154–5, 289, 298 f., 308, 365, 372
—original (*justitia originalis*), 143, 146, 167

Kairos, 80 ff., 96, 99 ff., 110, 115, 170, 278
Kingdom of God, 59, 66, 80, 118, 121, 137, 150, 151, 182, 206, 267
Knowledge, theory of (epistemology), scientific and religious, 65, 97–8,
99, 121, 140–1, 143–4, 208, 227–8, 231–3, 285–7, 346–7. See also
Reason, Revelation, Truth.

Law—moral, 41, 43, 49, 291, 296
—natural, 154, 314
—of the state, 371–2
Liberalism, 32, 54, 118, 119, 122, 140, 162, 168, 171, 237
Love, 47, 118 f., 121, 147, 150, 165, 202, 231, 280, 343, 385

Man, doctrine of, 95, 99, 102, 201–5, 218, 229–30, 233–4
Man in Society—Barth's view of, 204–11, 290–300
—Brunner's view of, 39–40
—Hromadka's view of, 68–71
—Niebuhr's view of, 153–6
—summary and critique, 355–9
Marx, younger pre-materialist, 27, 91, 94, 100, 104–6, 331
Materialism, 106, 213–4
Ministry to the Communist, 25, 47, 174–6, 381–7
Moral authority, 167. See also Law, moral.
Moralism in politics, 40–43, 49–50, 161–4

Nationalism, 103
Nazism, 53, 56, 58, 77, 83, 108, 158–60, 175, 272, 287, 300–1, 312,
322–4. See also Hitler.
Neutralism, 302–4, 315
New Deal, 124, 127, 147, 166.
Nihilism, 250 f., 328 f.

Order—in society, 155, 180, 296, 327
—of creation, 34 f., 36, 38, 292

Pilate, 269 f.
Planning in society, 157, 365–8
Political Theory and Action. See Theology of Politics, State, Power.
Post-Communist attitude, 333, 346

Power—and authority (*exousia*) in society, 83–4, 102, 113, 180, 292, 296–7, 307–12, 379–81
   —balance of, 153, 154–5, 360
   —of Communism. See Communism as political power.
   —control of, 42, 131, 160, 163, 359–64
   —economic, 129, 130–1
   —fact and problem in society, 101, 117–21, 128, 149, 151, 182, 269, 316
   —of Origin (Tillich), 78 ff.
   —revolutionary, 129, 326–34. See also Revolution.
Powerlessness, 25, 175–6, 378–9, 386
Pragmatism, 124, 147, 157, 161, 165, 314
Proletariat, its class and situation, 90 f., 105, 125, 127 f., 129, 132, 141, 148, 219, 247, 277 f., 331, 346
Property, 156
Protestantism, 85–6

Reason, place and limits of, 121, 140–44, 239, 247
Reconciliation, Redemption, Atonement—See Christ, Reconciler.
Religion, 134–9
      —radical (Niebuhr), 139, 145 n., 191
      —Marx-Feuerbach, criticism of, 21 f., 92 f., 113, 136–7, 212–6
Religionless or mature world, 338–48
Religious situation (Tillich), 86
Repentance, 56, 70, 73, 74 f., 142
Resistance to political power, 43–4, 48–9, 175, 297–8, 301, 310–12, 317, 334–7. See also Revolution.
Responsibility in society, 117, 145, 241, 244–5, 269, 282, 290 ff., 350–1, 359–62, 364–74
Resurrection, 146, 151, 174, 214. See also Christ.
Revelation, 51 f., 142 f., 184, 217, 218, 240, 246, 295, 346–8
Revelation, Book of, Ch. 13, 296
Revolution, Communist and general, 12, 23, 53–5, 62, 70, 112, 121 f., 127, 131, 139, 152, 169–74, 181–3, 277–9, 311, 320, 326–34, 340, 343. See also Power, revolutionary.
Romans, Epistle to, 177–82, 295–6, 307–8

Science, social and natural, see Knowledge.
Sermon on the Mount, 118 f.
Sin, 117, 217–8, 229, 244
Social Gospel, 118, 125

INDEX OF NAMES

PRAISE FOR THE TEACHER'S SECRET

'Beautifully written, entirely absorbing, and full of characters that live with you long after you finish reading, *The Teacher's Secret* is packed with heart and suspense... This brilliant book is a true page-turner, and I absolutely loved it.'

Jenny Ashcroft, author of *Beneath a Burning Sky*

'A delicately woven tapestry of interlinking stories... This is a big-hearted book about a small community and how small acts of kindness and courage, and the willingness to face the truth, restore the human spirit to a sense of new belonging.'

Joanne Fedler, author of *Secret Mothers' Business*

'Elegantly structured, unsettling, yet with moments of surprising wit - in this novel Suzanne Leal captures the life of a small community with real tenderness.'

Kathryn Heyman, author of *The Accomplice*

'Masterfully constructed, this moving novel warns us of our capacity to make or break the lives of those around us... Drawn with wit and clear-eyed affection, the inhabitants of this wonderful novel will remain with you long after you have put it down.' Mark Lamprell, author of *The Full Ridiculous*

'Leal's novel shows us, achingly and beautifully, the slippery nature of truth and the destruction that is occasionally wrought from good intensions.'

Maggie Joel, author of *The Safest Place in London*

'A rich interweaving of beautifully drawn characters told so gently and in such exquisite detail that they grew on me until I was lost in their world.'

Robin de Crespigny, filmmaker and author of
The People Smuggler

'*The 1*   mination of
one of   aracters and

relationships interwoven in a storyline that has the reader engrossed to the last page.'

Robert Wainwright, author of *Sheila*

'Suzanne Leal writes with her hand on her heart, writing according to its beat... translating the ordinary into the extraordinary. An Australian talent, universally understood.'

Charles Waterstreet, author of *Precious Bodily Fluids: A Larrikin's Memoir*

'Suspenseful, moving and full of heart. I couldn't put it down.'

Richard Glover, author of *Flesh Wounds*

'An eloquent story of a life thrown into disarray; it drew me in and held me, page after page.'

Rachel Seiffert, author of *The Dark Room*

PRAISE FOR BORDER STREET

'Utterly engrossing and moving... An exquisitely poised and intelligent unveiling of secrets; a book honouring the hidden, the intimate and the painfully unresolved.'

Gail Jones, author of *Five Bells*

'A book that looms closer with every page... By the end, you start seeing the characters on the street, and you hear their voices in your sleep.'

Markus Zusak, author of *The Book Thief*